Acclaim for Lawrence Lessig and
# REPUBLIC, LOST

"Lessig's vision is at once profoundly pessimistic—and deeply optimistic...Lessig's analysis of the distorting effects of money is...dead on."
—*New York Times*

"A well-reasoned argument on the structural problems now paralyzing American government."
—*Kirkus Reviews*

"REPUBLIC, LOST is a powerful reminder that this problem goes deeper than poor legislative tactics or bad character. As progressives contemplate how best to pick up the pieces after recent setbacks, a robust agenda to change how business gets done in the capital needs to be part of the picture. This time, we'd better mean it."
—*American Prospect*

"Comprehensive and persuasive...enjoyable to read."
—*Atlantic*

"One of the many charms of REPUBLIC, LOST is its sympathy for the people involved...With lawyerly precision, Lessig parses the problem."
—Bloomberg.com

"The real crisis facing American politics is what elected officials have to do to raise the money...That, roughly, is the theme of Lawrence Lessig's stirring book, REPUBLIC, LOST...Without a doubt, the Lessig plan (which has been carefully designed to pass constitutional muster) would be a vast improvement over the current system."
—WashingtonMonthly.com

Also by Lawrence Lessig

# REPUBLIC, LOST

*How Money Corrupts Congress—and a
Plan to Stop It*

★

# Lawrence Lessig

TWELVE

NEW YORK    BOSTON

Twelve
Hachette Book Group
237 Park Avenue
New York, NY 10017

www.HachetteBookGroup.com

Printed in the United States of America

RRD-C

Originally published in hardcover by Twelve.

First trade edition: October 2012
10 9 8 7 6 5 4 3 2

Twelve is an imprint of Grand Central Publishing.
The Twelve name and logo are trademarks of Hachette Book Group, Inc.

The Hachette Speakers Bureau provides a wide range of authors for speaking events. To find out more, go to www.hachettespeakersbureau.com or call (866) 376-6591.

The publisher is not responsible for websites (or their content) that are not owned by the publisher.

Library of Congress Catalog Number: 2011935711

ISBN 978-0-446-57644-4 (pbk.)

*To the million Arnold Hiatts that
this revolution will need*

# Contents

# Preface

"There is only one issue in this country," former MSNBC commentator Cenk Uygur told Netroots Nation, in June 2011. "Campaign finance reform."

For the vast majority of America, Uygur's comment is obscure. For a small minority, it is obvious. This book was written for that vast majority, drawn from the insights of that small minority.

As I have struggled to craft it, I have become driven by the view that practically every important issue in American politics today is tied to this "one issue in this country," and that we must find a way to show the connections. For both the Left and the Right, until this "one issue" gets fixed, there won't be progress on a wide range of critically important public policy issues. Until it gets fixed, governance will remain stalled.

The challenge is to get America to see and then act. Again and again I have been told by friends, "If you're going to do this, the story needs drama. There has to be good versus evil. You must tell story after story about venal corruption. Rod Blagojevich, Randy "Duke" Cunningham, Jack Abramoff—these are the figures who will rally America to respond."

Maybe. But what if the problem is not Blagojevich? What if Washington is not filled with evil souls trying to steal from the republic? What if the absolutely debilitating corruption that we face is a corruption caused by decent souls, not crooks? Could America rally to respond then? Can we get angry enough about small but systemic distortions that block the ability of democracy to work, if those distortions are the product of good people working in a corrupted system?

I am unsure. As I have worked over the past four years to understand this problem, I have become convinced that while a corruption of Congress is destroying the republic, that corruption is not the product of evil. There is great harm here, but no bin Laden. There are Jack Abramoffs and Duke Cunninghams, to be sure, but they are the exception, not the rule. And without great evil, I am not yet sure that we can muster the will to fight. We will, I fear, simply tolerate the corruption, as a host tolerates a parasite that is not life threatening. Until it is.

Yet I write with hope. If we understand the nature of this corruption, its solution will be obvious. The challenge, then, will be to build a movement to bring about that solution. Such a movement is possible. It has been built before.

But to build it will require a different kind of learning. This is not an academic book. I do not mean to enter an academic debate. It instead builds upon the insights of academics to address a different debate entirely: a political debate, within the domain of activists, that has been raging in parallel for almost a half century.

Each side in this debate talks past the other. The academic seeks a truth, but that truth is too often too obscure for citizens to grok. The activist seeks to motivate, but with stories that are too often too crude, or extreme. The activist is right that the problem is bad—indeed, worse than his focus on individual corruption suggests. But the academic is right that if the problem is bad, it is not bad because our government has returned to the Gilded Age. We are better than they were, even if the consequences of our corruption are much worse. For this is the paradox at the core of my argument: that even without sinning, we can do much more harm than the sinner.

This work takes me far from my earlier writing, though the hint of this book was clear in *Remix* (2008). I was driven to this shift when I became convinced that the questions I was addressing in the fields of copyright and Internet policy depended upon resolving the policy questions—the corruption—that I address here. I thus left copyright and Internet policy, and began a process to learn as much as I could about a vast and largely undefined field. That work has brought me back to Harvard, where I am now the director of the Edmond J. Safra Center for Ethics, and where I direct a five-year research project studying this "institutional corruption" generally. It has also pushed me to help forge a multipartisan political movement (described in the Appendix) to demonstrate the need, for the objectives of both the Right and the Left, for this fundamental reform.

Because such is the practice this reform will need: the willingness to move between the two very different worlds of the academic and the activist. I am not yet convinced that such a practice can work. I am certain it will evoke sharp criticism from the purists in each world. But if above that din, there are citizens who can glimpse a path to reform, that criticism is a small price to pay.

# REPUBLIC, LOST

# Introduction

There is a feeling today among too many Americans that we might not make it. Not that the end is near, or that doom is around the corner, but that a distinctly American feeling of inevitability, of greatness—culturally, economically, politically—is gone. That we have become Britain. Or Rome. Or Greece. A generation ago Ronald Reagan rallied the nation to deny a similar charge: Jimmy Carter's worry that our nation had fallen into a state of "malaise." I was one of those so rallied, and I still believe that Reagan was right. But the feeling I am talking about today is different: not that we, *as a people*, have lost anything of our potential, but that we, *as a republic*, have. That our capacity for governing—the product, in part, of a Constitution we have revered for more than two centuries—has come to an end. That the thing that we were once most proud of—this, our republic—is the one thing that we have all learned to ignore. Government is an embarrassment. It has lost the capacity to make the most essential decisions. And slowly it begins to dawn upon us: a ship that can't be steered is a ship that will sink.

We didn't always feel this way. There were times when we were genuinely proud—as a people, *and* as a republic—and when we proudly boasted to the world about the Framers' (flawed but still) ingenious design. No doubt, we still speak of the founding with reverence. But we seem to miss that the mess that is our government today grew out of the genius that the Framers crafted two centuries ago. That, however much we condemn what government has become, we forget it is the heir to something we still believe divine. We inherited an extraordinary estate. On our watch, we have let it fall to ruin.

The clue that something is very wrong is the endless list of troubles that sit on our collective plate but that never get resolved:

bloated and inefficient bureaucracies; an invisible climate policy; a tax code that would embarrass Dickens; health care policies that have little to do with health; regulations designed to protect inefficiency; environmental policies that exempt the producers of the greatest environmental harms; food that is too expensive (since protected); food that is unsafe (since unregulated); a financial system that has already caused great harm, has been left unreformed, and is primed and certain to cause great harm again.

The problems are many. Too many. Our eyes get fixed upon one among them, and our passions get devoted to fixing that one. In that focus, however, we fail to see the thread that ties them all together.

We are, to steal from Thoreau, the "thousand[s] hacking at the branches of evil," with "[n]one striking at the root."

This book names that root. It aims to inspire "rootstrikers." The root—not the single cause of everything that ails us, not the one reform that would make democracy hum, but instead, the root, the thing that feeds the other ills, and the thing that we must kill first. The cure that would be generative—the single, if impossibly difficult, intervention that would give us the chance to repair the rest.

For we have no choice but to try to repair the rest. Republicans and Democrats alike insist we are on a collision course with history. Our government has made fiscal promises it cannot keep. Yet we ignore them. Our planet spins furiously to a radically changed climate, certain to impose catastrophic costs on a huge portion of the world's population. We ignore this, too. Everything our government touches—from health care to Social Security to the monopoly rights we call patents and copyright—it poisons. Yet our leaders seem oblivious to the thought that there's anything that needs fixing. They preen about, ignoring the elephant in the room. They act as if Ben Franklin would be proud.

Ben Franklin would weep. The republic that he helped birth is lost. The 89 percent of Americans who have no confidence in Congress (as reported by the latest Gallup poll)[1] are not idiots. They are not even wrong. Yet they fail to recognize just why this government doesn't deserve our confidence. Most of us get distracted. Most of us ignore the root.

We were here at least once before.

One hundred years ago America had an extraordinary political choice. The election of 1912 gave voters an unprecedented range of candidates for president of the United States.

On the far Right was the "stand pat," first-term Republican William Howard Taft, who had served as Teddy Roosevelt's secretary of war, but who had not carried forward the revolution on the Right that Roosevelt thought he had started.

On the far Left was the most successful socialist candidate for president in American history, Eugene Debs, who had run for president twice before, and who would run again, from prison, in 1920 and win the largest popular vote that any socialist has ever received in a national American election.

In the middle were two "Progressives": the immensely popular former president Teddy Roosevelt, who had imposed upon himself a two-term limit, but then found the ideals of reform that he had launched languishing within the Republican Party; and New Jersey's governor and former Princeton University president Woodrow Wilson, who promised the political machine–bound Democratic Party the kind of reform that Roosevelt had begun within the Republican Party.

These two self-described Progressives were very different. Roosevelt was a big-government reformer. Wilson, at least before the First World War, was a small-government, pro-federalist reformer. Each saw the same overwhelming threat to America's democracy— the capture of government by powerful special interests—even if each envisioned a very different remedy for that capture. Roosevelt wanted a government large enough to match the concentrated economic power that was then growing in America; Wilson, following Louis Brandeis, wanted stronger laws limiting the size of the concentrated economic power then growing in America.

Presidential reelection campaigns are not supposed to be

bloody political battles. But Taft had proven himself to be a particularly inept politician (he was later a much better chief justice of the Supreme Court), and after Roosevelt's term ended, business interests had reasserted their dominant control of the Republican Party. Yet even though dissent was growing across the political spectrum, few seemed to doubt that the president would be reelected. Certainly Roosevelt felt certain enough of that to delay any suggestion that he would enter the race to challenge his own hand-picked successor.

A Wisconsin Republican changed all that. In January 1911, Senator Robert La Follette and his followers launched the National Progressive Republican League. Soon after, La Follette announced his own campaign for the presidency. Declaring that "popular government in America has been thwarted . . . by the special interests," the League advocated five core reforms, all of which attacked problems of process, not substance. The first four demanded changes to strengthen popular control of government (the election of senators, direct primaries, direct election of delegates to presidential conventions, and the spread of the state initiative process). The last reform demanded "a thoroughgoing corrupt practices act."

La Follette's campaign initially drew excitement and important support. It faltered, however, when he seemed to suffer a mental breakdown during a speech at a press dinner in Philadelphia. But the campaign outed, and increasingly embarrassed, the "stand pat" Republicans. As Roosevelt would charge in April 1912:

> The Republican party is now facing a great crisis. It is to decide whether it will be, as in the days of Lincoln, the party of the plain people, the party of progress, the party of social and industrial justice; or whether it will be the party of privilege and of special interests, the heir to those who were Lincoln's most bitter opponents, the party that represents the great interests within and without Wall Street which desire through their control over the servants of the public to be kept immune from punishment when they do wrong and to be given privileges to which they are not entitled.[2]

The term *progressive* is a confused and much misunderstood moniker for perhaps the most important political movement at the turn of the last century. We confuse it today with *liberals*, but back then there were progressives of every political stripe in America— on the Left and on the Right, and with dimensional spins in the middle (the Prohibitionists, for example). Yet one common thread that united these different strands of reform was the recognition that democratic government in America had been captured. Journalists and writers at the turn of the twentieth century taught America "that business corrupts politics,"[3] as Richard McCormick put it. Corruption of the grossest forms—the sort that would make convicted lobbyist Jack Abramoff wince—was increasingly seen to be the norm throughout too much of American government. Democracy, as in rule of the people, was a joke. As historian George Thayer wrote, describing the "golden age of boodle" (1876–1926): "Never has the American political process been so corrupt. No office was too high to purchase, no man too pure to bribe, no principle too sacred to destroy, no law too fundamental to break."[4]

Or again, Teddy Roosevelt (1910): "Exactly as the special interests of cotton and slavery threatened our political integrity before the Civil War, so now the great special business interests too often control and corrupt the men and methods of government for their own profit."[5]

To respond to this "corruption," Progressives launched a series of reforms to reclaim government. Many of these reforms were hopeless disasters (the ballot initiative and elected judges), and some were both disasters and evil (Prohibition and eugenics, to name just two). But mistakes notwithstanding, the Progressive Era represents an unprecedented moment of experimentation and engagement, all motivated by a common recognition that the idea of popular sovereignty in America had been sold. The problem was not, as McCormick describes, a "product of misbehavior by 'bad' men," but was instead now seen as the predictable "outcome of identifiable economic and political forces."[6]

That recognition manifested itself powerfully on November 5,

1912: The incumbent Republican placed third (23.2 percent) in the four-man race; the socialist, a distant fourth (6 percent); and Teddy Roosevelt (27.4 percent) got bested by the "new" Democrat, Woodrow Wilson (41.8 percent).

Yet only when you add together these two self-identified Progressives do you get a clear sense of the significance of 1912: almost 70 percent of America had voted for a "progressive." Seventy percent of America had said, "This democracy is corrupted; we demand it be fixed." *Seventy percent* refused to "stand pat."

A century later we suffer the same struggle, but without anything like the same clarity. A "fierce discontent," as Roosevelt described America in 1906, is once again raging throughout the republic. Now, as then, it gets expressed as "agitation" against "evil," and a "firm determination to punish the authors of evil, whether in industry or politics."[7] We look to a collapsed economy, to raging deficits, to a Wall Street not yet held to account, and we feel entitled to our anger. And so extreme is that entitlement that it makes even violence seem sensible, if only to the predictably insane extremes in any modern society.

Roosevelt was encouraged by this agitation against evil. It was, he said, a "feeling that is to be heartily welcomed." It was "a sign," he promised, "of healthy life."

Yet today such agitation is not a sign of healthy life. It is a symptom of ignorance. For though the challenge we face is again the battle against a democracy deflected by special interests, our struggle is not against "evil," or even the "authors of evil." Our struggle is against something much more banal. Not the banal in the now-overused sense of Hannah Arendt's *The Banality of Evil*—of ordinary people enabling unmatched evil (Hitler's Germany). Our banality is one step more, well, banal.

For the enemy we face is not Hitler. Neither is it the good Germans who would enable a Hitler. Our enemy is the good Germans (us) who would enable a harm infinitely less profound, yet economically and politically catastrophic nonetheless. A harm caused by a kind of *corruption*. But not the corruption engendered by evil souls. Indeed, strange as this might sound, a corruption crafted by good souls. By decent men. And women. And if we're to do anything about this corruption, we must learn to agitate against more than evil. We must remember that harm sometimes comes from timid, even pathetic souls. That the enemy doesn't always march. Sometimes it simply shuffles.

The great threat to our republic today comes not from the hidden bribery of the Gilded Age, when cash was secreted among members of Congress to buy privilege and secure wealth. The great threat today is instead in plain sight. It is the economy of influence now transparent to all, which has normalized a process that draws our democracy away from the will of the people. A process that distorts our democracy from ends sought by both the Left and the Right: For the single most salient feature of the government that we have evolved is not that it discriminates in favor of one side and against the other. The single most salient feature is that it discriminates against all sides to favor itself. We have created an engine of influence that seeks not some particular strand of political or economic ideology, whether Marx or Hayek. We have created instead an engine of influence that seeks simply to make those most connected rich.

As a former young Republican—indeed, Pennsylvania's state chairman of the Teen Age Republicans—I don't mean to rally anyone against the rich. But I do mean to rally Republicans and Democrats alike against a certain kind of rich that no theorist on the Right or the Left has ever sought seriously to defend: The rich whose power comes not from hard work, creativity, innovation, or the creation of wealth. The rich who instead secure their wealth through the manipulation of government and politicians. The great evil that we as Americans face is the banal evil of second-rate minds who can't make it in the private sector and who therefore turn to the massive wealth directed by our government as the means to securing wealth for themselves. The enemy is not evil. The enemy is well dressed.

Theorists of corruption don't typically talk much about decent souls. Their focus is upon criminals—the *venally corrupt*, who bribe to buy privilege, or the *systematically corrupt*, who make the people (or, better, the rich) dependent upon the government to ensure that the people (or, better, the rich) protect the government.[8]

So, too, when we speak of politicians and our current system of governance, many of us think of our government as little more than criminal, or as crime barely hidden—from Jack Abramoff ("I was participating in a system of legalized bribery. All of it is bribery, every bit of it") to Judge Richard Posner ("the legislative system [is] one of quasi-bribery") to Carlyle Group co-founder David Rubenstein ("legalized bribery") to former congressman and CIA director Leon Panetta ("legalized bribery has become part of the culture of how this place operates") to one of the Senate's most important figures, Russell B. Long (D-La.; 1949–1987) ("Almost a hairline's difference separates bribes and contributions").

But in this crude form, in America at least, such crimes are rare. At the federal level, bribery is almost extinct. There are a handful of pathologically stupid souls bartering government favors for private kickbacks, but very few. And at both the federal and the state levels, the kind of Zimbabwean control over economic activity is just not within our DNA. So if only the criminal are corrupt, then ours is not a corrupt government.

The aim of this book, however, is to convince you that a much more virulent, if much less crude, corruption does indeed wreck our democracy. Not a corruption caused by a gaggle of evil souls. On the contrary, a corruption practiced by decent people, people we should respect, people working extremely hard to do what they believe is right, yet decent people working with a system that has evolved the most elaborate and costly bending of democratic government in our history. There are good people here, yet extraordinary bad gets done.

This corruption has two elements, each of which feeds the other. The first element is bad governance, which means simply that our government doesn't track the expressed will of the people, whether on the Left or on the Right. Instead, the government tracks a different interest, one not directly affected by votes or voters. Democracy, on this account, seems a show or a ruse; power rests elsewhere.

The second element is lost trust: when democracy seems a charade, we lose faith in its process. That doesn't matter to some of us—we will vote and participate regardless. But to more rational souls, the charade is a signal: spend your time elsewhere, because this game is not for real. Participation thus declines, especially among the sensible middle. Policy gets driven by the extremists at both ends.

In the first three parts of what follows, I show how these elements of corruption fit together. I want you to understand the way they connect, and how they feed on each other. In the book's final part, I explore how we might do something about them.

The prognosis is not good. The disease we face is not one that nations cure, or, at least, cure easily. But we should understand the options. For few who work to understand what has gone wrong will be willing to accept defeat—without a fight.

# PART I

---- ★ ----

# THE NATURE OF
# THIS DISEASE

There are no vampires or dragons here. Our problems are much more pedestrian, much more common. Indeed, anything we could say about the perpetrator of the corruption that infects our government (Congress) we could likely say as well about ourselves. In this part, I frame this sense of corruption, to make that link clear, and to make its solution more obvious.

# CHAPTER 1

# *Good Souls, Corrupted*

In the summer of 1991, I spent a month alone on a beach in Costa Rica reading novels. I had just finished clerking at the Supreme Court. That experience had depressed me beyond measure. I had idolized the Court. It turns out humans work there. It would take me years to relearn just how amazing that institution actually is. Before that, I was to begin teaching at the University of Chicago Law School. I needed to clear my head.

I was staying at a small hotel near Jaco. In the center of the hotel was a large open-air restaurant. At one end hung a TV, running all the time. The programs were in Spanish and hence incomprehensible to me. The one bit someone did translate was a warning that flashed before the station aired *The Simpsons*, advising parents that the show was "antisocial," not appropriate for kids.

Midway through that month, however, that television became the center of my life. On Monday, August 19, I watched with astonishment the coverage of Russia's August Putsch, when hard-line Communists tried to wrest control of the nation from the reformer Mikhail Gorbachev. Tanks were in the streets. Two years after Tiananmen, it felt inevitable that something dramatic, and tragic, was going to happen. Again.

I sat staring at the TV for most of the day. I pestered people to interpret the commentary for me. I annoyed the bartender by not drinking as I consumed the free TV. And I watched with geeky awe as Boris Yeltsin climbed on top of a tank and challenged his nation to hold on to the democracy the old Communists were trying to steal.

I will always remember that image. As with waking up to the

*Challenger* disaster or watching the reports of Bobby Kennedy's assassination, I can remember those first moments almost as clearly as if they were happening now. And I vividly remember thinking about the extraordinary figure that Yeltsin was: bravely challenging in the name of freedom a coup that if successful—and on August 19 there was no reason to doubt it would be—would certainly result in the execution of this increasingly idolized defender of the people.

Every other player in that mix seemed tainted or compromised, Gorbachev especially. And compromise (what life at the Court had shown me) was exactly what the month away was to allow me to escape. So at that moment, Yeltsin was the focus for me. Here was a man who could be for Russia what George Washington had been for America. History had given him the opportunity to join its exclusive club. It had taken some initial courage for him to climb on, but on August 19, 1991, I couldn't imagine how he could do anything other than ride this opportunity to its inevitable end. If democracy seemed possible for the former Soviets, it seemed possible only because it would have a voice through the rough and angry Yeltsin.

That's not, of course, how the story played out. No doubt Yeltsin's position was impossibly difficult. But over the balance of the 1990s, the heroic Yeltsin became a joke. Perhaps unfairly—and certainly unfairly at the beginning, since his real troubles with alcohol began only after he became Russia's president[1]—he was increasingly viewed as a drunk. After his first summit with Yeltsin, Clinton became convinced that his addiction was "more than a sporting problem."[2] The public didn't even learn about the most incredible incident until two years ago: on a visit to Washington to meet with Clinton, Yeltsin was found by the Secret Service on a D.C. street in the predawn hours, dressed only in underwear, trying in vain to flag down a taxi to take him to get pizza.[3] Yeltsin fumbled his chance at history, all because of the lure of the bottle.

As clearly as I remember watching him on that tank on August 19, I remember thinking, over the balance of that decade, about the special kind of bathos that Yeltsin betrayed. He was handed a chance to save Russia from authoritarians. Yet even this gift wasn't enough to inspire him to stay straight.

Yeltsin is a type: a particular, and tragic, character type. No doubt a good soul, he wanted and worked to do good for his nation. But he failed, in part because of a dependency that conflicted with his duty to his nation. We can't hate him. We could possibly feel sorry for him. And we should certainly feel sorry for the millions who lost the chance of a certain kind of free society because of this man's dependency.

Such characters and such dependencies, however, are not limited to individuals. Institutions can suffer them, too. Not because the individuals within the institutions are themselves addicted to some drug or to alcohol. Maybe they are. No doubt many are. That's not my point. Instead, an institution can be corrupted in the same way Yeltsin was when individuals within that institution become dependent upon an influence that distracts them from the intended purpose of the institution. The distracting dependency corrupts the institution.

Consider an obvious case.

A doctor at a medical school teaches students how to treat a certain condition. That treatment involves a choice among a number of drugs. Those drugs are produced by a number of competing drug companies. One of those companies begins to offer the doctor speaking opportunities—relatively well paid, and with reliable regularity. The doctor begins to depend upon this income. She buys a fancier car, or a vacation house on a lake. And while there's no agreement, express or implied, about the doctor's recommending the drug company's treatment over others, assume the doctor knows that the company knows what in fact she is recommending. Indeed, it is amazing if you don't know this, that drug companies are able to track precisely which drugs a particular doctor prescribes, or not, and therefore adjust their marketing accordingly.

In this simple example, we have all the elements of the kind of corruption I am concerned with here. The institution of medical education has a fairly clear purpose—Harvard's is to "create and nurture a diverse community of the best people committed to leadership in alleviating human suffering caused by disease." That purpose requires doctors to make judgments objectively, meaning based upon, or dependent upon, the best available science about the benefits and costs of various treatments. If a doctor within that institution compromises that objectivity by weighing more heavily, or less critically, the treatments from one company over another, we can say that her behavior would tend to corrupt the institution of education—her dependency upon the drug company has led her to be less objective in her judgment about alternatives.

Of course, we can't simply assume that money for speaking would bias the doctor's judgment. There is plenty of research to show why it could, but so far that research is an argument, not proof.[4] It is at least possible that such an arrangement leaves the judgment of the scientist unaffected. Although, again, my own reading of the evidence suggests that's unlikely. But my point just now is not to prove the *effect* of money. It is instead to clarify *one conception* of corruption.[5] It is perfectly accurate to say that if the relationship between the doctor and the drug company affected the objectivity of the doctor, then the relationship "corrupted" the doctor and her institution.

In saying this, however, we need not be saying that the doctor is an evil or bad person. If our doctor has sinned, her sin is ordinary, understandable. And indeed, among doctors in her position, her "sin" is likely not even viewed as a sin. The freedom or latitude to supplement one's income is an obvious good. To anyone with kids, or a mortgage, it feels like a necessity. We can all, if we're honest, imagine ourselves in her position precisely. Ordinary and decent people engage all the time in just this sort of compromise. It is the stuff of modern life, to be managed, not condemned, because if condemned, ignored.

We manage this sort of corruption by, first, recognizing its elements and, second, evaluating explicitly whether the institution can afford the compromise it produces. We recognize its elements by being explicit about the range of influences that operate upon individuals within that institution—particular influences within, we could say, an economy of influence. Some of those influences may be too random to regulate. Some may be the sort that any mature understanding of human nature would say produced a dependency.

Where there is such a dependency, those responsible for the effectiveness of the institution must ask whether that dependency too severely weakens the independence of the institution. If they don't ask this question, then they betray the institution they serve.

By invoking this idea of *dependency*, I mean to evoke a congeries of ideas: a dependency develops over time; it sets a pattern of interaction that builds upon itself; it develops a resistance to breaking that pattern; it feeds a need that some find easier to resist than others; satisfying that need creates its own reward; that reward makes giving up the dependency difficult; for some, it makes it impossible.

We all understand how these ideas map onto Yeltsin's struggle. Few of us have not been harmed by, or not done harm as, an alcoholic. We get this dynamic. We have lived with it.

How these ideas map onto an institution, however, is something we need still to work out. Institutions are not spirits. They don't act except through individuals. Yet each of these ideas is at least understandable when we think of an institution in which key individuals have become distracted by an improper, or conflicting, dependency.

That distraction is the corruption at the core of this book. Call it *dependence corruption*.[6] As I will show in the pages that follow, it is this pattern precisely that weakens our government. It is this pattern that explains that corruption without assuming evil or criminal souls at the helm. It will help us, in other words, understand a pathology that all of us acknowledge (at the level of the institution) without assuming a pathology that few could fairly believe (at the level of the individual).

As an introduction to dependence corruption, consider a link between the idea and an example more directly related to the aim of this book.

Imagine a young democracy, its legislators passionate and eager to serve their new republic. A neighboring king begins to send the legislators gifts. Wine. Women. Or wealth. Soon the legislators have a life that depends, in part at least, upon those gifts. They couldn't live as comfortably without them, and they slowly come to recognize this. They bend their work to protect their gifts. They develop a sixth sense about how what they do in their work might threaten, or trouble, the foreign king. They avoid such topics. They work instead to keep the foreign king happy, even if that conflicts with the interests of their own people.

Just such a dynamic was the fear that led our Framers to add to our Constitution a strange and favorite clause of mine. As Article I, section 9, clause 8, states,

> [N]o Person holding any Office of Profit or Trust under [the United States], shall, without the Consent of the Congress, accept of any present, Emolument, Office, or Title, of any kind whatever, from any King, Prince, or foreign State.

The motivation for this clause was both contemporary to the Framers and a part of their history. At the time of the founding, the king of France had made it a practice to give expensive gifts to departing ambassadors when they had successfully negotiated a treaty. In 1780 he gave Arthur Lee a portrait of himself set in diamonds and fixed above a gold snuff box. In 1784 he gave Benjamin Franklin a similar portrait, also set in diamonds. The practice was common throughout Europe. During negotiations with Spain, for example, the king of Spain presented John Jay with a horse. Each of these gifts raised a reasonable concern: Would agents of the republic keep their loyalties clear if in the background they had in view these expected gifts from foreign kings? Would the promised or expected gift give them an extra push to close an agreement, even if (ever so slightly) against the interests of their nation?

The same fear was a part of England's past. The reign of Charles II was stained by the fact that he, and most of his ministers, received payments ("emoluments") from the French Crown while in exile in France. Many believed the British monarchy thus became dependent upon those emoluments, and hence upon France. Those emoluments were viewed as a form of corruption, even if there was no clear quid pro quo tied to the gifts.[7]

Likewise with the relationship of the British Crown to ministers in Parliament: The core corruption the Framers wanted to avoid was Parliament's loss of independence from the Crown because the king had showered members of Parliament with offices and perks that few would have the strength to resist.[8] Members were thus pulled to the view of the king, and away from the view of the people they were intended to represent.

In each of these cases, the concern was not just a single episode. It was a practice. The fear was not just that a particular minister might be bribed. It was that many ministers might develop the wrong sensibilities. The fear, in other words, was that a dependency might develop that would draw the institution away from the purpose it was intended to serve: The people. The realm. The commons.

Think about it like this: Imagine a compass, its earnest arrow pointing to the magnetic north. We all have a trusting sense of how this magical device works. When we turn with the compass in our hands, the needle turns back. It is to track the magnetic north, regardless of the spin we give it.

Now imagine we've rubbed a lodestone on the metal casing of the compass, near the mark for "west." The arrow shifts. Slightly. That shift is called the "magnetic deviation." It represents the error induced by the added magnetic field.

Magnetic north was the intended dependence. Tracking magnetic north is the purpose of the device. The lodestone creates a competing dependence. That competing dependence produces an error. A corruption. And we can see that error as a metaphor for the corruption that I am describing by the term *dependence corruption*.

If small enough, the magnetic deviation could allow us to believe that the compass remains true. Yet it is not true. However subtle, however close, however ambiguous the effect might be, the deviation corrupts.

Depending on the context, depending on the time, depending on the people, that corruption will matter. Repairing it, at least sometimes, will be critical.

# CHAPTER 2

## *Good Questions, Raised*

### 1.

It is late at night, a sleepless night, as all nights have been since the birth of your child. The kid is crying. You stumble into her room to change her. She is frantic, maybe afraid. You fumble in the dark for the pacifier, which will magically turn this anxious source of joy into a sleeping baby. You give her the pacifier. She starts sucking. And then an evil demon drops a single thought into your head, a question perfectly crafted to keep you up for the rest of the night: How do you know that plastic is safe?

And not just that plastic. What about the plastic of her cereal bowl? Or her bottle? Or the soft spoon you use to feed her? Or anything else that she puts in her mouth, which of course, for months of her life, is absolutely anything she can touch?

If you're like I was about a decade ago (and this is not a fact I'm proud of), you'll answer that question with a calming reassurance: *Obviously* the plastic is safe. We spend billions running agencies designed to ensure the safety of the stuff we put in our mouths. How could it possibly be that the safety of something a *baby* puts into his mouth could still be in doubt? A hundred years of consumer safety law haven't left something as obvious as that untested.

I would have delivered that lecture to myself with some pride. This isn't a political issue. There's no Republican in the U.S. Congress who believes that the products our children consume should be unsafe or untested. Instead, we have all come to the view that the complexity of modern society demands this minimal regulatory assurance at least.

Not all societies are yet at this place. The weekend my wife and I discovered she was pregnant with our first child, we were in China. In the paper that morning was the story of a Chinese businessman who had been convicted for selling sugar water as baby formula. Parents who had relied upon the assurances of safety printed on the bottles watched in horror as their children bloated and died. The owner of the factory defended himself in a Chinese court with words Charles Dickens might have penned: "No one forced these parents to use my formula. They chose to use it. Any deaths are their own fault, not mine."

But in fact, the demon pestering you as you lie awake in bed after putting your child back to sleep has asked a pretty good question. For years my wife imported our pacifiers from Europe. Until I began the research for this book, I never asked why. "BPA" (aka Bisphenol A), she said. In America, the vast majority of soft plastic for children contains BPA. In many countries around Europe that chemical has been removed from children's products.

Why?

Among the complexities in the development of a fetus is the precision of its timing. Certain things must happen at certain times, and ordinarily they do. At certain times, for example, exposure of the fetus to estrogen can be harmful. At those precise times, the fetus develops a protective layer, a sex-hormone-binding globulin, that blocks the fetus from its mother's estrogen.

In the mid-1990s, Frederick vom Saal, a professor of biological sciences now at the University of Missouri–Columbia, began to wonder whether the same blocking mechanism blocked man-made estrogenic chemicals as well. Those chemicals, in theory at least, could have the same harmful effect on the fetus. Did sex-hormone-binding globulins protect against those, too?

The answer was not good. "The great majority of man-made chemicals," vom Saal found, "are not inhibited from entering cells like natural estrogens are." Worse, vom Saal found, "the receptor in the cell that causes changes when estrogen binds to it [remember, changes that can, at specific stages of development, be extremely harmful] is very responsive" to synthetic estrogenic chemicals, including BPA.[1]

Armed with (and alarmed by) this finding, vom Saal and others started testing the actual effects of BPA on the development of mice. The findings confirmed their worst fears. And because the "molecular mechanisms at the cellular level [produce] no difference in the way that mouse and rat cells respond to BPA and the way that human cells respond to it,"[2] vom Saal believed he had tripped onto a potential health disaster. Almost everyone (95 percent) within the developed world now has "blood levels of [BPA] within the range 'that is predicted to be biologically active,' based on animal studies conducted with low doses of the chemical."[3] A study by the Harvard School of Public Health found that "BPA concentrations increased by 69% in the urine of subjects who drank from plastic bottles containing BPA."[4] Some studies have even detected BPA in the cord blood of newborns.[5] The consequences of this exposure according to this study range from "reduced sperm count to spontaneous miscarriages; from prostate and breast cancers to degenerative brain diseases; from attention deficit disorders to obesity and insulin resistance, which links it to Type 2 diabetes."[6] Indeed, just last year, "the White House task force on childhood obesity worried [that BPA] might be promoting obesity in children."[7] Its fear followed this extensive and growing research.

Vom Saal's conclusions are not his alone. Indeed, to give the issue prominence, more than thirty-six "of the world's best brains on BPA" signed "an unprecedented consensus statement [that] laid out [the] chilling conclusions" of the research.[8] In the view of these scientists, BPA is a danger already causing significant harm to children in developed nations, and will no doubt cause more harm in the years to come.

Not all scientists agree with vom Saal and his colleagues, however. Indeed, there are many who believe BPA is either harmless or not yet proven to cause harm in humans. Many of the studies of

BPA, these scientists believe, have been methodologically flawed. Indeed, the National Institutes of Health itself has acknowledged problems with some of the research.[9] Regulations that would ban BPA, these scientists believe, are an unnecessary burden that will only raise the cost of the products our children need (and yes, reader who has never had a child, children *need* pacifiers).

Among those insisting upon the safety of BPA is, not surprisingly, the industry that produces it. In December 2009, *Harper's* published a summary memo from a meeting of the "BPA Joint Trade Association." That meeting was intended to "develop potential communication/media strategies around BPA." Members at the meeting believed that a "balance of legislative and grassroots outreach (to young mothers and students) is imperative to the stability of their industry." Among the strategies discussed was "using fear tactics (e.g., 'Do you want to have access to baby food anymore?')," and urging that consumers should have choice (e.g., "You have a choice: the more expensive product that is frozen or fresh, or foods packaged in cans"). The association was concerned that the "media is starting to ignore their side," and "doubts obtaining a scientific spokesman is attainable." The memo identified the "holy grail spokesman" for the BPA industry in the minds of these committee members: a "pregnant young mother who would be willing to speak around the country about the benefits of BPA."[10]

Okay, so some say that BPA is dangerous. Some say it is not. You may be with me in the former camp, or you may be in the latter camp. Both views are fair enough.

But notice how your feelings change when you read the following:

Since vom Saal published his first study in 1997, there have been at least 176 studies of the low-dose effects of BPA. Thirteen of these studies have been sponsored by industry. The balance (163) have been funded by the government, and conducted at universities. The industry-funded studies have the advantage of being large scale. Most of the government-funded studies are smaller scale. Nonetheless, here are the results:

All of the large-scale studies found no evidence of harm. When added to the smaller-scale studies, this meant about 24 out of the 176 found no evidence of harm. But 152 of these studies did find evidence of harm. So from this perspective, we could say about 15 percent of the studies found the chemical harmless, while 85 percent found it potentially harmful.[11]

That doesn't sound good for BPA. And it does not get any better.

If you divide the studies on the basis of their funding, the results are even starker.

|  | HARM | NO HARM |
|---|---|---|
| **Industry Funded** | 0 <br> (0%) | 13 <br> (100%) |
| **Independently Funded** | 152 <br> (86%) | 11 <br> (14%) |

In a single line, none of the industry-funded studies found evidence of harm, while more than 85 percent of the independent studies did.

Researchers who conduct these industry-sponsored studies are of course "offended," as one director commented, "when someone suggests that who pays for the study determines the outcome."[12] She explains the difference by pointing to the "nature of the study," not "who pays for the studies." Independent studies "typically focus on hazards, or the intrinsic capacity to do harm," while industry-funded studies "are interested in determining the risks of exposure."[13]

Maybe. And maybe that's enough to explain the difference. But here is the point I want you to recognize: Some will read this analysis and conclude that BPA is unsafe. Some will read it and won't change their view of BPA in the slightest. But the vast majority will read this analysis and become less certain about whether BPA is safe. The presence of money with the wrong relationship to the truth is enough to dislodge at least some of the confidence that these souls once had.

And among those not so sure, at least some will have the reaction that I did, and do, every time I hand my kid a piece of plastic: It is absurd that in America I don't know if the thing I'm feeding my child with is safe—for her or for us.

## 2.

The next time you're holding your cell phone against your ear and notice your ear getting a bit warm, ask yourself this question: Is your cell phone safe? Does the radiation coming from that hand-held device—microwave radiation, emitted one inch from your brain—cause damage to your brain? Or head? Or hand?

The vast majority of Americans (70 percent) either believe the answer to the latter question is no or they don't know.[14] Part of that belief comes from the same sort of confidence I've just described— we've had cell phone technology for almost fifty years; certainly someone must have determined whether the radiation does any damage. Part of that belief could also come from reports of actual studies—hundreds of studies of cell phone radiation have concluded that cell phones cause no increased risk of biological harm.[15] And, finally, part of that belief comes from a familiar psychological phenomenon: cognitive dissonance—it would be too hard to believe to the contrary. Like smokers who disbelieved reports about the link between smoking and lung cancer, we cell phone users would find it too hard to accept that this essential technology of modern life was in fact (yet) another ticking cancer time bomb.

Yet, once again, the research raises some questions.

Depending on how you count, there have been at least three hundred studies related to cell phone safety—or, more precisely, studies that try to determine if there is any "biologic effect" from cell phone radiation. The most prominent of these is a recent, $24 million UN-sponsored study covering thirteen thousand users in thirteen nations for more than a decade. That study was deemed "inconclusive," but it did find that "frequent cell phone use may increase the chances of developing rare but deadly forms of brain cancer."[16] Specifically, the study found up to "40% higher incidence of glioma among the top 10 percent of people who" used their phone the most.[17] That qualification may give you comfort, at least if you don't think of yourself as one of those sad souls glued to their cell phones. But don't get too comfortable yet, because the study was conceived more than a decade ago, when "heavy use" was actually quite moderate by today's standards: thirty minutes a day put you in the highest category for the purposes of this study.[18] Indeed, as Dr. Devra Davis writes in her book *Disconnect* (2010), there's a very general problem with the established standards for cell phone usage: "Today's standards...were set in 1993, based on models that used a very large heavy man with an eleven-pound head talking for six minutes, when fewer than 10% of all adults had cell phones. Half of all ten-year-olds now have cell phones. Some young adults use phones for more than four hours a day."[19]

The concern that I want to flag, however, begins, again, when one looks at the source of these studies. Dr. Henry Lai of the University of Washington has examined 326 of these radiation studies. His analysis divides the studies into those that found some biologic effect and those that did not. Good news: the numbers are about even. Fifty-six percent of the studies found a biologic effect, while 44 percent did not. Not great (for cell phone users), but perhaps not reason enough (yet) to chuck your iPhone.

But Professor Lai then divided the studies into those that were funded by industry and those that were not. Once that division was made, the numbers no longer seemed so benign. Industry-funded studies overwhelmingly found no biologic effect, while independent studies found overwhelmingly that there was a biologic effect.

|  | BIOLOGIC EFFECT | NO BIOLOGIC EFFECT |
|---|---|---|
| Industry Funded | 27 (28%) | 69 (72%) |
| Independently Funded | 154 (67%) | 76 (33%) |

Lai's work is careful, but it has not yet been published in a peer-reviewed journal. Its conclusions, however, have been supported by important peer-reviewed work. In a paper published in 2007 in the journal *Environmental Health Perspectives*, researchers reviewed published studies of controlled exposure to radio-frequency radiation. They isolated fifty-nine studies that they believed meaningful, and divided those into ones funded by industry, funded by the public or charity, and funded in a mixed way.

Their conclusions are consistent with Lai's. As they wrote, "studies funded exclusively by industry were indeed substantially less likely to report statistically significant effects on a range of end points that may be relevant to health."[20] This conclusion added "to the existing evidence that single-source sponsorship is associated with outcomes that favor the sponsors' products."[21]

So how do these facts affect your view of cell phones?

Again, some will conclude that cell phones are dangerous. Some will continue to believe that they are safe. But the majority will process these facts by concluding that they are now no longer sure about whether cell phones are safe. The mere fact of money in the wrong place changes their confidence about this question of science.

## 3.

These two stories rely upon an obvious intuition—that money in the wrong places makes us trust less. My colleagues and I at Harvard wanted to test that intuition more systematically. Can we really show that money wrongly placed weakens the confidence or trust that people have in any particular institution? And if it does, does it have the same effect regardless of the institution? Or are some institutions more vulnerable—more untrustworthy—than others?

Our experiment presented participants with a series of vignettes in three different institutional contexts: politics, medicine, and consumer products. In each context, the cases differed only by the extent to which an actor's financial incentive was described to be dependent upon a particular outcome.

Across all three of the domains we tested, the mere suggestion of a link between financial incentives and a particular outcome significantly influenced the participants' trust and confidence in the underlying actor or institution. Doctors' advice was judged to be less trustworthy if the procedure they recommended was tied to a financial incentive. Politicians were judged to be less trustworthy if they supported a policy consistent with the agenda of contributing lobbyists. Researchers for consumer products were judged less trustworthy if their work was funded by an agency that had a financial stake in the outcome. And most surprisingly to us, these variations in the hypotheticals we presented also significantly influenced the participants' judgments *of their own* doctors, politicians, and consumer goods. Even the suggestion of one bad apple was enough to spoil the barrel.

In each of these contexts, of course, we might well say that the participants made a logical mistake. In none of the cases did we prove that the money was affecting the results. In none of the cases did we even suggest that it was. But logic notwithstanding, trust was affected merely because money was present in a way that *could have* biased the results. We infer bias from the structure of the case. Rightly or wrongly, this is how we read.[22]

## 4.

The field of "conflicts of interest" focuses on the question of when we should be concerned about dueling loyalties within a single decision maker or single institution. If, for example, you're a judge deciding a billion-dollar lawsuit brought against Exxon, the fact that you've got *any* financial connection to Exxon, however small, is enough to disqualify you from that suit. Your decision should depend upon the law alone. And one fear addressed by "conflicts" rules is that your loyalty might be split between the law and your own personal gain.

But come on—a single share of Exxon stock is enough to get a judge kicked from the case? Does anyone actually believe that a judge would throw a case because her stock might move from sixty dollars to sixty-one? Why does the law worry about such tiny things? Or, more sharply, why would it require a judge to step aside merely because, as the law states, her "impartiality might reasonably be questioned"? Shouldn't the test be whether the judge *is* partial? And if she is not partial, then shouldn't the question of whether people "might reasonably question her impartiality" be irrelevant? We don't lock people up in jail merely because other people "might reasonably" believe they're guilty. Why do we kick a judge from the bench?

Imagine a judge we know *is* impartial. Put aside how we know that; just assume that we do. If we know the judge is impartial, why should the fact that others might "reasonably" think otherwise matter? Sure, if we don't know, what others might "reasonably" think might be important. But what if we do know?

The answer to these questions is that uncertainty has its own effect. The law might say someone is innocent until proven guilty. But law be damned, if you learn that a school bus driver has been charged with drunk driving, you're going to think twice before you put your child on his bus. Indeed, even if you think the charge is likely false, the mere chance that it is true may well be enough (and rationally so) for you to decide to drive your kid rather than risk his life on the bus. The charge doesn't make the driver "guilty" in your head; but it certainly will affect whether you think it makes sense to let him drive your kid.

That's the same (Bayesian) principle that guides conflict-of-interest analysis.[23] The legal system doesn't assume that a judge is partial merely because her "impartiality might reasonably be questioned." But it does assume that the fact that her "impartiality might reasonably be questioned" will affect people's trust of the judicial system. And so to protect the system, or, more precisely, to protect trust in the system, the system takes no chances. As President William Howard Taft explained in his "Four Aspects of Civic Duty":

> This same principle is one that should lead judges not to accept courtesies like railroad passes from persons or companies frequently litigants in their courts. It is not that such courtesies

would really influence them to decide a case in favor of such litigants when justice required a different result; but the possible evil is that if the defeated litigant learns of the extension of such courtesy to the judge or the court by his opponent he cannot be convinced that his cause was heard by an indifferent tribunal, and it weakens the authority and the general standing of the court.[24]

The legal system thus avoids that chance. Or at least it takes the smallest chances it can. In this sense, following Professor Dennis Thompson, we can say that the "appearance standard identifies a distinct wrong, independent of and no less serious than the wrong of which it is an appearance"—because of this effect.[25]

But there's another side to this "impartiality might reasonably be questioned" standard that people often miss: the word *reasonably*. The question isn't whether any crazy person might wonder if a judge were biased. ("Your Honor, I notice you have the same birthday as the plaintiff, and I am concerned that might mean you are biased against Capricorns.") The question is what a "reasonable" person might think.[26] And so a reasonable question might be: Why stop at "reasonable"? If the objective is to protect the system, why not require recusal whenever someone in good faith at least worries that the judge is biased?

I learned about this side of the recusal rules the hard way. On December 11, 1997, the judge in the Microsoft antitrust trial appointed me a "special master" in that case. That meant I was to be a quasi, temporary, mini-judge, charged with understanding, and then making understandable, a complex technical question about how Windows was "bundled" with Internet Explorer. Microsoft didn't want a special master in the case, or at least they didn't want me. So almost immediately after the appointment, they launched a fairly aggressive campaign, in the courts and in the press, to get me removed. Their opening bid was that I used a Mac (on the theory that a neutral master would use Windows). It went downhill from there.

My first reaction to this firestorm (coward that I am) was to flee.

To resign. I didn't need the anger. I certainly didn't need the hate mail (and there was tons of that). But when I spoke to a couple of friends who were federal judges, they insisted that it would be wrong for me to resign. If a party could dump a judge merely by complaining, then parties could simply dial through all the judges until they found the one they liked best. The test, as I was told, was not whether a *party* could question my impartiality. The question was whether my "impartiality might reasonably be questioned." In their view, given the facts, it could not.

This story will help us understand the dynamic I described earlier in this chapter. In both cases, there was a factual question at stake: Is BPA, or are cell phones, safe? In both of those cases, there was a process by which that question was answered: scientific studies that presumably applied scientific standards to reach their results. But in both cases, there was also an influence present when conducting those studies that made at least some of us wonder. Why—except bias, one way or the other—would 72 percent of industry-funded studies find no danger from cell phones when 67 percent of independent studies found danger? Why would 100 percent of industry-funded studies find no harm from BPA while 86 percent of independently funded studies found some harm? And is it reasonable that someone would wonder about this scientific integrity given these differences?

That question at the very least reduces our confidence in the resulting claims of safety. Like a mom deciding to drive her kid to school rather than let him ride the school bus, that lack of confidence could also change how we behave. Again, not because we've necessarily concluded that something is unsafe, but because we now have reason to doubt whether something we thought safe actually is. That reason is the presence of an interested party, suggesting that it might have been interest, not science, that explains the difference in the result.

Put most simply: the mere presence of money with a certain relationship to the results makes us less confident about those results.

What follows from this put-most-simply fact, however, is not itself simple. The concern about conflicts must be "reasonable," as I've described, and there are many contexts in which we can't simply wish away the money that weakens our confidence. Sixty-three percent of drug trials are funded by the pharmaceutical industry.[27] We can't just pretend that's a small number, or wish the government would step in to fund trials on its own. Likewise with chemicals such as BPA or devices such as cell phones: It's a free country. The government should have no power to ban industry from studying its own chemicals or devices, and publishing to the world those results, at least barring fraud.

Instead, our response to this conflict, or potential conflict, is always going to be more complicated. We need to ask whether there is a feasible or reasonable way to win back the confidence that the presence of money takes away. Are there procedures that would remove the doubt of the reasonable person? Are there other ways to earn back that confidence?

## 5.

Many private institutions get this. Many structure themselves in light of it, taking the risk of this apparent corruption into account and pushing it off the table.

If you're old enough to remember the Internet circa 1998, you may remember thinking, as I did then, "This is a disaster. There's no good way to search this network without drowning in advertising muck." Then came Google, committed to the idea, and convincing in their commitment, that at least the core search results (not the "sponsored links" but the core bottom-left frame of a search screen) were true, that they reflected relevance as judged by some disinterested soul (maybe the Nets), not as bought by the advertisers. As the founders wrote at the time,

> We expect that advertising funded search engines will be inherently biased towards the advertisers and away from the needs of consumers.... [T]he better the search engine is, the

fewer advertisements will be needed for the consumer to find what they want.... [W]e believe the issue of advertising causes enough mixed incentives that it is crucial to have a competitive search engine that is transparent and in the academic realm.[28]

That commitment gave us confidence. It lets us trust the system, and trust Google.

The same with Wikipedia. Wikipedia doesn't accept advertising. As it is the fifth most visited site on the Internet, that means it leaves about $150 million on the table *every year*.[29] As a believer in Wikipedia, and the values of Wikipedians, this is a hard fact for me to swallow. The good (at least from my perspective) that could be done with $150 million a year is not trivial. So what is the good that the world gets in exchange for Wikipedia's abstemiousness?

As Jimmy Wales, founder of Wikipedia, described it to me, "[W]e do care that... the general public looks to Wikipedia in all of its glories and all of its flaws, which are numerous of course. But the one thing they don't say is, 'Well, I don't trust Wikipedia because it's all basically advertising fluff.'"[30]

So the Wikipedia community spends $150 million each year to secure the site's independence from apparent commercial bias. Wow.

Or again, think about the Lonely Planet series. Among the most popular travel books in the world (with 13 percent of the market share),[31] Lonely Planet has earned the trust of many. It is a reliable source for information about the unknown places you might visit. I use the books as often as I can.

But in gathering the information for its books, Lonely Planet needs to assure, both itself and its readers, that the reviews it is relying upon are trustworthy. And it strives to earn that trust with a very clear policy: "Why is our travel information the best in the world? It's simple. Our authors are passionate, dedicated travelers. They don't take freebies in exchange for positive coverage so you can be sure the advice you're given is impartial."

In all three of these cases, these private entities depend for their success upon the public trusting them. So they adopt rules that help them earn that trust. These rules alone, of course, are not enough. But they help. It is because of them that I have reason at least to give the institution the benefit of the doubt. Or, more important, it is because of these rules that I don't automatically assume financial bias whenever I see something I don't understand, or don't agree with. These clear and strong rules cushion skepticism; they make trust possible because they give the public a reason to believe that the institution *will* act as it has signaled it would act.

These freedom-restricting rules, moreover, are self-imposed. Search results with integrity were a competitive advantage for Google. That's part of why it made that choice. The same with Wikipedia: The Internet is filled with ad-driven information sites. Wikipedia's choice gave it a competitive advantage over others, and a community advantage as it tried to attract authors. Likewise with Lonely Planet: It wants a brand people can trust, as a way to sell more books. It therefore restricts its freedom to better achieve its goals.

In none of these cases was government regulation necessary. In none of the cases did some professional body, such as the Bar Association or the AMA, need to intervene to force the companies to do what was "right." "What was right" coincided perfectly with what was in the best interest of these entities. As Adam Smith famously said, they were "in this, as in many other cases, led by an invisible hand to promote an end which was no part of [their] intention."[32]

That's not always true of course. Indeed, as we'll see, pursuing self-interest alone, without the proper regulatory structure, is often fatal to the public interest. But here, private interests coincide with a public good. Government intervention was therefore not necessary.

I'm sure that with each of these entities, this freedom-restricting rule wasn't obvious, at least at the time it was chosen. Just at the time Google launched in a big way, the biggest competitor was ad-driven Yahoo. At the time, I'm sure everyone thought the future of Internet search was simply Yellow Pages on steroids. Wikipedians fight all the time about whether the restriction on advertising is actually necessary. And I'm quite sure that the editors at Lonely Planet have at least thought about how much cheaper their production costs would be if the reviewers got comp'd meals and lodging. My claim with each is not that the choice was easy or obvious. It is instead that the choice was made with the belief that the choice, regardless of the cost, was in the long-term interests of that institution.

In each case, these institutions recognized that to preserve a public's trust, they had to steel themselves against a public's cynicism. They had to starve that cynicism by structuring themselves to block the obvious cynical inference that money in the wrong place creates. Not money. Money in the wrong place. If properly cabined, or properly insulated, money within an institution (Google, Wikipedia, Lonely Planet) can be fine. It is when it is in a place where, as we all recognize, it will or can or could cause even the most earnest compass to deviate that we should have a concern.

# CHAPTER 3

## $1 + 1 =$

There's a frog at the center of a well-known metaphor about our inability to respond "to disasters that creep up on [us] a bit at a time."[1] The rap on the frog, it turns out, is false: frogs *will* jump from a tub of water as it is heated to boiling. (Trust me on this; please don't try it at home.) But the charge against us is completely fair: We don't do well with problems that don't scream their urgency. We let them slide. We wait for the dam to break.

The previous two chapters should suggest a related disability that is also fairly predicated of us: We don't do well responding to bads that stand between good and evil. We teach our kids the difference between good and evil. We craft blockbuster movies to test good versus evil. But to grow up is to recognize, and to live, the bad that stands between good and evil. And the challenge, always, is to motivate a response.

For while we respond appropriately to evil, we don't respond well to good souls who do harm. We don't identify the harm well. We don't act to stop it. Indeed, even when we see the harm clearly, we deny its most obvious source. We can't imagine this decent soul has caused it. So we scour the scene for the obviously corrupt or evil one, as if only the evil could be responsible for great harm.

Yet we all know better than this. We all recognize Yeltsin, or his character. It is our father. Or our mother. Or our uncle, or wife. Or us. We believe the dependency is his or her responsibility, not ours. We tell ourselves, There's nothing I can do. And so we don't.

It is because we are so familiar with this subtle form of bad— and with our weakness in the face of it—that we are in turn also so suspicious, or cynical, when certain puzzles confront us, and we see an obvious source—money in the wrong place.

The job of the decent souls we call "scientists" is to tell us truthfully whether BPA is safe, or whether cell phones will give us gray lumps behind the ears. But we're very quick to believe that even these good souls can be bought—again, not just by bribes, or through fraud, but in the subtle and obvious ways in which we all understand that money bends truth. So merely telling Americans that money is in the mix is enough for most Americans to jump to the ship *Cynical*. An institution that depends upon trust to be effective will thus lose that trust, and therefore become less effective, if it lets money seep into the wrong place.

I mark these as obvious points, yet we forget them, always. We know them; they guide how we live and negotiate our day-to-day life. But when we talk about the great failing that is at the center of this book, Congress, it is as if we return to the moral universe of kindergarten. We have an enormous frustration with our government. All sides try to identify the source of our frustration with this institution in the evil or stupid acts of evil or stupid people—senators, or worse, *congressmen*! Americans believe "money buys results" in Congress—almost literally. Some believe congressmen take bags of cash in exchange for changing their votes. They speak as if they believe that members of Congress entered public life because they thought public life was a quicker path to quick cash. They wouldn't have their son or daughter marry a member of Congress—at least the member of Congress who lives in their abstract thoughts.

Yet when we actually meet our congressman, we confront an obvious dissonance. For that person is not the evil soul we imagined behind our government. She is not sleazy. He is not lazy. Indeed, practically every single member of Congress is not just someone who *seems* decent. Practically every single member of Congress *is* decent. These are people who entered public life for the best possible reasons. They believe in what they do. They make enormous sacrifices in order to do what they do. They give us confidence, despite the fact that they work in an institution that has lost the public's confidence.

Don't get me wrong. Of course there are exceptions. Obviously some are more and some are less decent; some are more and some are less publicly minded. And no doubt, why politicians make the sacrifices they make is hard, psychologically, to understand. But however much you qualify the rosy picture I have drawn, the truth remains miles from the kind of machine of evil that most of us presume occupies our capital. Any account of the failure of our democracy that places idiots or felons in the middle fundamentally misses what's actually going on.

Instead, the story of our Congress is these two previous chapters added together:

1. We have a gaggle of good souls who have become dependent in a way that weakens the democracy, *and*
2. We have a nation of good souls who see that dependency, and assume the worst.

The first flaw bends policy. The second flaw weakens the public's trust. The two together condemn the republic, unless we find a way to reform at least one.

# PART II

# TELLS

None of us are expert—enough. We each may know a great deal about something, but none of us know enough about the wide range of things that we must understand if we're to understand the issues of government today.

For those bits that we don't understand, we rely upon institutions. But whether we trust those institutions will depend upon how they seem to us: how they are crafted, and whether they are built to insulate the actors from the kind of influences we believe might make their decisions untrustworthy.

We don't have a choice about this. We can't simply decide to know everything about everything, or decide to ignore the things that make us suspicious. We are human. We will respond in human ways. And we will *believe* long before scientists can *prove*. Thus we must build institutions that take into account what we believe, especially when those beliefs limit our ability to trust.

Including the institutions of government: We don't have a choice about *whether* to have government. There are too many interconnected struggles that we as a people face. There may well be a conservative or libertarian or liberal response to those struggles. But all sensible sides believe there's a role for government in at least some of these struggles, even if some believe that role is less than others.

When the government plays its role, we need to be able to trust it. Not trust that it will do whatever we want, for sometimes our party loses, and when it does, we lose the right to demand that the government do the right (from our perspective) thing. But whether we've won or lost, we need to trust that the government is acting for the (politically) correct reasons: liberal, if liberals have won; conservative, if conservatives have won; libertarian, if libertarians have won. We need to believe that the government is tracking the sort of interests it was intended to track. Or at least, as Marc Hetherington puts it, that the "government is producing outcomes consistent with [our] expectations."[1]

When the actions of government conflict with those expectations, we will look beyond trust, for other reasons, to see whether they might explain the puzzle. Other reasons, such as money in the wrong places. When we find it—when we see that money was in the wrong place—it will affect us. It will weaken our trust in government. It will undermine our motivation to engage.

In this section, I select four policy struggles and point to puzzles about each. I then stand these puzzles next to some facts about money that might or might not have affected each struggle. The drama here is not always as pronounced as with BPA or cell phones. But the exercise is crucial to understanding the kind of trouble our republic is facing.

# CHAPTER 4

# *Why Don't We Have Free Markets?*

Type 2 diabetes is a disease that causes the body to misuse its own insulin. Overproduction of insulin causes insulin resistance. Insulin resistance increases the level of free fatty acids in the bloodstream, and the level of sugar. Out-of-whack levels of fatty acids and sugar do no good. The direct harms are bad enough. Indirect harms include the loss of limbs, blindness, kidney failure, and heart disease.[1]

In 1985 only 1 to 2 percent of children with diabetes had type 2 diabetes. Of the adults with diabetes, 90 to 95 percent had type 2.[2] Over the past two decades, these numbers have changed, dramatically. Now it is children who, in at least some communities, "account for almost half of new cases of type 2 [diabetes]."[3] Among all new cases of childhood diabetes, "the proportion of those with type 2...ranges between 8% and 43%."[4]

In the view of some, the rise in type 2 diabetes among kids is tied to an "epidemic" rise in childhood obesity.[5] Today, 85 percent of children with type 2 diabetes are obese. That level, too, is rising.[6]

And obesity is rising not just among children. Between 1960 and 2006, the "percentage of obese adults has nearly tripled.... [T]he proportion...who are 'extremely obese' increased more than 600%."[7] Amazingly, less than a third of Americans ages twenty to seventy-four today are at a healthy weight.[8] That proportion is not going to improve in the near future.

Obesity-related disease costs the medical system $147 billion annually[9]—a greater burden than the costs of cigarettes or alcohol.

So what accounts for this bloat? How did we go from being a relatively healthy country to one certain to blow the highest proportion of GDP of any industrialized nation dealing with the consequences of one thousand too many Twinkies?

The most likely reason for this explosion in obesity is a change in what we eat. As people who know something about the matter will testify, we eat too much of the wrong stuff, and not enough of the right stuff: too much sugar, fat, processed food; not enough vegetables and unprocessed food. Between 1990 and 2006 the percentage of adults who ate five or more fruits and vegetables a day fell from 42 percent to 26 percent.[10] Americans now drink fifty-two gallons of soft drinks a year, with teenage girls getting 10 to 15 percent of their total caloric intake from Coke or Pepsi.[11] These choices matter to our bodies. They make us unhealthy and increasingly fat.

Why we make these particularly bad eating choices is a complicated story. We all (and especially women) work outside the home more than before. That means we have less time to prepare meals and more need for meals prepared by others. The others preparing those meals recognize that certain food qualities—the sweetness, the saltiness, the fattiness—will affect the strength of demand for that food. The ideal demand-inducing mix is all three together: think double-tall caramel latte.[12]

We're not about to empower federal food police, however, and neither are we going back to the 1950s, when more of us stayed at home cooking beets (or better). If we're going to make progress with this problem, we need to think about the parts of the problem that we can actually change.

The part that I want to focus on is the economics of what we eat. Or, more precisely, the economics of the inputs to what we eat. It's clear we eat a lot of sweet stuff. Since 1985, U.S. consumption of all sugars has increased by 23 percent.[13] But what's interesting is the mix of the sweet stuff we eat. It's not just sugar, or predominantly sugar. Increasingly it is high-fructose corn syrup, a sugar substitute. In 1980, humans had never tasted high-fructose corn syrup. In 1985 it accounted for 35 percent of sugar consumption. In 2006 that number had risen to over 41 percent.[14]

Why?

One simple answer is price. Natural sugar is expensive, relative to high-fructose corn syrup. So the market in sweeteners moves more and more to this sugar substitute. Or better, *races* to this sugar substitute. Forty percent of the products in your supermarket right now have high-fructose corn syrup in them.[15] That number is certain to rise.

Invocation of the "market" is likely to lead some to say, "Them's just the breaks." Markets are designed to channel resources to where they can be most efficiently used, and to push out inefficient inputs for more-efficient ones.

Yet lovers of the market should hesitate a bit here before they embrace this particular mix of sweetness. Indeed, an alarm for free-market souls should sound whenever anyone talks about the input costs from agriculture and related industries. Even for a liberal like me, it is astonishing to recognize just how unfree the market in foodstuff is. And it is embarrassing to reckon the huge gap between our pro-free-market rhetoric around the world and the actual market of government regulation of food production we've produced here at home. As Dwayne Andreas, chairman of Archer Daniels Midland (ADM), one of the most important beneficiaries of our unfree-food market, told *Mother Jones*: "There isn't one grain of anything in the world that is sold in a free market. Not one! The only place you see a free market is in the speeches of politicians. People who are not in the Midwest do not understand that this is a socialist country."[16]

*A socialist country.*

It's easy to see why this enormously wealthy capitalist celebrates this chunk of American socialism: he is a primary beneficiary. Headquartered in Illinois, ADM is a conglomerate of companies with revenues exceeding $69 billion in 2009. According to one estimate, at least 43 percent of ADM's annual profits are "from products heavily subsidized or protected by the American government." More dramatically, "every $1 of profits earned by ADM's corn sweetener operation costs consumers $10, and every $1 of profits earned by its ethanol operation costs taxpayers $30."[17]

Andreas is certainly right that few from the coasts (including the west coast of Lake Michigan) recognize just how pervasive this socialism is. We protect milk in America. *Milk*, for God's sake! "Most milk in the United States is marketed under…regulations known as 'milk marketing orders.' Currently, there are [ten] federal orders that regulate how milk is priced."[18]

That means there is a map controlled by government regulators that divides the country and sets the price. And by "most," that commentator means *almost 60 percent* of milk production under federal regulation, with most of the rest subject to state regulation.

This regulation is intended to subsidize dairy farmers. The Organisation for Economic Co-operation and Development (OECD) estimates that that subsidy increases the price of milk by about 26 percent. Cheese costs 37 percent more in the United States than elsewhere, again because of this regulation. Butter: 100 percent more in the United States than elsewhere. These differences are not trivial.

This system of subsidy dates back to the New Deal, when at least the government had the excuse of the phenomenally bad economics that seemed to rule the day. "Got a depression? Here's an idea: mandate higher prices!"

Since the 1930s the economics has improved. The politics has not. Richard Nixon hinted that he planned to abolish the price supports for milk. After receiving—because of the hints?—$2 million in campaign contributions from the dairy lobby, he changed his mind.[19] Since his flirt with free markets, no one has seriously thought to end this economic idiocy—because it is political genius. Highly organized special interests leverage their power to transfer wealth from consumers to farmers.

And not just dairy farmers. The government has intervened to protect shrimp producers against foreign competition.[20] It has blocked more-efficient Brazilian cotton producers from selling in the American market (by subsidizing American cotton farmers and paying off Brazilian farmers so they won't retaliate).[21] It has waged war to protect banana producers.[22] It has even imposed import restrictions and offered low-cost loans to protect peanut farmers (and no, Jimmy Carter is not to blame for that).[23]

This protection is not just for farmers. Republican president George W. Bush led the charge to protect steel in 2001.[24] So, too, do we protect domestic lumber firms from Canadian competition. According to the Cato Institute, this adds between fifty and eighty dollars per thousand board feet, pricing three hundred thousand families out of the housing market.[25] As University of Chicago professors Raghuram Rajan and Luigi Zingales estimate, "trade restrictions imposed in the 1980s . . . cost consumers $6.8 billion a year, while the value of government subsidies received by the industry over the same period amounted to $30 billion."[26]

Liberals are often untroubled by the idea of the government mucking about in the market. They like the idea of the government stepping in to help the weak. And certainly, as we non-farmers are likely to believe, farmers are among the poorest in our society. If a bit of milk regulation keeps a few cows on a dairy farm, latte-sipping Starbucks customers can afford it.

But these subsidies don't help poor farmers. Nor are they produced because of a concern for the poor. The biggest beneficiaries are the world's richest and most powerful corporate farmers.[27] Ten percent of the recipients of farm subsidies collect 73 percent of the subsidies—between 2003 and 2005, $91,000 per farm. The average subsidy of the bottom 80 percent? Three thousand dollars per farm.[28] And among those receiving large farm subsidies are Fortune 500 companies such as John Hancock Life Insurance ($2,849,799), International Paper ($1,183,893), and Chevron/Texaco ($446,914); many celebrities, such as David Rockefeller ($553,782), Ted Turner ($206,948), and Scottie Pippen ($210,520); and several prominent current and former members of Congress such as Chuck Grassley (R-Iowa; 1975– : $225,041), Gordon Smith (R-Ore.; 1997–2009: $45,400), and Ken Salazar (D-Colo.; 2005–2009: $161,084).[29]

The same story can be told about steel. If the United States wanted to help steel *workers* hurt because of shifts in the market for steel production, it could compensate them directly. But "instead of direct compensation to workers...[the] government imposed tariffs to protect fewer than nine thousand jobs in the steel industry"—which in turn was likely "to cost 74,000 jobs in steel-consuming industries."[30]

The list of anti-free-market interventions by our government is endless. But the particular regulations I want to focus upon here tie to the cost of sugar and high-fructose corn syrup (HFC). For the interventions with this are quite extreme, and they produce quite obvious effects. HFC is cheap relative to sugar for two very anti-free-market reasons: the first is tariffs; the second, subsidies.

*Tariffs*: Sugar in the United States is two to three times as expensive as in other countries. That's because the U.S. government protects the domestic sugar manufacturers with tariffs (there are all of forty sugar companies in the United States, just eight producing 75 percent of sugar, constituting 0.5 percent of farms in America, and employing a total of sixty-two thousand workers).[31] That tariff gives those manufacturers about $1 billion in extra profits a year. It costs the overall economy (through increased prices and inefficiency) about $3 billion.[32] Worst among those costs might well be the environmental damage to the Florida Everglades. For as we've pushed sugar production into Florida, it has poured millions of gallons of polluted water into the ecosystem.[33]

This protectionism hurts American business. (Every penny in increased sugar prices is estimated to cost at least $250 million in increased food costs.)[34] It hurts American jobs. (The Commerce Department estimates more than ten thousand jobs between 1997 and 2002.)[35] It hurts developing nations. (The State Department estimates that burden to be at least $800 million a year.)[36] And it obviously hurts America's selling of pro-free-trade ideology: our behavior makes a mockery of those important, wealth-producing ideals.[37]

This protectionism does, however, help at least one group beyond the sugar barons: corn producers. For the higher the cost of sugar, the safer the market for sugar substitutes such as HFC. Which explains why one of the biggest supporters of sugar tariffs is a company that doesn't produce any natural sugar: ADM. Sugar tariffs produce a "price umbrella" for HFC, protecting that enormously profitable business from a more natural competition.[38]

*Subsidies*: The shift to HFC, however, is not explained simply by the high cost of sugar. It is also explained by the low cost of corn. Corn in the United States is cheap relative to other nations because we subsidize its production. In the fifteen years between 1995 and 2009, the government spent $73.8 billion to ensure that farmers produced more corn than the market would otherwise bear.[39] That corn then got used to produce lots of high-fructose corn syrup, at an increasingly low price.

HFC is not even the most important effect of this policy by the government. Because corn is so cheap (and accounting for all the subsidies, some argue the cost of growing corn is actually negative),[40] cattle ranchers feed corn to their cattle. That's good for the ranchers (feeding cattle corn rather than grazing them on grass means more heads per acre and more profit on the bottom line). It's not so good for small farmers or for the cattle.

*Bad for small farms*: This subsidy encourages the decline of the family farm. Subsidized competitors drive out perfectly profitable smaller farms. Elanor Starmer and Timothy Wise, for example, have calculated that subsidized feed for hogs has "had the effect of reducing [factory farm] operating costs compared to those of smaller-scale, diversified operations."[41] That artificial cost advantage in turn may be driving further industrialization in the livestock production system—even though the cost of that system, if fully accounted, would be no better than smaller, more traditional farms.[42]

*Bad for cows*: Cows don't digest corn well. Their four stomachs evolved to digest grass. Corn typically makes them sick, as bugs brew in the poorly digested mix stewing in their stomachs. And so to deal with that sickness, farmers have to supplement corn feed with tons of antibiotics, twenty-five million pounds of them per year, eight times the total amount consumed by humans.[43]

This profligate use of antibiotics might strike you as weird. Before you use antibiotics, you have to get the permission of a doctor. Cattle, it turns out, have greater freedom than we do, in this respect at least. They are fed antibiotics prophylactically. No doctor needs to make sure that their use is actually warranted.

But doesn't that use then induce the spread of superbugs? you ask. For isn't the reason that we don't hand out antibiotics with every sneeze that we don't want to foster the strongest, antibiotic-resistant bacteria out there?

Right again. But public health concerns about the overuse of antibiotics get checked at the door of the Department of Agriculture. That agency has a long history of pushing for the widespread use of antibiotics.[44] And the consequence of that push, as many have argued, is that there's an explosion of drug-resistant bugs such as E. coli 0157:H7 and salmonella.[45] Were this book a movie, we'd now cut to a scene about a three-year-old boy who died after eating a hamburger, or a twenty-two-year-old dance instructor who can no longer walk.[46]

It gets worse. The strategy of the concentrated corn industry is not just to protect HFC. It is also to increase the demand for corn generally. Enter ethanol—perhaps the dumbest "green" energy program ever launched by government. Whole forests have been felled pointing out the stupidity of a subsidy to produce a fuel that is neither a good fuel (as in, it packs a good punch) nor, when you consider the cost of refining it,[47] a green fuel. As libertarian author James Bovard puts it, ethanol is "a political concoction—a product that exists and is used solely because of the interference of politicians with the workings of the marketplace."[48] One 2008 report estimated that the biofuel mandates of Congress would cost the economy more than $100 billion from 2005 to 2010.[49] That's sixty-five times the total amount spent on renewable energy research and development programs during the same period.[50]

So the government protects sugar, and the government subsidizes corn. As a result, more foods get made with high-fructose corn syrup, and more cattle get fed corn, meaning more cattle get fed antibiotics. The quantity of high-fructose corn syrup thus goes up in our diet, and the prevalence of dangerous bacteria goes up as well. And in complicated ways tied in part to these changes, it is at least plausible that one cruel consequence of these interventions in the market is that our kids get fat and sick.

Or, more sharply: the government distorts the market, which distorts what we eat, which distorts our kids' bodies and health.

So, why? What leads our government to such anti-free-market silliness?

There are many possible causes. Presidential campaigns begin in Iowa. Rural states are overrepresented in the Senate. Subsidies once started are difficult to end. And so on.

But as you try to reckon this mix of protections and subsidies, there is one fact to keep clear: The beneficiaries of these policies spend an enormous amount to keep them. The opponents spend very little to oppose them. The campaign spending of the sugar industry over the past two decades is high and growing.[51]

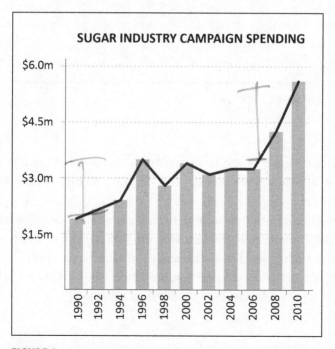

**FIGURE 1**

The lobbying and campaign spending of the corn industry is even higher.[52]

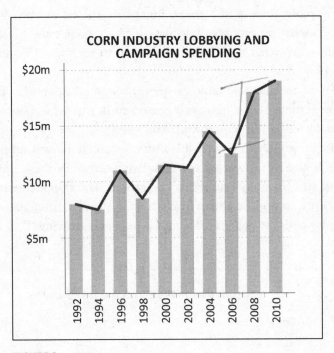

**FIGURE 2**

These numbers are large relative to other lobbying and campaign spending, even though they are tiny relative to the benefit they seek.

But I don't offer them here to prove anything about causation. Instead, the question that I mean these data to raise is simply this:

*Not*: Did these contributions buy the silliness we see?

*Instead*: Do these contributions affect your ability to believe that this policy is something other than silliness?

# CHAPTER 5

# Why Don't We Have Efficient Markets?

Imagine you drove into a small town just at the moment that a celebration was beginning. The town has a single street, creatively named Main Street. Behind the row of shops on one side of the street, imagine there's a steep drop-off to a river below.

All the action is in front of a restaurant on Main Street. The mayor is honoring the owner of that restaurant for her success and profitability.

As the son of an entrepreneur, I understand the pride of the owner. Success in business is hard. It only ever comes with hard work. And as a student of economics, it is easy for me to recognize the appreciation of the mayor and the town: successful business is the lifeblood of an economy. Everyone, whether liberal or conservative, should honor, celebrate, and protect such success.

But now imagine that you walked behind the restaurant and discovered a torrent of trash flowing from the back door, down the hill, and into the river. Imagine that torrent of trash flowed from a decision by the owner of the business: rather than paying to have her garbage collected, she simply dumped the garbage down the hill. And imagine, finally, that if you calculated the cost of garbage collection and subtracted it from the restaurant's profits, the restaurant would no longer have been profitable. It is profitable, in other words, only because it is not paying all of its costs.

Economists have a technical term for this kind of cost: *externalities*. Since time immemorial, economists have argued that such costs must be "internalized," meaning the people creating the costs must pay for what they create. Markets that don't internalize externalities are not, the economist insists, "efficient markets." Such markets might be profitable (for the businesses that don't have to pay for the costs they impose on others). But whether profitable or not, they are not efficient. An efficient market is one that fully pays its costs, and compensates for its benefits.

Put most simply, an externality is any effect that I have upon you that you and I haven't bargained about. If my friends and I have a party, the music from my stereo keeping you up late is an externality. If my family has a barbecue, and sparks from the fire turn your house into an inferno, those sparks are an externality. If I decide to raise hogs in my backyard, the smell from those lovely, cuddly creatures is an externality. In each case, the externality is something I do to you that you and I haven't agreed upon. In each case, you'd be perfectly right to complain.

But not with all externalities. Sometimes society likes the externality that I impose upon you, even if you don't. If I invent a better mousetrap, one that might well destroy your less-innovative mousetrap business, competition from me thus harms you; and you and I certainly didn't agree to that harm. Yet the law plainly encourages me to hurt you in precisely this way. (Sorry!) And finally, sometimes you will like the externality that I "impose" upon you. Imagine I renovate my house. That increases its value, and the value of the neighborhood. We didn't negotiate about whether I'd give you that extra wealth. I just did. The law doesn't seek to stop these externalities; the law *encourages* them.

The difference is between "negative" externalities and "positive" externalities. Negative externalities impose costs on others. Positive externalities create benefits for others, even if, as with competition, they make some people worse off. The public policy challenge with negative externalities is to avoid these imposed costs, by forcing the imposer to pay for them. The challenge with positive externalities is to ensure that the creator gets enough of the externalized benefits to have incentive to produce them in the first place.

To say that something is a "public policy challenge," however, is not to argue for a government program to solve it. Neighbors are pretty good at working stuff out. And social norms lead even the stranger on a highway to bus his tray at a restaurant. Likewise with externalized benefits: Just because painting my house makes you wealthier doesn't mean that justice requires a tax to give some of that benefit back to me. Often, both negative and positive externalities are manageable without some regulator stepping in the middle.

Many externalities are not manageable like this, however, and the government is needed then to avoid both the underproduction of positive externalities and the overproduction of negative externalities.

Consider, for example, the case of movies. Imagine a blockbuster Hollywood feature that costs $20 million to make. Once a single copy of this film is in digital form, the Internet guarantees that millions of copies could be accessed in a matter of minutes. Those "extra" copies are the physical manifestation of the positive externality that a film creates. The value or content of that film can be shared easily—insanely easily—given the magic of "the Internets."

That ease of sharing creates risk of underproduction for such creative work: If the only way that this film can be made is for the company making it to get paid by those who watch it, or distribute it, then without some effective way to make sure that those who make copies pay for those copies, we're not going to get many of those films made. That's not to say we won't get *any* films made. There are plenty of films that don't exist for profit. Government propaganda is one example. Safety films that teach employees at slaughterhouses how to use dangerous equipment is another.

But if you're like me, and want to watch Hollywood films more than government propaganda (and certainly more than safety films), you might well be keen to figure out how we can ensure that more of the former get made, even if we must suffer too much of the latter.

The answer is copyright—or, more precisely, an effective system of copyright. Copyright law gives the creator of a film (and other art forms) the legal right to control who makes copies of it, who can distribute it, who displays it publicly, and so forth. By giving the creator that power, the creator can then set the price he or she wants. If the system is effective, that price is respected—the only people who can get the film are the people who pay for it. The creator can thus get the return she wants in exchange for creating the film. We would be a poorer culture if copyright didn't give artists and authors a return for their creativity.

Since 1995, Congress has enacted thirty-two different statutes to further refine and strengthen the protection of copyright.[1] The frequency of these new laws has increased as digital technologies have put more pressure on the traditional architecture of copyright. But there's little doubt that the objective of this system of regulation is good and important for a free and flourishing culture.

So, fair enough. Congress has a reason to address this problem of positive externalities. The energy devoted to addressing this problem is consistent with that reason. Some intervention is plainly needed in this context. The government has plainly intervened some. Free riders (aka the "pirates") might want to block that intervention. But so far they've not succeeded in blocking this federal regulation. Congress has overcome resistance and internalized the benefits of these positive externalities.

But what about negative externalities? What has Congress done about them? As compared with its vigorous defense of the copyright industries, with thirty-two laws in sixteen years, what has it done to deal with the twenty-first century's equivalent to the restaurant owner at the start of this chapter: carbon pollution?

For, just like the restaurant owner, there are many within our economy who claim profits only because they ignore the cost of cleaning up the carbon they spew out their virtual back door. Take power companies that use coal to produce electricity: According to the Pew Center on Global Climate Change, the cost of capturing and sequestering carbon produced by coal-fired power plants is between $30 and $90 a ton. In 2003 more than 1.9 billion tons of carbon were spewed into the air by burning coal to produce electricity.[2] That means the cost to clean up the carbon those companies produced was between $280 and $840 *billion* in 2003 alone. The total profits of the coal and petroleum industry combined in 2003? $23.3 billion.[3]

These companies plainly produce negative externalities. They don't pay for the externalities they produce. Those externalities impose significant costs on our society and ecology. The most tangible are the health costs—estimated to be $100 billion per year.[4] The most profound are the contributions to the problem of climate change.

Now you might be a climate change skeptic. You might think, isn't the science about global warming contested? Aren't there scientists who doubt—and even deny—that carbon is harmful to our climate?

And of course, there is some contest. There are some scientists who doubt whether the harm from climate change is as great as Al Gore says it is, just as there are some economists who doubt whether the creators of culture need all the protection that the law of copyright now gives them.

But these two contests are radically different. If you took the average of every estimate by every scientist, skeptic or not, of the potential harm caused by climate change, and compared that to the average of every estimate by every economist, skeptic or not, of the harm caused to creativity by the Internet, climate change costs would be a mountain (call it Everest) and creativity costs would be a molehill (and you've not seen many molehills precisely because they're so small).

So then, while passing more than thirty laws over the past sixteen years to address the alleged harm to creativity caused by the Internet, how many times in the past fifteen years has Congress passed legislation to make carbon polluters cover the cost of their pollution? Or even the past twenty-five years?

Not once.

While the copyright free riders have failed to block externality-internalizing legislation affecting creativity, the carbon free riders have repeatedly succeeded in blocking the externality-internalizing legislation affecting climate change. Where the harm is almost certain, Congress does nothing. Where the harm is at best contested, Congress races to the rescue.

As a matter of principle, there is nothing political about the point my comparison is meant to draw. No sensible Republican would defend the restaurant owner at the start of this chapter. Nor would she say that a polluter shouldn't pay the cost to clean up his pollution. And while there's plenty to disagree about when deciding how best to clean up carbon pollution, there couldn't really be a principled reason to say we should not clean it up at all. Or, more strongly: if we are deploying federal courts to protect against the uncertain harm to Hollywood, we should be deploying someone or something to protect against the radically less uncertain harm to our economy and environment caused by carbon pollution.

Yet we don't. Why?

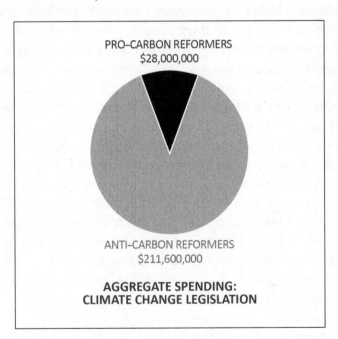

**FIGURE 3**

Here again, the political scientist might demur. There are many different causes, some good, some not so good. *Good*: Getting it wrong with climate change is costly (lost jobs, slowed economic growth). Getting it wrong with copyright is less costly (we don't get as much for free). *Not so good*: Key Democrats come from big-coal states. They're not about to willingly accept higher costs for energy, even if justified by good economic principles.[5] The carbon free riders have important allies. Copyright free riders, on the other hand, don't.

But as well as reasons good and not so good, there's another we cannot ignore. There is a radical difference in political funding by pro-reform advocates of both carbon and copyright.

Pro–carbon reformers get wildly outspent by anti-reformers. In 2009, pro-reform and anti-reform groups fought vigorously over whether Congress would enact a cap-and-trade bill to address carbon emissions. They didn't fight equally.[6] The reform movement spent about $22.4 million in lobbying and campaign contributions. The anti-reform movement spent $210.6 million.

An even more dramatic story can be told about copyright. Between 1998 and 2010, pro–copyright reformers were outspent by anti-reformers by $1.3 billion to $1 million—a thousand to one.[7] These are rough estimates, as transparency organizations don't

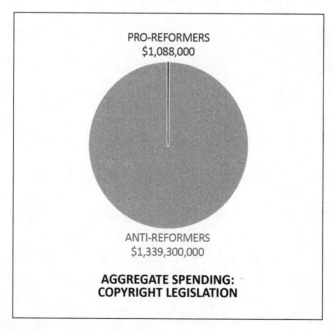

PRO-REFORMERS
$1,088,000

ANTI-REFORMERS
$1,339,300,000

**AGGREGATE SPENDING:
COPYRIGHT LEGISLATION**

FIGURE 4

aggregate copyright as a category. But even if I am wrong by a couple of orders of magnitude, the point is still correct: in both cases,
the anti-reformers outspend the pro-reformers by at least a factor of
ten.

So, again: Don't read these numbers to make any claim about
causation. Read them and ask yourself one question only:

*Not*: Did the contributions and lobbying buy this apparently
inconsistent result?

*Instead*: Do the contributions and lobbying make it harder to
believe that this is a principled or consistent or sensible result?

# CHAPTER 6

# Why Don't We Have Successful Schools?

Imagine a virus that spreads among kids, causing a certain kind of brain damage. The virus strikes kids at certain schools more than kids at other schools. It seems to strike rich kids less than poor. But it is pervasive, and spreading.

Then imagine that scientists discover a vaccine—a vaccine that might guarantee that no one, neither rich nor poor, will contract this brain-damaging disease. Imagine this vaccine is relatively inexpensive. Or, at least, the cost of the vaccine is a fraction of the cost of the damage done by the virus.

How long would it take before that vaccine spread to every kid in America?

We've argued throughout our history about just what government should do. Should there be a standing army? (Framers: no. Us: yes.) Should the government subsidize a partisan press? (Framers: yes. Us: no.) Should the federal government build highways? (Framers: no. Us: yes.)

But the one thing that everyone believes, at least now, is that the government has an essential role in ensuring a good education for our kids. Not everyone agrees on how. Some believe a voucher is all the government need do. Some believe it must mandate that everyone attend a public school. But within that wide range of means, all agree on the end: a safe and prosperous nation requires a well-educated youth.

We are failing in this. Miserably. In 1973 the United States was ranked high in the world in providing high-quality public education. We have fallen to fourteenth in reading among OECD countries (with math at twenty-five, and science at seventeen).[1] Things, of course, were not so great for many, many Americans in 1973. They are just bizarrely worse for almost all Americans today.[2]

One particular problem in the collection of challenges around public education has been how to improve the lot of the worst-off among us. Despite the fact that billions have been spent to improve our schools—indeed, a radical increase in spending since 1973—the performance (especially of the poorest among us) has flatlined. We've seen very little improvement, indeed a tiny improvement relative to the resources that have been expended.

Yet in the past decade, educators have begun to make progress. (The vaccine.) In very different educational contexts, a set of reforms has demonstrated that we can educate our children, including the poorest among us, to achieve college-bound competency. Indeed, in one long-term experiment in Harlem—in the worst district in Harlem—test results show students closing the race gap in performance.[3]

The key variable in these experiments is not who owns the school (whether public or private, whether a charter or not), or how big the classrooms are, or how many computers there are per student. It is instead a much more pedestrian, indeed, obvious, difference: teachers. For these reformers, the single most important component to successful education today is great teachers. Within the same school, and the same population, the difference between good and bad teachers can be a 300 percent difference in learning in a single year. According to Professor Eric Hanushek of Stanford's Hoover Institution, if we could eliminate just the bottom 6 to 8 percent of bad teachers, we could bring our results up to the standards of Finland, perhaps the best in the world.[4]

If you were convinced about the importance of teachers, you might wonder what stops school districts from getting better teachers. What stands in the way?

Many things, of course. We pay teachers a ridiculously small amount. In poor districts, we provide them with a ridiculously unequal range of resources. And as we'll see later on, whenever we try to get government service on the cheap, cheap is precisely what we get.

Without doubt, if we're going to fix education, we're going to have to be willing to pay good teachers more of what good teachers are worth.

At least some reformers believe, however, that low pay alone does not explain poor teacher performance. Some believe that there's another feature of our public education system that needs to be questioned: teacher tenure, which protects the worst (and the best) of public school teachers.

I mean that term, *teacher tenure*, precisely, so let's be clear about what it means. Everyone's heard about tenure. Tenure means a set of workplace protections that makes it extremely difficult to remove the tenured employee. Judges have tenure. Academics have tenure. And K-12 teachers in public schools have tenure.

As with any workplace employment innovation, however, tenure has its benefits and its costs. The benefits are independence. We give judges tenure so they can do their job without fearing punishment by the government. We give academics tenure so they can do their job (primarily research) without fearing punishment by the government or the university for pursuing politically unpopular research. And we give teachers tenure to protect them from the arbitrary and powerful control of school administrators. The thought in all these cases was that security would improve performance, by protecting the employee against arbitrary action by the employer.

That protection has costs. A bad judge can do really bad things—though, of course, except for the Supreme Court, bad decisions get reviewed by higher courts. A terrible academic can waste valuable resources—but at least college and graduate students select which teachers they'll have, and they can easily select away from the teachers ranked poorly. And a bad teacher can adversely affect the primary education of his kids.

These costs must be compared to the benefits that tenure provides. And where the costs outweigh the benefits, we shouldn't have tenure.

Now, obviously, I've got a personal conflict here. I am a professor. I have tenure. I believe tenure has been important to my ability to do my work. But I am completely open to being convinced that we don't need tenure in universities anymore. I'm less open to that argument with judges: the independence of the judiciary is critical, and essential if our democracy is to flourish.

Yet I'm skeptical about the argument for tenure for teachers. We know, based upon absolutely convincing evidence, that there are good teachers and bad teachers. We know, based on the same evidence, that bad teachers destroy educational opportunities for their kids. We know, based on common knowledge, that we're not about to give third graders a choice about which teacher they have for home room. And we know, based upon evidence and experience, that a system that protects failure will only encourage more failure. So if we know all these things, then we also know that the elaborate system of protections that school boards have agreed to may actually be inhibiting student success.

That's not to say that there should be no employment protection for teachers. There are lots of arbitrary and impermissible reasons for firing people that should be banned—race, gender, sexual orientation, religious affiliation, etc. But if the reformers are right, then principals need more freedom to filter out educators who are failing to perform. Just as a bus driver who fails to drive a bus safely, or an airplane pilot who lands at the wrong airport, or a lawyer who can't file his briefs on time, or an accountant who can't add, a teacher who can't demonstrate educational progress with his class should find a different job. Performance is at the core of efficient and effective business. It should be at the core of education as well.

If we could make performance the key to teacher retention and evaluation—*if*—then we would have a good chance to turn this failure of an education system around. Or, again, so these reformers insist. Not costlessly: we need to pay teachers more, or at least *good* teachers more. But with the kind of investment we already make in education, we could begin to close achievement gaps, and actually do what public education was meant to do: educate our kids and therefore our public.

Effective teacher performance is thus the vaccine at the start of this chapter. Poor teacher performance is the virus. We have the data to show that we now have a vaccine against this virus. We've had it for almost a decade.[5] Yet we have not deployed that vaccine broadly or systematically. Instead, politicians have continued to defend a system of tenure that is weakening the effectiveness of public education. Generations of hopelessness are being produced by this recalcitrance. What might explain the resistance?

There are lots of possible theories. Funding may be inadequate. No doubt it is wildly inadequate in poor neighborhoods. Moreover, poverty generally diminishes the educational opportunities of kids, as parents cannot provide a constructive environment for education. Perhaps testing has skewed the way we teach. Perhaps parents don't do enough to support young kids. And no doubt, better preschool interventions would radically improve performance overall.[6]

But there's one fact we can't ignore. The teachers' unions are among the largest contributors to the Democratic Party—by far. And the amount they've spent on "reform" outpaces that of the next-largest reform groups by two orders of magnitude.[7]

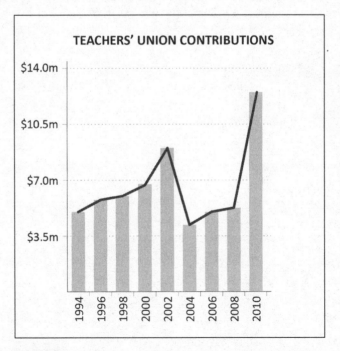

**FIGURE 5**

So, again, I am asking:

*Not*: Did the teachers' unions buy protection from more intensive performance evaluations?

*Instead*: Does the influence of the unions' spending weaken your ability to believe that the current pro-tenure policy makes sense?

## CHAPTER 7

# Why Isn't Our Financial System Safe?

America is still feeling the effects of the worst economic collapse since the Great Depression. That collapse was triggered in 2008 by a crisis on Wall Street. All of the major banks in America were drawn to the brink of bankruptcy. It took the largest intervention in the history of the nation to avoid a crisis likely to be worse than the Great Depression.

Tomes have been written about this crisis and its causes. Practically every single actor within our system of finance—from the borrowers to the lenders to the government overseeing it all—has been blamed by someone for the disaster. Some of that blame is politically motivated. Some of it is grounded in ignorance. But there is certainly enough to touch anyone of any consequence in this story, and more than enough to rock our confidence in these institutions intended to keep us financially safe.

The cause that I find least convincing, however, is irrationality. Some argue that it's just craziness that explains the crisis. That somehow, and inexplicably, everyone just became insanely greedy—irrationally borrowing more than they could repay, irrationally lending more than was prudent, irrationally ignoring the warnings of impending doom—and now that this fever has passed, we can look forward to another fifty years of financial stability. Like the measles or small pox, if you survive it, you don't get it again.

This is a criminally incomplete understanding of the disaster that we've just suffered. And while it would take a whole book to make that case convincingly, in the few pages that follow, I sketch one part of the argument with enough detail to make it relevant to the argument of this book.

For the core driver in this story was not craziness. It was rationality. The behavior we saw—from borrowers to lenders to Wall Street to government officials—was perfectly rational, for each of them considered separately. It was irrational only for the system as a whole. We need to understand the source of that irrationality—not an individual, but a systemic irrationality—to ask whether the policy judgments that produced it could even possibly have made sense.

That source is tied directly to regulation.[1] In my view, the single most important graph capturing the story of American finance was created by Harvard Business School professor David Moss (Figure 6).[2]

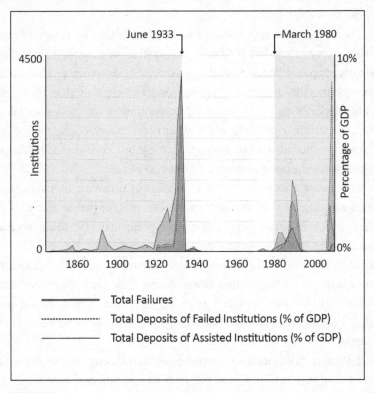

**FIGURE 6**

Moss explains the picture like this:

> Financial panics and crises are nothing new. For most of the nation's history, they represented a regular and often debilitating feature of American life. Until the Great Depression, major crises struck about every 15 to 20 years—in 1792, 1797, 1819, 1837, 1857, 1873, 1893, 1907 and 1929–33.
>
> But then the crises stopped. In fact, the United States did not suffer another major banking crisis for just about 40 years—by far the longest such stretch in the nation's history. Although there were many reasons for this, it is difficult to ignore the federal government's active role in managing financial risk. This role began to take shape in 1933 with the passage of the Glass-Steagall Act.... The simple truth is that New Deal financial regulations worked. In fact, [they] worked remarkably well.[3]

If you want to understand where the craziness began, we should begin where the "New Deal financial regulations" begin to end. This is the delta in the environment. Or it is at least the one self-conscious change that should be the first target of suspicion.

The most efficient entry into this argument is a quote from Judge Richard Posner. Judge Posner sits on the U.S. Court of Appeals for the Seventh Circuit in Chicago. He is among the most prolific legal academics and the most prolific judges in the history of the nation. He is certainly among the most influential. His book *Economic Analysis of Law* (1973) founded the law and economics movement. Since then he has written fifty more books, hundreds of articles, and thousands of judicial opinions. He was appointed to the federal bench by Ronald Reagan thirty years ago. Whatever we can say, we can be certain, Posner is no socialist.

Among Posner's fifty-some books are two that deal specifically with the financial crisis.[4] And at the core of Posner's argument is an insistence that we understand the rationality behind this insanity. As he writes, criticizing a government report on the crisis:

The emphasis the report places on the folly of private-sector actors ignores the possibility that most of them were behaving rationally given the environment of dangerously low interest rates, complacency about asset-price inflation (the bubbles that the regulators and, with the occasional honorable exception, the economics profession ignored), and light and lax regulation.[5]

This is the idea that I want to pursue here: that the gambling that Wall Street engaged in made sense to them given (1) "the environment of dangerously low interest rates," (2) "complacency about asset-price inflation," and (3) "light and lax regulation." My focus will be on (3) "light and lax regulation" and (2) "complacency about asset-price inflation." For our purposes, let us stipulate that (1) is also correct.

For, of all of the clues to this mystery, the one that should be most obvious is again the one that Moss's graph describes best: the economy that drove itself off the cliff was a financial system operating under different rules from the stable and prosperous financial system of the forty years before. Until the early 1990s the key financial assets of our economy were subject to the basic regulatory regime given to us by the New Deal. But beginning in the 1980s, critical financial assets of our economy were exempted from that basic regulatory framework.

The rules of that regime are impossible to describe in detail, but simple to summarize. The most important financial assets were subject to a rule that required they be traded publicly, transparently, and subject to antifraud requirements.[6] These rules achieved a number of objectives. First, they subjected traders to strong incentives to avoid fraud. Second, they kept key financial institutions from taking on too much risk. And third, they subjected the trades of critical financial assets to an important requirement of publicity—each time a financial asset was bought or sold, the market got something in return: information about the perceived value of the traded asset. That information helped the markets function more efficiently. Robust trading data produced robust prices; robust pricing ensured asset liquidity, at least during relatively normal times, which were many during the New Deal regulatory regime.

Beginning in the 1980s, however, and for our purposes, especially the 1990s, this regime changed. It didn't change for the assets that had been regulated by the New Deal rules: stocks and bonds. It changed instead for a new class of financial instruments, derivatives, a tiny portion of the market at first, but one that quickly, like the Blob, exploded onto the market, and consumed much of its value.

"Derivatives" are assets whose value is *derived* from something else, where "something" could mean literally anything. I could have a derivative that pays me if the price of gold falls below $1,000. I could have a derivative that pays me if the temperature in Minot, North Dakota, rises above one hundred degrees Fahrenheit. A derivative is just a bet entered into by two or more parties. The terms of the bet are limited only by the imagination of the parties.

By calling this a "bet," however, and by invoking remote American villages, I don't mean to question the economic wisdom behind derivatives. To the contrary: Derivatives serve a valuable purpose. As with any contract, their aim is to shift risk within a market to someone better able to carry it. That's a good thing, for the market, and the economy generally. That we've just seen an economy detonated by derivatives gone wild shouldn't lead us to ban (as if we could) these financial innovations. It should, however, lead us to be more careful about them.

At the birth of this innovation, however, no one was thinking much about being careful. Nor thinking clearly. Too many made an error of aggregation: even if derivatives enabled individuals to diversify risk, they couldn't reduce the risk for the system as a whole.[7] That didn't matter much at first, since the market for derivatives was initially tiny. A collapse in a tiny market doesn't do much systemic harm.

Technology soon changed all this, making it possible for the market in derivatives to explode. With the digital revolution distributing computing power to the masses, masses of financial analysts on Wall Street were able to use this computing power to concoct ever-more-complicated financial "innovations." With each of these concoctions, a new and fiercely competitive market would race to catch up. For a brief time, the innovator had an edge (and huge profit margin). But very quickly, others copied and improved on his invention, driving down profits, and driving innovators to find new derivative markets. (Here was a market with no real intellectual property protection, yet an insanely strong drive to innovate.) There were hundreds of financial instruments de jure, until the industry fixed upon a particularly rich and ultimately disastrous vein (home mortgages) and developed a whole series of assets backed by real estate mortgages.[8]

As this market in derivatives was growing, however, there was a constant question about whether and how derivatives would be regulated. With that question came a fight. One side of that battle thought that derivatives should be treated no differently from any other asset. The other side saw this as a chance to launch a project to deregulate financial assets generally.

The war for deregulation was waged by a (somewhat crude) libertarian, Mark C. Brickell. Though the nation had just suffered a derivatives-based financial crisis,[9] Brickell, a lobbyist for the derivatives industry, pushed the idea that the best response to the crisis was general policy to dismantle the New Deal regulations—not just with derivatives, but with every financial instrument within the economy.

Most thought Brickell's idea insane, and his campaign, hopeless. Nations reregulate financial services after a collapse; they don't deregulate. Nonetheless, Brickell pushed, and got his first true victory in January 1993, when "departing [Commodity Futures Trading Commission] chair Wendy Gramm delivered her 'farewell gift' to the derivatives industry, signing an order exempting most over-the-counter derivatives from federal regulation. (A few months later, she would receive her own farewell gift, being named a director of Enron, which was an active trader of natural gas and electricity derivatives.)"[10]

Victory at the CFTC, however, was just the first step. There were a handful of important pieces of legislation working their ways through Congress that would have heavily regulated derivatives. Brickell, as Gillian Tett describes it, "was relentless, and as the weeks passed, against expectations, his campaign turned the tide."[11] For Brickell got a completely unexpected gift in his campaign to deregulate derivatives: a new president, neither crude, nor libertarian, but a key ally nonetheless, Bill Clinton.

Clinton had campaigned with a strong strain of populist rhetoric. Wall Street was fearful that populism would translate into substantial regulation. Once in office, however, Clinton was eager to convince Wall Street that despite the rhetoric, he was no anti–Wall Street populist. His administration worked quickly to signal that he could love Wall Street as completely as the Republicans did. Almost seamlessly, as historian Kevin Phillips writes, "well-connected Democratic financiers stepped easily into the alligator loafers of departing Republicans."[12] By the end of 1994, and with tacit support by the administration, Brickell's campaign had killed all four of the antiderivatives bills in Congress.[13] And the campaign was not just legislative: the core agency charged with overseeing this industry, the SEC, was told by members of Congress to lay off. (When SEC chairman Arthur Levitt tried to introduce tougher conflict-of-interest rules for the accounting industry, Senator Phil Gramm, Senate Banking chair, "threatened to cut the SEC's budget.")[14] Finally, in 1999, President Clinton gave the industry its most important gift: he signed the law that abolished the Glass-Steagall Act,[15] thereby confirming the deregulation already effected by bank regulators. "[R]egulators essentially left the abuses of the 1990s to what Justice Cardozo had called the 'morals of the marketplace.'"[16] "Self-policing," as Tett put it, when describing an antiderivatives bill in 1994, had "won the day."[17]

This was not the only victory for the deregulation movement. Perhaps as important was the fact that the core instrument facilitating the derivatives market—asset-backed securities, where the asset was a mortgage—was exempted from any SEC oversight at all. In 1992 the SEC determined that these assets were not the sort that the Investment Company Act of 1940 had intended the SEC to regulate. By a rule, the SEC therefore exempted them.[18] But while these assets

may not have fit into the regulatory structures of the Investment
Company Act, it certainly made no sense to exempt them from any
of the traditional forms of financial oversight, by any agency at all.
Yet the then- (and now-?) dominant zeitgeist was not about to entertain a new regulatory structure to fill the gap created by the SEC,
and mortgage companies were certain to block any effort by any
agency to fill that gap. The assets were therefore left untouched.

These are not stories of public officials being bribed. Indeed, the
most complicating and difficult fact of this whole transformation is
how firmly, and independently, many of the key figures believed in
deregulation as an ideal. Some were motivated mainly, or partly, by
money. Some were motivated by a well-justified frustration with the
incredible incompetence of existing regulators and regulations. But
many were motivated by principles, even if, as I believe, those principles were incomplete and unrealistic. You can call the principled man
wrong, or even negligent. It is hard to call him evil.

We can see this moral complexity in perhaps the most famous
of the firefights that produced this extreme policy of deregulation.

By the middle of the Clinton administration, the volume in derivatives had grown to $13 trillion. (Compare: the total GDP of the
United States in 1998 was $8.7 trillion.) Some at the SEC wondered
whether the SEC should exercise jurisdiction over derivatives. To
the surprise of almost everyone, however, it was a weaker regulatory agency, the Commodity Futures Trading Commission (CFTC),
that initially took the lead.

The CFTC reasoned that derivatives functioned much like
"futures contracts," and futures contracts were already regulated
by the CFTC. So the agency, then headed by Brooksley Born, floated
the idea, in a draft release, that it should regulate derivatives, and it
circulated that release to other relevant federal agencies. The document reasserted the presumptive jurisdiction of the CFTC over the
market, and "float[ed] the idea of increased supervision."[19]

The reaction to Born's draft release was quick and harsh. As
Roger Lowenstein, a financial journalist who wrote for the *Wall
Street Journal* for more than a decade, describes it:

Every banker in Washington complained about the upstart CFTC. Following Wall Street's urging, Treasury secretary Rubin, a former cochairman of Goldman Sachs, was extremely hostile. A posse of regulators scheduled a meeting for late April, for the purpose of persuading Born to bury the release. Before the meeting, Larry Summers, Rubin's top deputy at the Treasury Department, called Born and berated her. Summers huffed, "There are thirteen bankers in my office. They say if this is published we'll have the worst financial crisis since World War II."[20]

By the April meeting, tempers had not cooled. Lowenstein:

[Alan] Greenspan got in Born's face, blowing and blustering until he reddened. Rubin, always more politic, spoke with controlled fury, as if Born's proposal were unsuited to his society. He repeated that the CFTC was out of its jurisdiction and asked if Born (who had been elected president of the *Stanford Law Review* in 1963, when most of the women in law firms were still pouring coffee) would like an education in the applicable law from Treasury's general counsel.[21]

Born persisted. She published the draft in May 1999, calling for more study. Greenspan, Rubin, and Summers reacted immediately, announcing that they would seek legislation to stop Born and her CFTC. Shortly thereafter, Born resigned. In November a government working group produced a report about derivative regulation and the CFTC. That report found that "to promote innovation, competition, efficiency, and transparency in OTC derivatives markets, to reduce systemic risk, and to allow the United States to maintain leadership in these rapidly developing markets," derivatives should be exempted from all federal regulation.[22] The following year, Congress overwhelmingly passed the Commodity Futures Modernization Act, which expressly forbade the CFTC from regulating derivatives, and expressly exempted derivatives from any other state law. Not surprisingly, as Gillian Tett describes, "the derivatives sector was jubilant."[23] But as the Financial Crisis Inquiry Commission concluded, the legislation "was a key turning point in the march toward the financial crisis."[24]

It's not clear that anyone had a clue about how big this market would be when the government first chose to ignore it. Professor Frank Partnoy has tried to characterize the scale of the regulatory change in a way that even lawyers can understand. As he explained to me, whereas in 1980, close to 100 percent of the financial instruments traded in the market were subject to the New Deal exchange-based regulatory regime, by 2008, 90 percent of the financial instruments traded in the market were exempted from it. If, as David Moss put it, "the simple truth [was] that New Deal financial regulations worked," they were not going to work for almost 90 percent of the assets traded in our financial markets. We had flipped from a presumptively public market of exchange to a market where only insiders knew anything real about how the market worked, or what the assets were worth. That was great for the insiders, giving them enormous power to leverage into extraordinary profits.[25] It was awful for the rest of us.

The decision to allow this economy of derivatives to run in secret was extraordinarily silly. For not only would secrecy weaken the efficiency of the market as a whole (since the public signal of price helps discipline a market),[26] but it would also lead to a kind of regulatory arbitrage: because regulation is costly, deals that were subject to the New Deal regulations would be recast into a form that could evade those regulations. Indeed, that's what happened: financial instruments that were "economically equivalent to many other financial instruments"[27] were substituted for those "other financial instruments," because unlike those "others," they were unregulated. As the Financial Crisis Inquiry Commission concluded, "[G]iven these circumstances, regulatory arbitrage worked as it always does: the markets shifted to the lowest-cost, least-regulated havens."[28]

Evading regulation has its own value. This led Nobel Prize–winning economist Merton Miller to the "insight" that "companies would do swaps not necessarily because swaps allocated risk more efficiently, but rather *because* they were unregulated. They could do swaps in the dark, without the powerful sunlight that securities regulation shined on other financial instruments."[29] Thus "much of the $600-plus trillion derivatives market exists," finance professor Frank Partnoy calculates, "because private parties [were] doing deals to avoid the law."[30]

A speed limit that applies to black cars only will not only incentivize the sale of colorful vehicles, it will also be a boon to the paint departments of auto body shops everywhere. That's the story of Wall Street in the 2000s: While some portion of the market for derivatives was no doubt driven by a genuine need for the particular flexibility of a derivative, a huge proportion was simply black cars being painted red. The winners in this new market were the drivers of these freshly painted cars, and the firms that had done the paint jobs (aka Wall Street). The losers were—surprise, surprise—the rest of us.

To say that the financial sector escaped the government's regulation, however, is not to say that the sector escaped regulation. As Alan Greenspan put it: "It is critically important to recognize that no market is ever truly unregulated.... The self-interest of market participants generates private market regulation."[31]

Even if the banks didn't have to worry about rules emanating from the CFTC, SEC, or Federal Reserve, they still had to worry about the constraints imposed upon them by the competitive market. The biggest firms on Wall Street were publicly traded. Rivals thus set the baseline for the profit each firm was expected to produce. As firms started down the path of risky behavior, the competitive market within which they operated pushed them even further. A conservative and sensible strategy is punished in such a market because, by definition, it doesn't produce the same return as a risky strategy. A risky strategy earns the market's reward.

These new instruments thus gave Wall Street firms a new opportunity to compete like hell against one another. But as they competed, they assumed risks that, while sensible for them alone, were not sensible for the economy as a whole. That's because, as Posner puts it, banks "do not have regard for consequences for the economy as a whole.... [T]hat is not the business of business. That is the business of government."[32]

It is this gap between the interests of the banks alone and the interests of the "economy as a whole" that explains the need for regulation. "Banks," Posner writes, "can be made safe by regulation, but that is *not their natural state*, and so if regulation is removed they may career out of control."[33] Thus, commenting upon Alan Greenspan's confession that he had expected the self-interest of Wall Street firms to be enough to induce them to behave properly, Posner writes:

> That was a whopper of a mistake for an economist to make. It was as if the head of the Environmental Protection Agency, criticized for not enforcing federal antipollution laws, had said he thought the self-interest of the polluters implied that they are best capable of protecting their shareholders and their equity. They are indeed the best capable of doing *that*. The reason for laws regulating pollution is that pollution is an external cost of production, which is to say a cost not borne by the polluting company or its shareholders, and in making business decisions profit maximizers don't consider costs they don't bear. Banks consider the potential costs of bankruptcy to themselves in deciding how much risk to take but do not consider the potential costs to society as a whole.[34]

The banks were thus freed of the burden of federal regulation, yet driven by the discipline of market regulation to assume far more risk than was good for the economy. As Posner concludes:

> Am I saying that deregulation *made* bankers and through them borrowers take risks that were excessive from an overall social standpoint? Yes, once we recognize that *competition will force*

*banks to take risks (in order to increase return) that the economic and regulatory environment permits them to take*, provided the risks are legal and profit-maximizing, whatever their consequences for the economy as a whole.[35]

This was also the conclusion of the Financial Crisis Inquiry Commission: "Unchecked, competition...can place the entire financial system at risk."[36] And indeed, as the commission concluded, in this case it did:

> More than 30 years of deregulation and reliance on self-regulation by financial institutions championed by former Federal Reserve chairman Alan Greenspan and others, supported by successive administrations and Congresses, and actively pushed by the powerful financial industry at every turn, had stripped away key safeguards, which could have helped avoid catastrophe.[37]

From the perspective of the economy as a whole, the banks thus took on more risk than was sensible. For the large banks, the risk was quite sensible—for them, at least when you count an implicit promise by the government to bail the banks out if the economy went south. Indeed, as Raghuram Rajan puts it, "What is particularly alarming is that the risk taking may well have been in the best ex ante interests of their shareholders."[38]

It was clear to most that the economy as a whole had this promise from the Federal Reserve. This was the "Greenspan put," which referred to the policy by the Federal Reserve to intervene to counteract a collapse in the market. A "one-sided intervention policy on the part of the Federal Reserve," as Marcus Miller and his colleagues put it, led "investors into the erroneous belief that they [were] insured against downside risk."[39] This is insurance, and as with all insurance, it could well have encouraged additional risky behavior.

Some believed the promise was even more specific than that. Why would sophisticated debt holders take such extreme risk? "The obvious explanation," Raghuram Rajan writes, "is that [they] did not think they would need to bear losses because the government would step in."[40] Simon Johnson and James Kwak point to at least one case in which the financial executives of one major bank calibrated the risk they would take based upon the government's decision to expand the bailout capacity of the Federal Reserve.[41] They and others have pointed to the discount the market gave big banks for their cost of capital as evidence that the market believed those banks "too big to fail": "Large banks were able to borrow money at rates 0.78 percentage points more cheaply than smaller banks, up from an average of 0.29 percentage points from 2000 through 2007."[42]

Harvey Miller, the bankruptcy counsel for Lehman Brothers, was even more explicit than this: As he told the Financial Crisis Inquiry Commission, hedge funds "expected the Fed to save Lehman, based on the Fed's involvement in [previous crises]. That's what history had proved to them."[43] Again, Rajan: "[T]he problem created by the anticipation of government intervention is that the bankers, caught up in the herd's competitive frenzy to cash in on the seemingly lucrative opportunity, are not slowed by more dispassionate market forces."[44]

The executives knew this. The pressures of the competitive market, however, made it impossible for them to do differently. As one CEO put it, "When the music stops, in terms of liquidity, things will be complicated. But as long as the music is playing, you've got to get up and dance. We're still dancing."[45]

Either of these accounts would explain the second condition that Posner described earlier: "complacency about asset-price inflation." It's easy to be complacent when you believe the government has your back—and especially when the market confirms that belief by giving you a break on the interest rate it charges.

In this sense, the story here is thus the story of both too little regulation and too much regulation.

*Too little*, since by relaxing the regulatory constraints, the government left the banks vulnerable to the constraints of competition. Those constraints forced the banks to take on more risk than was socially sensible, even if privately rational. In the terms of chapter 5, it forced the banks to ignore the externality of the risk their gambles would produce for the economy as a whole.

*Too much*, since the implicit guarantee of a bailout encouraged the banks to be "complacent about asset-price inflation." As Rajan writes, "the institutions that took the most risk were those that were thought to be too systemic to be allowed by the government to fail."[46] The implicit promise to socialize the risk, as Paul Krugman put it,[47] while allowing the banks to privatize the benefits was the consequence of an intervention by the government—certainly among the silliest in the history of finance, but an intervention nonetheless.[48]

The combination was deadly—for us, at least, if not for the banks. For, after the collapse, of course, the government did effectively bail out all but one investment bank, Lehman Brothers. The surviving banks, however, are ever larger and more profitable than they were before. Indeed, as Jamie Dimon, chairman and CEO of JPMorgan Chase, boasted about 2009, "This might have been our finest year ever."[49]

It is for these reasons that I believe the decision by our government to deregulate derivatives was foolish. When combined with the implicit and explicit promise to bail out failure, it encouraged a radical increase in risk that ultimately blew up the economy.

So what explains this foolish decision? What explains the power of these deregulatory ideas? Even Alfred Kahn, the architect of the very first deregulatory initiative during the administration of President Carter, could only shake his head decades later at the race to financial deregulation. Banks, he insisted, "were a different kind of animal.... They were animals that had a direct effect on the macroeconomy. That is very different from the regulation of industries that provided goods and services.... I never supported any type of deregulation of banking."[50] So why did everyone else, including supposedly progressive Democrats?

There is no simple answer. As I've argued, the ideology of deregulation flowed for many as a matter of principle. Alan Greenspan, for example, truly believed that markets would take care of themselves, that even regulations against fraud were unnecessary. Greenspan was wrong. He admitted as much. But he was not being guided by an improper dependence upon money. These were the beliefs of a true believer at work. They were not the beliefs of a hired gun.

And not just Greenspan: there were plenty in the army of financial deregulators who were true believers, not just mercenaries. It may well be, as John Kenneth Galbraith puts it, that "out of the pecuniary and political pressures and fashions of the time, economics and larger economic and political systems cultivate their own version of truth."[51] But these "versions" are still experienced as "versions of the truth," not outright fraud. "No conspiracy was necessary," as Simon Johnson and James Kwak put it in their 2010 book, *13 Bankers*: "By 1998, it was part of the worldview of the Washington elite that what was good for Wall Street was good for America."[52] As Raghuram Rajan writes, "Cognitive capture is a better description of this phenomenon than crony capitalism."[53]

Still, pure ideas are not the whole story. Not by a long shot. The campaign to deregulate the financial services sector was *a campaign*, even if it was also an ideology. When it began, none could have thought it would succeed. But soon after it began, as I describe in chapter 9, both Democrats and Republicans alike became starved for campaign funds. And as that starvation grew, both parties, but the Democrats in particular, found it made both dollars and sense to believe as the ideologues of deregulation told them to believe. It paid to believe. And that made believing easy. As the Financial Crisis Inquiry Commission put it:

> As [this] report will show, the financial industry itself played
> a key role in weakening regulatory constraints on institutions,
> markets, and products. It did not surprise the Commission that

an industry of such wealth and power would exert pressure on policy makers and regulators. From 1999 to 2008, the financial sector expended $2.7 billion in reported federal lobbying expenses; individuals and political action committees in the sector made more than $1 billion in campaign contributions. *What troubled us was the extent to which the nation was deprived of the necessary strength and independence of the oversight necessary to safeguard financial stability.*[54]

We could map this change simply by tracking the rise of certain members of the Democratic Party. New York senator Charles Schumer is an obvious example. "Over the five election cycles from 1989–90 to 1997–98, Schumer raised $2.5 million in contributions from securities and investment firms—more than *triple* the haul of the runner-up in the House."[55] Schumer's "success," as Jacob Hacker and Paul Pierson describe in their 2010 book, *Winner-Take-All Politics*, "was part of a major development in the evolution of the Democratic Party's finance: a big push to gain support on Wall Street."[56]

The money began to flow, and not just to the Democrats. As Johnson and Kwak describe, "from 1998 to 2008, the financial sector spent $1.7 billion on campaign contributions and $3.4 billion on lobbying expenses; the securities industry alone spent $500 million on campaign contributions and $600 million on lobbying." That's a faster growth in spending than with any other industry. Comparing the campaign contributions of the one hundred biggest contributing firms since 1989, we find contributions from firms in the financial sector total more "than the contributions of energy, health care, defense and telecoms *combined*."[57]

As that money flowed, the appetite for the insane policies of deregulation grew. And in line with the analysis of the previous chapters, the question we need to ask is whether we believe the campaign money had anything to do with this insanity. No doubt the ideology was widespread. But without the money, would it have prevailed?

No one can know the answer to that question for sure. But

there are some important clues. Take the case of Congressman Jim Leach, from Iowa, who was the leading Republican on the House Banking Committee in 1994. Leach was convinced that the derivatives market produced systemic risk to the economy. After the savings-and-loan crisis of the early 1990s, he issued a report that called for strong regulations of derivatives. That report was criticized by many in the industry. As one industry representative told the *Washington Post*, "I have a tough time conceiving of any event that would make derivatives the culprit of something that really crashed the system."[58] (Presumably, this is an easier thing for this industry representative to "conceive" of today.) Most people simply ignored Leach's report.

The interesting question isn't why the world ignored Jim Leach. It is instead why, as Frank Partnoy asks, "Leach [was] so different from his colleagues, who were uninterested in derivatives regulations? Why was Leach alone in publicly warning that derivatives markets were out of control and might cause a system-wide collapse?" Partnoy answers his own question: "The only discernible difference between Leach and other members of Congress was that Leach did not receive financial support from Wall Street.... Because he refused to accept contributions from political action committees, Leach could speak with an independent mind."[59]

No doubt we had enough ideological minds guiding government policy as it affected Wall Street. But did we have enough independent minds in government? And had we had more, would the government have made the same mistakes it made?

Or, in the terms of this section of the book, does the presence of the largest amount of campaign cash of any single industry affect your ability to believe this policy was guided by good sense rather than the need for campaign dollars?

## Where Were the Regulators?

At the end of her fantastic book *Fool's Gold* (2010), Gillian Tett quotes JPMorgan Chase's Jamie Dimon at a Davos event: "God knows, some really stupid things were done by American banks and American investment bankers.... Some stupid things were done...but it wasn't just the bankers. Where were the regulators in all this?"[60]

Later she quotes some of the original derivatives geniuses from JPMorgan reflecting to each other on the consequences of their "innovations": " 'It wasn't our job to stop other banks being so stupid!' another shot back. 'What about the regulators? Where were they?' "[61]

When I read those passages, however, my first thought was, "Wow. *This* is chutzpah."

"Where were the regulators?" Are you kidding, Jamie Dimon?

This is the son who has murdered his parents begging for mercy from the judge on account of his being an orphan. "Where were the regulators?" You got the regulators sent home!

The real story of the Great Recession is simply this: Stupid government regulation allowed the financial services industry to run the economy off the rails. But it was the financial services industry that drove our government to this stupid government regulation. They benefited *enormously* from this policy. And as carefully as I have tried to frame these puzzles in a way that might allow both sides some space, this case brings even me to the brink. Strain as I may, I find it impossible to believe that our government would have been this stupid had congressmen from both sides of the aisle not been so desperate for the more than $1 billion in campaign contributions given by individuals and groups affiliated with these firms, and the $2.7 billion spent by them lobbying.[62]

But let me try one last time:

*Forget* the question of whether the endless campaign funding bought this particularly silly regulatory result.

*Ask instead*: Does the fact that more than $1 billion was given affect your ability to believe that this insanely important if endlessly complicated area of regulatory policy was regulated sensibly? Does it affect your confidence or trust in the system? Or can you honestly say that the regulatory mistakes of the past three decades were unrelated to this, the largest single sector of campaign and lobbying contributions in our government? Raghuram Rajan writes, "The public has lost faith in a system where the rules of the game seem tilted in favor of a few."[63] Are you in that public? Does this pattern of contributions help put you there? *Yes*

# CHAPTER 8

# What the "Tells" Tell Us

When my colleagues and I tested whether apparent conflicts in the interests of professionals affected trust in the work of those doctors, researchers, and politicians, we didn't say that the apparent conflict was actually a conflict. We didn't tell the subjects that it actually affected the results, or that it was even reasonable to believe that it affected the results. People assumed it, and their confidence collapsed because of what they assumed.

When I described the conflict in research about the safety of BPA and cell phones, and linked that conflict to the source of funding, I didn't tell you that we had any good reason to believe this correlation proved anything. You assumed it, at least enough to weaken whatever confidence you had about whether those two products were safe.

In both cases, I needed only to point to the money—money in (what was perceived to be) the wrong place—for confidence to weaken. Not "money," but "money in the wrong place." Describe the architecture of incentives, and people will infer the causation. With no good reason, perhaps. But with a reliable regularity that cannot be denied, and certainly should not be ignored.

This same dynamic is true with each example of government policy that I have just described. Each is framed in a similar way: Given a fairly obvious public policy bias, actual policy was bent differently. Against free markets. Against efficient markets. Against effective education. Against safe financial markets. *Why* the policy was so bent, I didn't say. But after I round the story off in each case with an account of lobbying and campaign cash, you have a view about why. Or, at a minimum, you are less confident that the why has much to do with what makes good public policy sense.

These four examples are not small issues. Together, they have an effect. They confirm the view already held by the vast majority of Americans. In a poll commissioned for this book, 75 percent of Americans believe "campaign contributions buy results in Congress." *Three to one*, with Republicans (71 percent) just as convinced of this as Democrats (81 percent).[1] Puzzles plus money produce the view that the money explains the puzzles.

In a line: We don't trust our government. And until we create the conditions under which trust is possible—when, in other words, the presence of money in the wrong places doesn't inevitably make us doubt—this skepticism will remain. We can't help it. It will follow psychologically even if it doesn't follow logically.

But is the problem more than a problem of perception? Granted, the public reads the money as corruption. Is it corruption? Does it actually bend any results? If it doesn't, then maybe the problem is the perceiver and not what is perceived. Maybe the solution is a better understanding of the mechanisms of government, and why they ought to be trusted, rather than a radical change in how government gets funded. Maybe we, the people, are just confused?

# PART III

★

# BEYOND SUSPICION

*Congress's Corruption*

We have good reason to mistrust. The problem with Congress is not just appearance. It is real. It is the product of an economy of influence that we have allowed to evolve within our government, within our republic. That economy systematically draws members away from the focus, or dependence, they were intended to have. That dependence—as with vodka and Yeltsin—is a corruption. It is the corruption that is our government.

# CHAPTER 9

# *Why* So Damn Much Money

Midway through his extraordinary book *So Damn Much Money* (2009), Robert Kaiser, associate editor and senior correspondent at the *Washington Post*, reports a conversation with Joe Rothstein, campaign manager for former Alaska senator Mike Gravel. As Rothstein tells Kaiser:

> Money has been a part of American politics forever, on occasion—in the Gilded Age or the Harding administration, for example—much more blatantly than recently. But...: "the scale of it has just gotten way out of hand." The money may have come in brown paper bags in earlier eras, but the politicians needed, and took, much less of it than they take through more formal channels today.[1]

If we're going to understand the corruption that is our government, we need first to understand this change. What explains the explosion in campaign cash? What are its consequences? No doubt, things cost more today than they did in 1970. But the rise in campaign spending wildly outpaces the rate of inflation.[2] Between 1974 and 2008 "the average amount it took to run for reelection to the House went from $56,000 to more than $1.3 million."[3] In 1974 the total spent by *all* candidates for Congress (both House and Senate) was $77 million. By 1982 that number was $343 million—a 450 percent increase in eight years.[4] By 2010 it was $1.8 billion—a 525 percent increase again.[5]

Why? And how did this rise affect how Congress does its work? To answer these questions, we need to review a bit of recent history. There have been real changes in the competitiveness of American democracy that help account for the increase in the demand for campaign cash. This increase in demand in turn inspired a change in how campaign cash gets supplied. And that change in supply, I will argue, has radically altered how our democracy functions.

## Demand for Campaign Cash

If the political history of the twentieth century can be divided into three periods—a period before FDR, the period of FDR to Reagan, and the period of Reagan to Bush II—our picture of Congress, as taught to us in universities and as studied most extensively by scholars and political scientists, is the Congress of the middle period, FDR to Reagan. The Congress that gave us the New Deal. The Congress that enacted the Civil Rights Act. The Congress that would have impeached President Nixon.

This was a Democratic Congress. In the sixty-plus years between 1933 and 1995, Democrats controlled the House of Representatives in all but four years. It controlled the Senate in all but ten. If anything happened during this period, it was because the Democrats supported it. When things didn't happen, it was because they didn't support it strongly enough.

For most of this period, no sane Republican could imagine taking permanent control of both houses of Congress. Like runners before Roger Bannister cracked the four-minute mile, most Republicans, and most Democrats, simply believed that such an accomplishment was politically impossible. The parties had a certain character. The nation had a certain character, too. Those two characters were going to produce a political world in which Democrats controlled and Republicans cooperated. That was the "nature" of politics in America.

In the late 1960s, nature changed. The seeds to that change were sown by a Democratic president, elected with the second-largest contested Electoral College vote in American history: Lyndon Baines Johnson.

Johnson is likely the twentieth century's most important politician. Pulling himself up from almost nothing, by means none would be proud to confess, Johnson became a key leader of the Democrats in Congress. He knew better than most how to play the game of compromise that moves bills through Congress, and that moved him to the very top of the United States Senate.

When an assassin's bullet thrust him into the presidency, however, Johnson changed his game. In his first speech to Congress, he placed civil rights at the core of his new administration, and hence at the core of the values of the Democratic Party. The decision to do this was profoundly controversial. In a six-hour meeting before the speech, Johnson was advised strongly against making civil rights so central to his administration. As described by Randall Woods, Johnson was told, "Passage [of the Civil Rights Act]...looked pretty hopeless; the issue was as divisive as any...; it would be suicide to wage and lose such a battle." The safe bet was against the fight. Johnson replied, "Well, what the hell is the presidency for?"[6] These were not the words of a triangulator from the U.S. Senate, but of a man who had grown tired of that game, and wanted to try something new.

When he decided to make civil rights central to his party's platform, Johnson knew that he was forever changing the political dominance of the Democrats. His decision to pass the most important civil rights legislation in history was a guarantee that the Republicans would again become competitive. Yet his loyalty was more to truth, or justice, or his legacy—you pick—than to party politics. To that end, whichever it was, he was willing to sacrifice a Democratic majority of tomorrow in order to use the Democratic majority of today.[7]

I don't mean to suggest that racism made Reagan possible. To the contrary: it was a wide range of focused and powerful ideas, first born in the idealism of politicians such as Goldwater and public intellectuals such as William F. Buckley, that made the new Republican Party compelling. I remember well the power of those ideas. I was a rabid Reaganite, and the youngest elected member of a delegation at the 1980 Republican Convention.

But there's no doubt that this decision by Johnson strengthened the Republican Party by alienating a large number of not-yet-enlightened southern Democrats. That alienation encouraged a Republican return. And when Ronald Reagan rode a powerful set of ideals to power—none of them explicitly tied to race—he gave to all Republicans an idea that only dreamers in 1950 would have had: that their party could retake control of Congress. That it might once again become the majority party.

It was 1994 when this dream was finally realized. With the energy and passion of Newt Gingrich, with the ideals of a "Contract with America," and with a frustration about a young, triangulating Democratic president, the Republicans swept Congress. For the first time since 1954, the Republicans had control of both houses.

The Gingrich election changed everything: By putting the control of Congress in play, it gave both Republicans and Democrats something to fight to the death about. Whereas a comfortable, even if not ideal (for the Republicans, at least) détente had reigned for the prior forty-something years, now each side could taste majority status—or, perhaps more important, minority status. Congress was up for grabs. And between 1995 and 2010, control of Congress changed hands as many times as it had in the forty-five years before.

It was at this moment that the modern Congress—call it the "Fund-raising Congress"—was born. The Republicans came to power raising an unheard of amount of money to defeat the Democrats. Republicans in 1994 received $618.42 million (up from $534.64 million in 1992) in contrast to Democrats' $488.68 million (down from $498.45 million in 1992).[8] In the four years between 1994 and 1998, Republican candidates and party committees raised over $1 billion.[9] Never before had a party come anywhere close.

This fund-raising in turn changed what leadership in both parties would mean: if leaders had once been chosen on the basis of ideas, or seniority, or political ties, now, in both parties, leaders were chosen at least in part on their ability to raise campaign cash. Leading fund-raisers became the new leaders. Fund-raising became the new game.

Campaigns now were not just about who won in any particular district; they were also about which party would control Congress. This control has its own value—especially if, as John Lott argues, the government is handing out more favors, or, in the words of economists, "more rents."[10] Such rents drive demand for control. As corporate law scholars would describe it, they make the "control premium" all the more valuable.[11]

At the same time that demand for winning was increasing, the core costs of campaigns were increasing as well. Part of the reason for this change was the rising cost of media. But a bigger part was an advance in campaign technology. The machine of politics was more complicated and more expensive. "Campaigns dependent on pollsters, consultants, and television commercials," Kaiser notes, "were many times more expensive than campaigns in the prehistoric eras before these inventions took hold. . . . So congressmen and senators who used the new technologies . . . quite suddenly needed much more money than ever before to run for re-election."[12]

These two changes together—if not immediately, then certainly over a very short time—put the monkey on the back of every member of Congress. An activity, despised by most, that for most of the history of Congress was a simple road stop—fund-raising—now became the central activity of congressmen. Each member had to raise more, not just for his own seat but also for his own party. Yet because the most obvious solution to this increase in demand for campaign cash—collecting more from each contributor—was not legally possible, the only way to raise more money was to scurry to find more people to give.[13] Congress had tried to limit political expenditures in 1974.[14] The Supreme Court had struck down that limit, while upholding the limit on contributions. As Professor James Sample describes it, quoting Professors Pam Karlan and Sam Issacharoff, "The effect is much like giving a starving man unlimited trips to the buffet table but only a thimble-sized spoon with which to eat: chances are great that the constricted means to satisfy his appetite will create a singular obsession with consumption."[15]

"No rational regulatory system," Issacharoff writes, "would seek to limit the manner by which money is supplied to political campaigns, then leave...spending uncapped."[16] Yet ours did. And the result, as Josh Rosenkranz puts it, was a system that turned "decent, honest politicians [into] junkies."[17]

Junkies.

And as junkies, they became ever more disciplined in the feeding of their addiction. That discipline, in turn, changed them, and the political world they inhabited.

## Supply of Campaign Cash: Substance

As the demand for campaign cash rose, the political economy for its supply changed. The Fund-raising Congress became different from Congresses before. Its values and its ideals, at least as they related to raising campaign funds, were different.

One part of this difference was substantive: the political message of both parties changed in a direction that enhanced the ability of each to raise campaign funds.

*First,* the economic message of Democrats became much more pro-business.[18] Beginning almost immediately after the 1994 Republican sweep, leaders in the Democratic Party launched a massive campaign to convince corporate America that the Democrats could show them as much love as the Republicans traditionally had. As I described in chapter 7, President Clinton led the campaign, especially on Wall Street, as his administration worked feverishly to convince Wall Street funders that Democrats were as convinced of the need for deregulation as Republicans were. At least with respect to the economy, America didn't have two major parties anymore. Instead, as Dan Clawson and his colleagues wrote: "The country...has just one: the money party."[19] The Democrats' "populist tradition," Hacker and Pierson describe, "more and more appeared like a costume—something to be donned from time to time when campaigning—rather than a basis for governing."[20]

This change is familiar and extensively debated. So, too, is the

question of its causation. Many "new Democrats" defend the pro-
business shift on grounds of principle. Many more find this explanation a bit too convenient. But whether the initial shift was for
the money or not, as the shift in fact did produce more money, the
change was reinforced. Given the increasing dependency on cash,
the cause was conveniently ignored.

*Second*, and less frequently remarked, the noneconomic messages of both Democrats and Republicans became more extreme.
Conservatives on the Right became (even to Reagan Republicans)
unrecognizably right-wing. And many on the Left grabbed signature liberal issues to frame their whole movement. It may be true
that the Right moved more than the Left did,[21] but both sides still
moved.

The reasons for this shift are many, and complicated. But without hazarding a strong claim about causation, it is important to recognize that for both the Right and the Left, a shift to the extremes
made fund-raising easier. Direct marketers told campaigns that a
strong and clear message to the party base is more likely to elicit a
large financial response than a balanced, moderate message to the
middle. Extremism, in other words, pays—literally. As one study
summarized the research, "An incumbent's ideological extremism
improves his or her chances of raising a greater proportion of funds
from individual donors in general and small individual contributors
in particular. Extremism is not the only way to raise money, [...]
but] to some legislators, extremism is an advantage."[22]

But, you wonder, doesn't extremism hurt a candidate's chances
with swing voters?

Of course it does. But that doesn't matter if swing voters don't
matter—which they don't in so-called "safe seats." Safe seats are
gerrymandered to produce no realistic possibility for one party to
oust the other. Throughout this period, at least 85 percent of the
districts in the House remained safe seats. In those districts at least,
the fund-raisers had a comfortable cushion within which to message to the extremes. The demand for fund-raising plus the supply
of safe seats meant American politics could afford to become more

polarized, as a means (or at least a by-product) of making fund-raising easier.[23]

To claim that American *politics* became more polarized, however, is not to say that *America* became more polarized. Politically active Americans don't represent America. As Morris Fiorina and Samuel Abrams write, "The political class is a relatively small proportion of the American citizenry, but it is...the face that the media portray as an accurate image of the American public. It is not."[24]

Instead, the distribution of political attitudes for most Americans follows a classic bell curve. As Hacker and Pierson summarize the research, "the ideological polarization of the electorate as a whole—the degree of disagreement on left-right issues overall—is modest and has changed little over time,"[25] even though "the two parties are further apart ideologically than at any point since Reconstruction."[26]

Yet even though these activists are "not like most people," power in the American government gets "transferred to [the] political activists."[27] Not just because "only zealots vote,"[28] but increasingly because the zealots especially fund the campaigns that get people to vote. Fund-raising happens among the politically active and extreme, and that puts pressure on the extremists to become even more extreme. As Fiorina and Abrams put it, "the natural place to look for campaign money is in the ranks of the single-issue groups, and a natural strategy to motivate their members is to exaggerate the threats their enemies pose."[29]

In this odd and certainly unintended way, then, the demand for cash could also be changing the substance of American politics. *Could be*, because all I've described is correlation, not causation. But at a minimum the correlation should concern us: On some issues, the parties become more united—those issues that appeal to corporate America. On other issues, the parties become more divided—the more campaign funds an issue inspires, the more extremely it gets framed. In both cases, the change correlates with a strategy designed to maximize campaign cash, while weakening the connection between what Congress does (or at least campaigns on) and the potential needs of ordinary Americans. So long as there is a demand for endless campaign cash, one simple way to supply it is to sing the message that inspires the money—even if that message is far from the views of most.

## Supply of Campaign Cash: New Norms

An increasing pressure to raise money correlates not only with changing party policies, but also with radically different congressional norms.

Consider, for example, the case of Senator Max Baucus (D-Mont.; 1978– ), chairman of the Senate Committee on Finance, arguably the most powerful senator during the debate over the details of Obama's heath care program. Between 2003 and 2008, Senator Baucus raised more than $5 million from the financial, insurance, and health care industries—precisely the industries whose regulation he oversees.[30] According to Public Citizen, between 1999 and 2005, "Baucus took in more interest group money than any other senator with the exception of Republican Bill Frist."[31] Baucus is not embarrassed by this fact. Indeed, he should be proud of it. It is a measure of his status, and the power he yields. It is a way to demonstrate that power: they give to him because of it.

Compare Baucus to another powerful committee chairman, Mississippi senator John Stennis (D-Miss.; 1947–1989). As Robert Kaiser describes, in 1982, Stennis was chairman of the Armed Services Committee. That committee oversaw the spending of hundreds of billions of defense dollars. But when Stennis was asked by a colleague to hold a fund-raiser at which defense contractors would be present, Stennis balked. Said Stennis: "Would that be proper? I hold life and death over those companies. I don't think it would be proper for me to take money from them."[32]

The difference between Stennis and Baucus is not idiosyncratic. It reflects a change in norms. Stennis was no choirboy. But his hesitation reflected an understanding that I doubt a majority of Congress today would recognize. There were limits—even just thirty years ago—that

seem as antiquated today as the wigs our Framers wore while draft-
ing the Constitution. As Congressman Jim Bacchus (D-Fla.; 1991–
1995) said of the practice of raising money from the very people you
regulate, it "compromises the integrity of the institution."[33] After that
practice became the norm, Senator Chuck Hagel (R-Neb.; 1997–2009)
commented: "There's no shame anymore. We've blown past the ethical standards, we now play on the edge of the legal standards."[34]

Again, it is hard to say with integrity that one thing caused the
other. We just don't have the data to prove it. The most that we
can say is that the new norms make fund-raising easier just at the
moment when the demand for raising funds rises dramatically.
That should concern us.

## Supply of Campaign Cash: New Suppliers

The important story of the last thirty years, however, is not just about
political parties whistling a new (and more financially attractive)
tune. Nor is it about politicians getting more comfortable with lever-
aging power into campaign cash. The most important bit is the rise
of a new army of campaign cash suppliers happy and eager to oblige
policymakers with the wonder of their rainmaking techniques.

Some of these suppliers are relatively benign. Campaigns have
finance committees, with increasingly professional fund-raisers
at the top. These fund-raisers deploy the best techniques to raise
money. Those techniques may tilt the message of the campaign
slightly. But at least these fund-raisers are the agents of the candidate. They have just one boss, and their interest is in advancing the
interests of that boss.

Some of these suppliers, however, are not so benign. For some
are not agents of the candidate or the campaign. Instead, a critical
and newly significant part of this army of campaign cash suppliers
works not for the candidate, but for special-interest clients. Their
salary is paid not by a campaign, but by a firm that sells their services directly to interests eager to persuade policymakers to bend
policy in one way or another.

Enter the modern American lobbyist.

Lobbying, of course, is not new to the American republic. The moniker likely dates to President Grant, but the practice certainly predates him. Grant would sit with friends for hours in the lobby at the Willard Hotel "enjoying cigars and brandy."[35] Influence peddlers, or "those lobbyists,"[36] as Grant called them, would approach him while he sat there. Grant's sneer, however, suggests correctly that the relationship of these "peddlers" to democracy has always been uncertain, and for many, troubling. Georgia's constitution explicitly banned the lobbying of state legislators in 1877.[37] The Supreme Court tried to staunch at least one brand of lobbying three years before, in *Trist v. Child* (1874), when it invalidated contingency contracts for lobbyists. As the Court wrote,

> If any of the great corporations of the country were to hire adventurers who make market of themselves in this way, to procure the passage of a general law with a view to the promotion of their private interests, the moral sense of every right-minded man would instinctively denounce the employer and employed as steeped in corruption, and the employment as infamous. If the instances were numerous, open and tolerated, they would be regarded as measuring the decay of the public morals and the degeneracy of the times.[38]

"Degeneracy" notwithstanding, even without contingency contracts, the industry has thrived, especially as the reach of government has grown.

For most of the history of lobbying, the techniques of lobbyists, and their relationship to Congress, were, in a word, grotesque. Well into the twentieth century, lobbyists wooed members with wine, women, and wages. Congressmen were lavishly entertained. They frequented "cat houses" paid for by lobbyists.[39] They kept safes in their offices to hold the bags of cash that lobbyists would give them.[40] And late into the twentieth century, they were taken on elaborate junkets as a way to "persuade" members of the wisdom in the lobbyists' clients' positions.[41] If the aim of the lobbyist, as Kenneth Crawford colorfully described it in 1939, was to "burn [the] bridges between the voter and what he voted for,"[42] for most of its history, there were no obvious limits on the means to that burning.

Including flat-out bribes (which were not even illegal in Congress until 1853).[43] Throughout the nineteenth century, and well into the twentieth, lobbyists paid "consulting fees" to members of Congress—directly.[44] In the early nineteenth century, Congressman Daniel Webster wrote to the Bank of the United States—while a member of Congress voting on the very existence of the Bank of the United States—"If it be wished that my relation to the Bank be continued, it may be well to send me the usual retainers."[45] That example was not unique. Members of Congress would expressly solicit personal payments from those they regulated.[46] Crawford quotes a letter from Pennsylvania Republican George Washington Edmonds to the official of a shipyard dependent upon government contracts: "As you undoubtedly know, a Congressman must derive some of his income from other sources than being a member of the House, and in this connection I would like to bring to your attention the fact that my secretary and myself have a company in Philadelphia. Please put us on your inquiry list for materials in connection with ships."[47]  *House of Cards*

Yet when lobbying was this corrupt, perhaps counterintuitively, its effect was also self-limiting. Though these practices were not uncommon, they were still (at least after 1853) illegal. Lobbyists and members had to be discreet. There may have been duplicity, but there were limits. The payoffs could not be so obvious. And almost as a way to minimize the wrong, the policies bent by this corrupt practice had to be on the margins, or at least easily ignored. There are of course grotesque stories, especially as they touched land and railroads. But in the main, the practices were hidden, and therefore limited. They knew shame.

Today's lobbyist is not so rogue. It is an absurd simplification and an insult to the profession to suggest that the norms of the industry circa 1890 have anything to do with the norms of the profession today. The lobbyist today is ethical, and well educated. He or she works extremely hard to live within the letter of the law. More than ever before, most lobbyists are just well-paid policy wonks, expert in a field and able to advise and guide Congress well. Regulation is complex; regulators understand very little; the lobbyist is the essential link between what the regulator wants to do and how it can get done. Indeed, as we'll see more later, much of the lobbyist's work is simply a type of legislative subsidy.[48] Most of it is decent, aboveboard, the sort of stuff we would hope happens inside the Beltway. The ordinary lobbyist today is a Boy Scout compared with the criminal of the nineteenth century. He has as much in common with his nineteenth-century brother as Mormons have with their nineteenth-century founders.

Yet as lobbying has become more respectable—and this is the key—it has also become more dangerous. The rent seeking that was hidden and careful before is now open and notorious. No one is embarrassed by what the profession does, because everything the profession does is out in the open for all to see. Indeed, almost literally: since 1995 no profession has been required to disclose its activities more extensively and completely than lobbyists.

But as this practice has become more professional, its effect on our democracy has become more systemic. And the question we need to track is what that systemic effect is. The lobbyist today may be best understood as providing a mere "subsidy" to the legislature— advice, research, support, guidance for issues the legislators already believe in. But one of those subsidies has the potential to corrupt the whole process. As Robert Kaiser describes best, in at least the last thirty years, the demand for campaign cash has turned the lobbyist into a supplier.[49] Not so much from the money that lobbyists give directly—though lobbyists (and their spouses and their kids) of course give an endless amount of money directly. But instead from the funding they secure indirectly—from the very interests that hire them to produce the policy results that benefit those interests.

In a way that is hard to see (because so pervasive), and certainly hard to model (because so complex), lobbyists have become the center of an economy of influence that has changed the way Washington works. They feed a frantic dependency that has grown among members of Congress—the dependency on campaign cash—but they can feed that dependency only if they can provide something of value to their clients in return. The lobbyists are funding arbitrageurs. They stand at the center of an economy. We can draw that economy like Figure 7:

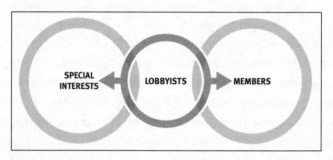

**FIGURE 7**

On the one side of this economy are the members, frantically searching for campaign cash. On the other side are interests that increasingly find themselves needing or wanting special favors from the government. As government grows, as it has, "its tentacles in every aspect of American life and commerce," then "no serious industry or interest can function without monitoring, and at least trying to manipulate, Washington's decision makers."[50] These manipulators make themselves essential to the extent that they provide a suite of essential services—including, for many, the channeling of campaign cash.

As Kaiser describes, "The more important money became to the politicians, the more important its donors became to them. This was a boon to [the lobbyists]. 'The lobbyists are in the driver's seat,' observed Leon Panetta. 'They basically know that the members have nowhere else to turn' for money....Lobbyists had become indispensable to politicians."[51]

At the center of this funding economy lie earmarks. Candidate Obama may have been right in 2008 when he said that earmarks are a very small portion of the overall federal budget—less than 2 percent of the 2005 budget.[52] But Senator McCain was certainly right when he said that the percentage itself is beside the point. The important question about earmarks isn't their absolute size relative to the federal budget. The important question is how easily the value of those earmarks can be privatized, so that, in turn, they can benefit the (campaign cash) interest of the congressman: If a congresswoman could secure a $10 million earmark benefiting Company X, how easily can some of the value of that $10 million be channeled back to her campaign? Not directly, and not illegally, but if a congressman is going to make the president of Acme, Inc., $10 million happier, is there some way that some of that "happiness" can get returned? How sticky can the favor be made to seem? How fungible? And most important, once the dance to effect that translation gets learned, how easily can it be applied to other policy issues, not directly tied to earmarks?

The answer to these questions is obvious and critical: If the only actors involved in this dance are members of Congress and the special interest seeking favor, then the dance is quite difficult, at least within the bounds of legality. But if there is an agent in the middle—someone who works not for the congressman but for many special interests seeking special favors from Congress—the dance becomes much, much easier, since there are obvious ways in which it can happen well within the boundaries of federal law.

To see how, we must first address an assumption that tends to limit imagination about how this economy of influence might work.

Too many assume that the only way that government power can be converted into campaign cash is through some sort of quid pro quo. Too many assume, that is, that influence is a series of deals. And because they imagine that a transaction is required, too many are skeptical about how vast or extensive such an economy of influence could be—first, because there are laws against this sort of thing, and second, because almost every single member of Congress, Democrat and Republican alike, strikes any one of us as clearly above this sort of corruption.

There are laws against quid pro quo bribery. These laws are, in the main, respected. Of course there are exceptions. Consider this key bit of evidence in the prosecution of Randy "Duke" Cunningham, the Vietnam War Top Gun fighter pilot turned congressman who promised in his 1990s campaign a "congressman we can be proud of" (Figure 8).

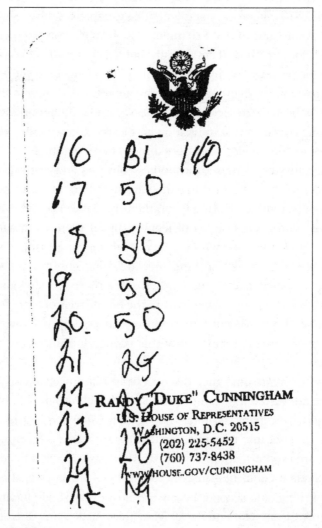

**FIGURE 8**

Look at the numbers: The first column represents the size of the government contract (in millions) the congressman was promising. The second column reports the size of the bribe (in thousands) necessary to get that contract. "BT" refers to a yacht. I'm no expert, but I know enough to say: this is not genius.

There are more Randy "Duke" Cunninghams or William Jeffersons in Congress, no doubt. But not more than a handful. I agree with Dennis Thompson that ours is among the cleanest Congresses in the history of Congress.[53] And if the only way that government power could be converted into campaign cash were by crossing the boundaries of criminal law, then there would be no book to write here. If the only possible "corruption" were the corruption regulated by bribery statutes, then I'd be the first to insist that ours is not a corrupt Congress.

Yet there is an obvious and overwhelming argument against the idea that corruption needs a transaction to work. Indeed, there is an argument—and it is the core argument of this book—that the most significant and powerful forms of corruption today are precisely those that thrive without depending upon quid pro quos for their effectiveness.

This argument can be proven in the sterile but powerful language of modern political science. Justin Fox and Lawrence Rothenberg, for example, have modeled how a campaign contribution "impacts incumbent policy choices," even if the candidates and funders can't enter into a quid pro quo arrangement.[54] But the argument is much more compelling if we understand the point in terms of our own ordinary lives. Each of us understands how influence happens without an economy of transactions. All of us live such a life all the time.

## Economies, Gift and Otherwise

Think about two economies, familiar to anyone, which we might call, taking a lead from Lewis Hyde, a gift economy and an exchange economy.[55]

A gift economy is a series of exchanges between two or more souls who never pretend to equate one exchange to another, but who also don't pretend that reciprocating is unimportant—an *economy* in the sense that it marks repeated interactions over time, but a *gift* economy in the sense that it doesn't liquidate the relationships in terms of cash. Indeed, relationships, not cash, are the currency within these economies. These relationships import obligations. And the exchanges that happen within gift economies try to hide their character as *exchanges* by tying so much of the exchange to the relationship. I give you a birthday present. It is a good present not so much because it is expensive, but because it expresses well my understanding of you. In that gift, I expect something in return. But I would be insulted if on my birthday, you gave me a cash voucher equivalent to the value of the gift I gave you, or even two times the amount I gave you. Gift giving in relationship-based economies is a way to express and build relationships. It's not a system to transfer wealth.

The gift economy is thus the relationship of friends, or family, or different people trying to build an alliance. It was the way of Native Americans completely misunderstood by their invading "friends." "An Indian gift," Thomas Hutchinson told his readers in 1764, "is a proverbial expression signifying a present for which an equivalent return is expected."[56] But the equivalence could never be demanded. And the equation could never be transparent.

An "exchange economy," by contrast, is clearer and in many ways simpler. It is the quid pro quo economy. The transactional economy. The this-for-that economy. It is the economy of a gas station, or a vending machine at a baseball park. In exchange for this bit of cash, you will give me that thing/service/promise. Cash is the currency in this economy, and as many of the terms of the relationship as possible get converted, or liquidated, into cash. It is the economy of commodification. It is an economy within which we live much of our lives.

As I've written elsewhere,[57] following the work of Yochai Benkler, Hyde, and others, there's nothing necessarily wrong with commodification. Indeed, there's lots that's great about it. As Lewis Hyde puts it,

> It is the cardinal difference between gift and commodity exchange that a gift establishes a feeling-bond between two people, while the sale of a commodity leaves no necessary connection. I go into a hardware store, pay the man for a hacksaw blade and walk out. I may never see him again. The disconnectedness is, in fact, a virtue of the commodity mode. We don't want to be bothered. If the clerk always wants to chat about the family, I'll shop elsewhere. I just want a hacksaw blade.[58]

There's plenty that's good about leaving important and large parts of your life simplified because commodified. The more bits that are simplified, the more time you have for relationships within the gift economies in which we all (hopefully!) live.

For in both economies, then, reciprocity is the norm. The difference is the transparency of that reciprocity. Gifts in this sense are not selfless acts to another. Gifts are moves in a game; they oblige others. In the economies that Hyde describes, the game in part is to obscure the extent of that obligation, but without extinguishing it. No one is so crass as to say, "I gave you a box of pearls; you need to give me something of equal value in return." Yet everyone within such an economy is monitoring the gifts given and the gifts in return. And anytime a significant gap develops, the relationship evinced by the gifts gets strained.

Against this background, we can understand Washington a bit better.

In the days of wine, women, and wealth, Washington may well have been an exchange economy. I doubt it, but it's possible. Whatever it was, however, it has become a gift economy.[59] For as the city has professionalized, as reformers have controlled graft more effectively and forced "contributions" into the open, the economy of D.C. has changed. If the law forbade D.C. from being an exchange economy, it could not block its becoming a gift economy. So long as

the links are not expressed, so long as the obligations are not liquidated, so long as the timing is not too transparent, Washington can
live a life of exchanges that oblige without living a life that violates
Title 18 of the U.S. Code (the Criminal Code, regulating bribery). As
Senator Paul Douglas (D-Ill.; 1949–1967) described it fifty years ago:

> Today the corruption of public officials by private interests
> takes a more subtle form. The enticer does not generally pay
> money directly to the public representative. He tries instead by
> a series of favors to put the public official under such a feeling
> of personal obligation that the latter gradually loses his sense of
> mission to the public and comes to feel that his first loyalties are
> to his private benefactors and patrons. What happens is a grad-
> ual shifting of a man's loyalties from the community to those
> who have been doing him favors. His final decisions are, there-
> fore, made in response to his private friendships and loyalties
> rather than to the public good. Throughout this whole process,
> the official will claim—and may indeed believe—that there is
> no causal connection between the favors he has received and
> the decisions which he makes.[60]

This is a gift economy. As Jake Arvey, the man behind Adlai Ste-
venson's political career, defined *politics*: "politics is the art of putting people under obligation to you."[61] Obligation, not expressed in
legally enforceable contracts, but in the moral expectations that a
system of gift exchange yields.

A gift economy is grounded upon relationships, not quid pro
quo. Those relationships grow over time, as actors within that economy build their power by developing a rich set of obligations that
they later draw upon to achieve the ends they seek. In this world,
the campaign contribution does not "buy" a result. It cements a
relationship, or as Kaiser describes it, it "reinforce[s] established
connections."[62] As one former lobbyist put it when asked why contributions are made: "Well, it isn't good government. It's to thank
friends, and to make new friends. It opens up channels of communication."[63]

It is within this practice of reciprocity that obligation gets built.[64] And as economist Michele Dell'Era demonstrates, the gifts necessary to make this system of reciprocity work need not be large.[65] What is important is that they be repeated and appropriate within the norms of the context. What is critical is that they are depended upon.

Unlike traditional gift economies, however, Washington is a gift economy not because anyone wants it to be. It is a gift economy because it is *regulated* to be. Having banned the quid pro quo economy, the market makers have only one choice: to do the hard work necessary to build and support a gift economy. The insiders must learn a dance that never seems like an exchange. Demands or requests can be made. (Day one: "Congresswoman, our clients really need you to see how harmful H.R. 2322 will be to their interests.") But those demands are unconnected to the gifts that are given. (Day two: "Congresswoman, we'd love to hold a fund-raiser for you.") Even congressmen (or at least their staff) can put one and one together. And even when the one doesn't follow the other, everyone understands how to count chits. There's nothing cheap or insincere about it. Indeed, the lobbyist is providing something of value, and the member is getting something she needs. And so long as each part in this exchange remains allowed, the dance can continue—openly and notoriously—without anyone feeling wrong or used.

For this economy to survive, we need only assume a rich and repeated set of exchanges, among people who come to know and trust one another. There has to be opportunity to verify that commitments have been met—eventually. In the meantime, there must be the trust necessary to enable most of the exchange to happen based on trust alone. It must be the sort of place "where one never writes if one can call, never calls if one can speak, never speaks if one can nod, and never nods if one can wink"—precisely how Barney Frank described D.C., borrowing from the words of Boston pol Martin Lomasney.[66]

As I've already described, the seed for the current version of this economy was earmarks. The lobbying firm retainers that secured these earmarks paid for the infrastructure that now gets leveraged to much greater and more powerful ends. Think of earmarks as the pianist's scales. They teach technique. But the technique gets deployed far beyond scales.

It wasn't always so. The modern earmarks revolution was born recently, and in a rather unlikely place. Its inventor was a McGovern Democrat, Gerald S. J. Cassidy, and its first target was a grant to support a nutrition research center at Tufts University in 1976. Cassidy and Associates "brought something new to an old game," Kaiser writes, "by stationing themselves at a key intersection between a supplicant for government assistance, and the people who could respond."[67] Once they did, the supplicants recognized they had tripped upon gold. There were thousands of organizations and individuals keen to get government money spent in a particular way. And if the will of these organizations could be achieved through the camouflage of the earmarking process, they'd be more than eager to pay for it. To pay, that is, both Cassidy (directly) and members of Congress (indirectly).[68] By 1984 there were fifteen university clients paying large monthly retainers to Cassidy's firm, and about a dozen more big companies—all seeking earmarks.[69]

Cassidy couldn't patent his brilliant insight (or at least he didn't—who knows what silliness the patent office would endorse). But as other lobbyists recognized just what was happening, other firms entered the market he originally staked out. Soon an industry was born to complement the practice (and profits) of the lobbyists of before: the product of that industry was a chance at channeling federal spending; the producers of that product were the lobbyists; the beneficiaries of that product were the lobbyists, congressmen, and the interests who might benefit from the earmark. For a time, Cassidy and his colleagues "could truthfully tell clients that they had never failed to win an earmark for an institution that had retained them."[70] *Never* is a sexy word in the world of political power.

As this economy grew, the lobbyists' role in fund-raising grew as well. As one lobbyist put it expressly, "I spend a huge amount of my time fundraising...A *huge* amount."[71] That behavior has been confirmed to me by countless others, not so eager to be on the record. "The most vital people" in this economy, Jeff Birnbaum reports, "aren't the check writers but the check *raisers*."[72] "Washington has thousands of lobbyists who raise or give money to lawmakers."[73]

At first, some of the old-timers in D.C. worried about the monster that Cassidy had helped birth. As Senator Robert Byrd (D-W.Va.; 1959–2010) put it:

> The perception is growing that the merit of a project, grant or contract awarded by the government has fallen into a distant second place to the moxie and clout of lobbyists who help spring the money out of appropriation bills for a fat fee.... Inside the Beltway, everyone knows how the game is played.... Every Senator in this body ought to be repulsed by the perception that we will dole out the bucks if stroked by the right consultant.[74]

The concern was not just among Democrats. Members from the middle era of the twentieth-century Congress from both parties were unhappy as they watched Congress become the Fundraising Congress. Senator John Heinz (R-Pa.; 1977–1991) asked, how could he explain to Pennsylvania universities that money was now handed out "not on the basis of quality, but on the basis of senatorial committee assignments."[75] Senator John Danforth (R-Mo.; 1976–1995) made a similar complaint.[76]

As the practice grew, the range and scale of the asks only increased, and the capacity of congressmen to decide on earmark requests *based on the merits of the request* declined substantially. My former congresswoman, Jackie Speier (D-Calif.; 2009– ), asked me to chair a citizens' commission to review earmark requests. Almost a dozen civic leaders from the district and I spent hundreds of hours poring over almost sixty specific requests. The topics of these requests ranged from streetlights to sophisticated defense technologies. The size ranged from the tens of thousands to the many, many millions.

What struck all of us on this commission was just how impossibly difficult it would be for anyone to weigh one request against another in a rational way. Moreover, we all were unanimous in our view that there was something inappropriate about for-profit companies asking for government help to better market or produce their products. Yet there were many requests of exactly that form, and thus many, many opportunities in districts unlike ours for the beneficiaries of those potential grants to make their gratitude known.

But isn't all this illegal? you ask. Even if the exchange merely increases the probability of a payment in return, isn't that enough to show quid pro quo corruption?

The answer is no, and for a very good reason: quid pro quo corruption requires intent. The guilty government official must intend to pay for the contribution made. That's the meaning of *pro*: this *pro* (for) that. But in the mechanism I'm describing, the repayment is attenuated, and there is no necessity that it even be intended. Indeed, as cognitive psychologists have now plausibly suggested using brain scan technology, it is quite plausible that "intent" to repay a gift happens completely subconsciously.[77] The member need not even recognize that she is acting to reciprocate for her action to be repayment for a previously recognized gift.

Indeed, the only way to clearly separate the gift to the member from the member's actions in return would be if such gifts were anonymous.[78] But of course, every contribution that matters today is as public as a pop star's latest affair. Without doubt, key staffers in every member's office know who supports their congressman and who doesn't. More likely than not, the key staffers have made sure of it.

The gifts within this economy go both ways. Sometimes it is the lobbyist who secures the gift. Sometimes it is the member who makes the gift, expecting the recipient will, as the moniker suggests, reciprocate.

How would this work?

A large proportion of earmarks have gone to nonprofit institutions. Nonprofit institutions have boards, and board members have an obligation to work for the interest of that institution. Sometimes that work includes fund-raising, especially fund-raising to support new buildings or new research ventures. Members of the board thus have an obligation to the institution to raise the funds to meet those objectives.

So imagine you're a board member of a small college in Virginia. Your board has decided to build a new science center. And just as you launch on this difficult task, your congresswoman secures an earmark to fund one building. You, as a board member, have now received a gift—from this congresswoman. A gift, not a bribe. You have no obligation toward that congresswoman. To the contrary, you have something better: you have gratitude toward her, for she has helped you and your institution.

That gratitude, in turn, can be quite lucrative—for the congresswoman. When you next receive a fund-raising solicitation from that congresswoman, it will be harder for you to say no and still feel good about yourself. She did a favor for you. You now should do a favor for her in return. The simplest way to return the favor is to send a check to her campaign committee. So you send a check—again, not necessarily even aware of how the desire to reciprocate has been induced by the congresswoman's gift. At no point in this process has any law been broken. The earmark was not a quo given in exchange for a quid. No promise of anything in return need have been made. The earmark is instead simply part of the economy. Representative Peter Kostmayer (D-Pa.; 1977–1981, 1983–1993) described this dynamic precisely, and his own recognition of its stench:

> I was once asked by a member of Congress from Pennsylvania to raise some money for the Pennsylvania Democratic Party, and he gave me a list of universities that had gotten big federal grants—academic pork. And he asked me if I would make

calls to the presidents of these universities across the state to get contributions. I decided I was uncomfortable doing it, and I didn't do it.[79]

My point just now is not to criticize what earmarks support, though I'd be happy to do that as well. Whether you think the spending makes sense or not, my point is to get you to see the dynamic that earmarks support. Or better, the *platform* they help build. That platform enables a certain trade. The parties to that trade are lobbyists, their special-interest clients, and members of Congress. Because that platform supports a gift economy, the trade it enables does not cross the boundary of quid pro quo corruption. The lobbyists never need to make any link explicit. They're proud of their "professionalism" in respecting that line. Indeed, they are surprised when anyone expressly crosses it. (Kaiser reports one example that reveals the understanding: The National Association of Home Builders was upset at a change made to certain pending legislation. In response, they expressly declared that there would be no further campaign contributions until the change was undone. "The statement raised eyebrows all over Washington. The NAHB had broken one of the cardinal rules of the game.")[80]

The gains in this system that each of the three parties in the system—lobbyists, their clients, and members of Congress—realize should be obvious. (Indeed, there is valuable theoretical work suggesting just why the lobbying game proves to be more valuable than the bribery game, and why we should expect, over time, a democracy to move from bribery to lobbying.)[81]

But to make understandable the enormous growth in this "influence cash," now leveraged by the "influence peddlers," we should enumerate it just to be clear:

- Members of Congress get access to desperately needed campaign cash—directly from the lobbyists, and indirectly, as facilitated by the lobbyists. They need that cash. That cash makes much simpler an otherwise insane existence, as it cuts back at least partially on the endless need of members to raise campaign funds elsewhere.

- The clients of the lobbyists get a better chance at changing government policy. In a world of endless government spending and government regulation, that chance can be enormously lucrative. As researchers at the University of Kansas calculated, the return on lobbyists' investment to modify the American Jobs Creation Act of 2004 to create a tax benefit was 22,000 percent.[82] A paper published in 2009 calculates that, on average, for every $1 that an average firm spends to lobby for targeted tax benefits, the return is between $6 and $20.[83] Looking at universities, John M. de Figueiredo and Brian S. Silverman found that universities with representation on the House or Senate Appropriations Committee see a 0.28 to 0.35 percent increase in earmarks for every 1 percent increase in lobbyist expenditures relative to universities without such representation.[84] Frank Yu and Xiaoyun Yu found that "compared to non-lobbying firms, firms that lobby on average have a significantly lower hazard rate of being detected for fraud, evade fraud detection 117 days longer, and are 38% less likely to be detected by regulators."[85] Hill, Kelly, Lockhart, and Van Ness have demonstrated how "lobbying firms significantly outperform non-lobbying firms."[86] All of these studies confirm what is otherwise intuitive: as the returns from lobbyists' investments increase, the willingness to invest in lobbyists will increase as well. Thus, as journalist Ken Silverstein puts it, while clients can pay retainers "easily reaching tens of millions of dollars...such retainers are undeniably savvy: the overall payout in pork is many times that, totaling into billions."[87]

- Finally, lobbyists get an ever-growing and increasingly profitable business. The lobbying industry has exploded over the past twenty years. Its growth and wealth match

almost any in our economy. In 1971, Hacker and Pierson
report, there were just 175 firms with registered lobbyists
in D.C. Ten years later, there were almost 2,500.[88] In 2009
there were 13,700 registered lobbyists. They spent more
than $3.5 billion—twice the amount spent in 2002,[89] rep-
resenting about $6.5 million per elected representative
in Congress.

And as the lobbying industry grows, D.C. gets rich, too. Nine
of Washington's suburban counties are now listed by the Census
Bureau as among the nation's twenty with the highest per capita
income.[90] As former labor secretary Robert Reich describes,

> When I first went to Washington in 1975, many of the restau-
> rants along Pennsylvania Avenue featured linoleum floors and an
> abundance of cockroaches. But since then the city has become
> an increasingly dazzling place. Today, almost everywhere you
> look in downtown Washington you find polished facades, fancy
> restaurants, and trendy bistros. There are office complexes of
> glass, chrome and polished wood; well appointed condos with
> doormen who know the names and needs of each inhabitant;
> hotels with marble-floored lobbies, thick rugs, soft music, granite
> counters; restaurants with linen napkins, leather-bound menus,
> heavy silverware.[91]

There are many in the lobbying profession, of course, who
deplore the state of the industry. They obviously don't want to
return to the old days. They instead want the industry to evolve
into the profession they dream it could be. As one lobbyist put it,
"Money does make a difference—and it has changed the character of this town.... The truth is that money has replaced brains
and hard work as the way for a lobbyist to get something done for
his client."[92] And many, including the American Bar Association's
Task Force on Federal Lobbying Laws, have recommended "so far
as practicable, those who advocate to elected officials do not raise

funds for them, and those who raise funds for them do not advocate to them."[93] As the ABA report states:

> [T]he multiplier effect of a lobbyist's participation in *fundraising* for a member's campaign (or the member's leadership PAC) can be quite substantial, and the Task Force believes that this activity should be substantially curtailed.... *[A] self-reinforcing cycle of mutual financial dependency has become a deeply troubling source of corruption in our government.*[94]

That follows the strong recommendation of President Bush's chief ethics lawyer, Professor Richard Painter:

> The best way to change the profession's reputation for abusing the system of campaign finance is to end lobbyists' involvement in campaign finance. When lobbyists bundle their own and clients' money to buy government officials' attention they undermine public confidence not only in government but also in the quality of lobbyists' advocacy and the merits of their cause. The bagman image erodes credibility even if credit is due for a lobbyist's intellectual ability, experience, and integrity.[95]

Until these reformers succeed in their reform, however, much of the value from the service of lobbyists will continue to derive not so much from the "bagman image" but from the fund-raising reality.

In this model of influence, campaign cash plays a complicated role. My claim is not that campaign cash buys any result directly. As Dan Clawson, Mark Weller, and Alan Neustadtl put it, "Many critics of big money campaign finance seem to assume that a corporate donor summons a senator and says, 'Senator, I want you to vote against raising the minimum wage. Here's $5,000 to do so.' This view, in its crude form, is simply wrong."[96]

Where lobbying does buy votes directly, it's a crime, and I've already said I don't think (many) such crimes occur.

Instead, campaign cash has a distinctive role, depending upon which of three buckets it finds itself within:

In the *first bucket* are contributions that are effectively anonymous. These are gifts, typically small gifts, that a campaign receives but doesn't meaningfully track. That doesn't mean they don't keep tabs on the contributor—of course they do, for the purpose of asking the contributor for more. I mean instead that they don't keep tabs on the particular issue or interest that the contributor cares about. This is just money that the campaign attracts, but that it attracts democratically. It is the support inspired by the substance of the campaign.

The *second bucket* is the non-anonymous contributions. These are the large gifts from people or interests whose interests are fairly transparent. PAC contributions fit in here, as do contributions by very large and repeated givers. For these contributions, the candidate knows what he needs to do, or say, or believe. If campaign contributions are an investment, as many believe, then these investments are made with a clear signal about the return that is expected.

Finally, the *third bucket* is most important for the dynamic I am describing in this chapter: that part for which a lobbyist can claim responsibility. Again, some of this is direct: the money the lobbyist gives. But the more important cash is indirect: the part bundled, or effectively coordinated or inspired by the lobbyist, which, through channels, the beneficiaries learn of. Everyone who needs to be thanked is thanked, which means everyone who needs to know eventually does.

As we move from bucket one to three, risks to the system increase.

Bucket one is the most benign and pro-democratic of the three. This is the part that the candidate's campaign inspires directly. It's the direct echo of the policies he or she advances. If there is pandering here to raise more cash, it is public pandering. It's the kind the opponent can take advantage of. It is the part that feeds political debate. And as Robert Brooks put it more than a century ago, "It is highly improbable that the question of campaign funds would ever have been raised in American politics if party contributions were habitually made by a large number of persons each giving a relatively small amount."[97]

Bucket two is where the risks begin. For here begins the incentive to shape-shift, and not necessarily in a public way. The understandings that might inspire contributions to this bucket can be subtle or effectively invisible. As Daniel Lowenstein writes, "From the beginning of an issue's life, legislators know of past contributions and the possibility of future ones.... All of these combine in a manner no one fully understands to form an initial predisposition in the legislator."[98]

Again, it's not easy to achieve such understandings effectively and legally. To the extent they're expressed, they're crimes. To the extent they're implied, they can be misunderstood. The rules regulating quid pro quo corruption don't block this sort of distortion. But they certainly make it much harder to effect.

Bucket three is where the real risk to the system thrives, at least so long as lobbyists are at the center of campaign funding. For here the relationships are complicated and long-standing, and their thickness makes it relatively simple to embed understandings and expectations.

We don't have any good data about how big each bucket is. The data we do have is (predictably) misleading because of (predictable) loopholes in the rules. My colleague Joey Mornin used the public records to try to calculate the size of bundled contributions.[99] He found large numbers overall. But even that careful analysis understates the influence, because the rules don't require a lobbyist to report a bundle if the event at which it occurs was jointly sponsored, and if each lobbyist was responsible for less than $16,000. So if ten lobbyists hold a fund-raiser at which they bring together $150,000, none of that need be reported.[100]

But critically, size is not necessarily the most important issue. Influence happens on the margin, and the most powerful are the contributors who stand there. Even if bucket three were small compared to buckets one and two, if it provided a reliable and substantial source of funds, then its potential to distort policy would be huge.

This point is important, and often missed. As economists put it, price is set on the margin. The economic actor with the most power is the last one to trade. ("What do I need to do to get the next $10,000?") Thus, even if small, bucket three is where the action is. The argument is parallel to one about technological innovation made by Judge Richard Posner:

> [T]he level of output in a competitive market is determined by the intersection of price and marginal cost. This implies that the marginal purchaser—the purchaser willing to pay a price no higher than marginal cost—drives the market to a considerable extent. It follows that a technological innovation that is attractive to the marginal consumer may be introduced even though it lowers consumer welfare overall; this is a kind of negative externality.[101]

In the context of contributions to a campaign, the same dynamic is true. The bending necessary to secure sufficient funds from bucket three may well make those giving to bucket one less happy. That's just the nature of these markets on the margin.

Campaign contributions in this model are thus not the only or even the most significant expenditure that special interests make. Indeed, lobbying expenditures (2009/2010) were four times as large as campaign expenditures in 2010. But though "themselves... never enough to create or maintain a viable government relations operation," as Clawson and his colleagues describe, contributions are a "useful, perhaps even a necessary, part of the total strategy."[102]

And finally, there is one more "useful, perhaps even necessary, part of the total strategy" that we cannot ignore: the power that one's future has over one's behavior today. This part was made obvious to me by an extraordinary congressman from Tennessee, Democrat Jim Cooper.

First elected to Congress in 1982 (at the age of twenty-eight), Cooper has a longer perspective on the institution than all but twenty-nine of its members.[103] Early into my work, Cooper captured one part of it for me with a single brilliant distillation. As he told me one afternoon, while we were sitting in his office overlooking the Capitol, with a portrait of Andrew Jackson overlooking us: "Capitol Hill is a farm league for K Street."

Cooper worries that too many now view Capitol Hill as a stepping stone to life as a lobbyist—aka K Street. Too many have a business model much like my students at Harvard Law School: They expect to work for six to eight years making a salary just north of $160,000 a year. Then they want to graduate to a job making three to ten times that amount as lobbyists. Their focus is therefore not so much on the people who sent them to Washington. Their focus is instead on those who will make them rich in Washington.

This, too, is an important change. In the 1970s, 3 percent of retiring members became lobbyists. Thirty years later, that number has increased by an order of magnitude. Between 1998 and 2004, more than 50 percent of senators and 42 percent of House members made that career transition.[104] As of June 2010, 172 former members of Congress were registered lobbyists.[105] In 2009 the financial sector alone had 70 former members of Congress lobbying on its behalf.[106] Indeed, as Jeffrey Birnbaum reports, there are members who are explicit about the plan to become lobbyists.[107] Ken Silverstein reports on one particularly pathetic example:

> While still a senator, [Bob] Packwood had confided to his fatal diaries that he regarded the Senate, where he dwelled for twenty-seven years, as but a stepping-stone to a more lucrative career as an influence peddler. Perhaps someday, he mused, "I can become a lobbyist at five or six or four hundred thousand" dollars a year. Less than a year after he resigned in disgrace, Packwood formed a firm called Sunrise Research and was making lavish fees representing timber firms and other corporate clients seeking lower business taxes.[108]

The system thus feeds itself. It's not campaign contributions that members care about, or not directly. It is a future. A job. A way to imagine paying for the life that other professionals feel entitled to. A nice house. Fancy cars. Private schools for the kids. This system gives both members and their staff a way to have it all, at least if they continue to support the system.

What exactly is the wrong in what they're doing, given the system as it is? The wannabe lobbyists get to do their wonky policy work. They get to live among the most powerful people in the nation. Their life is interesting and well compensated. And they never need to lie, cheat, or steal. What could possibly be bad about that? Indeed, anyone who would resist this system would be a pariah on the Hill. You can just hear the dialogue from any number of Hollywood films: "We've got a good thing going here, Jimmy. Why would you want to go and mess things up?"

# CHAPTER 10

# *What* So Damn
# Much Money *Does*

Consider two statements by two prominent Republicans. The first, by Senator Tom Coburn (R-Okla.; 2005– ): "Thousands of instances exist where appropriations are leveraged for fundraising dollars or political capital."[1]

The second, by former Federal Elections Commission chairman Bradley Smith: "The evidence is pretty overwhelming that the money does not play much of a role in what goes on in terms of legislative voting patterns and legislative behavior. The consensus about that among people who have studied it is roughly the same as the consensus among scientists that global warming is taking place."[2]

To be clear, Smith is a corruption denier, not a global warming denier. What he is saying is that the evidence from political science suggests—contrary to Senator Coburn and to the whole thrust of this book—that the money doesn't matter. Indeed, he says more than just that: He means to say that anyone who suggests that the money matters—to "legislative voting patterns and legislative behavior"—is as crazy as global warming deniers. That no honest scholar (let's put aside politicians) could maintain that we have any good evidence to suggest that there's a problem with the current system. That any honest scholar would therefore focus his work elsewhere.

I've found that people have two very different reactions to Chairman Smith's statement. The vast majority react in stunned disbelief: "Is he nuts?" is the most common retort. It is also among the kindest. Almost all of us react almost viscerally to corruption deniers, just as most (liberals, at least) react to global warming deniers.

A tiny minority, however, react differently. If they're careless in listening precisely to what Chairman Smith said ("money does not play much of a role in what goes on in terms of legislative voting patterns *and legislative behavior*"), they say something like this: "Yeah, it is surprising, but the data really don't support the claim that money is corrupting Congress." And if they're more on the activist side of the spectrum, and less on the academic side, they're likely to buttress this observation with something like "So *you*, Lessig, need to take this evidence seriously, and justify your campaign, since the facts don't support it."

I once confronted this latter demand in a bizarre Washington context. I had been invited to address a truly remarkable group called the Lib-Libertarians—a mix of liberal and libertarian D.C. souls who meet for dinner regularly to talk about common ideas. Most of them were lawyers. Some were journalists. And some were in various stages of the revolving and gilded door between government and the private sector.

I like liberals. (I am one.) I also like libertarians. (If we understand that philosophy properly, I am one, too.) So I carelessly assumed that my anti-money-in-politics argument would be embraced by the collected wise and virtuous souls of that dinner. It wasn't, by at least a significant chunk. For when I tried to brush off a version of Chairman Smith's claim, I was practically scolded by the questioner. How could I "possibly," he asked, "ignore these data?" How could I "honestly," he charged, "make an argument that doesn't account for them?"

That scolding is fair. I can't honestly make an argument that demands we end the corruption that is our government without honestly addressing "these data."

The Republican senator from Oklahoma is right (not the global warming denier, Senator James Inhofe [R-Okla.; 1994– ], but Coburn): There are thousands of "instances...where appropriations are leveraged for fundraising dollars or political capital." That defines the corruption that I have described in this book. Nothing in what I will say in this chapter will undermine that claim.

And Chairman Smith is also, in part at least, right. He is right that political scientists have not shown a strong connection between contributions to political campaigns and "legislative voting patterns." There is some contest about the question (much more than there is about global warming, I'd quibble), but it is fair to say that there is no consensus that the link has been shown.

Yet the aim of this chapter is to convince you that even if Smith is (partly) right—even if the political scientists can't see a connection between contributions and votes—that does not exonerate Congress from the charge of corruption. Why the political scientists can't see what the politicians do see is obvious enough, and clear. You can support the reform of Congress without denying the power of statistical regression. You can be a rootstriker even if you can't directly see the root.

## A Baseline of Independence

Though we describe our government as a "democracy," that's not precisely what our founders thought they had built. Indeed, for many (though not for all) at the founding, *democracy* was a term of derision, and the Constitution nowhere even mentions it. Instead, the Constitution speaks of a "Republic." Article IV of the Constitution even guarantees "to every State in this Union a Republican Form of government."

By a "Republic," our Framers meant a "representative democracy."[3] And one critical component of that representative democracy (the House) was to be directly elected by the people. (The president and Senate were independently elected.) These elected officers were not just potted plants. They were to deliberate and decide upon what was in the public interest. The *public* interest: the founding generation was obsessed with the distinction between private, or special interests (what Madison called "factions"), and the public or general good. They believed there was a distinction; they believed the job of the representative was to see it, and follow it.

To the Framers, this same distinction even applied to citizens. In their view, citizenship itself was a public office. As the holder of that office, each of us is charged with voting not to advance our own private interests, but instead to advance the public's interest. As Professor Zephyr Teachout summarizes the Framers' view: "In the worldview of the Framers—a view that persisted in constitutional case law for at least a hundred years—citizenship is a public office.... Citizens can be corrupted and use their public offices for private gain, instead of public good. They are fundamentally responsible for the integrity of their government."[4]

To modern ears, all this sounds a bit precious. What is the "public good"? And what would it mean for a citizen to vote in the public good, as opposed to in the interest of the citizen?

The answer (for us at least) is that there's no good answer, at least not anymore. And so did the Framers come to this answer fairly soon into the life of the new republic. Fairly quickly, as they saw representative democracy develop, most of them were convinced that their ideal of enlightened self-interest in governing was, in a word, naive.[5]

Yet the Constitution had a fallback.[6] Whatever the "public good" was, the House of Representatives (and after the Seventeenth Amendment, so, too, the Senate) was intended to have a specific dependency. As the Federalist Papers put it—oddly, because in this context, *dependent* is used in a positive sense, while in practically every other instance, the Federalist Papers use *dependent* and its cognates in a negative sense—that means a Congress "dependent upon the People alone."[7] *Dependent*—meaning answerable to, relying upon, controlled by. *Alone*—meaning dependent upon nothing or no one else.

So in a single line, in a way that frames the core of my claim that ours is a corrupt Congress, the Framers gave us a "republic"; to them, a republic was to be a "representative democracy"; a "representative democracy" was to be "dependent upon the People alone"; a representative democracy that developed a competing dependency, conflicting with the dependency upon the people, would be "corrupt."

That was their aim, as it sets the appropriate constitutional baseline.[8] To secure their aim, they then erected constitutional mechanisms to ensure this dependency. These mechanisms did two things: they weakened the likelihood of other dependencies, and they strengthened the force of the dependency upon the people.

Consider each in turn.

*1. The Framers weakened the possibility of competing dependencies by expressly blocking other corrupting ties.*

- The Ineligibility Clause (Article I, §6, cl. 2)—which Virginia's George Mason called "the corner-stone on which our liberties depend"[9]—made it impossible for the president to make members of Congress dependent upon him, by appointing them to civil office while also serving in the legislature, or by appointing them to offices that had been created (or the pay increased) during their tenure in Congress. New Jersey had a similar clause in its constitution, which tied the constitutional device expressly to a concern about "corruption":

    "That the legislative department of this government may, as much as possible, be preserved from all suspicion of corruption, none of the Judges of the Supreme or other Courts, Sheriffs, or any other person or persons possessed of any post of profit under the government... shall be entitled to a seat in the Assembly: but that, on his being elected, and taking his seat, his office or post shall be considered as vacant."[10]

- The Origination Clause (Article I, §7, cl. 1) expressly placed the power of the purse in the legislature, thereby weakening the opportunity of the executive to use federal spending to make legislators dependent upon him.[11]

- The Emoluments Clause (Article I, §6, cl. 2) weakened the opportunity of any "King, Prince, or foreign State" to make any member or officer of the United States dependent upon it, by banning gifts from such entities without the permission of Congress.

In all these cases, as Zephyr Teachout describes, the Framers were "drawing on the experience of England, where 'the [voters] are so corrupted by the representatives, and the representatives so corrupted by the Crown,'...to avoid financial dependency of one branch upon another."[12] Constitutional structure was deployed to avoid corrupting dependencies.

*2. The Framers also crafted devices to strengthen the force of Congress's dependency upon the people.*

- Requiring elections every two years for the House was explicitly understood to bind the House tightly to the people. (Federalist No. 57: "the House of Representatives is so constituted as to support in the members an habitual recollection of their dependence on the people.")
- The First Amendment's requirement that Congress listen to petitions "for a redress of grievances," meant Congress wasn't free to ignore the people, even after being bound.
- When the Framers recognized a part of Congress that was too far from "the People's" control, it weakened it. The delegates to the convention believed the Senate was more prone to corruption than the House (in part because of its small size). Madison thus recommended it "have less to do with money matters,"[13] to avoid an even stronger temptation to corruption.

This is the work of sophisticated constitutional architects all aimed at a single end: to establish and protect a link between Congress and "the People alone." A link. A dependency. A *dependency* sufficiently strong to ensure the *independence* of the institution.

It might sound a bit Newspeak to describe "independence" produced by "dependence." Yet we use the term in just this way all the time. We say we want an independent judiciary. That doesn't mean a judiciary that can do whatever the hell it wants. It means a judiciary dependent upon the law, and not upon the president, or politics, or whatever else you think might taint a judiciary. Independence in this sense simply means *the proper dependence*. And for our Framers, again, the proper dependence for a Congress was "upon the People alone."[14]

Of course, just because the Framers believed in something does not make it right. They (or many of them) believed in slavery. Most believed in bloodletting. They thought it absurd to imagine a woman as president.

It is fair, however, to use their ideas as the baseline against which to judge our own practices. That baseline might be unjust, no doubt. But if we believe the baseline is just, or sensible, then when there is deviation from that baseline, we should ask whether that deviation is something to praise. Does the change bring us to a better democracy? Or a better republic? Could we justify it—or even explain it—to the Framers? Or, with integrity, to ourselves?

## Deviations from a Baseline

Our current Congress is far from the Congress our Framers imagined. In a million ways. It doesn't deliberate together, as a whole. Members don't listen to other members during debate. Each representative represents at least twenty times the number of citizens that representatives at the founding did. Almost half of the Congress returned home after each election cycle in the first century of the republic. No more than 10 percent do so today.[15]

But the difference I want to focus on is the economy of influence that defines the life of a member. How is the republic altered because we have allowed this dependency to evolve? How would it be different if we found a way to remove it?

We can begin to answer this question with a simple exercise: Imagine yourself in your congresswoman's shoes. Imagine the life she leads. She has a campaign manager who tells her she needs to raise hundreds of thousands, maybe millions, of dollars, preferably long before the next election, so that no one in his right mind would even think about running against her. So each day she does her bit. A couple of hours here, a couple of hours there, on the phone with people she doesn't know, asking for money. The routine would be comical if it weren't so disturbing: A day on Capitol Hill is comprised of racing to vote on the floor of the House, to a quick drop in on a committee meeting, and then off the Hill to a fund-raising office with a telephone and an operator's headset, where, until the vote buzzer rings again, she will call and call and call again.

This life puts enormous pressure on a member. It is pressure that comes in part from the member herself (she wants to win), and in part from her staff, from her supporters, and from her party. And then she meets with a dizzying array of lobbyists, many of whom are eager to help relieve that pressure. How would that offer of "help" change what she thought, or what she did? How would it matter?

We don't need a Sigmund Freud here. We all recognize the drive deep in our bones (or, more accurately, our DNA) to reciprocate.[16] Some of it we see directly. Some of it we don't. The subconscious is guided by interactions of reciprocity as much as the conscious. We reciprocate without thinking. We are bent to those to whom we are obliged, even when we believe, honestly, that we are not. What Robert Brooks wrote over a century ago we can repeat today: "By far the worst evil of the present system is the ease with which it enables men otherwise incorruptible to be placed tactfully, subtly, and—as time goes on—always more completely under obligations incompatible with public duty."[17]

Sometimes the politicians admit as much. In 1905 an aging senator Thomas Collier Platt of New York "acknowledged receiving cash contributions to his campaigns from the insurance companies, and in return for that money he admitted that he had 'a moral obligation to defend them.' "[18]

Most of the time, however, they deny it. They insist that their judgment is independent of campaign cash. They insist they haven't been affected. "It is insulting," I've been told, "to suggest that my actions have been influenced by my contributors. They have not, and never will be."

America doesn't believe the denials. The vast majority of

Americans believe money buys results in Congress: 75 percent believe "campaign contributions buy results in Congress."[19] And this commonsense view is confirmed, albeit more subtly, by some current members of Congress, and more frequently by former members of Congress. In an excellent series, the Center for Responsive Politics has interviewed retired members of Congress about the influence of money in politics. Again and again, both Democrats and Republicans insist that of course the money matters. For example:

Rep. Joe Scarborough (R-Fla.; 1995–2001) (yes, *that* Joe Scarborough): "Across the spectrum, money changed votes. Money certainly drove policy at the White House during the Clinton administration, and I'm sure it has in every other administration too."[20]

Sen. Slade Gorton (R-Wash.; 1981–1987, 1989–2001) (Asked: Have you seen votes in the Senate where you just knew that certain votes were lining up certain ways because of the money?): "The answer to that question certainly has been yes."[21]

Rep. Tim Penny (D-Minn.; 1983–1995): "There's not tit for tat in business, no check for a vote. But nonetheless, the influence is there. Candidates know where their money is coming from."[22]

Rep. Mel Levine (D-Calif.; 1983–1993): "On the tax side, the appropriations side, the subsidy side, and the expenditure side, decisions are clearly weighted and influenced...by who has contributed to the candidates. The price that the public pays for this process, whether it's in subsidies, taxes, or appropriations, is quite high."[23]

Rep. Eric Fingerhut (D-Ohio; 1993–1995): "The completely frank and honest answer is that the method of campaign funding that we currently have...has a serious and profound impact on not only the issues that are considered in Congress, but also on the outcome of those issues."[24]

Sen. Bill Bradley (D-N.J.; 1979–1997): "We've reached a point where nothing but money seems to matter. Political parties have lost their original purpose, which was to bring people together…and instead they become primarily conduits for cash."[25]

Even when members think they're denying an effect, their denial just confirms that the effect is real. Former senator Slade Gorton, a supporter of the current system, commented, "It just seemed to me that those who were trying to buy influence on both sides were simply wasting their money."[26] Does that mean that those who bought on only one side were not wasting their money? Or as Representative Hamilton Fish IV (R-N.Y.; 1969–1995) commented: "I look at a contribution as a 'thank you' for the position I took, not as expecting that I would take a position in the future…. [It was] a reward, not a bribe."[27] But of course, we use rewards to induce people to do things they otherwise wouldn't do all the time. Why not here?

Most of us believe that the money has an influence. Former members from both political parties confirm it. That influence, we believe, bends the results of Congress from what they otherwise would have been. That constitutes, for the vast majority of Americans, proof enough of the corruption that is our government. This is the common view.

As I've said, our common view could be right. It could also be wrong. Indeed, as I describe in the section that follows, there is important scholarship that raises real questions about whether we can say that money in fact bends democracy in the way most of us feel it does. We need to confront that scholarship to see exactly what it sees, and exactly what it misses.

## 0. It Matters Not at All

Some believe that this dependence upon money does nothing. That it is harmless. Or at least, they insist, we have no good evidence that this dependence does anything, and since we've got no evidence, we've got no good reason to change it.

By "evidence," these conservatives (with a small $c$—they could well be politically liberal; my point is that they're scientifically conservative) mean numbers. Statistics. Regressions that show an input (campaign contributions) and an output (a change in votes). There is no good evidence, these scholars insist, that campaign contributions are changing political results. There may be many such contributions. Securing them may well occupy a huge chunk of a congressman's life. But we don't have the data to support the claim that this money is buying results that otherwise would not have been obtained.[28] As Frank Baumgartner and his colleagues summarize the research, there is "no smoking gun, no systematic relationship between campaign contributions and policy success."[29]

The most prominent work making this claim is by political scientists Stephen Ansolabehere, John M. de Figueiredo, and James M. Snyder. In an important paper published in 2003, "Why Is There So Little Money in U.S. Politics?,"[30] these authors question just about every strand of the commonsense view that money is buying results in Congress.

The most important bit of their argument for our purposes questions whether campaign contributions actually affect legislative decisions. Ansolabehere and his colleagues first collect about forty articles that tried to measure the effect of PAC contributions on congressional voting behavior. Looking across this range of studies, they conclude, "PAC contributions show relatively few effects." "In three out of four instances, campaign contributions had no statistically significant effects on legislation or had the 'wrong' sign. . . ."[31]

Ansolabehere and his colleagues then identified a number of statistical problems in some of the studies they collected. This led them to perform their own statistical analysis. That analysis used the voting score produced by the U.S. Chamber of Commerce as the dependent variable. They then estimated six models that mirrored the range of their original forty studies and that included campaign contributions among the independent variables.

Their conclusions are not good for the commonsense view (even if they sound promising for the republic). While they did find some evidence that contributions had an effect on voting patterns, that effect was small relative to other factors. Much of that effect, moreover, was eliminated once they controlled for voter preference. And once they controlled for legislator-fixed effects (such as the party of the legislator), they were able to "eliminate the effects of contributions entirely."[32] As they conclude: "Indicators of party, ideology and district preference account for most of the systematic variation in legislators' roll call voting behavior. Interest group contributions account for at most a small amount of the variation. In fact, after controlling adequately for legislator ideology, these contributions have no detectable effects on legislator behavior."[33]

In understanding the significance of this claim, we should first be very careful about what exactly is being argued here. Ansolabehcre and his colleagues are themselves careful to insist that they are not saying that contributions have no effect. Indeed, as one version of their paper asserts, "It is still possible that campaign contributions have significant effects on economic policies."[34] How would that happen, given the data they've studied?

> To raise sufficient funds, candidates might skew policies in ways preferred by donors. Campaign contributions might therefore act like weighted votes. And contributors, who are disproportionately wealthy, might have different policy preferences than the median voter.[35]

We'll return to this hypothesis later in this chapter. For now, just recognize that all that they are claiming is that the data don't show the link between PAC contributions and roll call votes, at least as reflected in the Chamber of Commerce rankings. That may be because there is no such link. Or it may be because the method they are using to find that link cannot detect one. In either case, what they are not saying is what the anti-reform think tank Center for Competitive Politics reports them as saying—viz., "a substantial majority of academic research on the subject has shown that there is little connection between contributions and legislative votes or actions."[36] "We don't see it" is not the same as "there is nothing to see."

Ansolabehere and his colleagues' conclusions, moreover, are not uncontested. Some political scientists do believe that there is a link between money and results that can be demonstrated by the numbers alone.[37] Thomas Stratmann, for example, conducted a meta-analysis of the same forty studies that Ansolabehere and his colleagues reviewed. That analysis rejected the conclusion that money does not affect results.[38] Sanford Gordon and his colleagues find that an executive's likelihood of contributing to political candidates is tied to how sensitive his or her salary is to firm profitability: the higher the sensitivity, the higher the likelihood of contributions, reinforcing the suggestion that the contribution is an investment rather than consumption.[39] Consistent with this result, in a study of PAC contributions related to the 1984 Deficit Reduction Act, Sanjay Gupta and Charles Swenson found that firms whose managers' compensation included earnings-based bonuses made larger PAC contributions, and that contributions generally were "positively associated with firm tax benefits."[40] Likewise, Atif Mian and his colleagues found that the voting patterns on the 2008 Emergency Economic Stabilization Act were strongly predicted by the amount of campaign contributions from the financial services industry.[41] Not exclusively, but partially, and certainly enough for us to wonder whether the money is queering results more generally. This work provides strong pushback against the theory that campaign contributions are mere consumption (and therefore don't affect results), and it explains how such investments could, consistent with the data, provide a return.[42]

But let's assume for the moment that Ansolabehere and his colleagues are right. Let's assume the data won't show a clear link between contributions and results. If that is true, does that fact exonerate Congress? Are the critics unfair, if Ansolabehere and his colleagues are correct?

The critics are not unfair. For, even if the political science skeptics are right, there are three undeniable effects of this economy of influence, each of them a reason for concern, and all three together a demonstration of the urgency there should be in solving it.

## 1. Distraction

First, and most obviously: the Fund-raising Congress is distracted.

If members spend up to 30 to 70 percent of their time raising money,[43] that means they have less time to do the sort of things members of Congress traditionally did. For example, deliberate. If you compared our Congress in 1792 to the British House of Commons in 1792, we'd fare pretty well. Today, Congress compared to today's Commons is an embarrassment. The British actually take time to deliberate as a body (as our Framers intended us to do). Our Congress does not. Or to read the bills: As Washington lobbyist Wright Andrews responded when asked about whether members read "most of the bills," "Most of the bills? [They read a]lmost none of them! Any member that was honest will tell you that."[44] (In a private session, Bill Gates reported that when he was a congressional page, he read "every bill." That may have been possible in the 1960s, even for mere mortals [which Gates plainly is not], but it is literally impossible today: the complexity of the bills Congress considers is vastly greater than in the past. The Senate version of the health care reform bill, for example, was more than two thousand pages long when introduced.)[45] Instead, the job of members is increasingly that of raising campaign funds. As Fritz Hollings (D-S.C.; 1966–2005) wrote after he retired from the Senate:

> I had to collect $30,000 a week, each and every week, for six years. I could have raised $3 million in South Carolina. But to get $8.5 million I had to travel to New York, Boston, Chicago, Florida, California, Texas and elsewhere. During every break Congress took, I had to be out hustling money. And when I was in Washington, or back home, my mind was still on money.[46]

Even twenty years ago, then–Senate majority leader Robert Byrd wanted reform for campaign finance because the Senate had become "full-time fund-raisers instead of full-time legislators."[47] "Members," as Anthony Corrado of Brookings describes, "are essentially campaigning and raising money all the time."[48] This is an important change. "For most of American history," Norman Ornstein and Thomas Mann write, "campaigns generally were confined to the latter half of election years."[49] Now that the campaign is permanent, the other work that was customarily done during the balance of the term must, in some ways, suffer.

The numbers support what common sense predicts. Between 1983 and 1997 the total number of non-appropriations oversight committee meetings fell from 782 to 287 in the House, and 429 to 175 in the Senate.[50] Total committee meetings tanked as well. Averages for each decade since the 1970s as shown in Figure 9:[51]

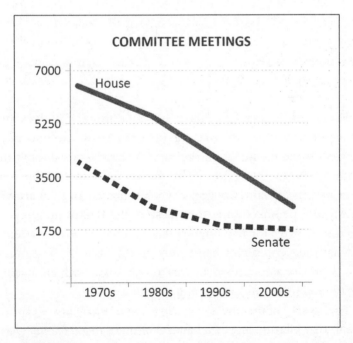

**FIGURE 9**

There has been a similar decline in the number of days in which Congress has been in session, at least in the House. Again, averaging the decades:[52]

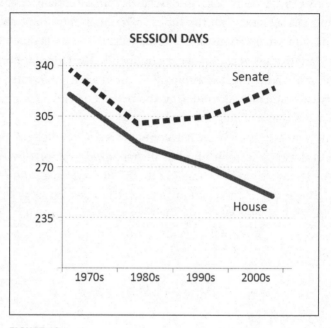

**FIGURE 10**

Maybe fewer days "in session" is a good thing, if it gives members more time in the district, and hence more time to understand their constituents. But even the idea of "in session" doesn't fully capture how the place has changed. As historian Gordon Wood describes, in the First Congress, when Congress was "in session," "nearly all" members sat at their desk in the Hall of Congress, listened to debates for five hours a day, and were "usually attentive to what their colleagues had to say on the floor of the House."[53] The "work" of a congressman was to deliberate—which means to debate, and listen, and argue, and then decide.

The "work" of members even "in session" today has no connection to that picture. Maybe a handful of times in a two-year period a majority of Congress will sit together in a single room listening to the debate about anything. The gathering of a majority of Congress today is almost exclusively ceremonial. It is practically never for the purpose the Framers envisioned: deliberation. Instead, bells, like those from elementary school announcing recess, ring; members race from wherever they are (which is most likely just off the Hill, making fund-raising telephone calls) to the floor; they are instructed by their staff as they enter the Chamber what the vote is and how they are to vote. They vote, and then they leave. As political scientist Steven Smith describes:

> On only the rarest of occasions, such as the debate over the 1991 resolution on the Persian Gulf War, do senators engage in extended, thoughtful exchanges before a full chamber. Instead, under pressure to attend committee meetings, raise campaign funds, meet with lobbyists and constituents, and travel home, senators deliberately minimize the time they spend on the floor.[54]

This change in the culture of Congress is radical when compared with the Framing. It is also radical when compared with Congress just thirty years ago. It has been criticized most by more-senior members. Republican senator Trent Lott (R-Miss.; 1989–2007), for example, describes Congress as having "had a different feel to it—there was a respect for chain of command; there was a respect for the institution."[55] In the words of Representative Tim Roemer (D-Ind.; 1991–2003): members "spend too much of their time dialing for dollars rather than sitting in their committee room and protecting the dollars of their constituents."[56] Likewise with Representative Pete DeFazio (D-Ore.; 1987– ): "You have to pretty much neglect your job.... You're spending all this time on telephones, talking mostly to people you don't know, you've never met."[57] And again, Representative Lee Hamilton (D-Ind.; 1965–1999):

> [T]he House has developed atrocious habits, [including] the fact that members only spend two or three days a week in Washington, [a] breakdown in the deliberative process that guarantees that all legislation is carefully scrutinized, and all

voices heard...the exclusion of the minority party, [and] failing to live up to its historic role of conducting oversight of the
Executive Branch.[58]

He concludes, "[N]o one today could make a coherent argument that the Congress is the co-equal branch of government the
Founders intended it to be."

No doubt it's too much to tie all of these failings to the rise of
fund-raising. And no doubt, for some, anything that keeps Congress
from regulating more must be a good thing. But at the very minimum, we can say with confidence that the fund-raising distracts
Congress from its work, and not surprisingly so. Any of us would be
distracted if we had to spend even just 30 percent of our time raising campaign funds. If you hired a lawyer to work for you, and you
saw that 30 percent of the time he billed you each month was actually time spent recruiting other clients, you'd be rightfully upset. If
you learned that teachers at a public elementary school that your
kids attended were spending 30 percent of their time running bake
sales to fund their salaries rather than teaching your kids how to
read, you'd be rightfully upset, too. So it doesn't seem crazy that we
should be rightfully upset that the representatives we elect to represent us spend even just 30 percent of their time raising funds to get
reelected rather than reading the bills they are passing, or attending committee meetings where those bills are discussed, or meeting with constituents with problems getting help from the Veterans'
Administration. At the very minimum, the Fund-raising Congress is
flawed because the Fund-raising Congress is distracted.[59]

## 2. Distortion

*Relative to the constitutional baseline*, the work of the Fund-
raising Congress is distorted.

At the end of a powerful and creative analysis of the effect of lobbying on policy outcomes, Frank Baumgartner and his colleagues
present data that contrast the public's view of "the most important

problem facing the country today" with data "reflecting the concerns of the Washington lobbying community."[60] The image is quite striking (Figure 11).

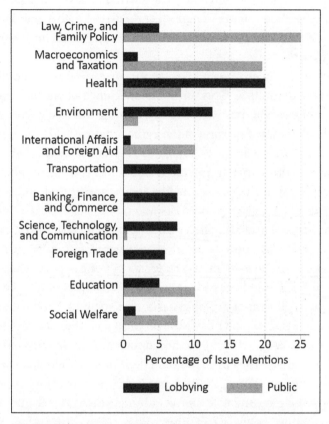

**FIGURE 11.** *Percent of lobbying cases compared to the average responses to the Gallup poll question "What is the most important problem facing the country today?"*[61]

This is a picture of "disconnect," as Baumgartner and his colleagues describe it. It is a "consequence of who is represented in Washington." "It may be," as the authors write, "that political systems built around majoritarianism work better for lower-income citizens. It's certainly the case that in the United States…inequities…are sharply exacerbated by the organizational bias of interest-group politics."[62]

The division between "majoritarianism" and "interest-group politics," however, might be too simple here. For even among democracies driven by "interest-group politics" (as opposed to majoritarianism), "disconnects" may be different. How much of that disconnect comes from the way elections in Congress get funded? Would the disconnect be less if the elections were funded differently? Would the distortion be as clear?

The most effective way to gauge this distortion is with perhaps the finest theoretical work in political science about lobbying in Congress over the past decade, and a work that seems at first at least to exonerate Congress of the cynic's charge.

In their 2006 paper, "Lobbying as Legislative Subsidy," Richard Hall and Alan Deardorff provide a model to explain just what lobbying in Congress does.[63] Lobbying, they argue, is best understood as a "legislative subsidy." Lobbyists don't try to flip their opponents. They work instead to solidify and help their base. Most of the work of lobbyists, they say, is directed toward getting people who already agree (at least in principle) to better support what they agree with. So lobbyists for unions, for example—and there are some: 1.26 percent of the lobbying dollars spent in 2009 were from labor spending[64]—don't waste their time trying to convert Mitch McConnell (R-Ky.; 1985– ) to the important role that unions have in our economy. They instead spend their time with Representative James Langevin (D-R.I.; 2001– ), or Senator Richard Durbin (D-Ill.; 1997– ), helping them to better advance their views that labor needs support. Lobbyists, in other words, try to *subsidize* the work of the members of Congress whom they like, by helping them do better the sort of stuff they already want to do.

This picture makes the process seem almost benign. If lobbyists are just supporting members, how could they be corrupting them? What's the harm? How could a free gift of aid consistent with what a member already wants to do hurt anything or anyone?

The answer is, in at least three ways—two of which (and the most important of which) Hall and Deardorff explicitly recognize, and the third of which follows directly from their model.

*First*, and as Hall and Deardorff acknowledge, "representation [can be] compromised without individual representatives being compromised."[65] It may well be that lobbyists do nothing more than help a member do what the member already wants to do. But not every issue the member wants to support has the same "subsidy" behind it.

If, for example, a member went to Washington after campaigning on two issues, the need to stop Internet "piracy" and the need to help working mothers on welfare, on day one she'd find a line of lobbyists around the block eager to help with the first issue, but none there to help her with the second. That difference would be for all the obvious reasons. And the consequence would be that her work would get skewed relative to her desires going in. At the end of two years, that member could well reflect that she supported only the issues she said she would support. But if she were only slightly more reflective, she'd recognize that the *proportion* of support she gave her issues was driven not by her own judgment about the relative importance of each, but instead by the weight of the subsidy, including, indirectly, of campaign funds.

*Second*, and related, the benign account underplays the way such a system of "subsidy" may in the end block effective access to representatives in government.

If there's one effect that money has that even supporters of the current system concede, it is on *access* to government.[66] As Larry Makinson puts it, "virtually everyone . . . accept[s] that money buys access to members."[67] The reason is clear enough. As former senator Paul Simon (D-Ill.; 1985–1997) describes it:

> If I got to a Chicago hotel at midnight, when I was in the Senate, and there were 20 phone calls waiting for me, 19 of them names I didn't recognize and the 20th someone I recognized as a $1,000 donor to my campaign, that is the one person I would call. You feel a sense of gratitude for their support. This is even more true with the prevalence of much larger donations, even if those donations go to party committees. Because few people can afford to give over $20,000 or $25,000 to a party committee,

those people who can will receive substantially better access to elected federal leaders than people who can only afford smaller contributions or can not afford to make any contributions.[68]

Indeed, as Clawson and his colleagues argue, "the principal aim of most corporate campaign contributions is to help corporate executives gain 'access' to key members of Congress."[69] And that's certainly its effect. As Representative Romano Mazzoli (D-Ky.; 1971–1995) put it: "People who contribute get the ear of the member and the ear of the staff. They have the access—and access is it. Access is power."[70]

Hall and Deardorff argue persuasively that if their theory of subsidy is correct, then all access is doing is enabling like minds to work together better—a "greater legislative effort on behalf of a shared objective, not a disingenuous vote."[71]

This description may be too sanguine. If the model of reciprocity that I described in chapter 9 is correct, then there is a shared interest among lobbyists, special interests, and members for the lobbyists to become a practically exclusive channel through which legislative change gets made (or blocked). We are nowhere close to this exclusivity now, but we need to recognize why everyone involved would like us to be. For the more the lobbyist becomes central, the richer the lobbyist becomes. This benefits the lobbyist. And the more the lobbyist becomes central, the easier it is for candidates to secure funding. This benefits the candidates. And the more the lobbyist becomes central, the easier it is for (some) special interests to trigger legislative change. This benefits these (relatively dominant) interests. For this exclusivity benefits not every special interest, but, as Hall and Deardorff recognize, only the special interests that can

afford the high costs, not only of organizing and making campaign contributions, but of paying professional lobbyists and financing the organizations that support them. Such resources are not equally distributed across groups. Business interests exhibit "tremendous predominance" in federal lobbying....

Hence, the hypothesis set forth here, that public interest groups without electoral assets can influence legislative behavior, does not imply that they countervail the influence of private interest groups and thereby correct the distortions.[72]

Or, put more directly: "Lobbying distorts the representative's allocation of effort in favor of groups sufficiently resource-rich that they can finance an expensive lobbying operation."[73]

I saw this dynamic firsthand. For many years, the focus of my work was on issues relating to copyright and the Internet. Often I would have the opportunity to speak directly to members of Congress about these issues. The most striking feature of those exchanges was not that members disagreed with me. It was that members didn't understand that there was another side to the issue. They had never even heard it. They were baffled when it was described to them. To them, the world was divided into those who believed in copyright and those who didn't. To meet someone who believed in copyright but didn't think the Motion Picture Association of America or the Recording Industry Association of America channeled the word of God (that's me) was, to say the least, anathema.

This wasn't because these members were stupid. They weren't. It wasn't because they were lazy. Most members of Congress work much harder than the majority of people, if you count all the junk they have to do, including fund-raising. Instead, this was simply because this different side was nowhere on the radar screen of these members. They hadn't heard it, because it hadn't had access.

Consider the lobbying that led to the recently enacted financial "reform" bill. In October 2009 there were 1,537 lobbyists representing financial institutions registered in D.C., and lobbying to affect this critical legislation—*twenty-five times* the number registered to support consumer groups, unions, and other proponents of strong reform.[74] A system that makes lobbyists the ticket to influence is a system that wildly skews the issues that will get attention. This, in time, will distort results.

Finally, the *third* reason this "legislative subsidy" model doesn't exonerate the current system is a dynamic that Hall and Deardorff don't discuss but that is also consistent with their model. In describing the "lobbying as legislative subsidy," Hall and Deardorff write: "The proximate objective of this strategy is *not* to change legislators' minds but to assist *natural* allies in achieving their own, coincident objectives."[75]

But what is this "nature"? How is it begot? How nourished? When a Republican member of Congress votes to raise the sugar tariff (as 35 Republican senators and 102 Republican members in the House did with the 2008 Farm Bill),[76] is that because that member ran on the platform that eight domestic sugar manufacturers should be protected from the free market? Or when frontline Democrats— meaning first-term members in closely fought districts, no more liberal or conservative than more-senior Democrats—on the House Committee on Financial Services voted to exempt car dealers from consumer protection legislation, while senior Democrats on the same committee did not, is that because those younger Democrats ran on a platform that consumers needed to be protected everywhere, except from used car dealers?[77]  WTF

What's missing here is an understanding of how "nature" gets made. For the relevant effect could be as much in anticipation as in response. And if it were in anticipation, then the methods that Ansolabehere and his colleagues deploy would not pick up the change. The money would not be buying a change in preferences; the change in preferences would be buying the money.

The best illustration of this dynamic is a comment by former representative Leslie Byrne (D-Va.; 1993–1995), recounting what she was told by a colleague when she first came to Washington: "I remember the comment of a well-known, big money-raising state delegate from Virginia. He said, 'Lean to the green,' and he wasn't an environmentalist."[78]

*Green Washing*

This is shape-shifting. It may well be unlikely that a lobbyist would waste his time trying to get a member to flip. There's too much pride and self-respect in the system for that. There's too much of an opportunity to be punished.

But if a lobbyist is important, or influential over sources of campaign contributions, then the effect of her influence could well be ex ante: a member could take a position on a particular issue in anticipation of the need to secure that lobbyist's support. That decision isn't a flip, for it isn't a change. It is simply articulating more completely the views of a member, as that member grows into her job.

Now obviously this dynamic won't work for everything. Certain issues are too prominent, or too familiar. But for a vast range of issues that Congress deals with, shape-shifting is perfectly feasible, because, for these issues, there's no visible change. As Representative Vin Weber (R-Minn.; 1981–1993) puts it, a representative keeps "a mental checklist of things [members] need to do to make sure their PAC contributors continue to support them."[79] Representative Eric Fingerhut (D-Ohio; 1993–1994) makes the same point: "[P] eople consciously or subconsciously tailor their views to where they know the sources of campaign funding can be."[80]

This dynamic is especially significant for smaller or more obscure issues. Again Vin Weber puts it: "If nobody else cares about it very much, the special interest will get its way."[81]

Likewise, Jeff Birnbaum: "It's the obscure and relatively minor issues that produce the most frenetic lobbying. And it is there, on the lucrative edges of legislation, that lobbyists work their ways. Lobbyists constantly obtain special exceptions or extra giveaways for their clients, and few other people ever notice."[82]

Again, Eric Fingerhut: "The public will often look for the big example; they want to find the grand-slam example of influence in these interests. [R]arely will you find it. But you can find a million singles."[83]

When the issue is genuinely uncertain, or just so obscure as not to be noticed, this lobbying can induce shape-shifting—away from the position the representative otherwise would have taken.

Such shape-shifting is perfectly consistent with Hall and Deardorff's model. Indeed, the conditions they identify where it does make sense for a lobbyist to try to persuade turn out to be precisely the sort of cases that Fingerhut, Birnbaum, and Weber are describing: obscure issues that a representative has no strong preference about, that are to be publicly voted upon, the results of which are uncertain.[84] As Martin and Susan Tolchin quote former congressman and governor James Blanchard (D-Mich.; 1983–1991), "In Congress, people feel strongly about two or three issues.... On almost all [other] issues, there's no moral high ground."[85]

Shape-shifting is thus one reason the effect of money on legislative voting would be invisible. It is distinct from another dynamic that would also be invisible to the regressions. The rankings of members by groups such as the Chamber of Commerce is based upon roll call votes. But roll call votes are the very end of a very, very long legislative process. A bill gets introduced. It gets referred to a committee. Very few of the bills referred to a committee get a hearing. Even fewer get referred to the floor for a vote. On the floor, there are any number of ways in which the proposal can be stopped. Or folded into something else. Or allowed to die. There is only one way to pass a bill in Congress, and a million ways to kill it.

But influence can be exercised—and hence a campaign contribution rewarded—in any of the stages of the potential life of a bill. If it is, it is invisible to the regressions. If a senator puts an anonymous hold on a bill, that doesn't enter any one ranking. If a chairman decides not to assign a hearing to the bill, he doesn't get tagged as a result. In a whole host of ways, legislative power can be exercised without a trace. And where it is exercised without a trace, the regressions cannot map cause and effect. As the House Select Committee on Lobbying Activities describes, "Complex government inevitably means government with bottlenecks at which pressure can be quietly and effectively applied.... The prevention of governmental action, and this is the aim of many lobbies, is relatively easy under these circumstances."[86] "Most issues," Baumgartner and his colleagues find, "do not reach those final stages and most are not highly publicized, even within the Beltway."[87] That means, again, the opportunity for invisible influence is great. Senator Larry Pressler (R-S.D.; 1979–1997) describes a particular example, drawn from the recent battle over health care:

There should have been an up or down vote on [single-payer health insurance], or a vote at least on cloture. There was neither. For some reason, it just went away. Barack Obama abandoned it completely, although he had said he was for it. Some Republicans are for it—I was for it way back and Nixon was for it...on a much more significant basis. Bob Packwood had a plan for it. But the point is, when they really started doing the health care bill, everybody disappeared who was for a single payer system. I would suspect that is because of the insurance companies' contributions, especially to the Democrats.[88]

Pressler's example could be multiplied a million times over. Indeed, it is almost too obvious to remark.

"You say," the skeptic insists, "that this competing dependency upon money draws the members away from what they otherwise would have done. But is there any evidence for this? Do we have a way to calibrate the extent of this distortion, or even any measure to demonstrate that there is distortion?"

There are two ways we might measure distortion. One maps the gap between what "the People" believe about an issue and what Congress does about that issue. Call this *substantive distortion*. The other way maps the gap between what Congress actually works on and what is important or, alternatively, what the people want them to work on. Call this *agenda distortion*.

The evidence for *substantive distortion* is compelling, at the level not of roll call votes—that's the fight we've just rehearsed—but of actual policy decisions. This is the story of "regulatory capture."[89] Consistent with the argument of this book, regulatory capture does not "imply that regulators are corrupt or lack integrity."[90] And even without proof of a contribution-based distortion, we know enough to conclude with very high confidence that the distortion at the level of policy is real and significant. A wide range of important work in political science makes it possible to argue with confidence that, first, there is a wide gap in the policy preferences of "the funders" and "the People," and second, in the face of that gap, Congress tracks not "the People" but "the funders."

The first work to make this point powerfully and clearly was by Princeton professor Larry Bartels. In a study of the correlation between U.S. Senate roll call votes and an index by Poole and Rosenthal designed to measure the ideological position of members across multiple dimensions,[91] Bartels concludes that "[i]n almost every instance, senators appear to be considerably more responsive to the opinions of affluent constituents than to the opinions of middle-class constituents, while the opinions of constituents in the bottom third of the income distribution have *no* apparent statistical effect on their senators' roll call votes."[92]

Princeton professor Martin Gilens extended Bartels's analysis substantially by examining about 1,781 national survey questions between 1981 and 2002.[93] These questions asked whether the respondent supported or opposed some particular change in U.S. policy, and then tracked whether in fact those changes occurred. Looking at all the survey questions, Gilens was able to demonstrate a significant difference between the likelihood that a measure would be enacted if the rich supported it and the likelihood when the middle class or poor supported it.

More striking was the comparison when looking at the subset of questions where the highest income group differed substantially in their views from the lowest (n = 887) and where the highest differed substantially in their views from the middle-income group (n = 498). What Gilens found here was amazing: while policymakers were responsive to the increasingly strong preferences of the highest-income groups (the more of whom supported a policy, the more likely it was to be passed), there was a "complete lack of government responsiveness to the preferences of the poor"[94] (meaning increasing support among the poor for a particular policy did not increase the likelihood of its passage). And middle-income voters "fare little better than the poor."[95]

This rather stark conclusion is the whole subject of Jacob Hacker and Paul Pierson's powerful book *Winner-Take-All Politics* (2010).

Hacker and Pierson frame their account by distinguishing between two kinds of societies, Broadland and Richistan. In Broadland, all income groups across some period of time are doing better, even if not necessarily at the same pace. In Richistan, only the very rich do better across that same period of time. The rest of society is either just holding on or falling behind.

Until about 1972 the United States, Hacker and Pierson argue, was Broadland. We then became Richistan. And not just in some slight or statistically meaningless sense, but instead, in as gross and extreme a sense as any comparable nation in the world.

Indeed, the best comparison to where we are today is not any other nation in the world, but rather to when we were on the cusp of the Depression. In 2007 the richest 1 percent of families were within a point of matching the share of income that the top 1 percent had in 1928.

These numbers are hard to make real, but here's a way to visualize them (Figure 12).

**FIGURE 12**

Between 2001 and 2006, the total income of all Americans added together grew. But it didn't grow proportionately. Not even close. For every dollar of added income, fifty-three cents of that dollar went to the top 1 percent of American households.[96]

It's even worse if you think about the top one-tenth of 1 percent

**FIGURE 13**

(0.1 percent): for income gains between 1979 and 2005, the top 0.1 percent received over 20 percent of all gains, while the bottom 60 percent received only 13.5 percent (Figure 13).[97]

In constant dollars, the average income of the top 0.1 percent (including capital gains) in 2007 was more than $7 million. In 1974 it was about $1 million. Their share of the pie grew from 2.7 percent to 12.3 percent—a four-and-a-half-times increase.[98]

For the top one-tenth of one-tenth of 1 percent (0.01 percent), it's even more extreme: the average after-tax income increased from about $4 million in 1979 to more than $24 million in 2005.[99] In Hacker and Pierson's terms, "Broadland was dead. Richistan was born."[100] Broadland is where most of the gains go to the bottom 90 percent of households; and Richistan is where most of the gains go to the top 1 percent. Indeed, were it not for the increase in hours worked over the past thirty years, the middle class would not have gained at all, and the lower class would have fallen behind, while the highest-income groups have exploded.[101] "The bottom went nowhere, the middle saw a modest gain, and the top ran away with the grand prize."[102]

Whenever anyone starts talking about inequality, the first reaction of many (at least on the Right but also in the middle) is to turn off. Our Constitution is not Soviet. We are not committed to the philosophy of Karl Marx, or even John Rawls. That there are rich and poor in America is a fact of American life. Some believe it explains the innovation in American life. And no set of clever graphs demonstrating "how the rich get richer" is going to move those who believe that the "unalienable right...[to] Life, Liberty, and the Pursuit of Happiness" includes the right to get rich faster than your neighbor.

Likewise, there are important differences between the wealth of the Gilded Age and the wealth today. The rich today are different. In 1929, as Rajan and Zingales put it, "70% of the income of the top .01% of income earners in the United States came from holdings of capital...The rich were truly the idle rich. In 1998, wages and entrepreneurial income made up 80% of the income of the top .01%."[103] The rich are not idle anymore. Indeed, they work harder than most of us: "in the 1890s, the richest 10 percent of the population worked fewer hours than the poorest 10 percent. Today, the reverse is true."[104]

My point in introducing Hacker and Pierson is not to reinforce the arguments of egalitarians, or the socialist Left. For the critical insight that they add to this debate is not that inequality is growing. It is instead *the reasons* that inequality is growing. Conservatives might well and consistently believe that there's nothing wrong with getting rich. But from the birth of conservative thought, conservatives have always objected to people getting rich because of the government. It's one thing to invent the light bulb and thereby become a billionaire (though, sadly, Edison wasn't so lucky). It's another thing to use your financial power to capture political power, and then use political power to change the laws to make you even richer.

So then what explains our move to Richistan? Is it geniuses producing endless wealth? Or is it government regulation that is protecting endless wealth?

Hacker and Pierson work hard to suss this out. Maybe the rich were better educated. Maybe that education produced this difference in rewards. But the rich in Hacker and Pierson's account are not what most people would call rich. The rich are the super-rich—the 0.1 percent or 0.01 percent. Those people are not better educated than the top 1 percent. Indeed, as Gilens finds, "fewer than one-third of Americans in the top income decile are also in the top education decile, and vice versa."[105] If there's a reason that we became Richistan, it's not because of Harvard or Berkeley or MIT.

It isn't raw smarts, or native talent. So, then what accounts for our leaving the happy world of Broadland and becoming Richistan?

According to Hacker and Pierson, and astonishingly: *changes in government policy.* A whole series of interventions by the government beginning in 1972 produced an enormously wealthy class of beneficiaries of those changes. This is not the neighborhoods of *Desperate Housewives.* Or even Hollywood or Silicon Valley. It is instead a kind of wealth that is almost unimaginable to the vast majority of Americans.

The biggest winners here are financial executives. As Nobel Prize–winning economist Joseph Stiglitz writes, "Those who have contributed great positive innovations to our society—from the pioneers of genetic understanding to the pioneers of the Information Age—have received a pittance compared with those responsible for the financial innovations that brought our global economy to the brink of ruin."[106] In 2004, "nonfinancial executives of publicly traded companies accounted for less than 6% of the top .01 percent of the income bracket. In that same year, the top 25 hedge fund managers combined appear to have earned more than all of the CEOs from the entire S&P 500."[107]

The next big winners were the top executives from the S&P 500 companies. In the 1970s the executives at the S&P 500 made thirty times what their workers did, and today make three hundred times what their workers make.[108] Their average salary was more than $10 million in 2007, about 344 times the pay of "typical American workers."[109] Likewise, as their salaries have skyrocketed, the position of the self-employed has collapsed. Between 1948 and 2003 "the self-employment rate in the United States fell from 18.5% to 7.5%"[110]—the second-lowest among twenty-two rich nations according to an OECD study.[111] The nation of our parents was defined by makers and innovators. We've become a nation defined not by the upwardly mobile entrepreneurs, but by Wall Street fat cats—the nation predicted by the apostle Matthew (13:12): "For whosoever hath, to him shall be given, and he shall have more abundance."[112]

So let's repeat the point in a single line, because it is critical to everything in this book: changes in government policy, Hacker and Pierson argue, account for the radical change in the distribution of American wealth. This isn't the rich getting richer because they're smarter or working harder. It is the connected getting richer because their lobbyists are working harder. No political philosophy—liberal, libertarian, or conservative—should be okay with that.

To be fair, this last step in the argument—linking the rich to the connected (by which I mean the funders)—is not a step that Hacker and Pierson explicitly make. Indeed, and surprisingly, they don't place campaign finance anywhere near the top of their program of reform. And while Gilens clearly references it, he is quite insistent that the work he has done so far cannot establish, at least at the level of confidence that a political scientist requires, exactly why policymakers respond to the rich more clearly than they respond to the poor.

Yet as Gilens acknowledges,

> [T]he most obvious source of influence over policy that distinguishes high-income Americans is money and the willingness to donate to parties, candidates, and interest organizations.... Since not only the propensity to donate but also the size of donations increases with income level, this figure understates—probably to a very large degree—the extent to which political donations come from the most affluent Americans.[113]

Senator Bob Dole (R-Kans.; 1969–1996) puts the point more directly: "Poor people don't make campaign contributions."[114]

The question we must ask as citizens, not political scientists, is what we will make of the data we've gotten so far. It is clear that government bends in the direction that the funders prefer, and against—often, but not always—the people. It is plausible, more likely than not, that this differential bending is because of the influence of this funding. If you considered the matter in the way the Framers did, accounting for the structural and predictable ways in which dependency might express itself, it is almost irresistible, *from their perspective*, that Congress betrays a competing dependency "on the funders"—competing, that is, with a dependency "on the People alone." The Framers were proud that they had ensured a two-year cycle of punishment and reward for the House. Yet the cycle of punishment and reward for funders is every day, not every two years. For two or three or more hours *every day*, as a member fund-raises, she feels the effect of the "votes" of funders. That feeling must at least compete and, given the data, conflict with the effect felt every two years in an election.

Indeed, it is here that the most striking weirdness of our current system makes itself plain. Our Constitution has been interpreted to require an almost obsessive attention to equality in voting. Judges are required to ensure that the weight of my vote for my member of Congress is "as nearly as practicable" equal to the weight of your vote for your member of Congress.[115]

That constitutional obsession ensures a kind of extreme equality on two days every two years—the primary (where there is one) and the general election. On those two days, the weight of my vote—the thing that was to ensure the dependency the Framers intended—is equal to yours. Both equal, down to the fraction of a percent equal.

Yet in between those two days, I, and thousands of others, also "vote" in another kind of election: the money election. In that election, I get to vote as often as I want, so long as my total "votes" to any particular candidate don't exceed $5,000; and $117,000 for all candidates, PACs, and political parties in an election cycle.[116] The limits don't apply to independent expenditures. So if I'm George Soros or the Koch brothers, I can spend an unlimited amount in addition to any amount I can contribute. And because of the Supreme Court's decision in *Citizens United v. FEC* (2010), discussed more later, corporations, too, have an unlimited right to spend as much as they want promoting or opposing any candidate.

In this second election—the election for these dollar votes— there is absolutely no concern about equality. For this competing dependency that we have allowed to evolve within the economy of influence of Congress, there is no effort to ensure that the forces within that economy are in any sense divided equally among citizens. Instead, this competing dependency gives some in our society an advantage over the rest in our society.

It is as if on Election Day, there were two ballots cast. In one ballot, every citizen got one vote. In the other ballot, every citizen got as many votes as he could buy—up to 5,000, with each vote costing a dollar. Now, even if you gave the first ballot the presumptive control of the result—maybe you weight the two ballots, with 90 percent for the one-person, one-vote ballot, and only 10 percent for the buy-as-many-votes-as-you-want-up-to-5,000 ballot—there would still be something bizarre and illicit in this two-ballot procedure. As journalist Jeffrey Birnbaum puts it, "Moneyed constituents possess higher status than constituents who merely vote."[117]And government policy is perfectly consistent with the effects that one would predict, given the different influence this system permits.[118]

This, you may recall, was precisely the way that Ansolabehere and his colleagues—the scholars most skeptical about the effect of money on politics—suggested that money may still be buying results. Again, as I quoted them at the start of this chapter:

> To raise sufficient funds, candidates might skew policies in ways preferred by donors. Campaign contributions might therefore act like weighted votes. And contributors, who are disproportionately wealthy, might have different policy preferences than the median voter.[119]

The evidence is pretty strong, at least for us citizens, that this is precisely what is happening.

Gilens ends his powerful essay by noting, "[T]here has never been a democratic society in which citizens' influence over government policy was unrelated to their financial resources." True enough. The troubling truth is in the final sentence to that paragraph: "But...a government that is democratic in form but is in practice only responsive to its most affluent citizens is a democracy in name only."[120]

Again, we should be clear about the scope of Gilens's claim here: He is speaking of cases where the views of the affluent conflict with the views of the majority. In that context, this is our democracy.

Of course no one is saying members of Congress are completely unresponsive to their constituents. That wasn't Gilens's point. It's not mine either. Indeed, there are plenty of data to suggest that in many cases there is a strong tie between what "the People" want and what Congress does. So while Mian and his colleagues do find that mortgage campaign contributions have a rising and significant effect on voting patterns, they also demonstrate that members were also responsive both to voter preferences and to special-interest campaign contributions.[121] No doubt, if our republic was meant to be dependent upon the people, there is much in the data to show that we are still, in important ways, a republic dependent upon the people. But not—and here is the critical point—upon, as the Federalists put it, "the People alone."

The question, however, is not whether Congress sometimes gets it right, any more than the question with an alcoholic bus driver is whether he sometimes drives sober. The question is why we allow Congress to often get it wrong. Even if you think the system is bent just slightly, it is still a bent system.

"But," defenders of the status quo argue, "don't unions or the AARP also have unequal influence? Is there something corrupt about that?"

The answer depends on the source of the influence. No doubt, there was a day when a union could reliably promise candidates millions of votes. That power translated into important political influence. But that is power that comes directly *from votes*. It is precisely the power that the intended dependency of our democracy, upon the people alone, was meant to credit. My point isn't that democracy requires equal influence. It is that the influence that is to express itself, however unequally, is the influence of votes in an election.

The same point applies to political parties. Across our history, political parties have had an enormous influence in controlling the direction and character of public life. That control has been a concern to many, especially liberals. " 'The system' is robust," Harvard professor Nancy Rosenblum has put it. "Candidates are dependent on parties, even apart from funding."[122] As she quotes Lincoln Steffens: " 'Isn't our corrupt government, after all, representative?' Steffens asked. He records a Philadelphia politician's puzzled confession: 'I'm loyal to my ward and to my—own, and yet—Well, there's something wrong with me, and I'd like to know: what is it?' "[123]

Parties, like unions, exercise their power in two ways. First, by mobilizing votes. Second, by concentrating economic power. The former is not troubling to the dependency theory of democracy. Power through votes is just what the doctor ordered. It is the power through money that raises the problem here. Avoiding "unequal influence" is not the objective. Preserving electoral influence is.

"Isn't that," the defenders continue, "just what money does? No one literally buys an election (anymore at least). The only thing money does is buy speech that helps persuade voters to one side in an election over another. If you don't object to unions driving members to the polls (literally, on buses), why would you object to spending money to try to persuade people to go to the polls (through television ads)?"

Great point. There's no doubt that the purpose of campaign funds is to persuade. And there's also no doubt that those funds persuade differently. Some of that persuasion comes from the television or radio ads a campaign is able to buy—getting a voter to support the candidate. Some of that persuasion comes from the ability to convince a challenger that a challenge is just not worth it—"There's no way we could raise enough money to overcome his war chest of one million dollars." All of that persuasion is benign from the perspective of a democracy dependent upon the people alone. Seen in this way, in other words, money is just part of a campaign to get votes.

The word *just* in that sentence, however, shouldn't be passed over too quickly. For one thing the current system plainly does is filter out a wide range of people who might otherwise be plausible and powerful candidates for Congress.[124] Under the current system, the ability to raise money is a necessary condition to getting party support. As Hacker and Pierson report about the Democratic Congressional Campaign Committee, "If a candidate proved a good fund-raiser, the DCCC would provide support....If not, the committee would shut him out."[125] The point was reportedly made quite clear by Rahm Emanuel when he was chairman of the DCCC: "The first third of your campaign is money, money, money. The second third is money, money, and press. And the last third is votes, press, and money."[126]

The more important point, however, is not about what the money does. It's about what has to be done to get the money. The effect of the money might be (democratically) benign. But what is done to secure that money is not necessarily benign.

To miss this point is to betray the Robin Hood fallacy: the fact that the loot was distributed justly doesn't excuse the means taken to secure it. Take an extreme case to make this critical point: Imagine a lobbyist signaled to a congressman that he could ensure $1 million in campaign funds so long as the congressman delivered a $10 million earmark for the lobbyist's client. Even if the $1 million is for the benign purpose of persuasion, there is an obvious problem in the deal made to secure it. The distortion is in the deal, not in the way the money is spent. The problem comes from the distortion necessary to secure the deal, not from the effect of the money spent in a campaign.

Of course, in this example the deal is a crime. And I've already said I don't think such crime happens (much). But the same point is true even if we substitute the more benign (as in legal) dance of the gift economy I described in the previous chapter for the quid pro quo game. Here again: If we assume the congressman has shape-shifted himself in all sorts of predictable ways for the purpose of ensuring funds for his campaign, even if that shape-shifting dance is not illegal, and even though the money he secures gets spent for the wholly positive purpose of persuading people in an election, that doesn't acquit the shape-shifting. For, again, the

problem is not the money; the problem is the distortion created
to produce the money. Senator Wyche Fowler (D-Ga.; 1987–1993)
tells a related story that makes the same point:

> The brutal fact that we all agonize over is that if you get two
> calls and one is from a constituent who wants to complain
> about the Veterans Administration mistreating her father, for
> the 10th time, and one is from somebody who is going to give
> you a party and raise $10,000, you call back the contributor.
> And nobody likes that. There's no way to justify it. Except that
> you rationalize that you have to have money or you can't cam-
> paign. You're not in the game.[127]

There's nothing wrong with the effect the $10,000 will have.
Nor is there anything wrong with the member calling back the
contributor. The wrong here—tiny in the scale of things but standing for the more general wrong—is the call not made.

Consider one final example. Birnbaum describes a congressman
in the mid-1980s who was undecided about whether to support
funding to build the B-1 bomber. Reagan was "frantic for support"
for the bomber, so the congressman was a "hot commodity." A
deal was struck to get the congressman's vote. What was his price?
A dam or some special funding for road construction in the district? No such luck (for his constituents). His price: "a VIP tour of
the White House for twenty or thirty of his largest and most loyal
campaign contributors."[128] Again, there's nothing wrong with the
White House giving VIP tours. But I suspect a constituent in this
congressman's district would be right to ask whether there wasn't
a better deal, for the district, that could have been made.

Once this distinction is made clear, the bigger point should be
obvious. We don't excuse a bank robber if he donates the money
he stole to an orphanage. Neither should we excuse a political
system that bends itself because of its dependency upon funders
just because it donates the proceeds it collects to funding political
speech. It is the bending, the distortion, the distraction, that is the

problem, and all that is produced by this competing dependency upon the funders rather than the people.

That's _substantive distortion_. The argument supporting it is long and complex. Length and complexity are certain to lose some souls on the way.

The argument for _agenda distortion_, however, is much simpler. Indeed, it can be made with a single case.

In the spring of 2011 the United States faced many public policy problems. We were in the middle of two wars. The economy was still in the tank: thirteen million Americans were unemployed, almost 15 percent were on food stamps, and 20 percent of kids were living in poverty. There was an ongoing battle about health care, and the public debt. There was a continuing fight over taxes. Likewise over immigration policy. Many wanted tort reform. Legislation to address global warming had still not been passed. Nor had an appropriations bill, or a budget. And a fight between Tea Party Republicans and the rest of Congress was bringing America to the brink of a government shutdown.

So within that mix, what issue would you say was "_the most consuming issue_ in Washington—according to members of Congress, Hill staffers, lobbyists and Treasury officials—"[129] at least as reported by the Huffington Post's Ryan Grim and Zach Carter?

A bill to limit the amount banks could charge for the use of debit cards: so-called "swipe fees."

This bill, addressing the question of "interchange rates," meaning the amount banks can charge retailers for the use of a debit card, was the leading issue for lobbyists. And therefore for Congress, too. As Grim and Carter describe, "a full 118 ex-government officials and aides [were] registered to lobby on behalf of banks.... [A]t least 124 revolving-door lobbyists" were lobbying on behalf of retailers. The issue dominated Congress's calendar. And beyond it, "a handful of other intra-corporate contests consume most of what remains on the Congressional calendar: a squabble over a jet engine, industry tussling over health-care spoils and the never-ending fight over the corporate tax code."

We all recognize that "Congress is zombified." Nothing gets done. Or at least, nothing relative to the issues that any objective measure would say were the most important issues for the nation to resolve. But "one of the least understood explanations," as Grim and Carter explain, "is also one of the simplest: The city is too busy refereeing disputes between major corporate interest groups." As Grim and Carter quote one anonymous moderate Democratic senator:

> I'm surprised at how much of our time is spent trying to divide up the spoils between various economic interests. I had no idea. I thought we'd be focused on civil liberties, on education policy, energy policy and so on.... The fights down here can be put in two or three categories: The big greedy bastards against the big greedy bastards; the big greedy bastards against the little greedy bastards; and some cases even the other little greedy bastards against the other little greedy bastards.

Why, you might ask, is Congress held hostage like this? Why can't it just focus on what it wants to focus on? I doubt there is a single member of the House or Senate who thought, "I'm going to go to Congress so I can 'divide up the spoils between various economic interests.'" So why don't they simply do what they went to Congress to do? ("Oh poor, poor me, I hate CBS." "So change channels!")

The answer is almost hidden in Grim and Carter's otherwise brilliant essay. As they write, "[T]he clock never ticks down to zero in Washington: one year's law is the next year's repeal target. Politicians, showered with cash from card companies and giant retailers alike, have been moving back and forth between camps, paid handsomely for their shifting allegiances."

Just to be sure you didn't miss the money point in this money quote: Congress, Grim and Carter claim, sets its agenda, at least in part, so as to induce funders to fund their campaigns. Who has time to deal with jobs, or poverty, or unemployment, or a simpler tax code? Where is the money in that? As Grim and Carter write, "Political action committees organized by members of the

Electronic Payments Coalition, a cadre of banking trade groups, dumped more than $500,000 into campaign coffers during January and February [2011] alone."[130]

This dynamic is perfectly consistent with Hall and Deardorff. There is plenty of persuading action on an issue not centrally salient to the public. It also follows directly from the excellent and extended analysis of Baumgartner and his colleagues of lobbying: "The bad news is that the wealthy seem to set the agenda," and "there's little overall correspondence between the congressional agenda and the public's agenda," and because of this "many issues never get raised in the first place."[131]

It is perfectly *in*consistent, however, with Chairman Smith's claim that the money doesn't affect "legislative behavior." Setting Congress's agenda is quintessentially "legislative behavior," and if it isn't money that explains this particular mix, then it is pure insanity.

I chose the more charitable reading: It is money that is affecting the agenda here. Money, in other words, that affects "legislative behavior."

## 3. Trust

But let's say you still don't buy it. Let's say you still believe (and I'm not going to hide it) *astonishingly* that the raising of the money within this lobbyist industrial complex, has no systematically distorting effect. That perhaps it distracts members of Congress, but so what? The less Congress does, you think, the better. The political scientists haven't proven that "money buys results," in your view. And my gift economy argument just doesn't persuade you, either.

Even if you assume that everything I've described is completely benign—that the policy decisions that Congress enacted when subject to the dependency upon funders as well as the dependency upon the voters is *precisely the same* as the decisions it would make if dependent upon the voters alone—there is still an undeniable whopper of a fact that makes it impossible simply to ignore this competing dependency upon the funders: trust.[132] The vast majority of Americans believe that it is money that is buying results. Whether or not that's true, that is what we believe.

This belief has an effect. Or better, it has a series of effects.

Its first effect is to undermine trust in the system. According to a 2010 Pew Research Center survey, "just 22% [of American voters] say they can trust the government in Washington almost always or most of the time, among the lowest measures in half a century."[133] Thirty years before, that number was 70 percent.[134] According to the American National Election Studies project at the University of Michigan, the public's perception of elected officials is near historic lows.[135] Whereas in 1964, 64 percent of respondents believed that government was run for the benefit of all and 29 percent believed that government was run for the benefit of a few big interests, in 2008, only 29 percent believed government was run for the benefit of all, and 69 percent believed it was run for the benefit of a few big interests. Similarly, whereas in 1958 only 24 percent of respondents believed that "quite a few" government officials were "crooked," in 2008 that percentage had increased to 51 percent.[136] A poll commissioned by Common Cause, Change Congress, and Public Campaign following the *Citizens United* decision found that 74 percent of respondents agreed that special interests have too much influence, and 79 percent agreed that members of Congress are "controlled" by the groups and people who finance their campaigns.[137] Only 18 percent believed that lawmakers listened to voters more than to their donors. Similarly, in 2008, 80 percent of Americans surveyed told the Program on International Policy Attitudes that they believed government was controlled by "a few big interests looking out for themselves."[138]

Loss of trust induces a second effect. It leads any rational soul to spend less time exercising her democratic privileges.[139] We're all busy sorts. Some of us have families. Some hobbies. Some treat our families as hobbies. But whatever the mix that drives our day, the belief that money is buying results in Congress is a sufficient reason for us to spend less time worrying about what Congress does—at least, that is, if we don't have money. What reason is there to rally thousands of souls to the polls if, in the end, the polls can be distracted by the money? How would you explain it to your kid? ("Willem, I don't have time to play soccer, I've got to go waste my time electing a member to Congress who won't have time to listen or do what the voters want.") The politically engaged sorts are always quick to spread scorn on the vast majority of Americans who don't pay attention to politics. But maybe it's not they who deserve the scorn. How ridiculous to waste time on elections when there are soup kitchens, or churches, or schools that could use our volunteer time? As Jeffrey Birnbaum puts it, "Rather than get mad and try to change the system...most Americans have given up."[140]

My claim about the relationship between trust and participation might be challenged by some. A large empirical analysis done by Steven J. Rosenstone and John Mark Hansen looking at survey data concludes that distrust of government does not reduce voter turnout.[141] This conclusion has been relied upon by many to suggest that levels of trust are independent of levels of participation.[142]

The trust that I am speaking of, however, is more accurately described as a view about efficacy: If one believes "money buys results in Congress," one is likely to believe that participation will be ineffective. And as Rosenstone and Hansen found, voters' feelings of "political efficacy" and "government responsiveness" have a large effect on voter participation.[143] Thomas Patterson has developed this view, arguing that "political efficacy" and confidence in government are strongly linked. Looking at the 2000 election, Patterson also found that distrust is linked to lower participation rates. Moreover, "of all the reasons Americans give for their lack of election interest, the most troubling is their belief that candidates are not very worthy of respect: that they are beholden to their financiers."[144]

A recent example confirms this point. One of the groups most affected by the explosion in cynicism is the group that was most benefited by the romance with Obama: Rock the Vote!, a nonpartisan nonprofit whose mission, according to Wikipedia, is to "engage and build the political power of young people." Founded in 1990, it has developed a range of techniques and new technology designed to register young voters, and turn them out "in every election." In 2008 the organization "ran the largest nonpartisan voter registration drive in history"—more than 2.25 million new voters registered, and there was a substantial increase in voter turnout among the young.[145]

But when Rock the Vote! polled its members about their plans for the 2010 election, the single largest reason that young people offered for why they did not plan to vote was "because no matter who wins, corporate interests will still have too much power and prevent real change."[146] That echoes the response that Representative Glenn Poshard (D-Ill.; 1989–1999) got when he asked a group of students why they do not trust government: "Congressman, just follow the money. You will know why we do not trust you."[147]

The belief that money is buying results produces the result that fewer and fewer of us engage. Why would one *rationally* waste one's time? In the Soviet Union, the party line was that the party was to serve the workers. The workers knew better. In America, the party line is that Congress is to serve the people. But you and I know better, too. And even if we don't actually know, our belief is producing a world where the vast majority of us disengage. Or at least the vast majority of you in the middle, the moderate core of America, disengage. Leaving the henhouse guarded by us polarized extremist foxes.

"But then maybe you should write a book trying to convince America that money is not buying results," the defender objects. "I mean, if Americans believed the earth was flat, that wouldn't be a reason to ban airlines from flying across the horizon."

You can write that book. If you think you have the data to prove that the existing system is benign—that it doesn't distort democracy, that the idea that representatives would actually deliberate is silly, that this competing dependency is a good thing, or at least harmless—then make my day. Meanwhile, my view is that even if America's judgment wouldn't pass peer review in a political

science journal, it's pretty damn insightful. We should listen to it
and do something about it rather than sitting around waiting for
the political scientists to deliver their gold-standard proofs.

The problem is trust—or, is at the least trust. As Marc Hetherington put it, "part of the public's antipathy toward government is
born of concern that it is run for the benefit of special interests. . . .
Measures that can change this perception should increase political trust."[148] We need to deploy those measures. But we can't until
we change what it is reasonable to believe—by removing the overwhelming dependency of members upon special-interest funding.
As Dennis Thompson has written, "Citizens have a right to insist,
as the price of trust in a democracy, that officials not give reason to
doubt their trustworthiness."[149]

"Officials" in this democracy have given us reason to doubt.

So let's survey the field of battle again. I began this chapter by
acknowledging two apparently conflicting Republican claims: On
the one hand, Senator Coburn claiming that there were "thousands
of instances . . . where appropriations are leveraged for fundraising
dollars." On the other, Chairman Smith claiming that "the money
does not play much of a role in what goes on in terms of legislative
voting patterns and legislative behavior."

There can be no doubt that the chairman is wrong at least about
"legislative behavior." Members spend between 30 percent and 70
percent of their time feeding this addiction. The majority of the
attention of Congress gets devoted to the questions that matter
most to their pushers (e.g., bank "swipe fees"). These two facts
alone demonstrate the extraordinarily important way in which the
money affects legislative behavior. No one could say that this effect
is benign.

The harder question is whether the money affects "legislative
voting patterns." Here, it is the testimony of another Republican,
Senator Larry Pressler (R-S.D.; 1979–1997), that is most helpful. As
he explained to me, whether or not the money matters in the very
last moment in the life (or death) of a bill, there is no evidence that

it does not matter in the million steps from the birth of a policy idea to the very last moments in the life (or death) of a bill. Instead, all the "evidence" here is to the contrary: People who live inside this system (e.g., former members) and people who study the life of this system (e.g., journalists such as Kaiser) all affirm that money is mattering here a very great deal. How could it not?

In the end, this debate is not really a disagreement among scholars. It is a fight pressed by those defending a status quo. In that fight, there is a Boris Yeltsin: an addict whose addiction is destroying his ability to do his job. That addict denies the addiction. But at some point the denial feels like the dialogue from any number of familiar works of fiction: "I can handle it." "It isn't affecting me or my work." "I understand how it might affect others. But it doesn't affect me." "I'm above it." "I can control it."

Right.

The corruption denier is in denial. It is time for us to move on.

# CHAPTER 11

# *How* So Damn Much Money
# *Defeats the Left*

On November 4, 2008, America voted to change its government. With the highest voter turnout in forty years, sixty-nine million Americans elected the first African American president, with twice as many electoral votes as his opponent, and almost ten million more of the total votes cast. House Democrats gained twenty-one seats, padding an already comfortable majority. And with the defection of one Republican, Senate Democrats gained enough seats to secure a filibuster-proof majority.

Obama's victory electrified the reform community. While no political liberal, his campaign had promised substantial change. Health care reformers were ecstatic to have a chance at real health care reform. Global warming activists thought they had elected a sexier version of Al Gore. And as Wall Street's collapse threw the economy over the cliff, America was very eager to hear Obama, the neo-Brandeisian, attack Wall Street. ("I will take on the corruption in Washington and on Wall Street to make sure a crisis like this can never, ever happen again";[1] "We have to set up some rules of the road, some regulations that work to keep the system solvent, and prevent Wall Street from taking enormous risks with other people's money, figuring that, 'Tails I win, heads you lose,' where they don't have any risk on the downside."[2]) If ever there was the opportunity for progressive change, this election seemed to promise it.

I was a strong supporter of Obama. Indeed, long before you likely had ever even heard the name Obama, I was a strong supporter of Obama. He was a colleague of mine at the University of Chicago. In 2000, Obama ran for Congress in the South Side of Chicago. The campaign was awful, yet after his defeat, Obama was optimistic. "It was a good first try," he assured me. If that campaign was a good first try, I thought, then he had even less political sense than I.

Despite that defeat, however, I backed every Obama campaign since. In one sense, that's not surprising. We were friends. But it was more than that. Like many who know the man, I believed there was something more than the typical politician here. I was convinced by Obama. More than convinced: totally won over. It wasn't just that I agreed with his policies. Indeed, I didn't really agree with a bunch of his policies—he's much more of a centrist on many issues than I. It was instead because I believed that he had a vision of what was wrong with our government, and a passion and commitment to fix it.

That vision is the great orator's summary of the argument of this book. In speech after speech, Obama described the problem of Washington just as I have, though with a style that is much more compelling. As he said, "the ways of Washington must change."

[I]f we do not change our politics—if we do not fundamentally change the way Washington works—then the problems we've been talking about for the last generation will be the same ones that haunt us for generations to come.[3]

But let me be clear—this isn't just about ending the failed policies of the Bush years; it's about ending the failed system in Washington that produces those policies. For far too long, through both Democratic and Republican administrations, Washington has allowed Wall Street to use lobbyists and campaign contributions to rig the system and get its way, no matter what it costs ordinary Americans.[4]

We are up against the belief that it's all right for lobbyists to dominate our government—that they are just part of the system in Washington. But we know that the undue influence of lobbyists is part of the problem, and this election is our chance to say that we're not going to let them stand in our way anymore.[5]

[U]nless we're willing to challenge the broken system in Washington, and stop letting lobbyists use their clout to get their way, nothing else is going to change.[6]

[T]he reason I'm running for President is to challenge that system.[7]

If we're not willing to take up that fight, then real change—change that will make a lasting difference in the lives of ordinary Americans—will keep getting blocked by the defenders of the status quo.[8]

It was this theme that distinguished Obama most clearly from the heir apparent to the Democratic nomination, Hillary Clinton. For Clinton was not running to "change the way Washington works." She stood against John Edwards and Barack Obama in their attack on the system and on lobbyists in particular. As she told an audience at YearlyKos in August 2007: "A lot of those lobbyists, whether you like it or not, represent real Americans. They represent nurses, they represent social workers, yes, they represent corporations that employ a lot of people. I don't think, based on my 35 years of fighting for what I believe in, I don't think anybody seriously believes I'm going to be influenced by a lobbyist."[9]

The "anybody" here didn't include the thousand or so in the audience, who moaned in disbelief as Clinton lectured them about what they could "seriously believe."

Instead, Clinton's vision of the presidency was much like her husband's (though, no doubt, without the pathetic scandals). She saw the job of president to be to take a political system and do as much with it as you can. It may be a lame horse. It may be an intoxicated horse. But the job is not to fix the horse. The job is to run the horse as fast as you can. Clinton had a raft of programs she promised to push through Congress. Nowhere on that list was fundamental reform of how Washington worked.

I was therefore glad, not so much that Clinton had lost (she is an amazing politician and, as her time as secretary of state has confirmed, an extraordinary stateswoman), but that Obama had won. For, as this book should make clear, it was my view, too, that the critical problem for the next president was the corruption we've been exploring here. Not because corruption is the most important problem. But because corruption is the gateway problem: until we solve it, we won't solve any number of other critical problems facing this nation.

I thought Obama got this. That's what he promised, again and again. That was "the reason [he] was running for President[—]to challenge that system."[10]

Yet Obama hasn't played the game that he promised. Instead, the game he has played has been exactly the game that Hillary Clinton promised and that Bill Clinton executed: striking a bargain with the most powerful lobbyists as a way to get a bill through—and as it turns out, the people don't have the most powerful lobbyists.

As I watched this strategy unfold, I could not believe it. The idealist in me certainly could not believe that Obama would run a campaign grounded in "change" yet execute an administration that changed nothing of the "way Washington works."

But the pragmatist in me also could not believe it. I could not begin to understand how this administration thought that it would take on the most important lobbying interests in America and win without a strategy to change the power of those most important lobbying interests. Nothing close to the reform that Obama promised is possible under the current system; so if that reform was really what Obama sought, changing the system was an essential first step.

The reason should have been obvious in 2009. In the very best of times, the Clinton model of governing will only have (very) limited success, so long as the current system of campaign funding remains and so long as markets in America remain concentrated. Reform shifts wealth away from some existing interest. That existing interest will therefore have an interest in fighting the reform. Indeed, if there were only one such entity with that interest, we could calculate quite precisely how much they'd be willing to spend to avoid the reform: whatever the status quo was worth; they'd be willing to spend up to (the net present value of) that amount to avoid any change.[11] As Kenneth Crawford put it during the New Deal, "Their bird is in the hand and they battle to keep it."[12]

So, for example, imagine there were only one oil company in the nation: if the net present value of being allowed to ignore the cost of carbon in the products that oil company sold were $100 billion, in principle, that oil company should be willing to spend $100 billion to avoid being forced to internalize the cost of carbon in the products it sold. In a system where money can influence politics, it is therefore not hard to understand why fundamental reform is not possible.

The story gets more complicated if there is more than one entity that benefits from the status quo. Then each faces what economists call a "free-rider problem." It may be good for each that the status quo is preserved, but it is better for each if the status quo can be preserved without that interest having to pay to preserve it. Each, in other words, would like to "free-ride" on the spending of the others to preserve the status quo. The interests thus don't naturally want to pay to avoid the reform. They instead need to coordinate to ensure that each pays its way.

This makes the case for reform much more promising (for the reformer at least) if markets are competitive. If there are a large number of entities comprising a special interest, it is much less likely that these entities could coordinate their fight to preserve the status quo. Thus in a competitive market, reform is simpler than in a concentrated, or monopolistic, market, if only because the targets of that reform have a harder time defending against it.

The problem for us, however, is that major markets in America have become heavily concentrated, and on key issues it has become much easier for allies to coordinate. Indeed, in the critical markets for reform—finance, for example—firms are more concentrated today than ever before. That concentration makes coordination much simpler.

As Barry Lynn has described this concentration:

- Colgate-Palmolive and Procter & Gamble split more than 80 percent of the U.S. market for toothpaste;
- Almost every beer is manufactured or distributed by either Anheuser-Busch InBev or MillerCoors;
- Campbell's controls more than 70 percent of the shelf space devoted to canned soups;
- Nine of the top ten brands of bottled tap water in the United States are sold by PepsiCo (Aquafina), Coca-Cola (Dasani and Evian), or Nestlé (Poland Spring, Arrowhead, Deer Park, Ozarka, Zephyrhills, and Ice Mountain);
- Wal-Mart exercises a de facto complete monopoly in many smaller cities, and it sells as much as half of all the groceries in many big metropolitan markets. [It] delivers at least 30 percent and sometimes more than 50 percent of the entire U.S. consumption of products ranging from soaps and detergents to compact discs and pet food;
- The world's supply of iron ore is controlled by three firms (Vale, Rio Tinto, BHP Billiton);
- A few immense firms like Mexico's Cemex control the world's supply of cement;
- Whirlpool's takeover of Maytag in 2006 gave it control of 50 to 80 percent of U.S. sales of washing machines, dryers, dishwashers and a very strong position in refrigerators;
- Nike imports up to 86 percent of certain shoe types in the United States—for basketball, for instance—and more than half of many others;
- As of March 2009, Google had captured 64 percent of all online searches in the United States;
- TSMC and UMC have together captured 60 percent of the world's demand for semiconductor foundry service—in which a company serves as a sort of printing press for chips that are designed and sold by other firms—and have concentrated that business mainly in one industrial city in Taiwan;
- Corning has captured a whopping 60 percent share of the business of supplying [LCD glass].[13]

These are just market concentration statistics. For antitrust purposes, they don't necessarily translate into market power (though they are certainly high), and it is market power that triggers the special limits of antitrust law. So by pointing to these concentrated markets, I'm not suggesting that the Antitrust Division of the Justice Department or the Federal Trade Commission is not doing its work.

These concentrated markets do, however, translate into a greater opportunity for coordinated political action: for the fewer corporations there are with interests at stake, the fewer it takes to persuade to support a campaign to defend those interests. Thus, concentrated markets may not necessarily signal economic risk, but they do raise the potential for political risk.[14]

This insight has led even free-market proponents such as Raghuram Rajan and Luigi Zingales to argue for a "political version of antitrust law—one that prevents a firm from growing big enough to have the clout in domestic politics to eventually suppress market forces."[15] We don't have that kind of antitrust today. Indeed, we have practically no limits on the ability of the capitalists to protect themselves from either reform or capitalism. Antitrust law (as interpreted in light of the First Amendment) exempts conspiracies for the purpose of changing the law, even if the change is simply to protect the conspirators.[16] Thus, no matter what reform a new government might try, there is a well-funded and well-connected gaggle of lobbyists on the other side. Those lobbyists know that politicians will listen to their arguments quite intently, because their arguments about good policy carry with them (through the complicated dance that I described in chapter 9) campaign cash. These lobbyists thus get to go to the front of the line. Their concerns get met first, long before the concerns of the voter.

No example better captures this dynamic than the fight over health care reform. The president made the reform of health care a priority in the campaign. He made it a priority in his administration. From his first days in office, Obama and his team strategized on how they could get reform passed. And how they got that reform passed shows plainly (if painfully) where the power in this system lies.

Obama had made promises about health care in the campaign. The "public option" was one such promise. Though the details were never precisely set, the idea was simple enough: The government would offer a competing health care plan that anyone would have the freedom to buy. That option would thus put competitive pressure on private insurance companies to keep prices low. It may well have been that no one ever bought that public option plan. That doesn't matter. The aim wasn't to nationalize health insurance. The aim was to create competitive pressure to ensure that the (highly concentrated) health insurance market didn't take advantage of a national health care program to extort even greater profits from the public.

Again, how was never specified. Sometimes Obama spoke of the health care plan that members of Congress received. Sometimes he spoke of a "new public plan." As the campaign website described:

> The Obama-Biden plan will create a National Health Insurance Exchange to help individuals purchase new affordable health care options if they are uninsured or want new health insurance. Through the Exchange, any American will have the opportunity to enroll in the new public plan or an approved private plan, and income-based sliding scale tax credits will be provided for people and families who need it.[17]

Likewise, at a speech at the University of Iowa on March 29, 2007: "Everyone will be able to buy into a new health insurance plan that's similar to the one that every federal employee—from a postal worker in Iowa to a congressman in Washington—currently has for themselves."

Or again, three and a half months later, to the Planned Parenthood Action Fund on July 17, 2007: "We are going to set up a public plan that all persons, and all women, can access if they don't have health insurance."

Or again, five months later, to the Iowa Heartland Presidential Forum on December 1, 2007: "We will set up a government program, as I've described, that everybody can buy into and you can't be excluded because of a pre-existing condition."

And these promises continued after the campaign. During the president's weekly address on July 17, 2009: "Any plan I sign must include an insurance exchange: a one-stop shopping marketplace where you can compare the benefits, cost and track records of a variety of plans—*including a public option to increase competition and keep insurance companies honest*—and choose what's best for your family."[18]

But whether that plan or another, the idea that there would be some backstop for all of us was a central plank in the campaign.

So, too, was doing something about the high cost of prescription drugs. The pharmaceutical industry (PhRMA) is the third most profitable industry in America.[19] One reason it is so profitable is the monopoly the government gives it in the form of drug patents. Those patents are necessary (so long as drug research is privately financed), but there has long been a debate about whether they get granted too easily, or whether "me-too" drugs get protection unnecessarily. (A me-too drug is a new drug that performs very similarly to a drug it is intended to replace. Patents for such drugs may be unnecessary since the cost to society of a patent is large [higher prices], and the added benefit from the me-too drug is small.)

Patents, however, are not the only government-granted protection from an otherwise free market that the drug companies receive. In addition to patents, the government sometimes promises not to use its market power to "force" drug companies to offer lower prices to the government. I put that word in scare quotes, because of course there's no coercion involved. Instead, it is just the workings of an ordinary market, where large buyers pay less than small buyers. Ordinary souls understand this to be the difference between wholesale and retail: The wholesaler pays less per unit than retail prices. But when the wholesaler is really, really big, that means it can leverage its power to get really, really good prices from the seller.

Thus talk of "market power" and "forcing" shouldn't lead you to think that anything bad is happening here. A seller is "forced" to sell to wholesalers at lower prices in just the sense that you are "forced" to pay $3.50 for a latte at Starbucks. If you don't like the price, you can go someplace else. If the seller doesn't like the price the wholesaler demands, the seller can just say no. People might not like what the market demands. But most of us don't get a special law passed by the government to exempt us from the market just because we don't like what it demands.

The drug companies, however, did. In 2003, Congress passed President Bush's biggest social legislation, the Medicare Prescription Drug, Improvement, and Modernization Act.[20] This massive government program—estimated to cost $549 billion between 2006 and 2015,[21] and not covered by any increase in taxes—was intended to benefit seniors by ensuring them access to high-price drugs. It also had the effect of benefiting the drug companies, however, by ensuring an almost endless pipeline of funds to pay for the high-cost drugs that doctors prescribe to seniors.

The best part of Bush's plan (for the drug companies at least) was a section called Part D, which essentially guarantees drug companies retail prices for wholesale purchases.[22] The law bars the government from negotiating for better prices from the drug companies. Thus, while the government is not permitted to use its market power to get lower prices from the drug companies, the drug companies are permitted to use their (government-granted) market power (from patents) to demand whatever price they want from us.

This is not a simple issue. Sane and independent economists will testify that it is very hard to determine exactly what price a government should be able to get its drugs for. For just as there is a problem with a monopoly (one seller), there is a problem with monopsony (one buyer). Permitting a monopsonist to exercise all of its market power can certainly cause social harm in just the way that permitting a monopolist to exercise all of its market power can cause social harm.

My point, however, is not to map an economically ideal compromise—even assuming there is one. It is instead to track the president's position on these complicated policy questions. For when Congress passed the Prescription Drug Act, there was no ambiguity in Barack Obama's reaction. He was outraged. As he said on the floor of the Senate, this was just another example of "the power and the profits of the pharmaceutical industry...trump[ing] good policy and the will of the American people." It was "a tremendous boon for the drug companies." And as he added, "When you look at the prices the Federal Government has negotiated for our veterans and military men and women, it is clear that the government can—and should—use its leverage to lower prices for our seniors as well. Drug negotiation is the smart thing to do and the right thing to do."[23]

Obama continued the criticism during his campaign. On the Obama-Biden website, the campaign stated: "Barack Obama and Joe Biden will repeal the ban on direct negotiation with drug companies and use the resulting savings, which could be as high as $30 billion, to further invest in improving health care coverage and quality."

And the example was the subject of the campaign ad named "Billy":

Narrator: "The pharmaceutical industry wrote into the prescription drug plan that Medicare could not negotiate with drug companies. And you know what, the chairman of the committee, who pushed the law through, went to work for the pharmaceutical industry making $2 million a year."
The screen fades to black to inform the viewer that "Barack Obama is the only candidate who refuses Washington lobbyist money," while the candidate continues his lecture:
"Imagine that. That's an example of the same old game playing in Washington. You know, I don't want to learn how to play the game better, I want to put an end to the game playing."[24]

So just as clearly as the public was led to think that Obama's reform would include a public option, the public was also led to think that Obama's reform would never include another "tremendous boon for the drug companies" in the form of a(nother) free pass from the forces of the market.

On both fronts, of course, we were wrong.

As the story is told by Jonathan Cohn of the *New Republic*, Obama took on health care almost as "a test": "Could the country still solve its most vexing problems? If he abandoned comprehensive reform, he would be conceding that the United States was, on some level, ungovernable."[25]

But the question was *on what terms* America would be governed. As Cohn writes: "Obama had promised to change the way Washington does business. No more negotiating in the anterooms of Capitol Hill. No more crafting bills to please corporate interests. But Obama also wanted to pass monumental legislation. And it wasn't long before the tension between the two began to emerge."[26]

This statement is almost right, but not quite. Certainly Obama had promised to end the practice of "crafting bills to please corporate interests." ("[U]nless we're willing to challenge the broken system in Washington, and stop letting lobbyists use their clout to get their way, nothing else is going to change.")[27] But that's different from promising to give up politics. ("No more negotiating in the anterooms of Capitol Hill.") There's nothing wrong with negotiating, and with compromise, so long as the driving force in that compromise is the single dependency that this democracy is to reveal: the people. Maybe voters in Nebraska need something from California before they can support health care. There's no sin in making that deal.

The sin, as Obama described it, and as I certainly believe it, is when forces not reflecting the people force compromise into the system. It is the *"undue* influence of lobbyists"[28]—undue because not tied to the proper metric for power within a democracy.

Yet the story that Cohn tells is the story of such "undue

influence" again and again. The administration strikes a deal to get PhRMA's support for the bill. The price? A promise to protect PhRMA in just the way President Bush did with the Prescription Drug Act: no bargaining to lower prices. The administration estimated that a health care bill would increase the revenue to the drug companies by $100 billion. This deal struck by Obama with the lobbyists from PhRMA assured PhRMA that it would keep much of that increase.

The same with the "public option." The Congressional Budget Office had estimated that a public option would "save the government around $150 billion,"[29] by putting competitive pressure on insurance companies to keep their rates low. That competitive pressure seemed to many only fair, as insurance companies, like PhRMA, were about to get a big boost from the bill: a requirement that everyone have insurance. But alas, as Cohn describes, "That money would come out of the health care industry, which prevailed upon ideologically sympathetic (and campaign-donation-dependent) lawmakers to intervene. They blocked a bill until Waxman [dropped the public option]."[30]

The lesson here is obvious. There are "institutional constraints" on change in America. Central to those "constraints" is, as Cohn lists it with others, "the nature of campaign finance."[31] And what is its "nature"?: that "corporate interests" (Cohn's words) "use lobbyists and campaign contributions to rig the system and get [their] way, no matter what it costs ordinary Americans"[32] (Obama's words). Here that "nature" "cost ordinary Americans" up to $250 billion: apparently the price we have to pay for reform to please these corporate masters, given the "nature of campaign finance."

After health care passed, *Washington Post* columnist Ezra Klein wrote with praise that Obama had "succeeded at neutralizing every single industry"[33]—insurance, PhRMA, the AMA, labor, and even large businesses. Klein meant that term *neutralizing* precisely: that Obama had succeeded in balancing the forces of each powerful interest against the other, with the result that his reform (however hobbled it was) would pass.

That meaning for the term *neutralizing* was made ambiguous, however, by the title that the editors gave to the essay ("Twilight of the Interest Groups"), a title that suggested that Klein was arguing that Obama had weakened the power of the interest groups. That he had in fact, as promised, "fundamentally change[d] the way Washington works."[34]

Glenn Greenwald picked up on this hint, and as is his style, picked on it in a merciless way. As he wrote,

> If, by "neutralizing," Ezra means "bribing and accommodating them to such an extreme degree that they ended up affirmatively supporting a bill that lavishes them with massive benefits," then he's absolutely right.
>
> Being able to force the Government to bribe and accommodate you is not a reflection of your powerlessness; quite the opposite.
>
> The way this bill has been shaped is the ultimate expression—and **bolstering**—of how Washington has long worked. One can find reasonable excuses for why it had to be done that way, but one cannot reasonably deny that it was.[35]

Greenwald's criticism of Klein is debatable. The criticism of Obama, however, is completely fair. Had President Hillary Clinton passed health care as Obama did, she would deserve great praise. That Obama passed health care the way Clinton would have does not earn him the same great praise. Rather than "take up the fight" to "change the way Washington works," Obama has simply "bolstered" "how Washington has long worked." That's not what he promised.

The story is very much the same with just about every other area of major reform that Obama has tried to enact. Consider, for example, the reform of the banks.

I've already described the reckless behavior of the banks—encouraged as it was by idiotic government regulations—that threw the economy over the cliff in 2008. Reckless from the perspective of society, not from the perspective of the banks. In my view, following Judge Richard Posner, the banks were behaving perfectly rationally: if you know your losses are going to be covered by the government, gambling is a pretty good business model.

Reform here therefore needed to focus on the incentives to gamble. The government needed to ensure that it no longer paid for the banks to use other people's money to gamble with our economy. After spending an enormous amount of public funds to save the banks so as to save the financial system, we should at least ensure that we don't have to save the system again.

From this perspective, the fundamental flaw in the system is one that conservatives often harp upon in the context of welfare: the system created a "moral hazard problem." With welfare, the conservative's concern is that unemployment payments (intended to cushion the burden of losing a job) may encourage people not to seek a job. With the financial system, the conservative's concern should be that the promise of a government bailout will encourage the banks to behave more recklessly.

Indeed, the evidence of this moral hazard is quite compelling. Banks in the United States have gotten huge in the past ten years. They've gotten only bigger after the most recent crisis.[36] Before the crisis, each bank could reasonably hope that if it got into trouble, the government would help it. After the crisis, that hope is now a certainty.

The market as it is means large banks are still able to gamble with more confidence than small banks. It also means that these large banks are therefore a less risky borrower than small banks (since there's no risk they'll be allowed to go bankrupt), and can therefore borrow money on the open market for a discount relative to small banks. Again, as Simon Johnson and James Kwak calculated the advantage in 2009: "Large banks were able to borrow money at rates 0.78 percentage points more cheaply than smaller banks, up from an average of 0.29 percentage points from 2000 through 2007."[37]

"In the period since" the crisis, as Oliver Hart and Luigi Zingales summarize a study by economists Dean Baker and Travis McArthur: "the spread had grown to 0.49 percentage points. This increased spread is the market's estimate of the benefit of the implicit insurance offered to large banks by the 'too big to fail' policy. For the 18 American banks with more than $100 billion each in assets, this advantage corresponds to a roughly $34 billion total subsidy per year."[38]

A $34 *billion* subsidy per year: that's 500,000 elementary school teachers, or 600,000 firefighters, or 4.4 million slots for kids in Head Start programs, or coverage for 4 million veterans in VA hospitals.[39] We don't spend that money on those worthy causes in America. We instead effectively give that money to institutions that continue to expose the economy to fundamental systemic risk while paying the highest bonuses to their most senior employees *in American history*.

As the system now works, when the banks' gambles blow up, we bail them out. The bailouts, plus an endless stream of (almost) zero-interest money (if one could call $9 trillion in loans from the Federal Reserve a "stream"), gave the banks the breathing room they needed to avoid bankruptcy, and the fuel they needed to earn the massive profits to pay back the bailout, and also pay their senior executives their bonuses. In 2009, investors and executives at the thirty-eight largest Wall Street firms earned $140 billion, "the highest number on record."[40]

This is a system of incentives crafted by government regulation—both the regulation to permit the gambling and the regulation to guarantee the losses. Together, it has created the dumbest form of socialism known to man: As Paul Krugman has described it, "socializ[ing] the losses while privatizing the gains,"[41] benefiting the privileged while taxing all the rest. And we should say, following Zingales, "[I]f you have a sector...where losses are socialized but where gains are privatized, then you destroy the economic and moral supremacy of capitalism."[42]

Banks are rational actors. They would not expose our economy to fundamental systemic risk if it didn't pay—them. And it wouldn't pay them if they believed that they would go bankrupt when their gambles blew up. So the single most important reform here should have been to end this "moral hazard problem" for banks. And the one simple way to do that would have been to guarantee that banks wouldn't be bailed out in the future.

The reform bill that passed Congress in 2010 tried to make that guarantee. But that guarantee is not worth the PDF it is embedded within. If any of the six largest banks in the United States today faced bankruptcy, the cost that bankruptcy would impose on America would clearly justify the government's intervening to save it. In the face of that collapse, it would be irrational for the government not to save it. "No matter how much we try to tie our hands," Zingales writes, "when a major crisis comes it is impossible to stop the politicians from intervening."[43] Real reform cannot depend upon irrational tough love. Real reform depends upon making it make sense that the government lets the gamblers lose, so the gamblers know it makes sense for them to stop gambling.

The simplest way to achieve this real reform would be to force banks back to a smaller size.[44] A promise by the government not to bail out banks is credible only when banks are small. It is not credible when banks are "too big to fail." Thus, as Simon Johnson and James Kwak recommend:

> (1) A hard cap on the size of financial institutions: no financial institution would be allowed to control or have an ownership interest in assets worth more than a fixed percentage of U.S. GDP. The percentage should be low enough that banks below that threshold can be allowed to fail without entailing serious risk to the financial system. "As a first proposal, this limit should be *no more than 4 percent of GDP*, or roughly $570 billion in assets today."
>
> (2) A lower hard cap on size for banks that take greater risks, including derivatives, off-balance-sheet positions, and other factors that increase the damage a failing institution could cause to other financial institutions. "As an initial guideline, an investment bank (such as Goldman Sachs) should be effectively limited in size to two percent of GDP, or roughly $285 billion today."[45]

This reform would have produced a market of banks that were not so big that the government would have to save them. These banks would therefore live life like any other entity in a competitive market, keen to make money, but careful not to take on unnecessary or extreme risk. The market would thus be the ultimate and efficient regulator, because the market would not forgive failure. Bankruptcy would be the remedy for failure, not a blank check from the Federal Reserve.

Yet the banks fought this obvious reform with fury, and succeeded. As Lowenstein describes it, "Wall Street institutions emerged from the crisis more protected than ever."[46] "For better or worse," as Tyler Cowen wrote after the reform bill was passed, "we're handing out free options on recovery, and that encourages banks to take more risk."[47] Hacker and Pierson quote "two *New York Times* reporters describing Wall Street executives as 'privately relieved that the bill [did] not do more to fundamentally change how the industry does business.' "[48] Sebastian Mallaby "put [it most] simply": "government actions have decreased the cost of risk for too-big-to-fail players; the result will be more risk taking. The vicious cycle will go on until governments are bankrupt."[49]

How was this non-reform reform bill passed?

Contributions by groups opposed to even the much tamer reform bill that Congress passed were more than $25 million, two and a half times the contributions of groups supporting the reform. Likewise, lobbying in 2010 by interests opposed to reform was more than $205 million. Lobbying by interests supporting reform: about $5 million.[50] The result: The critical reform necessary to secure our economy has not been made. Our banks were too big to fail in the past. They have only gotten bigger, with even more certainty that they will not be permitted to fail in the future.

Former chairman of the SEC Arthur Levitt describes the dynamic perfectly:

During my seven and a half years in Washington...nothing astonished me more than witnessing the powerful special interest groups in full swing when they thought a proposed rule or a piece of legislation might hurt them, giving nary a thought to how the [battles over corporate reform] might help the investing public. With laser-like precision, groups representing Wall Street firms...would quickly set about to defeat even minor threats. Individual investors, with no organized labor or trade association to represent their views in Washington, never knew what hit them.[51]

In the words of perhaps the twentieth century's greatest philosopher, David Byrne: "same as it ever was."

Finally, if the point isn't clear enough, consider one last example: climate change regulation.

The 2008 campaign happened against the background of a profound awakening of awareness about the dangers from climate change. Al Gore was behind much of this new awareness—not because any single soul slogging across the world giving thousands of Keynote (not PowerPoint) talks about a problem is enough to solve it, but when the power of those talks got amplified by the talent of a filmmaker such as Davis Guggenheim, that became a recipe for a real change in awareness. The film won an Oscar. Gore won a Nobel Peace Prize. Both political parties, and both candidates, insisted that *they* were the candidate, and *theirs* was the party, to fight global warming. Senator McCain had long maintained, contrary to many Republicans, that he believed global warming was real, and something the government had to address. Senator Obama could say the same, and made climate change legislation a central plank of his campaign.

So when Obama won by a landslide, and with a majority in the House and a supermajority in the Senate, environmental activists were ecstatic: here, finally, was a chance to get something done about arguably the most important public policy problem facing the globe.

In the first two years of the Obama administration, environmental groups did whatever they could to support the administration's efforts to get a bill. After they contributed close to $5.6 million in the 2008 elections, and spent $22.4 million lobbying Congress in 2009 (compared with $35.6 million spent by opponents of reform in the 2008 election, and $175 million spent lobbying Congress in 2009),[52] the House produced an extremely compromised "cap-and-trade" bill.[53]

Even that bill, however, couldn't survive the onslaught of special-interest money. On July 22, 2010, Senate Majority Leader Harry Reid announced that the cap-and-trade bill was dead. And thus, no global warming legislation will now be passed during at least the first term of Obama's administration.

In each case, the story is the same. The interests that would be affected by the **CHANGE** that Obama promised lobbied and contributed enough to block real change. Not completely, but substantially. Seven billion dollars have been spent lobbying this Congress during the first two years of the Obama administration, almost $1 billion more than was spent in the last two years of the Bush administration.[54] That money blocks reform. It will always block reform, at least so long as the essential element to effecting reform, Congress, remains pathologically dependent upon the campaign cash that those who block reform can deliver. As Al Gore has described it, "The influence of special interests is now at an extremely unhealthy level.... It's virtually impossible for participants in the current political system to enact any significant change without first seeking and gaining permission from the largest commercial interests who are most affected by the proposed change."[55]

Robert Reich makes the same point: "As a practical matter, this means that in order to enact any piece of legislation that may impose costs on the private sector, Congress and the administration must pay off enough industries and subsets of industries... to gain their support and therefore a fair shot at winning a majority."[56]

The president gets this. He waged a campaign committed to changing it. He promised us that changing it was "why [he was] running." He challenged us to "take up the fight"[57] with him.

Then the president surrounded himself with an army of tiny minds whose vision of governance was Clinton's, not Obama's. And in the tyranny of those tiny minds, the reform that Obama promised died.

When critics like me attacked this retreat, the administration defended itself by claiming the president was never a "leftist." But the problem with this administration is not that it is too conservative. And certainly not that it is too liberal. The problem with this administration is that it is too conventional. It has left untouched the corruption that the president identified, which means that it has left as hopeless any real reform for the Left.

# CHAPTER 12

# *How* So Damn Much Money *Defeats the Right*

The most important political movement in the second half of the twentieth century began in 1964. A wildly popular Democratic president, Lyndon Baines Johnson, was not going to be defeated by any Republican. The Republican Party therefore let the nomination go to the least likely Republican to win, Arizona's senator Barry Goldwater. Goldwater waged a campaign to mark out a new political movement. His ideals resonated with just a few then. But they were the seeds of a revolution for the Republican Party, at least when properly cultivated by Ronald Reagan a decade later.

Reagan's first run for the presidency was also a defeat. On November 20, 1975, he announced he would challenge a wildly unpopular president of his own party, Gerald Ford. No one knows for sure whether Reagan really thought he could win. But no one expected that he would come so close to dislodging a sitting president. In 1980 he was the logical pick for his party's nomination. He easily defeated the unpopular incumbent, Jimmy Carter.

People forget how important ideas were to Ronald Reagan. By the end of his term, his opponents had painted him as little more than an actor on a very important stage. But I doubt we have had a president in the past fifty years who more carefully and completely thought through a philosophy for governing and government. Reagan was more an academic than even the professor president, Barack Obama. Whether you like his ideas or not, they were ideas.

If you doubt my claim, then just listen to the extraordinary collection of radio lectures Reagan delivered between January 1975 and October 1979. Said to have been written completely by him himself, scrawled on yellow legal pads in his office in Pacific Palisades,

California, without the help of aides or clerks, these thousand-plus three-minute shows mapped a series of arguments about the major issues of the day. They were not cheap shots at current events. They were not fluffy rhetoric masking empty ideas. They were instead conclusive evidence of a president with a plan. Again *ideas.*

At the core of these ideas was a suspicion of government. Again and again, Reagan returned to the theme of a government gone wild. His claim was not that bureaucracies were filled with evil souls or idiots. The problem, instead, was good intentions gone bad. And not because the bureaucrats didn't work hard enough (though Reagan didn't often predicate "energy" of government employees). It was instead because there was something inevitable about the failure of big government. We needed a world where people relied more on themselves, Reagan argued. A world where government helped too much was a world where people did too little. Liberty, like muscle, had to be exercised. The Nanny State would inevitably weaken liberty, good intentions notwithstanding.

Lost liberty, however, wasn't Reagan's only concern. He worried as well about an inevitable inertia within big government. Once we let government get too large, Reagan feared, we would inevitably lose control of a certain political, or public choice, dynamic. As Reagan described, quoting (who he said was) Alexander Fraser Tytler: "A democracy cannot exist as a permanent form of government. It can only exist until the voters discover they can vote themselves largesse out of the public treasury. From that moment on the majority always votes for the candidate promising the most benefits from the treasury—with the result that democracy always collapses over loose fiscal policy."[1]

As a predication, I take it that most would agree with Reagan in at least this respect: we have driven our government to the brink of bankruptcy—and if Gary Becker and Richard Posner are correct, over the brink.[2] Total debt held by the public today is around $9 trillion. That number will increase by between $1 trillion and $2 trillion each year until 2020 at least. If it does, then by

2020, half of federal tax revenue will go simply to servicing the debt.[3] (Fiscal) prudence is not our middle name.

Yet however strongly we can agree with where things went, with all due respect to the most important political figure in my lifetime, we should push a bit more to understand just why things went where they went. Reagan spoke as if the engine driving our inevitable destruction were the rapaciousness of the masses and the bureaucrats—the masses, as they "vote themselves largesse out of the public treasury"; the bureaucrats, as they relentlessly pushed to regulate an ever greater scope of human activity.

When you look to the causes of the massive explosion in government debt, however, it's hard to see "the masses" as responsible for much of anything. Instead, the overwhelming dynamic in income in America over the past two decades has been rising inequality, which "government taxes and benefits have actually exacerbated[—]an outcome witnessed in virtually no other nation."[4] Sure, the Medicare Prescription Drug, Improvement, and Modernization Act was designed to help the middle class. But Part D was a $49.3 billion gift to big PhRMA.[5] Sure, health care reform will help millions of uninsured, but it was also a $250 billion gift to PhRMA and the insurance industry.[6] Sure, Obama pledged $700 billion to save Wall Street and another $800 billion to stimulate the economy. But it was the banks that received the vast majority of that bailout (and more important, the $9 trillion of effectively zero-interest loans from the Fed). Fewer than $75 billion was ever intended to go to homeowners, and in the end, less than $4 billion actually did.[7]

The engine behind this spending, or at least the most horsepower, came not from the masses, but from the special interests. And these interests could leverage their power to achieve this rapaciousness because—in part at least—of the "self-reinforcing cycle of mutual financial dependency" between members of Congress and the lobbyists, as the American Bar Association's Lobbying Task Force put it.[8]

Reagan couldn't see this in the early 1970s when his philosophy was finally set. The dynamic hadn't quite taken hold. No doubt there was "rent seeking"—efforts by special interests to secure favors through the government that they couldn't get through the free market. But then, the level of this rent seeking was nothing close to the level that is now the new normal. It's not the game that has changed. It is the scale. Reagan can be forgiven for missing this scale.

Likewise with the alleged rapaciousness of bureaucrats. It's easy to see how Reagan's fear was engendered. In the early 1970s, Nixon, a Republican, had established the Environmental Protection Agency (EPA), the Occupational Safety and Health Administration (OSHA), the Consumer Product Safety Commission (CPSC), and the Mining Enforcement and Safety Administration (MESA), and had expanded the Office of Management and Budget (OMB). As these regulators got going, there was a wide range of new stuff regulated. That flurry of activity could easily have seemed like a trend. As if the agencies would take off, regulating untethered to the mother ship.

But agencies regulate only so far as Congress allows. And as it turns out, the reasons that Congress might have for allowing the scope of regulation to grow are more than a simple pro-regulatory bias.

We'll see this point more in the pages that follow. But for now, imagine a follower of Ronald Reagan who wants to achieve three core Reagan objectives. First, he wants to shrink the size of government. Second, he wants to simplify the U.S. tax system. Third, he wants to make sure that markets are allowed to be efficient.

What are the systemic challenges this Reaganite would face within the current economy of influence that is D.C.? What would block him, and his (Tea) Party, from their ends?

## 1. Making Government Small

When Al Gore was vice president, his policy team had a proposal to deregulate the Internet. As a "network of networks," the Internet lives atop other physical networks. In 1994 some of those networks were telephone networks; some were (promised to be) cable networks. The bits running on the telephone lines (both the dial-up connections and DSL) were governed by Title II of the Communications Act of 1934. The bits running on cable lines were regulated by Title VI.

Title II and Title VI are very different regulatory regimes. One has an extensive regulatory infrastructure (Title II); the other has a very light (with respect to access at least) regulatory infrastructure (Title VI). So Gore's idea was to put both kinds of Internet access under the same regulatory title, Title VII, and to give that title the smallest regulatory footprint it could have. Not no regulation, but much less regulation than is contemplated today by "network neutrality" advocates.

Gore's team took the idea to Capitol Hill. One aide to Gore summarized to me the reaction they got, "Hell no! If we deregulate these guys, how are we going to raise any money from them?"

As I said, Reagan often spoke as if it were the bureaucrats who were pushing to increase the size of government. These bureaucrats, like roaches, would push and push and push until they regulated absolutely everything they could.

What Reagan didn't think about is how members of Congress—even Reagan Republicans—might themselves become the roaches. How they both, Republicans and Democrats alike, have an interest in extending the reach of regulation, because increasing the range of interests regulated increases the number who have an interest in trying to influence federal regulation. And how is that influence exercised? Through the gift economy enabled by Santa, the lobbyist.

Now, of course no one would say that Congress regulates simply for the purpose of creating fund-raising targets—though that was the clear implication of Ryan Grim and Zach Carter's story about the perennial battles among potentially large funders that get waged in Congress.[9] But souls on the Right—especially those enamored of incentive theories of human behavior—should recognize that it is more likely Congress's thinking about targets of fund-raising that affects the scope of government power rather than bureaucrats angling to increase the scope of their work. That having lots of targets of regulation is actually a good way to have lots of targets for fund-raising. And thus, so long as fund-raising is a central obligation of members of Congress, there is a conflict between the interests of small government activists and the interests of the fund-raising-dependent congressmen.

This point is even clearer when you think about it from the perspective of the targets of this fund-raising. According to one survey, almost 60 percent of the time when members of Congress meet with regulators and other government officials, "they do so to help their friends and hurt their political opponents."[10] That fact produces "fear," this study concludes, in the minds of business leaders. That "fear...drives most business leaders to contribute to campaigns. It's also why most say donors get more than their money's worth back for their political 'investments.' "[11]

Martin Schram asked former members about that fear. As he describes it,

> I asked, "just what do you suppose the lobbyist is thinking when he or she gets a telephone call in which a senator or representative who sits on a committee that oversees the lobbyist's special interest is asking for a large contribution." [W]hen pressed... the Members pondered it, and then often voiced the same basic, obvious conclusion: "The lobbyist must figure that he or she has no choice but to contribute—or risk being shut out."[12]

This dynamic is common. One Joyce Foundation study found that "four fifths of [individual donors] said that office holders regularly pressured them for contributions."[13] Almost 84 percent of corporations reported that candidates pressured them for contributions at least occasionally; 18.8 percent said this happened frequently.[14] Even the reformers reportedly practice this extortion. As Clawson describes, one "PAC officer reported that though John Kerry (D-Mass.; 1985– ) makes a public issue of not accepting PAC contributions, his staff had nonetheless called the corporation to say that Kerry expected $5,000 in personal contributions from the company's executives."[15]

"The longer I stay in Washington," reporter Jeff Birnbaum writes, "the more I believe the protection-money racket is a good metaphor for what a lot of campaign giving is about."[16] A protection racket, or a gift economy—you pick, but each of which depends upon the other side's having something to give. And the key for reformers on the Right to see is that the more the government's fingers are in your business, the more the politicians have to "give." "Donors coerce politicians," as Clawson puts it, "and politicians coerce donors."[17]

The same dynamic explains the organization of Congress. Newt Gingrich "believed that the more committees and subcommittees a person can be on, the more attractions they can acquire to present to contributors."[18] Of course, as I've already reported, the attendance at hearings of those committees has also fallen off dramatically. But that's consistent with an account of the growth of committees that looks more to the influence of committee membership on potential funders than to the importance of the actual work of the committees. As Martin Schram reported after interviewing former members of Congress, "lawmakers freely acknowledged that they and their colleagues often sought assignments to certain 'cash cow' committees primarily because members of those committees are able to raise large amounts of campaign money with little effort."[19] Here is the purest example of regulating to raise money, open and notorious in the current context of Congress.

The lesson is simple: Getting a smaller government is difficult enough. Getting a smaller government when members have a direct financial interest in a bigger one might well be impossible.

## 2. Simple Taxes

It has been a central plank of the Republican Party since before Ronald Reagan that our system taxes too much, and too complexly.

Simpler, "lower taxes" has been the common and consistent refrain. Of course, sometimes that refrain has been translated into lower taxes, at least for some. But the aspirations of many on the Right (and sometimes even on the Left, such as Jerry Brown in the 1992 presidential election) that we move to a flat tax, so simple it could be completed on a postcard, have not been realized.

Why? Who benefits from complex taxes? And how could that benefit possibly outweigh a universal push for simplicity?

To understand the nature of tax law in America, you have to understand one simple point: its complexity is a feature, not a bug. From the perspective of those closest to crafting the code, complexity offers a host of opportunities that simplicity simply can't. Some of those opportunities are legitimate: the chance to better target taxing to achieve economic goals. But many are completely illegitimate. And for the illegitimate, when simplicity is pushed, complexity pushes back harder.

The most obvious, if most trivial, example of this is the very system for collecting taxes. In 2005 the State of California started experimenting with a system they called "ReadyReturn." The ReadyReturn system treated taxes the way Visa treats your credit card bill. Rather than demanding that you fill out a form listing all the times you used your Visa over the prior month, and then sending a check to Visa for the total, Visa sends you a bill that lists all the charges you made, and the amount Visa thinks you owe it. Of course you're free to challenge any charge on the bill. Credit card companies are pretty good about removing them. But obviously, given that Visa knows every charge you've made, it makes more sense for them to fill out your bill than for you.

Advocates for the ReadyReturn asked, Why aren't taxes the same? For the vast majority of taxpayers, the government, like Visa, knows exactly how much the taxpayer owes. Wages are reported to the government by employers. Interest and dividend payments are reported by banks. For most Americans, that's all there is to the annual tax ritual. So why not a system that sent the taxpayer a draft tax form that was already filled out? As with the Visa statement, the taxpayer would be free to challenge it. But for the vast majority of taxpayers, no change would ever be needed.

Not necessarily a postcard, but just as simple.

In 2005, following a plan sketched by Stanford Law professor Joe Bankman, California implemented an experimental system like this for taxpayers with just one employer and no complicated deductions. The reviews were raves. As one report put it: "Most of the taxpayers who voluntarily participated in a test run of the state's Ready Return program said it alleviated anxiety, saved time and was something government ought to do routinely. More than 96% said they would participate again."[20]

So the following year, the state taxing authorities decided to expand the experiment. But very quickly, they hit a wall. Strong legislative opposition was growing to oppose this effort at tax simplification.

Why? From whom? Well, not surprisingly, from those who benefit most from a world where taxes are complex: consumer tax software makers, who sell programs to consumers to make completing complex taxes easier.[21] Leaders in the California legislature blocked a broad-based rollout of this immensely popular improvement in the efficiency of the California tax system because it would hurt the profits of businesses who sold software to make California's existing and inefficient tax system more efficient.

Now, again, this is small potatoes. And it has nothing directly to do with Congress (though a similar program at the federal level has been stalled at the IRS for similar reasons). But it illustrates the discipline we need to adopt if we're to understand why obvious problems don't get fixed. Sometimes problems pay. When they pay enough, those who benefit will work to block their being fixed.

This lesson we've seen before. But the more invidious story about complex taxes is actually quite a bit different, and much more significant.

The taxes that most of us think about are quite general. Most pay the same sales tax. And while the rates for income taxes are different depending upon your income, the impression the system gives is that broad classes of taxpayers pay the same basic rates. The tax code, to the uninformed, is a set of rules. Rules are meant to apply generally.

In fact, our tax code is riddled with the most absurd exceptions. Special rates that apply to "all corporations incorporated on January 12, 1953, in Plymouth, Massachusetts, with a principal place of business in Plymouth, employing at least 300 employees as of 2006"—that is, a case where "all" means "one." Special exceptions to depreciation rules, or to deduction limitations.

These exceptions are proposed and secured by lobbyists. Indeed, lobbyist firms specialize in providing the "service" of securing these special benefits. The firm Williams and Jensen, for example, advertises that it has "the primary mission of advancing the tax policy interests of clients" and claims to have a "results-oriented approach, proven by outcomes," including "creating new tax code provisions to help finance a client's project" by "securing special effective dates and exemptions when Congress adopts tax law changes."[22] A paper by Brian Richter and his colleagues demonstrates convincingly one clear example of such a special tax benefit that gave one (and only one) NASCAR facility accelerated tax depreciation for their racetrack. The company secured that benefit through about $400,000 in fees paid to the lobbyist firm.[23] Richter's paper then provides an incredible empirical analysis of lobbying disclosure data to show that "firms that lobby are able to accelerate their tax depreciation at faster rates than firms that do not lobby."[24]

In light of this finding, it is not "surprising that [corporations] spend...money on lobbying since it has a quantifiable payoff in at least one important area, taxes."[25] "For firms spending an average of $779,945 on lobbying a year, an increase of 1 percent in lobbying expenditures produced a tax benefit of between $4.8 million to $16 million."[26] That's a 600 percent to 2,000 percent return—not bad for government work!

This, too, is something we've seen before. Yet it is just one-half of the two-part dance that, unless stopped, will drive our taxing system into bankruptcy.

The key to the dance is this: When you get a targeted tax benefit, you don't get to keep it forever. Instead, because of the rules governing how our budget gets drafted (so-called "PAYGO rules"),[27] each of these special benefits "sunsets" after a limited period. Because of these sunsets, each must be reconsidered every time a budget gets drafted.

Sunsets sound like a good idea. Indeed, some seem to treat them as a panacea for all the ills of a government. But when you begin to think more carefully about the obvious incentives, or political economy, that sunsetting creates, their virtue becomes a bit more ambiguous. For every time a "targeted tax benefit" is about to expire, those who receive this benefit have an extraordinarily strong incentive to fight to keep it. Indeed, we can say precisely how much they should be willing to pay to keep it. If the tax benefit is worth $10 million to the company, they should be willing to spend up to $10 million to keep it.

Professor Rebecca Kysar has framed the point most effectively in the context of "tax extenders"—the term used for temporary tax provisions. In a paper published in 2006 in the *Georgia Law Review*, she described the obvious (though apparently missed by those who created these sunsets) incentives a system of sunsets produces. As she wrote, "The continual termination of certain tax benefits and burdens creates occasions for politicians to more easily extract votes and campaign contributions from parties affected by the threatened provision."[28]

They do this by "increas[ing] the amount of rent available for extortion."[29] (Remember, "rent" refers to the surplus produced by government regulation, which different interests fight over—with the interest at issue here including the politician.) Increasing "extortion"-inducing "rents" produces only one thing: more extortion!

That wasn't exactly the purpose of these sunsets, either when pressed generally (as they were, most importantly, by President

Carter) or specifically in the context of taxes. Indeed, the first tax extenders were created as a genuine compromise to test whether a controversial predication about tax revenue was true. In 1981, Congress enacted Reagan's idea of a credit for research and development. Some on the Left doubted the credit would produce the revenue the Reaganites predicted. As a compromise, the credit was made temporary, so that the actual effect could be measured.[30]

Harmless enough—as were other original sunsets for tax provisions, all either experiments or addressing a temporary problem (such as the benefits granted to employees working in or near the World Trade Center affected by the attack on 9/11).[31] But if the road to hell is paved with good intentions, then the paving here has certainly worked. For the numbers should give us a clue as to why these intended sunsets were never actually going to happen. In the first twenty-five years of the life of tax sunsets, only two were allowed to expire—and one of those was renewed in the next session of Congress, with a retroactive gift given to cover the lapse.[32]

The lie to this game becomes clear, Kysar argues, when you look again at the very first "tax extender." For, whatever skepticism there was at the beginning, most economists agree that this Reagan idea was a brilliant one. The tax credit really did produce more growth and revenues than it cost. It was perfectly tuned to induce growth and investment—precisely the purpose any such benefit would have.

So once that point had been proven, why didn't Congress just make it permanent? We had run the experiment. The data showed that the benefit made good economic sense. Why go through the game of renewing a good idea every two years?

The answer, Kysar suggests, has lots to do with the nature of the beneficiaries. "The principal recipients of the research credit," Kysar writes, "are large U.S. manufacturing corporations." In many cases, the credit "cuts millions of dollars from the tax returns of a single corporation." So, obviously "[t]hese business entities are more than willing to invest in lobbying activities and campaign donations to ensure the continuance of this large tax savings."[33]

And they do. And the politicians they make these donations to have recognized this. And the lobbyists with clients eager to ensure that these extenders are extended have recognized this.

And these flashes of recognition have now produced one of the most efficient machines for printing money for politicians that Washington has ever created—by focusing and practicing and concentrating the money to inspire ever more tax burdens on those who don't organize well (you and me) so as to fund ever-lessening tax burdens on those who organize perfectly well (the largest corporations and the very rich). Mancur Olson would not have been happy that he was so right.[34]

The pattern is obvious. As Kysar quotes one lobbyist:

> With the extenders, you know you always have someone who will help pay the mortgage. You go to the client, tell them you're going to fight like hell for permanent extension, but tell them it's a real long shot and that we'll really be lucky just to get a six-month extension. Then you go to the Hill and strike a deal for a one-year extension. In the end, your client thinks you're a hero and they sign you on for another year.[35]

The cost of this game is only growing. In December 2010, the *Wall Street Journal* reported on "extender mania." As they described, in the 1990s there were "fewer than a dozen" tax extenders in the U.S. tax code.[36] Now there are more than 140. The *Journal*, however, didn't even notice the dynamic at the core of Kysar's argument. But to you it should be obvious. The system is learning, evolving, developing an ever-more-efficient way to create the incentive for people to contribute to campaign coffers: create a mechanism that threatens a tax increase unless a reprieve can be bought, and at least among those who can afford the reprieve (meaning the lobbyists and the funders), you can be certain that that reprieve will be bought. December 2010 saw the huge battle over whether "Bush tax cuts" would be extended for the very rich. But that was just a small part of the struggle that was actually going on. It was instead a gaggle of special benefits that got magically extended, through a dance that included billions spent on campaigns and lobbyists by those who got the special benefit.

And thus have we produced the inverse of the world that Reagan predicted when he said he quoted Tytler. But with us, at least in the context of taxes, the problem is not the voters' voting themselves "largesse out of the public treasury." The problem is Congress's learning how it can threaten the richest in our society with higher taxes, so as to get them to give the endless campaign cash Congress needs. So, modifying Tytler just a bit, we could say:

> A democracy cannot exist as a permanent form of government. It can only exist until the ~~voters~~ [congressmen] discover they can vote themselves largesse ~~out of the public treasury~~ [by playing around with the tax code]. From that moment on the majority [in Congress] always votes [to sunset the tax benefits of] ~~the candidate~~ [the citizens and corporations] promising the most benefits ~~from~~ [to] the[ir campaign] treasury—with the result that democracy always collapses over loose [tax] policy.

New York real estate mogul Leona Helmsley famously said, "We don't pay taxes. Only the little people pay taxes."[37] Now you have a sense just why.

But what about Reagan's 1986 tax reform? you ask. You've already called it his most important tax legislation. Didn't it radically simplify that tax code? Doesn't that prove your theory wrong?

Would that it did. Reagan's 1986 reform was brilliant. It was bipartisan, and real reform. It eliminated a world of tax breaks and special deals. It seemed to signal (to the hopelessly naive at least) that the special interests had lost. Reagan the reformer (with the help of key Democrats in Congress) had radically transformed the mother of all special-interest legislation: the tax code.

Almost overnight, however, everything undone by the 1986 reform was replaced very soon after. As Hacker and Pierson describe, "If you take a good look at the tax code now, you'll see that it is chock-full of new tax breaks, far more expensive than the ones eliminated with such fan fare."[38]

I once was on a conservative talk show, talking about just these issues. "You're wrong," the Glenn Beck wannabe scolded me, "all our problems would be solved if we had a flat tax."

"Maybe," I responded. "But how are you going to get a flat tax? What congressmen are going to give up the benefits they get from having a bunch of rich people and corporations coming to them each year begging for more tax benefits?"

The tax system is many things. It is first a revenue system for our government. But it is also an indirect revenue system for congressional campaigns. The critical insight here is to see just how *complexity in the system is an enabler* of the latter, even if it is intended to be the former. It is because no one understands the system that targeted benefits are relatively cost-free to those who give them. No one has the time even to recognize how this dynamic shifts the tax burden to those who can least defend against it. And more important for those who want a simpler tax system: Too few see how this dynamic ensures that simplicity is never achieved. One tax rate for everyone would give no one a special reason to write a check to their congressman. That's all you need to know to understand why we're never going to get one tax rate for everyone. So long as tax favors can inspire campaign funds, the game of tax favors will continue.

Thus again we could say: Getting a system of simpler taxes is difficult enough. Getting a system of simpler taxes when Congress has a direct financial interest in complexity might well be impossible.

## 3. Keeping Markets Efficient

Theorists and principled souls on the Right are free-market advocates. They are convinced by Hayek and his followers that markets aggregate the will of the public better than governments do. This doesn't mean that governments are unnecessary. As Rajan and

Zingales put it in their very strong pro-free-market book, *Saving Capitalism from the Capitalists* (2003), "markets cannot flourish without the very visible hand of the government, which is needed to set up and maintain the infrastructure that enables participants to trade freely and with confidence."[39] But it does mean that a society should try to protect free markets, within that essential infrastructure, and ensure that those who would achieve their wealth by corrupting free markets don't.

Yet often the biggest danger to free markets comes not so much from antimarket advocates (the Communists and worse!) as from strong and successful market players eager to protect themselves from the next round of strong and successful market players. As Rajan and Zingales describe: "Capitalism's biggest political enemies are not the firebrand trade unionists spewing vitriol against the system but the executives in pin-striped suits extolling the virtues of competitive markets with every breath while attempting to extinguish them with every action."[40]

The perpetual danger is that this competition will be "distorted by incumbents,"[41] because of an obvious fact not about markets, but about humans: "Those in power...prefer to stay in power. They feel threatened by free markets"[42]—even if it was free markets that gave them their power!

This is not a new point. Adam Smith, founding father of the modern free-market movement (even if, like most founding fathers, his work is only indirectly and partially understood by those who follow him most vigorously), famously condemned the very heroes of free-market wealth: "People of the same trade seldom meet together, even for merriment and diversion, but the conversation ends in a conspiracy against the public, or in some contrivance to raise prices."[43]

It was from this recognition that Smith offered his rule for interpreting any proposal by successful incumbents for regulating the market. Such proposals, Smith said, "ought never to be adopted till after having been long and carefully examined, not only with the most scrupulous, but with the most suspicious attention."[44]

For such proposals "come...from an order of men, whose interest is never exactly the same with that of the public who generally have an interest to deceive and even oppress the public, and who accordingly have, upon many occasions, both deceived and oppressed it."[45]

Thus, as an example, Rajan and Zingales point to Congress's aid for the tourism industry after 9/11: "The terrorist attacks affected the entire tourism industry. But the first legislation was not relief for the hundreds of thousands of taxi drivers or restaurant and hotel workers, but for the airlines, which conducted an organized lobbying effort for taxpayer subsidies."[46]

Principled souls on the Right thus worry about how to protect, as Rajan and Zingales put it, capitalism from the capitalists. As Rajan writes in his own work, "The central problem of free-enterprise capitalism in a modern democracy has always been how to balance the role of the government and that of the market. While much intellectual energy has been focused on defining the appropriate activities of each, it is the interaction between the two that is a central source of fragility."[47]

This is a worry because there are only two things we can be certain of when talking of free markets: first, that new innovation will challenge old; and second, that old innovation will try to protect itself against the new. Again and again, across history and nations, the successful defend their success in whatever way they can. Principles—such as "I got here because of a free market; I shouldn't interfere with others challenging me by interfering with a free market"—are good so long as they don't actually constrain. Once they constrain, the principles disappear. And once they disappear, the previously successful use whatever means, including government, to protect against the new. This was one of the problems the Progressives fought against: "To destroy this invisible government, to dissolve the unholy alliance between corrupt business and corrupt politics is the first task of the statesmanship of the day."[48] This is one of the battles that should join progressives of the Left and free-market advocates on the Right.

Rajan and Zingales offer a range of remedies to secure a free society from this type of market protection. The most interesting I've described: the notion of a political antitrust doctrine, a doctrine that aims at blocking not only inefficient economic behavior, but also concentrations in economic power that could too easily translate into political power. In this, their work echoes Louis Brandeis, who opposed "bigness" not just for (mistaken) economic reasons, but more important, because of the view that "in a democratic society the existence of large centers of private power is dangerous to the continuing vitality of a free people."[49] It also echoes the battles by Presidents Jefferson and Jackson centuries ago, who both fought the first Bank of the United States, because both "saw a powerful bank as a corrupting influence that could undermine the proper functioning of a democratic government."[50]

But the one point that Rajan and Zingales strangely leave aside is the effect of the corruption I've described here on the capacity for capitalists to corrupt capitalism. So long as wealth *can be* used to leverage political power, wealth *will be* used to leverage political power to protect itself. This was Teddy Roosevelt's view: "Corporate expenditures for political purposes...have supplied one of the principal sources of corruption in our political affairs."[51] But however clever political antitrust might be, a more fundamental response would be to weaken the ability of wealth to leverage political power. Never completely. That would not be possible. But at least enough to weaken the return from rent seeking, perhaps enough to make ordinary innovation seem more profitable.

Any reform that would seek to weaken the ability of wealth to rent-seek would itself be resisted by wealth. So long as private money drives public elections, public officials will work hard to protect that private money. And if you doubt this, look to Wall Street: never has an industry been filled with more rabid libertarians; but never has an industry more successfully engineered government handouts when the gambling of those libertarians went south. When threatened with our existence, none of us—including principled libertarians—will stand on principle. The Right needs to recognize this as well as the Left.

All three examples point to a step in arguments from the Right that too many too often overlook. I've been in the middle of literally thousands of arguments in which someone on the Right (and I was that person for many years) invoked a common meme: something like "This problem too would be solved if we simply didn't have such a big/invasive/expensive government."

Maybe. But the point these three examples emphasize is that you can't simply assume away the problem you've identified. If you believe big or expensive government is the problem, then what are you going to do to change it? *How* are you going to shrink it? What political steps will you take toward the end that you seek?

My sense is that too many on the Right make the same mistake as many on the Left. They assume that change happens when you win enough votes in Congress. Elect a strong Republican majority, many in the Tea Party believe, and you will elect a government that will deliver the promise of smaller government and simpler taxes—just as activists on the Left thought that they could elect a strong Democratic majority and deliver on the promise of meaningful health care reform, or global warming legislation, or whatever other reform the Left thought it would get.

What both sides miss is that the machine we've evolved systematically thwarts the objectives of each side. The reason for the thwart is different on each side. Change on the Left gets stopped because a strong, powerful private interest uses its leverage to block changes in the status quo. Change on the Right gets stopped because strong, powerful public interests, Congress, work to block any change that would weaken their fund-raising machine.

The point is not that the Right agrees with the Left. They don't. The ends that both sides aim for are different.

But even if the Left and the Right don't share common ends, they do share a common enemy. The current system of campaign funding radically benefits the status quo—the status quo for private interests and the status quo of the Fund-raising Congress.

The same dynamic will thus work against both types of reform. Private interests will flood D.C. with dollars to block change that affects them. And government interests, as in congressmen, will keep the grip tight on large, intrusive, complicated government, in part because it makes it easier to suck campaign dollars from the targets of regulation.

The existing system will always block the changes that both sides campaign for. Both sides should therefore have the same interest in changing this system.

This is not a new point, though it is strange how completely it gets forgotten. In 1999, Charles Kolb, a Republican and former George H. W. Bush administration official, led the Committee for Economic Development (CED) to take a major role in pushing for campaign finance reform. The CED describes itself as "a non-profit, non-partisan business led public policy organization." Since 1942 the CED has pushed for "sustained economic growth." It has been well known for pushing for that growth from a relatively conservative position.

Central to its mission since 1999 has been the argument that the existing system of campaign funding is broken. As it wrote in its first campaign financing report,

> The vast majority of citizens feel that money threatens the basic fairness and integrity of our political system. Two out of three Americans think that money has an "excessive influence" on elections and government policy. Substantial majorities in poll after poll agree that "Congress is largely owned by the special interest groups," or that special interests have "too much influence over elected officials." Fully two-thirds of the public think that "their own representative in Congress would listen to the views of outsiders who made large political contributions before a constituent's views."
>
> These findings, typical of the results of public opinion surveys conducted in recent years, indicate a deep cynicism regarding the role of money in politics. Many citizens have lost

faith in the political process and doubt their ability as individuals to make a difference in our nation's political life. Americans see rising campaign expenditures, highly publicized scandals and allegations regarding fundraising practices, and a dramatic growth in unregulated money flowing into elections.[52]

The CED was "deeply concerned about these negative public attitudes toward government and the role of money in the political process." It was "also concerned about the effects of the campaign finance system on the economy and business." For "[i]f public policy decisions are made—or appear to be made—on the basis of political contributions, not only will policy be suspect, but its uncertain and arbitrary character will make business planning less effective and the economy less productive."

The solution, the CED argues, is for business to be less tied to campaign fund-raising. "We wish," as the report states, "to compete in the marketplace, not in the political arena."[53] Because, again, that competition doesn't create wealth or produce new jobs. It just fuels the very rent seeking that all good conservatives should oppose.

The CED does. More should.

Special interest control
gov.

Solution: change campaign
finance
    —Smaller banks
    — tax overhead
    — lobbiest

# CHAPTER 13

# *How* So Little Money *Makes Things Worse*

At the start of the Soviet Union, the average salary of members of the Politburo was said to be not far from the salary of the average worker.[1] This equality expressed an ideal within the Soviet system—the ideal that the USSR was a workers' state and that state employees, even leaders, were no better than other workers.

That expression was a lie. While the formal salary of members of the Politburo was close to the average salary for Soviet workers, the *effective* salary was much, much higher. Members of the Politburo got vacation homes (dachas), access to Western stores, government-issued cars with drivers, foreign publications, better health care, and better opportunities for their kids. Meaning government employees were in effect actually *highly* paid relative to the average worker, or anyone else in Soviet life. The only way to make more in the Soviet system was to be a criminal (assuming there was a sharp distinction between members of the Politburo and criminals).

America isn't the Soviet Union. But in a weird way, our Congress is quickly becoming a kind of Politburo. Tenure for members of Congress now exceeds the average tenure of members of the Politburo. (House: ten years. Senate: twelve years.[2] Politburo: just over nine years.[3]) And more troubling is the way that Congress effectively inflates its salary. Through games quite Soviet, many members of Congress live like millionaires, even though their take-home salary is the same as the very best students who graduate from Harvard Law School *in their first year practicing law*.

Now let me be clear about the criticism I intend to offer in this chapter. The salaries of key officials in our government strike many as high. Some believe them too high. The last amendment to our Constitution was for the very purpose of blocking any salary increase for members of Congress until after an election. It is a common populist refrain among critics of government that the "bureaucrats" are paid too much. Even worse, members of Congress.

The populist view is wrong. What we know from economics, and from experience with governments across the world, is that if you underpay government officials *relative to their talents or their peers*, they will find ways to supplement their income. Those supplements are not cost-free, even if they cost the Treasury nothing. They sometimes involve outright bribes. (Norman Ornstein explains the "inexplicable petty corruption of powerhouses like Dan Rostenkowski and Ted Stevens . . . by their belief that they were making such immense sacrifices to stay in public service.")[4] But in America, at least with members of Congress and senior members of the administration, that sort of bribery is not the problem. The real danger is that policy gets bent, through the unavoidable influence spread by those who need the favor of government. If, as Congressman Jim Cooper told me, "Capitol Hill has become a farm league for K Street," then no one should doubt that players on a farm league do everything they can to get to the majors.

Yet the purpose of this chapter is not to argue that we should increase the salaries of government officials. We should. But so, too, should people stop smoking and stop "breakfasting" at Dunkin' Donuts. There's a limit to what's possible. I recognize that limit here. I'm not going to fell trees on the fool's errand of trying to persuade you to rally with me to increase Barney Frank's pay.

Instead, the point of this chapter is to underline why the fact that we underpay government officials will make it much harder to change how Congress now works. The very mechanisms that we have evolved to compensate for our undercompensated government workers make change through ordinary political means enormously difficult, and, just maybe, impossible.[5]

## The Ways We Pay Congress

Some in Congress don't give a squat about how much they're paid. Some don't care because they're millionaires. (Indeed, 44 percent of members of Congress are millionaires, compared with 1 percent of the American public.)[6] Some of them spent millions to get to Congress in the first place. To them, government service is a luxury good. They are proud to serve. They'd be proud to serve even if the salary were zero (or negative—which it is for most who self-fund their campaigns).

Others don't care about how much they're paid because they're married to wealthy spouses. That spousal income is sometimes completely benign. (Senator Ron Wyden's [D-Ore.; 1981– ] wife owns the Strand bookstore in New York City. There are not many policies that get bent by the influence of used-book store owners.) Sometimes it is much less benign. (When Indiana senator Evan Bayh [D-Ind.; 1999–2011] was elected to the U.S. Senate, his thirty-eight-year-old wife, a junior law professor at Butler University and a mid-level attorney at Eli Lilly, got appointed to the board of the insurance company that would become WellPoint. No doubt Susan Bayh is a talented soul. But as the website TheStreet commented when the appointment was made, "Her work background at the time she was appointed...would have been surprising, given that she had no insurance experience and was relatively young and inexperienced to serve as a director on a multibillion-dollar board."[7] One can't help but wonder whether that appointment would have been made but for the marriage, or whether the policies of the senator weren't affected by the affiliations of the spouse.[8]) But in most cases, these members with wealthy spouses are not likely looking for ways to make things easier financially for themselves.

Finally, some members don't care about the size of their salaries because they come from inexpensive districts, and don't have kids, and do okay on the salary Congress provides. They share an apartment in D.C. with a colleague. They come home as frequently as they can. They find JCPenney to be an especially talented fashion designer.

Put all of these three types of congressmen aside. In what follows, I'm not talking about them.

Instead, think about those who aren't rich, who don't have a high-income-earning spouse, and who don't come from rural West Virginia. Think about a member from Seattle, or Boston, or San Francisco. Imagine that member needs to keep a home in the district, but brings her family to D.C. Imagine her spouse is a schoolteacher, and they've got three kids. Think about what a member like that does.

There are a number of ways that members like these can cope with the salary they get. Some cut costs by living in their office—literally, sleeping on a couch and showering in the gym. Some simply suck it up, and serve for a relatively short time before returning to private life. And some do something more—by securing a future for themselves that compensates for the (relatively) low pay of their present.

The motives of the members in this group need not be questioned. Many just simply can't afford perpetual service to a low-paying government, at least if they're going to afford to raise a family. Or at least, if they're going to raise a family the way their family might reasonably expect, given their talents and the comparable opportunities. Whatever the pressure, the question I mean to raise is about the work these members do after their life in Congress. Because if their plan is to enter the influence market that D.C. has become, then they can't help but develop a dependency upon that market doing well. It's not just the need to keep future employers happy. That's a possible but, I think, distant concern that would rarely extend its reach into the day-to-day work of the job.

Instead, the real problem is imagining a soul like this voting to destroy a significant chunk of the value of this influence industry— which fundamental reform of the type that I discuss in chapter 15 would do. For if lobbyists weren't able to channel funds to campaigns, and hence, if congressmen didn't depend upon lobbyists to get them the resources they need to run, then the value of lobbying services would decline. Lobbyists' market power would decline. And hence the ability of lobbying firms to pay former members of Congress millions would disappear. If "Capitol Hill is a farm league for K Street," then imagine asking players on a baseball minor-league team whether salaries for professional baseball players should be capped, and you will quickly get the point.

Of course there are members who would ignore that consequence. Of course there are some who would do the right thing, regardless of how it affected them personally. But fortunately or not, members of Congress are humans. They are much more likely to develop all sorts of rationalizations for keeping alive the system that will keep them millionaires. You think you wouldn't? You think they are so different from you?

Life after Congress is thus one reason why members would be reluctant to think about fundamentally changing the economy of influence that governs D.C. today.

A second reason is much more contemporary (with a member's tenure), and much more disgusting.

Members of Congress are not members of the Politburo. Unlike with members of the Politburo, the salary of a member of Congress is basically it. They don't get a housing stipend. For most of them there are no fancy government limos driving them from one place to another. There's no summer dacha. There are no free flights on government planes. As for most of us, their salary is their salary.

But unlike for most of us, their salary is not all they get to live on. Rather, members of Congress have perfected a system that allows them to live a life a bit more luxurious than a first-year associate at a law firm. And the way they do this ties directly to the need to raise campaign cash.

Many members of Congress (at least 397, according to the Center for Responsive Politics) [9] have leadership PACs. A leadership PAC is a political action committee that raises money from individuals, and other PACs, and then spends it to support candidates for office. Members of our Congress stand in the well of the House handing one another checks for up to $5,000. Such checks are the glue that keeps the system together.

Raising money, however, costs money. These costs are the expenses that a leadership PAC incurs. A member of Congress might want to take a potential contributor to dinner. That costs money—especially today in D.C., which now has some of the most expensive restaurants in the United States. Or if the member really wants to impress the potential contributor, she might take him on a golfing trip, or to a "retreat" in a work-inducing location such as Oahu. These things cost money, too. So the leadership PAC must raise money to spend money to raise money.

But much of the way the leadership PAC spends its money benefits, in a perverse sort of way, the member of Congress. A member from California, not independently wealthy, with a spouse who doesn't work, and who is trying to raise three kids, doesn't have much money for fancy dinners if the family lives near D.C. Even less if the family stays in the district and the member has to maintain two residences.

So how does that member get to go to fancy restaurants?

He sets up a leadership PAC, and all doors are open. As Jeff Birnbaum reports, "More than one lawmaker...was willing to declare almost any lobbyist-paid meal a fund-raiser as long as the host of the dinner didn't just pick up the check but also provided one as well—eventually."[10]

The numbers here are really quite amazing. In the 2010 election cycle, leadership PACs collected more than $41 million in contributions.[11] But there's no actual obligation that members spend this PAC money on other members. So here's just some of the delicious/disgusting (you pick) tidbits that public records reveal:

- "[Thirty] Democrats and 17 Republicans...collected $1.07 million collectively without spending a dime on other candidates."

- "A committee created by Rep. Rodney Alexander (R-La.) [2003– ], called Restore Our Democracy, collected nearly $100,000 this [2010] cycle and spent nearly two-thirds to finance his participation with donors or friends in two Mardi Gras balls. . . . Alexander's committee has not used any funds directly for an election campaign."
- Two-thirds of expenditures of then–House minority leader John Boehner (R-Ohio; 1991– ) have gone toward fund-raising costs, which included "fine meals and trips to luxurious resorts," . . . "including $70,403 at the Ritz-Carlton in Naples, Florida, and more than $30,000 at Disney" resorts.
- House majority leader Steny Hoyer (D-Md.; 1981– ) spent more than $50,000 on "travel with donors to resorts" in the 2010 election cycle, including $9,800 on entertainment tickets and limousines.
- House minority whip Eric Cantor (R-Va.; 2001– ) raised $2.1 million for his leadership PAC, and spent $136,000 on golf events, baseball games, skiing, and restaurants. In November 2009 his leadership PAC spent $30,000 "on a Beverly Hills fundraising event."[12]
- Rep. Charlie Rangel (D-N.Y.; 1971– ) used funds from his leadership PAC to commission a portrait of himself.[13]

All this luxury would go away if Congress were to end special-interest fund-raising as the means to getting reelected. Members would have to live on the salary they got. They would have to pay for their own dinners. Holidays would be at Ocean City (New Jersey), not Oahu or the south of Florida.

Now, again, I'm sure there are members of Congress who'd be okay with this. I'm sure many would be happy to make do with the salaries they got.

But I'm equally sure that there are many who recognize that a congressional pay raise is not in the offing, and that living life on $187,000 is not what they bargained for. Some who recognize this might well decide to leave office. But many more would fight the reform of this system to its death.

There's no easy way to figure out if a candidate for Congress is either (a) the sort who's going to be happy living frugally, or (b) the sort who's going to pretend he'll be happy, but then live life taking every advantage he can. Other countries get this, and rather than risk it, they pay their representatives a high, but competitive rate. Ministers in Singapore, for example, rated the least corrupt country (tied with Denmark and New Zealand) by Transparency International, make about $1 million a year.[14]

But this problem is not likely to be fixed anytime soon. (And raising salaries without also fixing the way we fund elections would certainly be no solution.) But if we're not going to decide that members of Congress make too little; if we're not going to recognize that underpaying people only gets us bad people, or turns good people bad, then the prospect that we're going to get members of Congress to vote to support a new system of campaign finance just got much, much worse. For the choice to make Washington clean is now a choice to make a member poor.

## The Benefits of Working for Members

The bigger challenge, however, may not be with the 535 members, or, more precisely, the proportion of the 535 who are not rich or who didn't marry rich or who don't live in West Virginia. The bigger challenge may be with their staff, and with the staff of every major regulatory bureaucracy.

Here, again, we've opted for government on the cheap. Staffers on Capitol Hill get paid on average between $29,890.54, for a staff assistant, and $120,051.55, for a chief of staff. The maximum salary earned by any staffer is $172,500. (Forty-three staffers earned this level of pay in 2010.)[15] The chairman of the SEC earned $162,900 in 2009. The average starting salary for an attorney at the SEC is $78,000.[16] By contrast, the starting salary for an analyst working in investment banking on Wall Street with just a bachelor's degree is from $100,000 to $130,000 after bonus.[17] As study after study has concluded, we pay government employees too little.[18] The same is true for state and local governments.[19]

So why, then, do government officials choose to work for so little?

No doubt some of them do it because they believe in public service. They could get a job anywhere, but they work for the government because they want to do something that does something for America. General Petraeus is not wanting for employment options. Neither was David Walker, the former (and fantastic) comptroller general of the United States. These are people who serve because service is in their DNA.

There are many souls like this throughout American society. They are soldiers who work for less because they believe they are working for something more. They are teachers who work for less because they believe they are working for something more. Doctors at NIH, lawyers at the Justice Department, federal judges—the government is filled with people who do what they do for reasons other than money. We are fortunate to have such people among us. We should think hard about how to have more.

Not every staffer working on Capitol Hill, however, is working for nothing because she believes in something. And not every regulator at the SEC is earning less than his equal on Wall Street because he believes his work will make society a better place.

Instead, living in the "farm league," some of those people see their time on the Hill, or within major regulatory agencies, as an investment. They work for six or eight years as a staffer to a major committee, then they cash out and become a lobbyist. An experienced staffer leaving Capitol Hill can expect a starting salary of about $300,000 per year. Some senior staff members have been known to secure salary and bonus packages of $500,000 or more. If the senator whom a staffer worked for is still in office, the staffer can receive as much as $740,000.[20] Heads of agencies do much better: In 2011, Michael Powell, former chairman of the FCC, became chief lobbyist for Comcast, and was reported to be making more than $2.2 million per year. In the same year, FCC commissioner Meredith Attwell Baker left the commission to join Comcast after voting to approve Comcast's merger with NBC Universal.

This gap in salaries is an enormous change. In 1969 a "newly minted lobbyist with solid Capitol Hill experience could count on making a touch more than the $10,000 they earned as congressional staff. Today, the congressional staffer making $50,000 can look at a peer making five or six times that much as a lobbyist."[21]

The prospects are even better if you enter the revolving door. Start your career as an associate at a law firm, leave to spend a few years as a staffer on the Senate Committee on Banking, Housing and Urban Affairs, and return to that law firm as a principal making hundreds of thousands if not millions a year, where you will represent numerous financial institutions before the Senate.[22] As of 1987, "most of the administrative assistants or top congressional staffers in the House spent 5.5 years working in Congress." A decade later, the average tenure had fallen by more than 25 percent.[23] Between 1998 and 2004, 3,600 former congressional aides had "passed through the revolving door."[24]

In both of these types of cases, the government employee traded her experience for cash. And as the amount of cash that gets traded goes up, more and more will enter government service with that trade in mind.

Again, sometimes this trade is completely benign. After World War II, fighter pilots became commercial pilots. They were paid (practically) nothing to risk their lives to protect America. Then they were paid lots more because of the experience they'd earned while serving to protect America. No one thinks that the prospect of becoming a commercial pilot somehow compromised the service of the military pilot. Indeed, to the contrary: the lucrative post-service salary made it easier to get great pilots to serve in the war.

Sometimes, however, that trade is not at all benign.

Consider, for example, the lobbying firm PMA Group, Inc., created and run by staff alumni of Representative John Murtha (D-Pa.; 1974–2010). In 2008 that firm persuaded 104 different House members to add separate earmarks into the defense appropriations bill worth $300 million to PMA Group clients. These same lawmakers have received $1.8 million in campaign donations from the lobbying firm since 2001. When these deals came to light in 2009, the PMA Group closed shop. Its founder, former Murtha aide Paul Magliocchetti, pled guilty to illegally laundering political contributions, and was sentenced to twenty-seven months.[25]

Or consider a second example: When an artist records an album, the artist gets the copyright. For many years, the recording industry has wanted that rule changed, so that the company making the recording, by default, gets the copyright. This is no small matter: for many artists, and their heirs, the copyright to the recording is the most important right they get. In 1999, Mitch Glazier, the chief counsel to the Subcommittee on Courts and Intellectual Property in the House of Representatives, is said to have inserted into a bill of technical corrections to the Copyright Act a fairly fundamental change: an amendment that classified many recordings as "work made for hire" (meaning the record company, not the artist, would by default get the copyright). Immediately after he allegedly did this, Glazier left Capitol Hill and became senior vice president of governmental relations and legislative counsel for the Recording Industry Association of America.[26]

Our government is shot through with examples like this, far beyond the problems with Congress. A huge proportion of the "staffers" who support the military move seamlessly from private defense contractors to the government and back again, keeping their security clearance, doing the same sort of work, but sometimes at a high salary (when private) and sometimes at a low salary (when for the government). The rotation balances out to a very nice salary on average, but many would not be in this service if the private part didn't complement the public.

Again, maybe sometimes this accommodation is completely harmless. Much more often, these relationships earn the insiders something special, whether it is special access to members of Congress that a lobbyist firm then sells to clients, or a special relationship that an ex-staffer can use to influence an enforcement decision, or simple friendship so that their arguments will be given greater credibility than those of others, and can be used to delay action on an issue.[27]

The best evidence of this influence is a recent paper that studied the effects on a staffer turned lobbyist when the member that former staffer worked for left Congress. Drawing upon the extensive data provided by the lobbying disclosure reports, political scientist Jordi Blanes i Vidal and his colleagues were able to calculate that a lobbyist with experience in the office of a senator sees a 24 percent drop in lobbying revenues immediately after that senator retires.[28]

When you look at these numbers, it is hard to understand them as anything except direct evidence of the channels of influence that the current system buys. In other words, the value of these lobbyists was to a significant extent a function of their connections. But why? Why was the connection so valuable to the firm, if the connection itself wouldn't translate into significant legislative benefit to the clients of the lobbying firm?

There's nothing evil in the story of these staffers turned lobbyists. Or at least, there need be nothing evil. These are not people securing bribes; they are not even necessarily working against the ideals they believe in. Indeed, most of them are doing jobs they love. In this sense, they're living an American dream, honorably and honestly, in the vast majority of cases.

The issue here is not whether these people are good. The issue is whether the system they work within is corrupt. Does it tend to distract members from their constituents? Does it build a dependency that conflicts with the dependency intended?

Of course it does. Or at least, most Americans would be justified in believing it did. This is just another example of how the current system differs fundamentally from the system our Framers intended. It is another example of a difference that matters.

# CHAPTER 14

# Two Conceptions of "Corruption"

S o now I have to do some work. Some law work. I've walked you through an understanding of the corruption that is our government. That understanding differs from the standard story. It is more complex, more human, more difficult to change.

Now I need to tie that more complex story back to some legal doctrine. For our Supreme Court seems to say that there's very little that Congress could do, constitutionally, to fix the problems I've described. Congress can, constitutionally, remedy "corruption," the Court says. But the Court's understanding of "corruption" excludes the problems I've described. It should not, and in the balance of this chapter, I try to make this point bulletproof.

I do this as an act of respect. The Supreme Court is not, in the sense I have described, corrupt. Quibble as we might about its sensitivity to politics, the Court is a gem of institutional integrity. If the Court just reflected a bit on why it had that integrity, it would understand a bit more why it must give Congress the opportunity to secure the same for itself.

The ordinary meaning of *corruption*—at least when we're speaking of government officials, or public institutions—is clear enough. *Corruption* means bribery. Taking this (money) in exchange for that (special favor or privilege from the government). Quid pro quo.

In this sense, Congressman Randy "Duke" Cunningham (R-Calif.; 1991–2005) was corrupt. The government charged that he took over $2.4 million in exchange for securing contracts from the Defense Department. Duke was convicted, and sentenced to eight years and four months in prison.[1]

In this sense, Congressman William J. Jefferson (D-La.; 1991–2009) was corrupt. In a raid on Mr. Jefferson's home, federal agents found $90,000 wrapped in aluminum foil in his freezer. He was charged with receiving up to $400,000 in bribes and alleged to have sought much more.[2] In 2009 he received the largest prison sentence for corruption in the history of the United States Congress: thirteen years.

These are both classic instances of bent and bad souls. They are the stuff the U.S. Criminal Code was written for.

And not just the Criminal Code. Since *Buckley v. Valeo* (1976) it has been clear that Congress has the power to do more than just criminalize quid pro quo bribery. It also has the power to ban contributions that might raise the suspicion of quid pro quo bribery. *Buckley* held, and no decision has ever doubted, that Congress has the power to ban large contributions to a campaign, at least when it is reasonable for people to wonder whether those large contributions are really just disguised bribes. As the Court said in *Buckley*:

> Of almost equal concern as the danger of actual quid pro quo arrangements is the impact of the appearance of corruption stemming from public awareness of the opportunities for abuse inherent in a regime of large individual financial contributions. In *CSC v. Letter Carriers*, the Court found that the danger to "fair and effective government" posed by partisan political conduct on the part of federal employees charged with administering the law was a sufficiently important concern to justify broad restrictions on the employees' right of partisan political association. Here, as there, Congress could legitimately conclude that the avoidance of the appearance of improper influence "is also critical ... if confidence in the system of representative Government is not to be eroded to a disastrous extent."[3]

Thus, even to avoid just the public's *perception* that members may be selling their office, Congress has the power to limit the extent to which one person can signal his support (through contributions) for a political candidate.

This is not an insignificant power. The liberty to contribute to the campaign of another is an important free speech liberty. To be able to say, "I support Mr. Smith," not only in words, but also with your money, is to be able to show just how much you support Mr. Smith. That liberty is the freedom to signal intensity, in a way that's credible and real. No government should have the power to remove that liberty. At least not completely.

Yet despite the importance of that liberty, the Supreme Court has upheld Congress's power to limit it so as to avoid the mere impression that something more than simple praise is going on. So important is it to our political system that the people not reasonably believe corruption is the game that Congress has the power to restrict this political speech.

Call this *type 1 corruption.* As I've described, the law regulating type 1 corruption permits Congress to block it (through bribery and illegal influence statutes), and to block contributions that raise a reasonable suspicion of it.

But if there's a type 1 corruption, there is also type 2. And thirteen chapters into this book, this second sense should already be clear.

Here's an example to refresh the recollection: think about the independence of a judiciary. The job of a judge is to follow the law. Some say that in Japan, judges follow more than the law.[4] Japanese judges, these scholars argue, are sensitive not only to what the law says, but also to whether a particular decision is likely to upset the government. They pay attention to this extrajudicial concern because (at least these scholars claim) the government controls the promotion of judges on the basis of their "behavior." And so, if you're a Japanese judge and don't want to end up in some regional court in the countryside, you need to be certain not to anger those who decide where you'll serve by deciding a case in a way that goes against their (fairly transparent) interests.

I don't know whether these charges are correct—they likely are, given the integrity of the source, but many (in Japan at least) deny it. But imagine they were correct, because if they were, they'd provide a perfect example of the second type of corruption I intend to flag here. One dependency, upon the law, is in tension with a second dependency, upon the will of the government. Or, again, the independence of the judges, the freedom to decide cases dependent only upon the law, is weakened because of this second, conflicting dependency, upon the retaliating will of the government.

We could make the same point without picking on the Japanese. Think about the system that many states use to select their judges: contested elections. Certainly one of the dumbest of the Progressives' (and President Jackson before them) ideas, this system has now spiraled into the most extreme example of campaign cash weakening the public's trust of a crucial arm of government. In the 2008 cycles, state supreme court candidates from across the nation raised $45.6 million, seven times the amount raised in the 1990 cycle.[5] This money yields "unprecedented pressure from interest groups [on judges] to make decisions that are based on politics,"[6] not law, as former Supreme Court Justice Sandra Day O'Connor writes. (Remember, O'Connor is no commie: appointed by Ronald Reagan, she was one of the most important conservative justices on the Rehnquist Court.) With "so much money go[ing] into influencing the outcome of a judicial election," she continues, "*it is hard to have faith that we are selecting judges who are fair and impartial.*"[7]

And indeed, we don't "have faith." In a survey conducted in 2002, 76 percent of Americans said they thought "campaign contributions influence judicial decisions."[8] Seventy percent of surveyed judges expressed concern that "in some states, nearly half of all supreme court cases involve someone who has given money to one or more of the judges hearing the case."[9] Indeed, almost half (46 percent) of the state court judges surveyed in that 2002 survey said they believe "contributions have at least a little influence."[10] Seventy-nine percent of Texas attorneys believe that "campaign contributions significantly influence a judge's decision."[11] That number in particular makes sense to me: one of my students reported on a study he had conducted that included one Texas judge who begins each hearing by asking the lawyers to identify their firm, and then, in front of everyone present, opens his contribution book to check whether that firm had contributed to his reelection.[12]

The suspicions of 76 percent of Americans, 70 percent of surveyed judges, 46 percent of state judges, and 79 percent of Texas attorneys are borne out by the empirical studies of judicial voting behavior and contributions. Professor Stephen Ware, for example, studied Alabama supreme court decisions from 1995 to 1999 and found "the remarkably close correlation between a justice's votes on arbitration cases and his or her source of campaign funds."[13] A 2006 study by *New York Times* reporters Adam Liptak and Janet Roberts found that over a twelve-year period, Ohio justices voted in favor of their contributors more than 70 percent of the time, with one justice voting with his contributors 91 percent of the time.[14] One example from Louisiana is particularly amazing:

> Justice John L. Weimer, for instance, was slightly pro-defendant in cases where neither side had given him contributions, voting for plaintiffs 47 percent of the time. But in cases where he received money from the defense side (or more money from the defense when both sides gave money), he voted for the plaintiffs only 25 percent of the time. In cases where the money from the plaintiffs' side dominated, on the other hand, he voted for the plaintiffs 90 percent of the time.[15]

"That's quite a swing," note the reporters. Yeah. No kidding.

In both the Japanese and the American cases of tarnished judicial independence, the system that queers independence is a system of corruption. Like the compass that deviates because of an interfering magnetic field, the influence of the government (Japan), or the influence of campaign funders (state courts in America), corrupts the independence the judiciary intends. It weakens the fairness of that system. It weakens public trust.

This is *dependence corruption*, and as applied to Congress, the concept should be obvious: As with every other branch of our government, the Framers intended Congress to be "independent." But as with the judiciary, "independent" didn't mean free to do whatever it wanted. Instead, as I described in chapter 10, an "independent Congress" was to be one that was properly "dependent upon the People alone."[16] That dependency was to be enforced by rapid and regular elections (every two years for the House). It was to be protected, for example, by blocking the executive from making appointments to Congress, and blocking foreign princes from giving gifts to Congress. And more. The Constitution is filled with devices designed to ensure that Congress track the truth a democracy intends it to track: the people. An "independent Congress" is thus a representative body that remains dependent "upon the People alone."

That independence gets corrupted when a conflicting dependency develops within Congress. A dependency that draws Congress away from the dependence that was intended. A dependency that makes Congress less responsive to the people, because more responsive to it. In this second sense of corruption, it is not individuals who are corrupted within a well-functioning institution. It is instead an institution that has been corrupted, because the pattern of influence operating upon individuals within that institution draws them away from the influence intended.[17]

But aren't you just talking about a fancier version of quid pro quo corruption? you ask. Or, put better: If we eliminated all quid pro quo corruption, wouldn't we also eliminate all dependence corruption?

No. Dependence corruption is not the aggregate of many smaller cases of quid pro quo corruption. The two may overlap, but they are not coextensive. To solve the one is not to solve the other. To regulate one is certainly not to regulate the other.

To see this critical point (critical to the argument of this book at least), consider just one example:

Imagine that a company, call it Bexxon, let it be known that it intended to spend $1 million in any congressional district to defeat any representative who believed that the federal government should enact climate change legislation. This spending would be independent of any candidate's campaign. As the Supreme Court has defined it, because it occurs in "the absence of prearrangement and coordination,"[18] it would not fall within the range of speech properly regulable as campaign contributions. It is an "independent expenditure."

If a representative learned of that intent, and decided to shape-shift and adjust her view about the need for climate change legislation—for example, by dropping a pledge to support climate change legislation from her website, or removing her sponsorship on a prominent bill—there'd be little doubt that that change was because of Bexxon's expressed intent. But there'd also be little doubt that that change was not an instance of quid pro quo corruption. There's no agreement. There's no act to carry out an agreement. There's simply an expressed intent, and an action in response to that intent that preserves the political position of a politically vulnerable representative.

Similarly, it's obvious the motive of this representative in adjusting her view is not the motive of Randy "Duke" Cunningham or William J. Jefferson. The question she asked herself was not whether and how to benefit her own pecuniary interest. It was instead how to benefit her own political interest. Her focus was on the best means to avoid an enormous influx of campaign funding that might well succeed in bringing her political life to an end.

I've already described how this shape-shifting is harmful to our republic, even though the thing the shifting tries to secure—more money for political speech—is pure. If there are compromises to ensure the funding, the compromise is the harm. If there is distortion to secure the funding, the distortion is the harm.

That there is distortion—or, again, more precisely, that it would be completely and absolutely reasonable to believe there is distortion—is the argument I made in chapter 10. "The funders" are not "the People"; why would you expect the dance necessary to attract "the funders" to be the same dance necessary to attract "the People"? It is reasonable to believe there is a gap between "the funders" and "the People," if only because in the most critical cases, the vast majority of contributions to a congressional campaign are not even from "the voters" in that district. At one point, Representative John Murtha (D-Pa.; 1973–2010) had raised over $200,000, with only $1,000 coming from his district.[19] OpenSecrets.org reports that 67 percent of John Kerry's contributions in his 2008 reelection to the Senate came from out-of-state donors. His Republican opponent received 73 percent of his funding from outside Massachusetts.[20] MapLight reports that between January 2007 and March 2010, 79 percent of contributions to California state legislators came from out-of-district contributors.

Even if you ignore this "out-of-district" effect, it is clear "the funders" are not "the People." As Professor Spencer Overton puts it, "Individuals with family incomes over $100,000 represented 11% of the population in 2004, cast 14.9% of the votes and were responsible for approximately 80% of the political contributions over $200."[21] Only 10 percent of American citizens give to political campaigns; less than 0.5 percent are responsible for the majority collected from individuals.[22]

This gap between contributors and voters means that responsiveness to one is not necessarily responsiveness to the other. Or, again, the sort of thing you need to do to make contributors happy is not the sort of thing you need to do to make voters happy.

And so, once again: while it might not convince a political science department, in my view, we have enough to say that this competing dependency upon "the funders" is also a conflicting dependency with "the People." Or that it is, in other words, an instance of dependence corruption.

This conception of dependence corruption helps make sense of the important distinction suggested by J. J. Wallis between what he calls "venal corruption" and "systematic corruption."[23]

Venal corruption, as Wallis puts it, is "the pursuit of private economic interests through the political process. [It] occurs when economics corrupts politics."[24] Systematic corruption is in a sense the opposite, "[m]anipulating the economic for political ends.... [It] occurs when politics corrupts economics."[25] Or, again:

> In polities plagued with systematic corruption, a group of politicians deliberately create rents by limiting entry into valuable economic activities, through grants of monopoly, restrictive corporate charters, tariffs, quotas, regulations, and the like. These rents bind the interests of the recipients to the politicians who create the rents. The purpose is to build a coalition that can dominate the government.[26]

With both forms of corruption, one could focus upon the bad souls effecting the corruption, or upon the institutions that make it possible.

The rhetoric of the Progressives focused upon "bad men rather than on bad institutions."[27] But their remedy was structural changes that would make it "more difficult for the few, and easier for the many, to control."[28] The common thread in the enormously diverse movement from Teddy Roosevelt to Louis Brandeis was a focus upon corruption. The common remedies for this diverse movement were changes that would make government more responsive to a democratic will.[29]

For conservatives (and the Framers), the focus was on bad institutions that would encourage bad men. The remedy, in their view, to systematic corruption was to "[f]irst...eliminate...the pressure to create special corporate privileges by enacting constitutional provisions requiring legislatures to pass general incorporation laws [rather than special (and privileged) corporate charters]. [Likewise, to forbid] state and local investment in private corporations."[30] The intent was "to reduce the political manipulation of the economic system...by reducing the payoff to political machinations."[31]

Throughout the literature exploring this dichotomy, however, there is an underdeveloped conception of responsibility with each conception of corruption. It's plain enough how both forms of corruption can occur when the actors involved in each intend it. There's no such thing as an accidental bribe. And when we think about Zimbabwe, it's hard to imagine Mugabe not meaning to produce the systematic dependency his regime has produced.

Yet when we think about these conceptions of corruption against the background of the (federal) government today, it is harder to believe that either conception of corruption is really common or pervasive. I've said again and again that I believe Randy "Duke" Cunningham's crimes are rare. And it's hard to imagine the government as even competent enough to plan a system where private industry has to become essentially dependent upon it.

Venal and systematic corruption might flourish, however, without either being expressly intended. That's the lesson of dependence corruption. It builds a platform upon which both venal and systematic corruption can emerge without having to believe that individuals acting on that platform had a motive remotely as evil as Randy "Duke" Cunningham's or William Jefferson's.

To see this, think again about the dynamic of this platform: the crucial agent in the middle, the lobbyists, feed a gift economy with members of Congress. No one need intend anything illegal for this economy to flourish. Each side subsidizes the work of the other (lobbyists by securing funds to members; members by securing significant benefits to the clients of the lobbyists). But that subsidy can happen without anyone intending anything in exchange—directly. "The system" permits these gifts, so long as they are not directly exchanged. People working within this system can thus believe—and do believe—that they're doing nothing wrong by going along with how things work.

Sometimes this going-along produces benefits that seem venally corrupt. Because of a loophole in the tax system (one that has existed since the 1960s), managers of hedge funds don't pay ordinary income tax on the money they earn from hedge funds. Instead, their "carried interest" gets taxed at 15 percent.[32] Thus, though the top ten hedge fund managers in 2009 made, on average,

$1.87 billion, they paid a lower tax rate on that income than their secretaries.[33] Obama promised to change this. But that change was blocked. It's very hard not to understand the very richest in our society enjoying the same tax rate as individuals earning between $8,000 and $34,000 as anything other than a kind of venal corruption. Yet again, no one needs to have intended any quid pro quo to produce this result.

Likewise, sometimes this going-along produces benefits that seem systematically corrupt. That was the example I described with Al Gore's proposed Title VII of the Communications Act—a government regulating for the purpose (in part at least) of producing a dependency by citizens (or corporations) on the government, and thus producing a willingness to turn over wealth to the government (through campaign funds). So, too, with the complexity of tax policy, or the constant role the government plays in agricultural policy. All of these may well be instances of a government deploying its power to create client dependencies, which in turn it deploys to keep itself in power. But here again, all this could be produced without anyone crossing any criminal line.

The clearest recent example of this sort of systematic corruption is the case of the Republicans the last time they controlled Congress. In 1995, Tom DeLay (R-Tex.; 1985–2006), majority leader in the House of Representatives, launched the "K Street Project." The "brainchild of Grover Norquist," the K Street Project "embraced the idea that trade associations, lobby shops, law firms, and corporate offices in Washington should be run by Republicans."[34] DeLay is said to have personally told corporate "executives not to send Democrats to try to lobby him."[35] Gingrich and DeLay had curried favor with business, and as Kaiser comments about the role in 1996 and 1998, "they obviously expected favors in return in the form of contributions. The mutual dependence between Capitol Hill and K Street was now firmly established."[36]

DeLay's behavior was extreme, and to some, ultimately criminal. In 1995 the *Washington Post* reported on a "book" that [DeLay] kept on a table in the anteroom of his Capitol Hill office, which listed "friendly" and "unfriendly" companies, industries, and associations.[37] Lobbyists would use the book to determine whether DeLay would meet with them—"friendlies," yes; others, no—and the cheapest way to keep on the right side of that line was campaign cash.

Not all of this behavior by these Republicans was illegal (though DeLay was convicted of money laundering).[38] Yet it all produced a kind of systematic corruption. Indeed, so tempting was it to the Republican leadership to feed this dependency that after coming to power, the caucus very quickly decided to give up on its stated goal of shrinking the size of government, so that it could use the power of majority status to more effectively pursue its goal of securing control of the government. As Kaiser describes it:

> Republicans took over the House Appropriations Committee determined to cut the government down to size. Their ambitions were soon compromised. Jim Dyer, the staff director of the committee under Congressman Bob Livingston of Louisiana, who became chairman of Appropriations in 1995, recalled what happened. Gingrich initially supported Livingston's efforts to impose discipline on spending, Dyer recounted, but in the face of perceived political necessity, the leadership wavered. Cutting spending was good, but Gingrich, Armey, DeLay, and others quickly realized that "we have another aspect to our existence here, which is that we must use the Appropriations Committee as a resource to protect our vulnerables, because once we got into power, we wanted to stay in power."[39]

In this way, dependence corruption is an enabler for both venal and systematic corruption. A feeder drug. It makes both venal corruption easier, and systematic corruption more likely. It does this by creating conditions that feel normal, or justified, but that breed both forms of corruption. Knowing that there are members of Congress dependent upon campaign cash, private interests exploit that dependency, by seeking special benefits from the government ("rents") and returning the favor ever so indirectly with campaign contributions. And knowing that they are so dependent upon private support, members of Congress will work to keep their fingers in as much of private life as possible, if only to ensure that there are souls interested in securing sensible regulatory policy (in the way such policy is secured—through the proper dance of campaign funding). Because this is "just the way things are done," no one need feel guilty, or evil, by participating in this system. Jack Abramoff was evil. But a lobbyist arranging a fund-raising event for a target member of Congress is "just doing his job."

It's this distinction, I believe, that Representative Tony Coelho (D-Calif.; 1979–1989) was trying to draw in what otherwise seems a bizarrely weird comment. As he told Robert Kaiser, "The press always tries...to say that you've been bought out. I don't buy that....I think that the process buys you out. But I don't think that you individually have been bought out, or that you sell out. I think there's a big difference there."[40]

There is a big difference. Individuals live within a system that demands certain attentions. Certain sensibilities. As those sensibilities are perfected, the representative begins to function on automatic pilot. And when she bends, she's not bending because of a particular interest. She's bending because of a process she has learned, and perfected. As Kaiser puts it, these are "ordinary people responding logically to powerful incentives."[41] There's nothing else to do. It isn't selling out. It is surviving.

Dependence corruption also helps throw into relief a (possible) blindness in the Supreme Court's recent authority, apparently limiting the reach of campaign funding regulation. That at least was the implication of the Court's (now-infamous) decision in _Citizens United v. FEC_ (2010).

In *Citizens United*, the Supreme Court held that corporations had the same right to make independent campaign expenditures that individuals had. This means corporations have the right to spend an *unlimited* amount of money promoting or opposing a candidate, so long as the expenditures are not coordinated. Not surprisingly, we have seen an explosion in independent expenditures since that decision. Comparing 2010 to the last off-year election, spending is up more than 460 percent.[42]

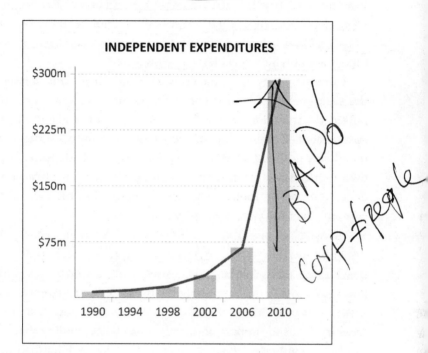

**FIGURE 14**

The Court reached its conclusion not because it held (in this case at least) that corporations were "persons," and, for that reason, entitled to First Amendment rights. Instead, the opinion hung upon the limits of the First Amendment. The question, as the Court addressed it, was whether Congress had the power to limit this kind of political speech.[43] The First Amendment says that Congress "shall make no law... abridging the freedom of speech." It doesn't say "...the freedom of speech of persons." As the Court interpreted that right, it was about what Congress could and couldn't do, not about who got the benefit of what Congress couldn't do. And Congress, the Court held, had no power to limit this kind of political speech.

There is an important kernel of truth in the Supreme Court's opinion. Congress shouldn't have the power to silence or burden any political speech based upon who or what is uttering it. Whether the speech is from a person, or a corporation, or a dolphin, should be irrelevant: Congress should not be in the business of balancing or silencing speech of any kind on the basis of some theory about which speech is to be preferred.[44]

And thus, in my view, the corporate speech actually at issue in the case—a video about Hillary Clinton, produced by a nonprofit political corporation—should have been free of regulation by the government. Citizens United, Inc., should, in my view, have had the liberty to spend whatever corporate funds it had to advance its own quirky view about why Clinton should not have been president. In its result, then, in the precise context of the facts of the case, the decision was, in my view, correct.

Likewise, in my view, was the Court correct in holding that Congress shouldn't have the power to suppress speech for the purpose of "equalizing" speech. That was the theory behind *Austin v. Michigan* (1990), the case explicitly overruled in *Citizens United*. *Austin* had held that Michigan could ban corporations from using treasury funds to support or oppose a candidate, finding that such funds "can unfairly influence elections."[45] That holding had been read to support the idea that the category of corruption included both quid pro quo corruption and what we could call inequality corruption.

But to call inequality corruption is just to create confusion.[46] Inequality in speech *may* be corruption. But not necessarily. If, for example, Michigan had banned political organizing by unions, arguing that unions' power to turn out votes was "unequal" to the power of other interest groups in the state, that inequality would have nothing to do with corruption, at least in a system intended to be dependent upon votes. Regulating it would be improper. The aim of campaign finance regulation should not be, therefore, in my view at least, "to level the playing field among interests that vie for support and attention."[47] Its only aim should be to end corruption.

The Court was therefore right, in my view, to reject the "equality" conception of corruption. But it was wrong to imply the only relevant conceptions of corruption are "equality" and "quid pro quo" corruption. Justice Kennedy's opinion made it sound as if the only corruption that Congress could remedy, at least through regulations on political speech, was type 1, quid pro quo, corruption. Or, again, that venal corruption is the only legitimate target of speech-restricting regulation. Systematic corruption is not.

For an originalist, this is bizarre. As Zephyr Teachout's and J. J. Wallis's work makes clear, the single most important corruption that the Framers were working to cure was systematic corruption, not venal corruption. That was the problem that plagued the English so completely, as "the ability to tie the interests of the financial community to the policies of the government through the medium of the national debt and corporate charters allowed the Crown to extend its influence and undermine the independence of Parliament."[48] As J. G. A. Pocock describes it:

> The King's ministers were not attacked for sitting in Parliament, but they were attacked for allegedly filling Parliament with the recipients of government patronage. For what was universally acknowledged was that if the members of the legislature became dependent upon patronage, the legislature would cease to be independent and the balance of the constitution would become corrupt. Corruption on an eighteenth-century tongue—where it was an exceedingly common term—meant not only venality, but disturbance of the political conditions necessary to human virtue and freedom.[49]

Such "disturbance" occurred when one power had the ability to weaken the independence of another.

The puzzle for the Framers, then, was not how to police the perpetual problem within any government—bribery, or quid pro quo deals. The challenge was to craft a government in which each department was sufficiently independent to protect itself against systematic corruption by another, and to protect the people against systematic corruption by the government.[50] From that perspective, the important question is whether we could call deviation from that dependency "corruption"—at least in the language of the Supreme Court.

In my view, the answer to this question is obviously yes. Dependence corruption is plainly corruption. It also plainly infects the political system for the same reasons that quid pro quo corruption does. In both cases, the consequence of the corruption is to draw the legislature away from the reasons it should be considering. With quid pro quo corruption, the effect is to draw attention to personal and venal reasons. With dependence corruption, the effect is to draw attention to a competing dependency.

Justice Kennedy's apparent argument for limiting the concept of corruption to quid pro quo is perhaps best captured in two closely related passages from *Citizens United*. First, to the suggestion that there may be a corruption beyond quid pro quo corruption, tied to the special influence that money has within our political system, Justice Kennedy quotes an earlier opinion of his: "Favoritism and influence are not...avoidable in representative politics. It is in the nature of an elected representative to favor certain policies, and, by necessary corollary, to favor the voters *and contributors* who support those policies."[51]

Notice the words *and contributors*. Without those two words, Kennedy's statement is certainly true. The claim could be made even more strongly: favoring the policies that one's constituents favor *is the essence of* representative democracy (or at least one dominant conception of it). It was for the purpose of establishing precisely this sort of dependency of representatives on constituents that the Framers created frequent elections in the House.

But by adding the words *and contributors*, Kennedy makes the statement not only not obvious, but also, in my view, plainly wrong. The Framers did not intend to make representatives dependent upon contributors. Representatives were to be dependent upon voters, or, more generally, "on the People alone." And while it is conceivable—assuming many contingencies—that a dependence upon "contributors" could in effect be the same as a dependence upon voters, as I've just demonstrated, there is no doubt that under our current system of campaign finance, there is no such overlap between the interests of "the People" and "the funders."

This gap between a dependence upon the people and a dependence upon contributors has two effects. One is the distortion in policy described in chapter 10. To chase funders, you have to do different tricks from the ones you do to chase voters. Those different tricks at least sometimes yield different policies.

The second effect is on the public's trust. The public isn't stupid. It recognizes that the focus of the politician is elsewhere. Every other year there's lots of screaming at the public, lots of messages on TV, many of them extremely negative. But once the campaigns are over—once, as Obama powerfully put it, the "confetti is swept away...and the lobbyists and the special interests move in"[52]—the focus shifts back to the funders. The public is therefore not unreasonable in believing that it is the funders, not the voters, who call the shots. The public is not crazy when it loses faith in its democracy.

Justice Kennedy, however, denies this effect on the public's trust. In a second critical passage from *Citizens United*, Kennedy writes:

> The appearance of influence or access...will not cause the electorate to lose faith in our democracy. By definition, an independent expenditure is political speech presented to the electorate that is not coordinated with a candidate....The fact that a corporation, or any other speaker, is willing to spend money to try to persuade voters presupposes that the people have the ultimate influence over elected officials. This is inconsistent with any suggestion that the electorate will refuse "to take part in democratic governance" because of additional political speech made by a corporation or any other speaker.[53]

Notice the nature of this claim. Here, one of our nine lawyers in chief is making a claim not about the law or about some complex legal doctrine that needs the keen legal insight that we presume our Supreme Court justices to possess. He is instead making a statement about cause and effect: a representation about facts in the world. An effect (the voters' losing "faith in our democracy") won't be produced by the challenged cause ("the appearance of influence or access"). And as one does for South African president Thabo Mbeki's statement that HIV doesn't cause AIDS, one wants to know, upon what authority did the justice make this claim? On what factual basis did the Court rest this factual judgment?

The answer is none. The Court had no evidence for its assertion. It didn't even purport to cite any. Instead, Justice Kennedy tried to negate the suggestion that there could be such a link by invoking a point of logic: all the money does is to buy campaign advertisement; a campaign "presupposes that the [voters] have the ultimate influence over elected officials." That logical fact of "ultimate influence," Kennedy argued, demonstrates the social-psychological fact that "the electorate [will not] lose faith in our democracy."

I've already addressed the logical gap in this argument in chapter 10: even if the money simply buys political speech, if procuring it or inspiring it to be spent requires distortion in the work of government, that distortion is reason enough to be cynical about the government.

Consider now the psychological gap in Kennedy's argument: Attitudes don't follow logic alone. Or, at least in this case, they need not follow from the very narrow chain of reasoning highlighted by the Court. It is perfectly plausible that an individual would look at our current system and lose faith in that system, even if the system "presupposes that the voters have the ultimate influence."

The point bears emphasis. Imagine the following political system: Every citizen gets to cast a vote to determine which candidate for Congress gets to be a member of Congress. But the Politburo or Exxon or George Soros or Glenn Beck (you pick) gets to decide who will be the candidates for Congress. No doubt, the voters in this system "have the ultimate influence" over which candidates get selected. But the voters in this system have no influence over who the candidates will be.

No one would say that this system was a democracy just because voters had "the ultimate influence." For a democracy, as we understand the term today, must ensure not only an equal vote at the time of election, but also that no improper or illegitimate or undemocratic influence sets up who will be the candidates that the voters "have the ultimate influence over." We all recognize the illegitimacy today of a poll tax. But what about a politicking tax, a tax that a candidate must pay as a condition of being a candidate. Why is it wrong to filter *voters* on the basis of who can pay and who cannot, but not wrong to filter *candidates* on the basis of who can pay and who cannot?

The citizens of this republic are perfectly entitled to have lost faith in this democracy. Justice Kennedy's lecture in logic to justify this faith-destroying economy of influence fails as a matter of logic, and a measure of reality.

If Congress has the power to restrict speech to limit quid pro quo corruption, and the reasonable appearance of quid pro quo corruption, it ought, in principle at least, to have the power to restrict speech to limit dependence corruption as well.

If quid pro quo corruption is regulable because we presume such bribes distract legislators from their proper focus, on legislation that serves the public interest, then dependence corruption raises the same concern, this time at the level of the legislature.

If Congress can regulate to keep individual legislators from making decisions that are dependent upon venal rather than public interests, it ought to be free to regulate to keep the legislature as a whole from making decisions based on improper dependencies.

If it can act to ensure that individual legislators don't act, or seem to act, on an obviously improper dependency, it ought to be free to act to ensure that the legislature itself not act, or seem to act, on a different, but equally improper, dependency. Here is the place where logic ought to matter. And here, the logic justifying the one speech restriction justifies the other.

Again, in principle. My claim is not that a law restricting speech to protect against dependence corruption is necessarily valid, or even a good idea. As with any speech regulation, the first question is whether there are other, less restrictive means of achieving the same legislative end. So if Congress could avoid dependence corruption by, say, funding elections publicly, that alternative would weaken any ability to justify speech restrictions to the same end. The objective should always be to achieve the legitimate objectives of the nation without restricting speech. My point is simply that the legitimate objectives should plainly include what the Framers thought they had achieved: congressional independence by eliminating dependence corruption.

We know enough to state with confidence what most Americans have felt in their guts for a very long time: the people can fairly believe that the core institution of this democracy, Congress, is corrupt. Not in the old-fashioned way. There aren't safes on Capitol Hill filled with bags of cash. It is instead corrupt in a new and more virulent way. Zephyr Teachout jokes, "More bribery, less corruption." There's a deep insight in that clever quip.

We are fair to believe that this corruption blocks Congress from reforms on the Left and on the Right. It instead cements Congress to a debilitating status quo. What wins in the market is too often not what "a free market" would choose, but what a market bent by tariffs and subsidies and endless incumbency protective regulation defaults to. Call that "crony capitalism." Our tax system is an abysmal inefficient mess not because of idiots at the IRS or on the Joint Committee on Taxation, but because crony capitalists pay top dollar to distort the system to their benefit. We don't have real financial reform, because millions have been spent to protect bloated banks. We don't have real health care reform, because the insurance companies and pharmaceutical companies had the power to veto any real change to the insanely inefficient status quo.

Adam Smith never defended crony capitalism. Neither did Friedrich Hayek, or Milton Friedman, or William F. Buckley, or Barry Goldwater, or Ronald Reagan. Franklin Delano Roosevelt almost did, but he was shaken back to his senses by his own Supreme Court. And the best of the principles in the New Deal Democratic Party would have agreed with Smith, Hayek, Friedman, Buckley, Goldwater, and Reagan: a government in which policy gets sold to the highest bidder is not long for greatness.

As I write these words, Gallup's latest "confidence in Congress" poll finds only 11 percent who have confidence in this Congress.[54] *Eleven percent.* At what point do we declare an institution politically bankrupt, especially an institution that depends fundamentally upon public trust and confidence to do its work? When the czar of Russia was ousted by the Bolsheviks, he had the confidence of more than 11 percent of the Russian people. When Louis XVI was deposed by the French Revolution, he had the confidence of more than 11 percent of the French. And when we waged a Revolutionary War against the British Crown, more than 11 percent of the American people had confidence in King George III.

We all must confront this disease if we're to overcome it. Our Congress is politically bankrupt. It struts around as if all were fine, as if it deserved the honor that its auspicious Capitol building inspires. It acts as if nothing were wrong. As if the people didn't notice.

We have lost something profoundly important to the future of this republic. We must find a way to get it back.

# PART IV

# SOLUTIONS

Our Congress has been corrupted; its independence, weakened. This corruption can be seen from two sides: from the side of Congress and from the side of the people.

From the side of Congress, the corruption weakens the focus on the people, as it strengthens the focus on the funders. As Barry Goldwater (R-Ariz.; 1953–1965, 1969–1987) put it:

> Senators and representatives, faced incessantly with the need to raise ever more funds...can scarcely avoid weighing every decision against the question, "How will this affect my fund-raising?" rather than "How will this affect the national interest?"[1]

From the side of the people, the corruption confirms the irrelevancy of democracy. We are taught our place. We find other things to do. We focus on strategies to make us less dependent upon an entity that is distracted from us. We learn not to waste our time, because the message these distracted souls send is, You are not my real concern.

Both sides are bad, but in different ways. Yet we can respond to both in a similar way: by removing the distraction that thwarts their independence.

The changes that would accomplish this are not hard to describe. How we effect them, however, is. The gap in the Framers' original design is obvious enough. The types of reform that would fill that gap are obvious as well. But how one motivates a political response sufficient to fill it is incredibly difficult to imagine. I am not convinced it is possible, even though the next chapters map four different strategies we could try. I have my favorite among these four, but none are probable.

If this change is possible, it will take a series of unprecedented events. We've only ever seen major reform as the reaction to major quid pro quo corruption. But as the corruption I've described here doesn't manifest itself in drama, I am not even sure we could imagine the event that would inspire the change we need.

Instead, this reform will depend upon equally extraordinary, but much less dramatic, events, moments that defy belief as a way to focus attention in a way that might affect beliefs.

The first time I recognized such a moment, I was watching TV. Bill O'Reilly was Jon Stewart's guest on *The Daily Show*. As a liberal, my job is to despise O'Reilly. As a former conservative, I find that job harder than it should be. I get that there's a *Star Wars* metaphor in this somewhere, but the ambiguity made me particularly eager to watch a clear hero, Stewart, tangle with the denouncer of "pinheads," O'Reilly.

Stewart was interviewing O'Reilly about his new book, *Pinheads and Patriots* (2011).[2] Midway through the interview, Stewart asked O'Reilly this:

> When are we going to come together and deal with the corruption at the heart of all these problems?

Astonishingly, O'Reilly agreed:

> They spend so much time raising money and kissing butt, they don't even think about problem solving. But it cuts both ways. The liberal pinheads are just as bad as the right-wing pinheads.

Rarely—okay, almost never—do these two figures agree about something. But here was agreement: upon "the corruption at the heart of all these problems." *Corruption. Heart. All these problems.*

As you've already seen, I couldn't say it better myself.

# CHAPTER 15

# Reforms That Won't Reform

O ur democracy does not have just one problem that one single reform would fix. There is a long list of reforms that we need. I would happily join with others to push for this long list. But there is a beginning to that list, and we need to be clear about what that beginning is. In this chapter, I address two reforms many believe to be sufficient. To be reform enough.

They are not.

## The Incompleteness of Transparency

In 1973, regulators at the EPA were struggling with ways to get Americans to care more about fuel efficiency. In August of that year the agency published a voluntary protocol for calculating fuel economy values, and a label format for manufacturers choosing to display the calculated values. Those protocols have undergone a number of changes. The most recent version requires a label like the one in Figure 15.[1]

The insight here was brilliant. Give consumers an understandable chunk of data and let them use it to regulate their own behavior. Some won't care about the cost of gasoline. They'll ignore the label. But others will care. And on the margin, their care will push more car manufacturers to do the thing the EPA wanted: improve the fuel efficiency of the nation's fleet.

About the same time the EPA was innovating with transparency, good-government sorts were struggling with ways to get Americans to care more about good (as in clean) government. What could

**FIGURE 15**

regulators do to protect democracy from the embarrassment of corruption? How could they mobilize a public to demand cleaner government?

Their answer (amending the Federal Election Campaign Act of 1971) was massive, if largely invalidated (by *Buckley v. Valeo* [1976]). But the one part that survived *Buckley* looked, in principle at least, a lot like the EPA fuel economy standards: disclosure. Federal law now required that all political contributions greater than $200 be recorded and disclosed. More significantly, the information disclosed would include whom someone worked for, making it possible to aggregate contributions on the basis not just of zip codes, but of industry codes and corporations.

So here's the product of that bit of sunlight, for contributions to Democratic congressman Mike Capuano, a local hero representing Cambridge, Massachusetts. To spare a forest, I've simply aggregated the contributions by the firm the contributors worked for.[2]

| ORGANIZATION | PAC ($) | CITIZENS ($) | TOTAL ($) |
|---|---|---|---|
| Triumvirate Environmental | 0 | 44,650 | 44,650 |
| Telecommunications Insight Group | 0 | 40,780 | 40,780 |
| Machinists/Aerospace Workers' Union | 30,000 | 0 | 30,000 |
| Genzyme Corp. | 7,500 | 15,100 | 22,600 |
| Feeley & Driscoll | 0 | 20,700 | 20,700 |
| Eli Lilly & Co. | 16,000 | 2,000 | 18,000 |
| FMR Corp. | 10,000 | 8,750 | 18,750 |
| Liberty Mutual Insurance | 10,000 | 5,250 | 15,250 |
| Raytheon Co. | 10,000 | 4,950 | 14,950 |
| Citigroup Inc. | 0 | 14,500 | 14,500 |
| Science Research Laboratory Inc. | 0 | 14,450 | 14,450 |
| Mintz, Levin et al. | 0 | 13,600 | 13,600 |
| Wilmerhale LLP | 0 | 12,800 | 12,800 |
| Intl Brotherhood of Electrical Workers | 12,500 | 0 | 12,500 |
| UNITE HERE | 12,000 | 0 | 12,000 |
| Government Insight Group | 0 | 12,000 | 12,000 |
| Goulston & Storrs | 0 | 11,650 | 11,650 |
| New York Life Insurance | 11,000 | 0 | 11,000 |
| Somerville | 0 | 10,950 | 10,950 |
| Suffolk Construction | 0 | 10,350 | 10,350 |
| United Food & Commercial Workers' Union | 10,000 | 0 | 10,000 |
| National Education Assn. | 9,000 | 1,450 | 10,450 |
| American Assn. for Justice | 10,000 | 0 | 10,000 |
| Icon Architecture Inc. | 0 | 10,000 | 10,000 |
| National Assn. of Realtors | 10,000 | 0 | 10,000 |
| United Transportation Union | 10,000 | 0 | 10,000 |
| Service Employees International Union | 10,000 | 0 | 10,000 |
| American Dental Assn. | 13,500 | 0 | 13,500 |
| Interpublic Group | 0 | 15,750 | 15,750 |
| ACS Development | 0 | 9,800 | 9,800 |

*continued*

| ORGANIZATION | PAC ($) | CITIZENS ($) | TOTAL ($) |
|---|---|---|---|
| Forest City Enterprises | 5,000 | 4,800 | 9,800 |
| Nixon Peabody LLP | 1,000 | 8,750 | 9,750 |
| Roberts, Raheb & Gradler | 0 | 9,600 | 9,600 |
| IBE Trade | 0 | 9,600 | 9,600 |
| Sager Foundation | 0 | 9,600 | 9,600 |
| Merck KGaA | 9,500 | 0 | 9,500 |
| National Treasury Employees' Union | 10,500 | 0 | 10,500 |
| Honeywell International | 9,500 | 0 | 9,500 |
| Harvard University | 0 | 9,300 | 9,300 |
| DLA Piper | 3,000 | 6,250 | 9,250 |
| Barletta Construction | 0 | 9,200 | 9,200 |
| Camb Health Alliance | 0 | 11,700 | 11,700 |
| J. J. Vaccaro | 0 | 9,200 | 9,200 |
| Federal Realty Investment Trust | 0 | 8,900 | 8,900 |
| Cetrulo & Capone | 0 | 8,900 | 8,900 |
| Dimeo Construction | 0 | 8,700 | 8,700 |
| Airline Pilots' Assn. | 9,500 | 0 | 9,500 |
| American Hospital Assn. | 7,500 | 1,000 | 8,500 |
| Massachusetts Mutual Life Insurance | 10,000 | 0 | 10,000 |
| Palmetto Group | 0 | 8,000 | 8,000 |
| O'Neill, Athy & Casey | 0 | 10,750 | 10,750 |
| Robinson & Cole | 1,500 | 6,150 | 7,650 |
| Amalgamated Transit Union | 7,500 | 0 | 7,500 |
| Brotherhood of Locomotive Engineers | 7,500 | 0 | 7,500 |
| Amgen Inc. | 5,000 | 2,500 | 7,500 |
| American College of Emergency Physicians | 7,500 | 0 | 7,500 |
| American College of Surgeons | 7,500 | 0 | 7,500 |
| Carpenters & Joiners Union | 7,500 | 0 | 7,500 |
| Brown Brothers Harriman & Co. | 0 | 7,400 | 7,400 |
| Alternate Concepts Inc. | 0 | 7,400 | 7,400 |
| Edwards, Angell et al. | 2,400 | 4,900 | 7,300 |

*continued*

| ORGANIZATION | PAC ($) | CITIZENS ($) | TOTAL ($) |
|---|---|---|---|
| Scansoft Inc. | 0 | 7,200 | 7,200 |
| Commonwealth of Massachusetts | 0 | 7,060 | 7,060 |
| International Assn. of Fire Fighters | 7,000 | 0 | 7,000 |
| Global Companies | 0 | 7,000 | 7,000 |
| National Air Traffic Controllers' Assn. | 7,000 | 0 | 7,000 |
| Sheet Metal Workers' Union | 12,000 | 0 | 12,000 |
| Textron Inc. | 7,000 | 0 | 7,000 |
| Beal Co. | 0 | 5,800 | 5,800 |
| Manulife Financial | 6,500 | 250 | 6,750 |
| Ads Ventures | 0 | 6,650 | 6,650 |
| Partners Healthcare | 0 | 15,400 | 15,400 |
| Rasky/Baerlein Group | 0 | 6,550 | 6,550 |
| Haleakala National Bank | 0 | 6,100 | 6,100 |
| Endo Pharmaceuticals | 6,000 | 0 | 6,000 |
| Metlife Inc. | 6,000 | 0 | 6,000 |
| RMD | 0 | 6,000 | 6,000 |
| Roche Holdings | 6,000 | 0 | 6,000 |
| National Assn. of Home Builders | 6,000 | 0 | 6,000 |
| Nat'l Assn./Insurance & Financial Advisors | 6,000 | 0 | 6,000 |
| Marty Meehan for Congress Cmte. | 6,000 | 0 | 6,000 |
| Boeing Co. | 6,000 | 0 | 6,000 |
| Zipcar Inc. | 0 | 5,800 | 5,800 |
| BBH & Co. | 0 | 5,800 | 5,800 |
| Goodwin Procter LLP | 0 | 5,900 | 5,900 |
| Comcast Corp. | 1,000 | 5,000 | 6,000 |
| Century Bank | 0 | 5,300 | 5,300 |
| Trinity Financial | 0 | 5,300 | 5,300 |
| CWC Builders | 0 | 5,300 | 5,300 |
| New England Development | 0 | 5,300 | 5,300 |
| Winn Development | 0 | 5,300 | 5,300 |
| Boston University | 0 | 5,900 | 5,900 |

*continued*

| ORGANIZATION | PAC ($) | CITIZENS ($) | TOTAL ($) |
|---|---|---|---|
| AECOM Technology Corp. | 1,000 | 4,200 | 5,200 |
| Kearney, Donovan & McGee | 0 | 5,150 | 5,150 |
| Credit Union National Assn. | 5,000 | 0 | 5,000 |
| Bart's Bridge PAC | 5,000 | 0 | 5,000 |
| American Optometric Assn. | 5,000 | 0 | 5,000 |
| KPMG LLP | 5,000 | 0 | 5,000 |
| American College of Cardiology | 5,000 | 0 | 5,000 |
| American Assn. of Orthopaedic Surgeons | 5,000 | 0 | 5,000 |
| BRIDGE PAC | 5,000 | 0 | 5,000 |
| National Rural Letter Carriers' Assn. | 5,000 | 0 | 5,000 |
| Ocean State PAC | 5,000 | 0 | 5,000 |
| Maloney Properties | 0 | 5,000 | 5,000 |
| Marine Engineers Beneficial Assn. | 5,000 | 0 | 5,000 |
| American Academy of Ophthalmology | 5,000 | 0 | 5,000 |
| American Council of Life Insurers | 3,000 | 2,000 | 5,000 |
| Biogen Idec | 5,000 | 0 | 5,000 |
| Seafarers International Union | 5,000 | 0 | 5,000 |
| Teamsters' Union | 5,000 | 550 | 5,500 |
| American Federation of Teachers | 5,000 | 0 | 5,000 |
| Penguin PAC | 5,000 | 0 | 5,000 |
| Operating Engineers' Union | 10,000 | 0 | 10,000 |
| Silk PAC | 5,000 | 0 | 5,000 |
| Ironworkers' Union | 5,000 | 0 | 5,000 |
| Laborers' Union | 5,000 | 0 | 5,000 |
| USA Farm Worker PAC | 5,000 | 0 | 5,000 |
| National Assn. of Letter Carriers | 5,000 | 0 | 5,000 |
| National Beer Wholesalers' Assn. | 5,000 | 0 | 5,000 |
| Donoghue, Barrett & Singal | 0 | 5,000 | 5,000 |
| Synergy PAC | 5,000 | 0 | 5,000 |
| United Parcel Service | 5,000 | 0 | 5,000 |

What does this list say?

Many people experience this sort of question the way they'd experience the formalities of an eighteenth-century ball: eager to avoid embarrassment, because they believe there must be insight or wisdom here. But put your humility aside for a second: What are these data telling us? We see contributions from employees of UPS. But we also see contributions from the Teamsters. We can say unions support the congressman. But we can also wonder why the lawyers do. The sheer volume seems to scream, "There's something here to see!" But the more we look, the less we understand. The more we study, the more questions get raised.

There's a fundamental difference between the EPA sticker and the product of the FEC: the one conveys information in a usable manner; the other conveys facts that are often likely to confuse. The one helps us make decisions; the other leaves us more uncertain. The one says something; the other cannot. In an economy in which members of Congress must raise millions to keep their jobs, a perfect record of those contributions tells us both too little and too much. Too much because we're as likely to jump from some stray fact to a conclusion it can't support ("He took money from the banks; he must be bought by the banks"). Too little because if the real action is in the relationship between the funders and the lobbyists, then the mere fact of a contribution doesn't reveal that real action. A donation of $2,500 given by an executive on his own, outside of a relationship with a lobbyist, means something completely different from $2,500 given by an executive as part of a campaign directed by a lobbyist to secure support for a congressman just as he's considering what to do about a particular bill.

This incompleteness doesn't mean that transparency rules should be abolished. Of course they should not. Having a record of contributions is critically important to avoiding more grotesque forms of corruption. And no doubt, given the astonishing drop in disclosure by "independent" entities participating in political campaigns, Congress should certainly work quickly to close the disclosure gap. (In 2004, 97.9 percent of groups making electioneering communications disclosed their donors; in 2010, 34 percent did.)[3]

But a detailed record of contributions in a system that depends fundamentally upon an endless stream of contributions will not on its own produce the reform we need. It will not secure congressional independence.

For, perversely, the system simply normalizes dependence rather than enabling independence. There's no shame in the dance. There's no embarrassment from being on the list. There is instead an endless stream of "gotcha" journalism linking a decision to a contributor, with almost no integrity on either side. That "gotcha" in turn feeds the already profound cynicism that Americans have. Like snippets of flirtation between a significant other and someone else, they fuel emotion, not understanding. Passion, not truth.

And then there's another, more fundamental problem with relying upon transparency alone: transparency assumes that the influence in the system comes with the gift. That if you want to know how much Company X influenced Congressman Y, you need only look at the contributions of X to Y (by employees of X, or through independent expenditures of X to support Y).

But as economists Marcos Chamon and Ethan Kaplan argued in a paper titled "The Iceberg Theory of Campaign Contributions," the influence from campaign contributions may well be independent of the amount actually spent. Instead, the influence on any particular candidate, they maintain, could also depend on the credible threat of expenditures to benefit the candidate's opponent.[4]

The effect on the incentives of a candidate, for example, of a $10,000 contribution to the candidate could be the equivalent to the effect on incentives from a $2,000 contribution to that same candidate, if the $2,000 contribution were bundled with a credible threat to contribute $8,000 to the candidate's opponent. The threat creates its own incentive. The more credible the threat, the greater the incentive.

Threats, however, are not reported on any campaign disclosure form. In the example just given, the $2,000 contribution would be reported; the $8,000 threat would not. The $2,000 is thus the visible tip of the iceberg, while the $8,000 is the bulk, hidden from the public's view.

This dynamic was confirmed to me by former senator Larry Pressler (R-S.D.). "By pouring money into the opponent's coffers," Pressler explained, "it is a signal that there could be more." For example,

> National Public Radio has a lot of financial supporters—very major wealthy people. I was also a supporter, but I thought they needed to reform some of their internal things. But whenever I would try to do something about that, all of a sudden contributions would show up in my potential opponent's campaign. NPR is a very powerful organization. They don't give money themselves, but they have a lot of very wealthy supporters. And somehow, miraculously, that money shows up. It is a clear signal, and the message is received.[5]

Chamon and Kaplan wrote in the pre–*Citizens United* world, where the maximum "corporate contribution" through a corporate PAC was $5,000 per cycle. The significance of their insight in a post–*Citizens United* world, however, is much greater. For the power of a potential threat is limited by the maximum contribution allowed. After *Citizens United*, limits on independent expenditures are removed. And while the threats must still be independent, there are many ways that corporate wealth can be translated into significant political influence that would never be revealed by any system of disclosure alone. Indeed, as a poll of Hill staffers in 2011 reveals, this has been precisely the effect.[6]

Imagine again, for example, that Exxon let it be known that it was willing to spend up to $1 million in any congressional district to elect representatives who were skeptical of global warming science. Or imagine that Google let it be known that it would run up to $1 million in online ads to defeat global warming skeptics. Neither position would necessarily be "coordination" sufficient to render the expenditures non-independent: both announcements could be made well before candidates were even chosen by parties. Yet, if the iceberg theory is correct, in neither case would all the money have to be spent in order to have its intended effect. Moogle might actually spend only $1,000, and it might report that amount. But its influence would be far beyond what it reported, so long as its threat was credible.

The point is that transparency is being asked to carry too much weight in this reform fight. It is being depended upon to do too much. Not only does the "information" revealed not necessarily inform, but the most important influences in the system would not necessarily be revealed. No doubt, an efficient system will show us lots that will concern many. In this, it functions as the Webcam on the Deepwater Horizon functioned: displaying in graphic detail the sludge being dumped into the Gulf. But as with the Deepwater Horizon, the solution is not a better camera. It is a regime that stops the sludge.

That's the commitment those dedicated to transparency must make. If the problem we face is the inevitable distortion that dependence corruption produces, we need to focus on ways to end that corruption. Seeing it more clearly, as the brilliant souls at the Sunlight Foundation and MapLight make possible, is necessary. Their work has certainly motivated many (including me), and will certainly motivate more. But if seeing it is all that we do, then it is just as likely to drive many more of us over the brink of cynicism. "You've shown me clearly now what I already believed. Now I'm even more certain that there's no reason for me to be here." But as San Francisco supervisor Harvey Milk said, "You gotta give 'em hope." A perpetual stream of political muck made transparent is not hope.

## The (Practical) Ineffectiveness of Anonymity

The incompleteness of transparency has led some to suggest its opposite: anonymity. If the core problem with money in a democracy is the risk of corruption, whether in the crude quid pro quo form or the more subtle dance of a gift economy, then maybe the simplest way to solve that corruption is to make all donations anonymous *to the members as well as the public.* Obviously, laws banning quid pro quo corruption need to remain, but if we could make it impossible (or really, really difficult) for a member to know who gave his campaign what, we would make it impossible for the member to give favors in exchange for the gifts that have been given.

Put aside for a moment the obvious question—how could you ever really make a donation anonymous to the recipient?—so that the contours of this ingenious solution are clear. If the problem with money in politics is that the money will bend policies, this requires that the politicians know something about who their money comes from. Add anonymity, and that essential condition gets removed. Remove that essential condition, and it just could not be true that "money buys results."

The inspiration for this idea comes from the nineteenth century's solution to a similar problem with money in politics: vote buying. Until the late nineteenth century, voting was public: a voter would openly and publicly cast his (and it was just his) ballot. That publicity was thought to be an essential part of the integrity of the vote. It may have been, but publicity was also an essential element to vote buying, a very common practice in nineteenth-century democracy.[7] Because I can see exactly how you vote, you can easily sell your vote to me.

Enter anonymous voting, which made it impossible legally for me to be confident about how you, the voter, votes. No doubt, you could promise me that you'll vote as I wish, but you could just as well promise the same thing to the other side. The price I'd be willing to pay, then, for your vote is much, much less (discounted for the possibility that you've also sold your vote to the other side). And by lowering the price, this ingenious reform lowered the significance of vote buying substantially.

That's the same intuition behind anonymity in contributions. Sure, I could tell you that I contributed $10,000 to your campaign.

But if you couldn't be sure, there wouldn't be much reason for you to respond. My incentive to give would thus be weakened substantially—at least if the motive of my gift were to buy a particular result. That decline in incentives would thus weaken the market for buying policy.

Professors Bruce Ackerman and Ian Ayres have done the most to describe this system, and in describing it, they have developed an elaborate system for protecting this anonymity.[8] The two critical elements are, first, an anonymous donation booth, which takes in contributions and then divides those contributions into random amounts, which it then passes along to the candidates; and two, the right to revoke any contribution once made. It is this second element that does most of the work: for even if you watched me make the contribution to your campaign, I would still have an opportunity to revoke that contribution the next day. Once again, you're free to trust me when I say I haven't revoked it. But just as with vote buying, the need for trust will severely weaken the market.

The Ackerman/Ayres solution is ingenious. Indeed, its biggest danger is that it might work too well: without substantial public funding, it could severely limit the amount of money contributed to campaigns, at least if the contributions were for the purpose of influencing legislation. (This was the result from one well-known example with anonymous contributions to judicial elections in Florida.[9] Once contributions were made anonymous, contributions dried up.)

My concern with this solution is not whether it would actually work. It would, in my view, for the architecture is genius. My concern instead is about whether it would *be perceived to work*. For, if the core problem that dependence corruption creates is the perception among voters that "money buys results in Congress," then fighting that perception requires a system that the voters would understand, and believe. Yet we live in a nation where people don't even believe that voting machines are counting ballots accurately. To imagine the public understanding the brilliance of the anonymous donation booth, and believing that, in fact, there is no way for large contributors to prove they've made (and haven't revoked) a contribution, is, I believe, unrealistic. The mechanics are too complex; the sources of suspicion are too great. Even serious scholars criticizing the plan haven't grasped its basic mechanics. To expect more from the average American is to expect too much.

That's not to say it shouldn't be tried; it should. It's not to say we shouldn't see whether the mechanism could be clearly explained; we should. But the change here is huge, and the gamble even bigger.

There is a smaller change that we could make with a larger potential payoff.

# CHAPTER 16

# *Reforms That Would Reform*

If the independence of our Congress has been weakened—if the intended dependence "upon the People alone" has been compromised by a competing dependence upon the funders—the solution to this corruption is to end the compromise. The simplest way to do that would be to make "the funders" "the People." A reform, in other words, that reduces the gap between "the funders" and "the People," so that none could believe that the actual influence of the one was substantially different from the intended influence of the other. *Substantially* different. No system is going to eliminate the gap completely. But as Robert Brooks commented more than a century ago, "under a system of small contributions from a large number of people, it would matter little even if some of the contributors were not wholly disinterested."[1]

Over the past fifteen years, three states have experimented with reforms that come very close to this idea. Arizona, Maine, and Connecticut have all adopted reforms for their own state government that permits members of the legislature (and of some statewide offices) to fund their campaigns through small-dollar contributions only. Though the details of these programs are different, the basic structure of all three is the same: candidates qualify by raising a large number of small contributions; once qualified, the candidates receive funding from the state to run their campaigns.

Arizona, Maine, and Connecticut are very different states—politically, demographically, and culturally. But despite their differences, these "clean money," or "voter-owned," elections have had important success. Candidates opting into these public funding systems spend more time talking to voters than to funders. They represent a broader range of citizens than the candidates who run with private money alone. And they have succeeded in increasing the competitiveness of state legislative elections, making incumbents if not more vulnerable, then at least more attentive.[2]

If America were to adopt any one of these programs to fund elections in Congress, it would be an enormous improvement over the current system. But I believe we can do even better. These bold and important experiments have taught us something about what works, and what doesn't. They have also made salient the sources of key opposition.[3]

The principal objections to these state programs are two. First, any system that selected a fixed funding amount per legislative district would be attacked as either arbitrary, too generous, or not generous enough. I share the anxiety of many with any system in which bureaucrats pick the amount of money available to candidates within an election. Elections should be free of that potential for abuse.

Second, some are troubled with the idea of "their money" being used to fund political speech that they oppose. This is not a concern of mine, but I do respect the concern and understand it.

We can solve both of these problems within the architecture of small-dollar-funded elections. In the balance of this chapter, I describe how.[4]

## The Grant and Franklin Project

Assume with me that every voter in America produces at least fifty dollars in revenue to the U.S. Treasury. Ninety percent of Americans pay some tax revenue to the federal government.[5] And we can assume the percentage of voters who pay some tax revenue is even higher.

Given this assumption, consider the outline of a system to finance political campaigns that would not produce the cynicism that stains the current system:

*First*, we convert the first fifty dollars that each of us contributes to the federal Treasury into a voucher. Call it a "democracy voucher." Each voter is free to allocate his or her democracy voucher as he or she wishes. Maybe fifty dollars to a single candidate. Maybe twenty-five dollars each to two candidates. Maybe ten dollars each to five candidates.[6] The only requirement is that the candidate receiving the voucher must opt into the system.

*Second*, if the democracy voucher is not allocated, then it goes to the political party to which the voter is registered. If the voter is not registered to a party, then it goes to supplement funding for the infrastructure of democracy: voting systems, voter education, and the Grant and Franklin Project.

*Third*, voters are free under this system to supplement the voucher contribution with their own contribution—up to $100 per candidate. One hundred dollars is nothing...to about 2 percent of the American public. It is a great deal of money to everyone else.

*Fourth*, and finally, any viable candidate for Congress could receive these contributions if he or she agreed to one important condition: that the only money that candidate accepted to fund his or her campaign would be democracy vouchers and contributions from individuals of up to $100 per citizen. That means no PAC money and no direct contributions from political parties. The only external funds such a campaign would receive would be democracy vouchers plus, at most, one Ben Franklin per citizen.

There are a bunch of ways to tinker with the elements to this design. We could (and, in my view, should) increase the voucher amount and add the presidency. I've excluded that office for now, but no reform would be complete without it. We could also add the ability of political parties to contribute. I'd be for that—political parties are critically important stabilizing and energizing tools for democracy—but I've left them out for the moment (partly because they add an important complication: How would you create a voluntary limit to the amount each individual gave to a political party and avoid that being channeled improperly to the candidates?). Likewise, we could limit the voucher contributions to candidates within your own district. (Wisconsin did this at the end of the nineteenth century.)[7] That, too, may make more sense of the project to reinforce constituent dependencies. But this, too, I've left out for the moment, again for the purposes of keeping the idea simple and clear.

This design has a number of essential features:

First, it is voluntary. Candidates opt into the system, just as presidential candidates have (or have not) opted into the existing system to fund presidential campaigns. By making it voluntary, we avoid an almost certain invalidation by the Supreme Court on the basis of *Buckley*. Contribution limits, the Court said, are fine, so long as the limit is related to a reasonable perception of quid pro quo corruption.[8] But $100 would be too low a limit for this Court.

Second, unlike practically every other plan to fund political campaigns publicly, this plan does not allow "your money" to be used to support speech you don't believe in. The money that gets allocated here is money tied to you. It's the "first fifty dollars" you send to the federal Treasury. Whether through income tax, or gas tax, or cigarette tax—it doesn't matter. You caused the money to enter the federal system. You get to allocate it to whomever you wish. Others will allocate their money differently. But no one will be able to complain that his money is being used to pay for political speech he doesn't believe in.

Third, unlike most systems to fund publicly political campaigns, this system permits contributions in addition to the public funds. If the Obama campaign taught us anything, it taught us the importance of allowing citizens to have skin in the game. If you choose to give a candidate $100 rather than spending that money on designer jeans, that says something about your commitment to the candidate. It binds you to his campaign much more strongly than if you simply said you supported him, or allocated your (otherwise unusable) democracy vouchers to him. This is the brilliant insight in Spencer Overton's analysis of the "Participation Interest" in campaigns.[9] Give something and you get committed.

Fourth, unlike most systems to fund political campaigns publicly, this one would inject an enormous amount of money into the system. If every registered voter participated in this system, it would produce at least $6 billion in campaign funds per election cycle ($3 billion a year). Some portion of that would flow to candidates. The balance would flow to political parties. In 2010 the total amount raised and spent in all congressional elections was $1.8 billion. The total amount contributed to the two major political parties was $2.8 billion. Compare: Within a reasonable range, we can be confident the new system has a shot at being competitive with the existing one. As a candidate, you would not have to starve to be good. Or, more controversially, you could be good and still do well.

Now, put aside a million questions for the moment and focus on the single most important thing this system would buy: if a substantial number of candidates opted into this system, then _no one could believe that money was buying results._

Subject to one critical assumption, which I will return to shortly, if enough representatives were elected under this system, then whenever Congress did something stupid, it would be because there were more Democrats than Republicans, or more Republicans than Democrats, or more pinheads than patriots. But whatever the reason, it would not be because of the money. No sane soul could believe that special-interest money was driving a result. Every sane soul could instead believe that the mistakes were democratic mistakes, correctable through a democratic response. This system builds a treadmill that gets politicians to worry first about what we, the voters, want. The politician gets on this treadmill the first moment she decides to run for office. From that moment until the election, she is collecting the votes (as in campaign funds) that she needs to wage an effective campaign. And on Election Day, she collects, or so she hopes, the votes she needs to win. Her primary focus is on the source of those votes: the people of her district, not the special interests.

This reform is the key to everything else that follows. Regardless of what you believe America's most important problems are, you need to see this as the first problem that needs to be solved.

But, you say, $6 billion? That's a lot of money, isn't it? Can we afford it?

It is. For you and for me. For the republic, it certainly isn't, for two reasons.

First, if it has its intended effect, this reform will make it possible for us to spend many times less than $3 billion a year. Take just one example: In 2009, the Cato Institute estimated that the U.S. Congress spent $90 billion on "corporate welfare." Corporate welfare, as they defined it, was "subsidies and regulatory protections that lawmakers confer on certain businesses and industries."[10]

We have corporate welfare largely because we have privately funded elections. The "welfare" is the payback, indirect and legal, but payback nonetheless.

So let's imagine we could eliminate just 5 percent of that payback, by eliminating the need to pay anyone anything, since elections are no longer funded by large private contributions. Five percent of $90 billion a year is $9 billion an election cycle—more than the $6 billion needed to fund the system every election cycle. Here is an investment that would easily repay itself.

Second, $3 billion a year isn't a lot if it gives us even just a 20 percent chance of fixing our democracy.

For just think about how much we spend every year to "support democracy" around the world. Some of that spending (a small part) is direct. Much more of that spending (a huge part) is indirect. We've waged the longest war in American history to "make democracy possible in Iraq." The total cost of that war? More than $750 billion. And that's just the money. Put aside the 4,500 patriots who have given their lives to that theory of democracy building.

If we're willing to spend $750 billion (so far) to make democracy in Iraq possible, we should be willing to spend one-twenty-fifth of that to make democracy in America work.

Will it work? We don't see lots of evidence that trust in government increases when politicians adopt campaign finance reform. Why would this be any different?

It is fair to be skeptical about any reform working here. As Nate Persily and Kelli Lammie have demonstrated,[11] we have little actual evidence to support the idea that cleaning up elections increases the public's trust.

It is also fair to be skeptical about whether Persily and Lammie's results generalize to every type of campaign finance reform. After all, none of the changes in the system for financing federal elections have changed the underlying (and corrupting) economy of influence. Indeed, the most prominent (transparency) has just made it more prominent. It is therefore not surprising that trust doesn't rise when these changes are made. These changes are different, however, from the changes of the Grant and Franklin Project. It alone would change the economy of influence of elections and give the people a reason to think differently.

But what's to stop the bundling of the democracy vouchers just as contributions are bundled today? And if they were bundled, wouldn't we still have the same problem we have today?

In a word, no. The problem with American democracy is not that people try to aggregate their influence. It is that the influence they aggregate is so wildly disproportionate to the influence the system intended—votes. If a bundler succeeded in pulling together one hundred thousand souls to contribute their vouchers to a particular candidate, no doubt that bundler would have some important influence. But her influence is a better proxy for "the People" she has inspired than is the proxy of the bundler who today collects $5 million from a handful of wealthy, connected souls. *Better*, not perfect. But my bet is that it would be better enough.

Which leads to the final important qualification, or what I called before the "one critical assumption":

The history of campaign finance reform is water running down a hill. No matter how you reform, the water seems to find its way around the obstacle. Block large contributions from individuals, and they become soft contributions to parties. Block soft contributions to parties, they become bundled contributions coordinated through lobbyists. And on it goes. In each case, a brilliant reform has been defeated by some new clever technique to ensure that money continues to have more salience in our political system than votes.[12] As Robert Brooks wrote a century ago, "it must be admitted that the ablest corruptionists sometimes show skill little short of genius in devising new schemes to avoid the pitfalls of existing law."[13]

It would be hubris to pretend that there is any single and final solution to this problem. I don't make that assumption here. I do believe, however, that the architecture of this solution is better than the architecture of most of the solutions offered during the past forty years, all of which depended upon either silencing, limiting, or dampening someone's desire to speak.

This one doesn't. The Grant and Franklin Project doesn't forbid anyone from running their own ads. It doesn't force any candidate into the system. It doesn't stop the likes of Citizens United, Inc., from selling videos attacking anyone. This is not a solution that says *speak less*. It is a solution that would, if adopted, allow people to *speak more*.

Yet in that may lie its Achilles' heel. For, as I've already remarked, the effect of the Supreme Court's decision in *Citizens United* has been to encourage a massive growth in "independent" political expenditures—with "independent" in quotes because whether they are indeed independent or, just as important, whether they are perceived to be independent is an open question. And indeed, even with 100 percent participation in the Grant and Franklin Project, it is conceivable that these "independent" expenditures would simply evolve into another kind of dependency. Rather than obsessively focusing on how to raise campaign funds, the candidates in this new system would be obsessively focusing on how to ensure the right kind of "independent expenditures" by very powerful special interests. The candidates would smile and tell us all that their campaigns were funded by clean contributions only. And that would be true. But all the dirty work in the campaigns would be done by "Americans for a United Future" or "Veterans Against Feline Abuse" or "United We Stand Forever" or whatever. On the margin, these independent campaigns would determine who won and who lost. And as the margin is the game, this world enabled by *Citizens United* could well defeat all of the independence that the Grant and Franklin Project was meant to buy.

In my view, Congress should have the power to regulate against this sort of dependency as well. But if the Supreme Court sticks to its (indefensibly narrow) view of what corruption is, then even if we win this battle for funding reform, we could still lose the larger war. For the numbers here are quite staggering: Remember the $6 billion? If the Fortune 400 spent just 1 percent of their 2008 profits on "independent" political expenditures, that would be more than $6 billion. Or, put differently, just 1 percent of corporate profits could defeat the independence this system was meant to buy.

Even if this is true, however, it doesn't change the essential first step in a strategy for reform. It may well be that we need constitutional reform to ensure congressional independence. But if we do, we need first to build a constituency for congressional independence. Right now we have no such constituency. Right now there are few clean-money candidates in Congress. And until the time that a majority of our candidates are clean, we won't have the political strength to make that constitutional change.

So, again: I am not promising that ending the addiction brings with it an end to all the troubles that confront this democracy. I am only insisting that ending the addiction is the first step to addressing those troubles.

There are details galore to work out. There are comparisons to make and lessons to learn. But, for now, my aim is to talk strategy. If you believe, as I do, that our Congress is corrupted; if you believe that corruption can be solved only by removing its source; and if you believe that at least some version of a small-dollar campaign system is the essential first step to removing corruption at its source, how could we do it? What steps can we take? What is the strategy that makes this revolution possible?

# CHAPTER 17

# *Strategy 1*

## The Conventional Game

The first steps to a cure could be made by simple statute. One vote in each House of Congress, a signature by a president, and a bill that would radically remake the economy of influence that is D.C. could be passed. No changes to the Constitution would be necessary. No insanely large commitment of funds from the Treasury required. For about the amount of money we spend *every weekend* at the Pentagon, we could create a workable system where "the funders" were "the People."

The House of Representatives came close to passing such a bill in the fall of 2010: the Fair Elections Now Act. That bill would have allowed candidates to opt into a system that limited contributions to $100 per citizen, matched, after the candidate qualified, four to one by the government.

This bill isn't my favorite design. But it is close to the design of the program in Connecticut, Maine, and Arizona, and those states have demonstrated the great value of "clean," or "voter-owned," elections. Even if not perfect, the bill would have been a critically important change. And if we could get so close in the House, maybe we don't need anything really fancy here. Maybe some letters to the editor, and some pressure on congressmen to sign up. If this single bill could really change D.C., why point attention anywhere else?

If I thought there were a chance we could get this bill passed in both Houses of Congress, I'd put all my worrying about the details of the bill aside and push for it.

But there are a number of reasons to be skeptical about this possibility—the first, and most important: Why was it so close to passing in the House?

The answer in part is because it was so certain not to pass in the Senate. There are many who supported the bill who would have thought twice if they actually believed it was going to pass. To be on the side of clean elections is valuable, in some districts at least, with some constituencies. There's no doubt that it pays, at least there, to be seen on the side of reform.

It's another matter entirely, however, to imagine actually living under that system of reform. The one thing every incumbent has done under the current system is win. The one thing no incumbent can be certain of is that he can win under a radically different system. It is very unlikely congressmen are going to want to give this up, voluntarily.

Moreover, as I've already described, the devil they know is not the only thing they would have to give up. The existing system for many members of Congress is just a stepping stone, not to higher political office, but to a lobbying firm. At least some now see their six or eight years in Congress as the apprenticeship for the real job coming later. Not all members of Congress, or even most—but I do think that almost all members are uncertain about what their future will be, and almost all of them are therefore keen to keep their options open.

Likewise, and again, as I've already described, a radical change in the way campaigns get funded would mean an even more radical change in the business of fund-raising. That, in turn, would eliminate many of the cushy write-offs members now get as they flail about trying to raise campaign funds. Many who now support the legislation would think twice about whether to enact it when they recognized its most significant consequence for them would be that they would have to live on the salary of a first-year lawyer in a Wall Street firm.

Finally, let's not forget the elephant in the room. There is a professional class of policy manipulators in this picture. They're called lobbyists. A very large percentage of those lobbyists are going to recognize that if elections were funded by citizens, and not by the funds they channel to candidates, their power, and therefore their wealth, would collapse.

*[handwritten margin note: Ulost like tax Peop.]*

These professional policy manipulators will have an overwhelming interest in stopping this legislation. And while there is only one way to pass a bill, there are a million ways to block it. We can count on these manipulators using every weapon they have to block this bill. Why wouldn't they? Wouldn't you, if you saw that the total value of your industry were about to collapse?

These four reasons all point to a common lesson in the history of warfare: You don't beat the British by lining up in red coats and marching on their lines, as they would on you. You beat them by adopting a strategy they've never met, or never played. The forces that would block this bill work well and effectively on Capitol Hill, and inside the Beltway. That is their home. And if we're going to seize their home, and dismantle it, we need a strategy that they're sure is going to fail.

Yet we need it to win.

# CHAPTER 18

# Strategy 2

## An Unconventional (Primary) Game

We need a bit of peaceful terrorism. No guns. No bombs. No hijacked airplanes. Instead, peaceful, legal action that terrifies the enemy. We know who the enemy is. They live within the Beltway. They depend upon the status quo. We need to give them a reason to flee the status quo that is more compelling than the comfort of things as they are.

The single most terrifying idea for an incumbent is a primary challenge. As I described in chapter 9, the vast majority of seats in Congress are safe seats. Safe seats mean the general election is just a coronation. And so, too, the primary: well-disciplined parties teach young and up-and-coming candidates not to rock the primary boat. Wait your turn, and you'll get a turn. Step out of line, and a thin red or blue line will keep you out.

Peaceful terrorism would disturb this comfortable pattern. It would produce primary challenges. But not by other politicians. Instead, by citizen politicians: candidates who affirmatively state that their purpose is not to become a politician. Their purpose instead is to push an incumbent to do the right thing.

Now, that idea alone won't go far. Local challenges by people who expect to draw 10 percent (if lucky) from an incumbent aren't exactly newsworthy. But an interesting loophole in the Constitution as written does provide a very interesting news hook, and a chance to rally a much larger force.[1]

Here's a quiz: What's required to be elected to the House of

Representatives? You'd think that one requirement is that you be a resident of the district from which you're to be elected. In fact that is not true. All the Constitution requires is that at the time of the election, you "be an Inhabitant of that State in which [you] shall be chosen." That means you could live in San Francisco, but run for Congress in LA. Or run in LA, and in San Francisco. And in Oakland and Sacramento and Eureka.

You get the idea. There's nothing in the Constitution that forbids a single candidate from running in multiple districts at the same time. Of course, she couldn't become the congresswoman from multiple districts. But her candidacy could be waged in multiple districts at the same time, all under a single, clear platform: that she (and the others who are doing the same) will remain in the race so long as the incumbent does not commit publicly to supporting citizen-owned elections.

To make this work, the supercandidate must be a certain kind of soul. She must be a prominent, well-liked leading citizen from the state who is, again, and this is important, *not a politician*. Indeed, the party organizing and supporting these peaceful terrorists must demand that the candidates affirm that they have no intention to run for office again for at least five years, except in this supercandidate role. To be credible, this must be seen as the act of a disinterested citizen whose only objective is to change the system for others. Not the objective of becoming a congressman or other politician. Like a juror called into service for a limited time, these supercandidates would be called into service for a limited time, with a promise to go home.

But if, across key states, this movement could organize a handful of prominent souls to join in this challenge candidacy—businesspeople, scientists, former presidents of universities, even lawyers— then the protest could begin to resonate. In the first round in 2012, in the early primaries, the campaign could target a handful of districts where incumbents had not committed to citizen-owned elections. Those candidates could all leverage their candidacy off of a common and free set of Internet resources. The districts would be selected on the basis of which were most likely to produce a result. Producing a result early on would feed more candidates in more districts later in the primaries. And then once the primaries were over, the campaign could shift to the general election: targeting seats that were not safe, where even a single point could flip the seat from one party to the other.

The advantage of this system is the advantage of all terrorism, good and evil. Incumbents are deeply risk-averse. They are quick to position themselves to avoid a fight. And so if this campaign could launch in a convincing and transparent way, many would shape-shift. They would position themselves in a manner that avoided any potential challenge. Much of this peaceful war could be fought before even a single virtual shot was fired.

The advantage, too, is that this may be the most effective technique against the so far least-engaged party in this debate, the grass-roots Republicans. Citizen-owned elections are an extremely popular idea among both grass-roots Republicans and Democrats. Indeed, in a number of polls I've seen, the idea is more popular among Republicans than among Democrats. That's because, for many Republicans, the idea of special-interest influence is *the corrupting force* in government today. Everything they complain about is tied to that idea.

Beltway Republicans are different of course. The party of Tom DeLay had to make some pretty awful deals with the devil in order to raise the money they needed to win. They've developed a fairly complicated, cognitively dissonant account that justifies selling government to the highest bidder.

Outside the Beltway, citizen Republicans aren't similarly burdened. Citizen Republicans care about the ideals of the party. And those ideals resonate well with the objective of removing the influence of cash in political campaigns. Citizen Republicans identify with those who attack systematic corruption—government that organizes itself to hand out favors to the privileged so as to strengthen its own power. Just such large-scale corruption is precisely the evil that small-government Republicans seek to fight.

Thus, these peaceful terrorist candidates in Republican primaries could help break the partisan logjam that has blocked this reform from moving in Washington. Just a few victories may be enough to move the leadership of the GOP to a more principled position.

Critical to this strategy is that while these campaigns are waged in partisan primaries and, in some cases, as a third party in a general election, the platform for this campaign must stand beyond partisanship. Everyone within this peaceful terrorist conspiracy must sign on to the same basic principles. To leverage the campaign effectively, everyone must point back to the same basic principles. In Republican primaries, the reason these principles matter may be different from the reason in Democratic primaries. But the principles must be the same.

So how many would it take?

Let's pick a round number: Let's say we're looking for three hundred. A hundred for each party in key state primaries. Then a hundred in reserve for the general election.

Those hundred in each party need not enter every race, of course. There are lots of incumbents already credibly committed to key reform on both sides of the aisle. But they would enter every primary where the incumbent was not committed. In some states (small states with committed incumbents), that would mean we would need no candidates. In some states, we would need lots of candidates. But overall we would need a platoon of citizen candidates committed to one election cycle, to stand on a single platform, to restore the possibility of democracy in America.

What are the chances this could work? Let's be wildly optimistic: 5 percent.

So then, what's next?

# CHAPTER 19

# *Strategy 3*

## An Unconventional Presidential Game

In his first press conference after his "shellacking" in the 2010 congressional elections, President Barack Obama said this about his party's defeat: "We were in such a hurry to get things done that we didn't change how things got done. And I think that frustrated people."[1]

Count me as Frustrated Citizen No. 1. I've already explained why "chang[ing] how things got done" was so important to our democracy. I've already described why I believed Obama intended to make that change central to his administration. That he didn't is an enormous failing of his presidency, at least so far.

And the failure is not just for Obama. It's also for us. We are Charlie Brown. Lucy has told us again and again that she is the Lucy of change. Again and again, we have trusted her. Again and again, we have been misled.

At some point, the dissonance begins to register, and Americans no longer even hear the claim. Or they hear it, but they hear it simply to confirm what they are already predisposed to believe: here is yet another politician talking about "change" who cannot be trusted as far as I can throw him.

Obama, I fear, was the last straw. Other candidates in that race, and in campaigns before, had made change an element of their brand. But Obama made it the core. It was what the whole campaign was about: change. A change from Bush. A change in the way Washington works. A change in the way politics is done.

Yet two years into this administration, and the word *change* feels like a bad joke. In critical domains of contested policy—foreign policy and the way we conduct the war, in particular—there has been no change. The role of money in campaigns? Absolutely no change. The way the work of Washington gets done? None.

I don't mean to overstate the criticism. For better (my view) or worse (maybe yours), Obama is not Bush. There is plenty that is radically different today from four years ago, and plenty that is extraordinary about this man. (Think about his speech about race during the 2008 campaign, or his speech to the nation after the Arizona assassinations. Reagan has nothing on this incredible inspiration.)

Yet even if these past two presidents are not the same, it is fair to criticize the current president for not being sufficiently different. His campaign was the classic bait and switch: he attracted us in the primaries with a promise of something different from Hillary Clinton, but he has executed with the same playbook as Hillary Clinton's.

This was a betrayal. It has consequences for more than Barack Obama. It has consequences for the politics that could make real change possible. After Obama, there are only two ways that a reform presidency might work. Each of these is unlikely, though one is actually happening as this book goes to press.

It is hard for this Democrat to accept, but in 2011, the reform party in America is not the Democratic Party. We had that moniker on January 20, 2009. Obama then fumbled it, and the Tea Party picked it up and ran. Earmarks were blocked in the 2011 budget because the Tea Party insisted upon it. There is an Office of Congressional Ethics, the only independent watchdog ensuring that members live up to the ethical rules, because the Tea Party insisted upon it. Whatever else that party does, it has done a great deal with these two changes alone.

As we enter the election of 2012, it is the Tea Party again that has the chance to insist upon a presidential candidate who will push for real change. And as this book goes to press, there is at *never heard of he even did he even run?*

least one candidate who is demanding the kind of change that I
have described: former governor Buddy Roemer (R-La.). Roemer ~~FAIL~~
has focused his campaign on a single issue: the role of money in
politics. He has committed to taking no more than $100 from any-
one. He will take no PAC contributions. He will disclose every contribution regardless of the amount to any organization that wants
to audit. "Free to Lead" is the slogan of his campaign. And his promise is to leverage the mandate he would receive into a demand to
change Congress.

*thus never even heard of him*

In launching his campaign, Roemer embraced four principles
that must guide any legislation designed to restore independence to
Congress. As he described these principles in a lecture at Harvard:

> First, no system for funding campaigns should try to silence
> anyone or any view. This was the kernel of truth in the Court's
> *Citizens United* decision. The fact that it is a corporation that is
> speaking does not by its nature make the speech any less valu-
> able or important to our system of democratic deliberation. We
> need to hear all sides, especially the sides we're least likely to
> agree with.
>
> Second, no system for funding campaigns should force any
> citizen to support political speech that he or she doesn't believe
> in. Once a candidate is elected, of course, his or her salary is
> paid by the government. And I'm sure that all of you have, like
> I, cringed at the words of at least some of those whose salary
> we pay. But there's a fundamental distinction between paying
> the salaries of government officials, and paying for the cam-
> paign of political candidates. Even if government money must
> be used to support such campaigns, we must assure that it is
> not used to advance ideas that are contrary to the taxpayer who
> is funding it.
>
> Third, no bureaucrat in Washington should be in the busi-
> ness of deciding how much any campaign for Congress deserves
> to get. We can't have a system where government decides the
> allowance that challengers to the government will get to wage

their challenge. Instead, it is the people who should decide
how much anyone should get to run his or her campaign.

 And finally, any system must permit—indeed, encourage—
individuals to give at least a small amount of their own money
to support the campaigns that they believe in. If Barack Obama
taught us anything, it was the extraordinary energy and importance that would come from getting millions to commit at least
a small amount. Politics is not passive anymore. The Internet
has made it possible for everyone to have skin in the game.[2]

*Berney Sanders*

These principles are consistent with a number of programs to
fund the independence of Congress. They are consistent with the
Grant and Franklin Project. And if Roemer succeeds in his campaign,
and translates these four principles into law, the fourth American *Far!*
revolution (after 1776, 1800, and 1865) will have been achieved.
Roemer's would be the most important presidency since FDR.

There are, however, two significant doubts that will dog
Roemer's campaign. The first is practical: Can a candidate raise
enough money if he takes only $100 from any citizen? The pundits
notwithstanding, no one knows the answer to that question. No
doubt in 1980 it would have been impossible to fund a national
campaign on such meager resources. But in the Internet era, whole
governments are brought down with less real resources committed. It is perfectly plausible to me that if Roemer becomes credible,
his low-budget campaign could take off, launched not so much by
expensive campaign ads, but by the energy that built Facebook and
Twitter.

Yet in the quintessential catch-22, because most believe you
can't win a campaign with contributions capped at $100, they
won't credit a campaign with contributions capped at $100. The
view "he can't win" makes it likely "he can't win," even if a majority of souls would support him were they convinced he could win!

A different kind of credibility, however, is a second significant
doubt. Not because Roemer lacks credibility on this issue: He

was elected governor of Louisiana on a similar platform. He made reforming Louisiana government his primary task. Instead, the lack of credibility here goes back to Obama: Will America even entertain the promise of yet another presidential candidate that he (or she) is going to "take up the fight," as Obama put it, to fundamentally change the system? Are we Charlie Brown? Or have we finally learned that Lucy will always pull the football away?

It is impossible to answer that question just now. But the very possibility that no candidate could convince the American public that he or she was credibly committed to fundamental change forces us to look further. Is there another way to use the presidential election cycle to leverage fundamental change into our government?

Losing the president as an agent of change is a huge loss. Presidential elections are important to focus America, and not just because the president is the president. But instead, because of the primary system, presidential elections have the chance to overcome a fundamental problem with American politics today: attention span. We were once a nation that listened to multiple-hour-long speeches by our politicians.[3] We're now a nation that can't stomach more than thirty seconds at a time. That change may well signal the decline of American politicians. It may be that most Americans today would be quite happy to listen to Lincoln/Douglas-style debates (which were three hours long, with the opening speaker given sixty minutes, the respondent ninety minutes, and the opening speaker thirty minutes to reply)—but I doubt it. The bigger reason is us: We don't have time or patience for long explanations. It is a tiny fraction of this nation that would spend even an hour listening to a political argument.

Or, more accurately, an hour at any one sitting. For the magic of presidential campaigns is that they spread the messaging over a long period of time. The same point gets repeated—repeatedly. At first it isn't heard. Or if it is heard, it isn't understood. Or if it is understood, it isn't acted upon. But after the ten-millionth repetition, in the context of the tenth or fifteenth primary, finally, the point is understood. In our multitasking way, we've become quite good at picking up a lot in tiny bites over extended periods of time. The presidential primary system was made for just such an attention span. Presidential primaries were made for Twitter.

Thus if we're trying to imagine how to get the American democracy to demand the change necessary to remove this fundamental corruption from our government, Obama's failure presents a difficult choice. We must find a way either to make a transformational candidate for president credible, or to get America to engage in politics outside the ordinary cycles of ordinary presidential elections.

Let's start with the first: How could a candidate for president credibly signal to the American public that his or her exclusive focus would be to remove this fundamental corruption from our government? How could she make that the only issue that mattered? Or more precisely, how could she frame the issue so people recognized that though there were a million other issues that mattered more, this issue must be resolved first?

Here's one path:

Imagine a candidate—a credible nonpolitician, someone who has made her mark in business, or as a creator, or as something that allows people to have confidence in her. The candidate enters a New Hampshire primary. The candidate makes a single two-part pledge: if elected, she will (1) hold the government hostage until Congress enacts a program to remove the fundamental corruption that is our government, and (2) once that program is enacted, she will resign.

What that program is, of course, will be a central focus of the campaign. We needn't worry about the details here, though Roemer's four principles would be an important place to start. And how we can trust that she will actually resign will be an obsessive focus of every news show from the launch until the election. But a credible candidate challenging the president with a single message of "change"—this time, change you can *really* believe in—would have at least a 10 percent chance of capturing the imagination of that single state.

There are more details to describe in this, but before I do, let me lay out the balance of the plan:

If that candidate did respectably in New Hampshire, then all bets would be off. Even a modest showing would spark an enormous amount of energy—both good and bad. Good, as more and more would be rallying to the plan of reform; bad, as a bunch of party loyalists on the other side would see this challenger as an effective way to weaken the other party's candidate for president.

That latter fact then suggests the second part to this strategy: assuming it achieves some resonance and respectability, it will strike many that the plan should not be exclusive to one party. So then, imagine a second candidate—again, a credible nonpolitician, someone who has made her mark in business, or as a creator, or as something that allows people to have confidence in her—but this time from the other party. This candidate makes the same promise—she, too, will (1) hold Congress hostage until it passes fundamental reform, and then, she, too, will (2) resign once that reform is enacted.

Again, if this candidate can make a respectable showing in a primary, all bets are off. The race would quickly be recast as not the familiar battle among familiar politicians, all arguing the same, inherently unbelievable blather. It would instead be a battle between the reformers, Republican and Democrat, and the candidates of the status quo. Those status quo politicians will, Lucy-like, insist that they really, really, really will make "change" their mission this time. But in the face of a real alternative, it will be very easy to undermine that argument.

As such a campaign moves toward the conventions, both parties will face a difficult choice. They could each decide to rebuff the reform movement, by rejecting the change candidate and nominating a normal candidate who tries to make the promise of reform believable. But they each recognize that if they do that, the other party can grab the mantle of reform by embracing the reform candidate. And of all the years when it would not make sense to be on the side of the status quo, I suggest, 2012 (like 1912 before it) is high on that list.

The alternative both parties face is to embrace the reform candidate, and make the difference in the ticket hang upon the vice-presidential candidate. For, of course, when the reform president resigns, it will be the vice president who takes over. The choice between the parties will then be the choice between these two vice presidents. Or again, once the reform of this fundamentally corrupt system has been enacted, we turn the business back to the normal politicians.

That's the strategy. Assuming (big assumption) it worked (as in it got a reform president elected), how could it work (as in change the system)? How exactly could a president hold a government hostage?

My assumption is that going into the election, both reform candidates, the Republican and the Democrat, have agreed on a package of reform. And on the same package of reform. This bit is critical, because constitutional reform—which, even if we don't touch the Constitution, this, in effect, is—is precisely the sort of change that must cut across a wide range of America. A single package promoted by both candidates would provide that sort of credibility. And when either candidate wins (as, of course, one is guaranteed to win), that candidate will be able to say with authority that America has spoken and these are the reforms that she demands.

That fact alone, I suggest, would have enormous power in Congress. I can't imagine any member with the courage to stand up against the results of such an election. I can't imagine the body growing the backbone necessary for it to defend continuing its corrupt ways. My sense is that both parties would be keen to get this reform president out of the way. And the cheapest, simplest way to do that would be to enact the package on the first day of the new Congress. Deny the new president the privilege even of moving into the White House, by delivering on Inauguration Day the package the people have demanded.

Imagine, however, that Congress is more resistant. Imagine it refuses to pass the package. What could the president do then?

Ordinarily, a president is radically constrained in what he or she can do. That constraint comes from the recognition that at some point she will need Congress. The single most important mistake in George W. Bush's administration was failing to recognize the need to work with Congress. Recognizing that need limits the freedom that a president would otherwise have.

In our scenario, that constraint is relaxed. The president needs Congress to do just one thing: pass this bill. Tradition has collected within the reach of the president an enormous array of power that she could deploy for the purpose of coercing a reticent Congress. The president has the power to impound spending—why not the salaries of Congress? He has the power to veto any bill—why not every bill until Congress relents? And while the costs of shutting down the government are huge, and borne by many who can't bear them, both candidates could promise to keep the essential entitlements untouched during the transition.

But what about all the other stuff a president does? you ask. What about being commander in chief? Or serving as head of state? Who would perform those duties during this constitutional regency?

The elected president. The elected president is the president. She has all the powers of the president, and during the term in which she serves, she executes those powers fully. I don't mean this officer to be compromised in any way, except in the term during which she chooses to serve. Her term ends when Congress ratifies the changes that the people have demanded. At that point, she returns to private life and hands the government back over to the politicians. She is a regent president, holding office until the democracy grows up.

But why should she resign? you ask. After all, she's actually succeeded in getting Congress to change the fundamental corruption that is its system. She sounds like a great person to serve as president. Why would we bench our star player?

The candidate's promise is the essential element necessary to make her a credible change candidate. She needs to commit to reform in a way that makes it plain she intends to reform. If she doesn't commit to that, or if she doesn't carry through with her commitment, then she's Lucy, and once again we're Charlie Brown.

Moreover, her succeeding in getting this legislation passed would not necessarily make her a great president. Indeed, the attitude and inflexibility necessary to succeed in this role is precisely, I would argue, the wrong attitude and flexibility necessary to succeed as president. No successful president has ever done it alone. Not FDR, or Lincoln, or even Washington—all of them depended upon rich and serious engagement with all sides of an issue. That engagement requires humility, flexibility, and good political sense.

That's not our reform, or regent president. As romantic and Hollywoodesque as she would seem, if she tried to carry that rigid and absolute character over into every sphere of presidential leadership, she would fail. A great president is not a great reformer. We have to recognize this, and separate the two. And that's precisely what this plan is intended to do.

What are the chances this would work? Let's be wildly optimistic: 2 percent.

So, what's next?

# CHAPTER 20

## *Strategy 4*

## The Convention Game

(const. convention)

It has never happened. Or maybe it did, once. At the founding. But beyond that single example, we've never had a transformation effected by a federal constitutional convention.

In 1787 the best bet about the future of the United States was that the Union would dissolve and generations of internal wars would begin. America—or better, the "united States"—had won their (and at the time, the plural possessive was all anyone would dare to utter) war against Britain. But they had all but lost the peace. States refused to support the confederation. Congress had no power to deal with a wide range of crucial issues. And in the state legislatures, corruption was rampant.[1] The Framers feared becoming their parents: "Look at Britain," instructed Patrick Henry, "see there the bolts and bars of power; see bribery and corruption defiling the fairest fabric that ever human nature reared."[2] "[I]f we do not provide against corruption," George Mason warned, "our government will soon be at an end."[3]

The Constitution in effect at the time made change seem quite unlikely. Article XIII of the Articles of Confederation stated:

Every State shall abide by the determination of the united States in congress assembled, on all questions which by this confederation are submitted to them. And the Articles of this confederation shall be inviolably observed by every State, and the union shall be perpetual; nor shall any alteration at any time hereafter be made in any of them; unless such alteration be agreed to in a congress of the united States, and be afterwards confirmed by the legislatures of every State.

And while everyone might well have agreed that things were bad, there is more chance of getting the Senate today to agree to a carbon tax than to imagine the thirteen states agreeing to a fundamental alteration in the Articles of Confederation.

So our founding fathers decided to break the rules. After the failure of a conference at Annapolis in 1786, Congress convened a new conference to be held in Philadelphia in 1787. The "sole and express purpose" of that conference was to promise amendments to the Articles of Confederation to "render the federal constitution adequate to the exigencies of Government & the preservation of the Union."[4]

*Amendments.* Not a new Constitution. But quickly the organizers of that convention convinced those present (and not every state even deigned to send a delegate) to meet in secret. (No WikiLeaks to fear.) The windows were shut. And for almost three months the Framers banged away at a document that we continue to revere today.

They took to this exceptional path because they recognized that sometimes an institution becomes too sick to fix itself. Not that the institution is necessarily blind to its own sickness. But that it doesn't have the capacity, or will, to do anything about it.

Sometimes an institution, like an individual, needs an intervention, from people, from friends, from outside.

Our Framers recognized this about their government. They had just lived it. But they also recognized the disruption and danger that come from revolution. Instability at some point is death, even if too much stability is also death. It may well be, the Framers thought, that the only way to restrain Washington was with "a well regulated Militia" (and hence the Second Amendment). But they hoped that restraint could be achieved through more peaceful means.

So the Framers added to our Constitution one more way out.

Obviously, to them at least, the people always retained the right to "alter or abolish" their government. That was the premise of the Declaration of Independence, and they didn't mean to deny that principle through their new Constitution—especially since the authority to enact that new Constitution (by violating the terms of the Articles of Confederation) depended upon it. (Indeed, as Kurt Lash argues, "it is at least plausible the Preamble and Assembly Clause presented by Madison to the First Congress were intended to explicitly recognize the people's right to assemble in convention and alter or abolish their Constitution."[5] Reflecting a similar understanding, Edmund Pendleton said at the Virginia ratifying convention that if Congress refused needed amendments, "we will assemble in Convention; wholly recall our delegated powers, or reform them so as to prevent such abuse."[6])

In addition to these extraconstitutional means of constitutional reform, however, the Framers added two more tools that were internal to the Constitution itself: First, a simpler method by which Congress could initiate amendments to the Constitution. Second, a more complicated method by which "a convention" could propose amendments to the Constitution.

Under the first path, Congress proposes an amendment to the Constitution, if two-thirds of Congress agree. Under the second path, Congress calls "a convention for proposing Amendments" if two-thirds of the state legislatures ask it to. Amendments proposed either way get ratified if three-fourths of the states agree.

The first path has been the exclusive path for all twenty-six amendments to our Constitution. Every amendment has been first proposed by Congress and then ratified by the states.

The second path has never been used. Indeed, in the first one hundred years after the founding, there were only ten applications calling for a convention submitted by the states to Congress.[7] But even though no convention has been called, the calls for a convention have had an important reformatory effect, most famously in the context of the Seventeenth Amendment (making the Senate elected), when the states came within one vote of calling for a convention, and Congress quickly proposed the amendment the convention would have proposed.[8]

Even though it has never happened, however, a constitutional convention is the one final plausible strategy for forcing fundamental reform onto our Congress.[9] It is also the most viable grass-roots strategy for forcing reform onto the system. It's going to be easier to organize movements within the states to demand fundamental reform than it will be to organize Congress to vote for any particular amendment to the Constitution to effect that reform. And more important, it's going to be much easier to get a conversation about fundamental reform going in the context of a call for a convention than it will be through any other plausible political means.

The reason is an important strategic opportunity that a call for a convention would offer and that a demand for an amendment would not: different souls with different objectives could agree on the need for a convention without agreeing on the particular proposals that a convention should recommend. Some might want an amendment to give the president line-item-veto power. Some might want a balanced-budget amendment. Some might want term limits. Some might want to abolish the Electoral College, or ban political gerrymandering. And some might want to demand a system for funding elections that restores integrity and independence to Congress (me!).

All of these different souls could agree at least on the need to create the platform upon which their different ideas could be debated. That platform is the convention. And if the convention then recommended some of these changes, those changes would be sent to Congress to be sent to the states for the purpose of ratification. They would remain invalid, mere "propos[als]," until they were ratified by thirty-eight states.

Thirty-eight states. That is an almost impossibly large proportion of America—so large as to offer the first best reason that we should not fear this process. There are easily thirteen red states and thirteen blue states in America today. One chamber in each of thirteen states is enough to block any amendment. Neither side needs to fear that the other is going to run away with our Constitution.

Instead, in my view, this process could well give America the single best hope for a sustained conversation about what changes this democracy needs to restore integrity and trust to the system. The many months that it would take to build a movement within the states would give citizens in each of these states a chance to think about why such reform is necessary. The furious intensity of debate that would be directed against the very idea of a convention would make it almost impossible for any thinking American to miss what was at stake. And then the convention itself could provide a remarkable opportunity—if properly structured—for real reform to be considered and debated. There is no other process that could come close, in my view, to exciting the attention this issue needs and the reflection and deliberation it deserves.

Yet the convention is reviled by scholars and by insiders on the Left and Right alike. The process, they insist, is too uncertain. Too dangerous. A convention once convened could "run away,"[10] these scholars say (to where, exactly?). The whole process is just too radical and untested for a mature and stable democracy.

This campaign against a constitutional convention is motivated by principle as well as by politics.[11] There are some who are genuinely fearful of the uncertainty that such a procedure would raise. But as I will explain, the danger motivating that fear is completely avoidable. Others are not interested in avoiding that danger, because their real objection is political: the strongest movements for a convention in our lifetime have been movements from the Right. The most recent of these was a call for a convention to require a balanced budget. By 1989, thirty-two states had petitioned Congress to make that call (two short), before Alabama rescinded its petition and the movement apparently died.[12]

What's clear, however, is that the Framers intended the convention clause to address precisely the problem that we face today. When the convention first turned to the amending power, many thought Congress should have only a limited role in passing amendments, since it would be Congress that "would be the very occasion for moving to amend."[13] The insiders are not going to fix this mess. We need instead a movement from the outside. (The same insight motivated Lincoln, when he called for constitutional amendments through the convention procedure, because he wanted "amendments to originate with the people themselves.")[14] The convention clause was meant to channel such a movement. Again, not exclusively. The Framers did not intend to abolish the Declaration of Independence's self-evident right "to alter or to abolish" a government, regardless of the procedures specified. Instead, they intended to provide at least one (relatively) regular procedure to complement that right.

But how this complement is to be invoked is famously uncertain. Who sets the rules for the convention? How are delegates selected? What defines the agenda? Are there any limits to what it can decide?

Answering these questions is of course a necessary and proper step to any responsible constitutional amending process. And the Constitution is quite explicit about how such "necessary and proper" means are to be specified: Article I, section 8, clause 18, says that it is Congress that has the power "[t]o make all Laws which shall be necessary and proper for carrying into Execution the foregoing Powers, and all other Powers vested by this Constitution in the Government of the United States or in any Department or Officer thereof."

"All other Powers vested by this Constitution" certainly includes the power to call a convention. This simple and plain text at the core of our constitutional design gives to Congress all the power it needs to ensure an orderly and sensible procedure for initiating and conducting a convention.[15]

And indeed, Congress has come very close to exercising this sensible judgment precisely. When it seemed plausible that enough states would call for a convention to consider an amendment to require a balanced budget, Senator Orrin Hatch introduced an eminently sensible bill that would have provided all the procedure necessary to form and conduct a convention. This bill (Senate Bill No. 40, from the Ninety-ninth Congress[16]) specified the procedure by which a call by a state for a convention would be recognized. It specified the procedure by which a convention would be constituted—including how many delegates each state would elect and (my favorite bit of the bill) a requirement that no senator or representative "be elected as delegate."[17]

Every reasonable question raised by scholars about how a convention would be constituted and run has been addressed by this very reasonable bill. Not all scholars, however, accept the answers that this bill would give. In particular, though Senator Hatch's bill explicitly permits states to ask for the convention to narrow its agenda to particular topics, these scholars insist not only that the convention cannot be so limited, but that any call for a limited convention is invalid. As Walter Dellinger puts it, "[e]ven when the applying state legislatures seek only to limit the convention with respect to subject matter, the case against the validity of the applications is still persuasive."[18]

This can't be correct. The only convention America has ever seen was a convention called for a limited purpose: the convention that gave us the Constitution itself. And the consistent practice among states has always been to recognize the validity of a limited call for a convention.[19] There is not a single sentence reported anywhere that suggests that the Framers intended to proscribe the manner in which a convention could be called. No doubt, they wanted that convention to be a national body. No doubt they wanted it to consider issues that affected the nation as a whole. But there is simply nothing to support the claim that they meant there to be an unwritten requirement that any call for a convention be made with the magic words "We, the Legislature of X, hereby petition Congress to call a convention to consider any amendment to the Constitution whatsoever." To the contrary, at least some at the convention expected "future conventions to be rather limited affairs."[20]

Now, of course, the only example of a convention in our history is also an example of a convention that exceeded the limits of its call. And that's precisely what concerns many people about the idea of calling for a convention: How could we be sure that the convention didn't propose radical changes to our Constitution? What would stop fundamentalists from repealing the separation of church and state? Or antiabortionists from reversing *Roe v. Wade*? Or crazies on the Left mandating government ownership of the Internet?

But let's keep this argument clear.

First, the fact that the limits on a call for a convention have been exceeded does not show that a call for a limited convention is invalid, any more than the fact that banks have been robbed shows that bank managers have no right to lock their vaults. To the contrary: The call for a limited convention could be perfectly valid. The invalid part is the exceeding of those limits. The question of the proper remedy for invalidity is distinct from the question of whether the line drawn is valid. Thus, as the historical practice shows, states, in my view, are perfectly entitled to narrow the scope of issues they'd like a convention to consider, *and* Congress, in my view, is perfectly entitled to specify the scope of the convention's work consistent with the proper limits expressed by states, *even if* no one can control what actual amendments a convention proposes.

Second, the same tradition that permits the calls for a convention to be limited also shows that conventions sometimes ignore those limits. But the critical question is this: *With what consequence?* As our first constitutional convention plainly recognized, because it had exceeded the scope of its authority, it had no authority to change anything on the basis of its proposed Constitution alone.[21] Instead, as James Wilson put it, the Framers conceived of themselves as "authorized to *conclude nothing*, but . . . at liberty to *propose anything*."[22] James Madison made the same point in Federalist 40. Indeed, the anti-Federalists (who opposed the Constitution) worked hard to invalidate the work of the convention by arguing that the convention had no right to propose a constitution because that exceeded the mandate of the convention. The anti-Federalists failed. Again, as Madison and others responded, the convention didn't rest upon any "right" to propose anything. They merely asked that the Congress refer their proposal to state conventions to be considered and ratified if the states so chose.

That is precisely the same "danger" that we would face today. (For we have *never* seen a "runaway" convention that purported actually to change the Constitution on its own.) A convention called for the purpose of considering amendments to restore the independence of Congress, but that instead proposed an amendment to abolish the Electoral College, would have no right to demand that Congress do anything with its work. Congress would be free, of course, to take up the amendment itself. But it would also be free to ignore it.

The point, as Paul Weber and Barbara Perry convincingly argue, is that we need to think about this "danger" in political terms, not legal terms.[23] The question is, How likely is it that the proposals of a runaway convention—a convention that expressly ignored limitations called for by the very states that had called for the convention—would nonetheless be ratified by three-fourths of the states?

It is not likely. At all. But if it happens, then it would happen only because that runaway convention had come up with the same sort of world-changing brilliance that our Framers did. And if it did, then why wouldn't we want the states to ratify it? Or put more strongly: If an "illegal proposal" were so strong as to overcome its own illegitimacy, and rally the support of thirty-eight states, it would have to be an incredible proposal! Not an incredible proposal for the Left or for the Right. To win the approval of thirty-eight states would require a proposal that cut across both Left and Right. What possible reason is there for us to fear a change that was supported by such a substantial majority?

Thus the states, in my view, are perfectly entitled to ask Congress to narrow the scope of the convention it convenes. The Congress, in my view, is perfectly entitled to set the agenda of that convention consistent with those requests. Congress restricts the convention only at its peril. The states impose too many restrictions on the call for a convention only at the convention's peril. If a state says that it asks Congress to consider one topic only, then Congress will convene a convention only if thirty-four states make the same proposal. The movement for a convention requires a bit more flexibility. No doubt it is reasonable not to want a convention to roam wherever an academic would want. But it is politically foolish—if indeed the state wants a convention—to forbid it from at least discussing issues that might not yet seem compelling to that petitioning state.

These questions, however, do lead me to suggest a possible compromise. One way to avoid this runaway fear, while preserving the opportunity for states with different concerns to join with a common purpose (to have a convention), would be for the petition calling for the convention itself to also call on Congress to set certain limits to the scope of the convention. Here's an example:

> The State of Utah, speaking through its legislature, pursuant to Article V of the Constitution, hereby petitions the United States Congress to call a convention for the purpose of proposing Amendments to the Constitution of the United States of America.
>
> Furthermore, Utah would propose that convention consider amendments to strengthen the veto power of the president by, for example, among other possible solutions, giving him a "line-item-veto" authority.
>
> Furthermore, Utah requests that its proposal notwithstanding, Congress restrict the agenda of the convention to considering only those matters enumerated by at least 40 percent of the states calling for the convention.
>
> And finally, Utah requests that Congress exclude from eligibility as delegates to the convention any current Member of Congress.

This proposal explicitly calls for a convention for proposing amendments. It explicitly enumerates the particular type of amendment the state wants considered. But it asks Congress to filter out any subject that doesn't have at least twenty states behind it. And it includes the (in my view, crucial) clause that no sitting member of Congress may be a delegate to this convention.

If thirty-four states passed a version of this application, then Congress would be required to call a convention. It would be entitled to set an agenda for the convention consistent with the 40 percent clause. And it would be entitled to ban members of Congress from being delegates to the convention.

That part is the easy work here. The hard work would be building the movement to support a convention. That building will take time, and a particularly risky strategy—at least for the movement. Like the transformative-president strategy, it is slow and deliberate; it happens state by state; it doesn't assume the world pays attention all at once, but instead, it understands that people come to understanding in their own time and, increasingly, in 140-character missives. It would take a couple of years at least to get within striking distance of thirty-four states' making the call. That's plenty of time to educate and persuade.

But unlike the race for the presidency, this political battle doesn't fit into any existing media category. So it might be hard to get the earned-media necessary to make it work. If Rhode Island passed a resolution, and then Washington, and then Iowa, those would be the first steps, but on a path that most don't even recognize exists.

Likewise, unlike the race for the presidency, this battle wouldn't have a candidate. There'd be no single (or even two) souls for the public to love or hate. There'd be no intrigue or scandal for the media to focus on.

Yet both of these weaknesses may actually be strengths. Such a movement needs to live beneath the radar at first. Like the Internet itself, it needs to develop in a world where all the experts say that it's impossible, so that those who understand the world only through the experts ignore it as it develops. Likewise, it needs to develop by exercising the civic power of ordinary citizens. We've seen people devote endless hours to a single person; we need the same devotion to an ideal, or a cause. The discipline of a campaign that needs to rely upon a million volunteers is precisely the discipline constitutional reform needs. And a convention, even an Article V convention, especially.

The campaign would need a common infrastructure—a platform upon which strategy and substance could be worked out. And more important, an infrastructure that would develop a campaign that could move from state to state, or from state to states, as states passed the resolution making the call.

That platform need not be heavily staffed. Indeed, it needs to grow with the discipline of our own revolutionaries: small, apparently disorganized citizens fighting for liberty. A general, a staff to support infrastructure, and a call for citizens to engage are everything the system needs.

That platform would prove itself as it targeted state legislatures, and delivered. With each victory, attention would grow. The list of supporters would become more engaged. That engagement would attract others. And if it could be kept authentic, removed from the control of either party in D.C., it might yet spark the inspiration such reform needs.

Indeed, if I were to design the movement, I would place at the top of its requirements that it be a *citizens'* movement only. Of course we welcome the support of anyone—politicians, corporations, foreigners, even dolphins. But the work necessary to make this succeed must come from citizens alone. And more precisely, citizens who pledge that they are not seeking a role in Congress. Let no one doubt the integrity of those participating in this movement. Remove any question of ulterior motive.

As I've talked about this idea in literally hundreds of places around the country, the single most pressing objection is the fear of American ignorance—the belief that Americans are too ignorant to inform or direct a constitutional convention, and that therefore we should not give them the chance.

Americans are ignorant about politics and our government no doubt. Less than a third of us know that House members serve for two years, or that senators serve for six.[24] Half of us believe foreign aid is one of the top two federal expenditures. It is actually about 1 percent of the budget.[25] Six years after Newt Gingrich became Speaker, only 55 percent of us knew the Republicans were the majority party in the house, a rate just slightly better than the result if monkeys had chosen randomly.[26]

So, ignorant we are. But we're not stupid. Indeed, for all the reasons this book has collected, remaining ignorant about politics and our government is a perfectly rational response to the government we have. The question isn't what we know. The question is what we're capable of knowing, and doing, if we have the right incentives, and the right opportunity.

Yet I've also come to see that there's no arguing people out of their fear of this ignorance. The only opportunity is to show them something that convinces them of something different. So here's the biggest gamble that I would place in this plan:

As we push for states to call for Article V conventions, we should simultaneously be convening shadow conventions in each of these states. These shadow conventions would not be casual or ad hoc. Instead, they would be built according to a common plan developed by the organizing platform for this movement. Think of it as a convention in a box, which would map how the convention should be crafted. In my view, drawing upon a rigorous technique first developed by Professor James Fishkin, these shadow conventions should be constituted themselves as *deliberative polls*.[27]

A deliberative poll?

To understand a deliberative poll, you must first ignore the word *poll* in the title. The aim of a deliberative poll is not just to figure out what people think. The aim instead is to figure out what people would think if they were informed enough about the matter that they were being polled about. Think of it as a jury, only better: the sample is large and representative (at least three hundred for a large population), and the process begins by providing participants with the information they need to speak sensibly about the matter they are addressing.

In this case, the deliberative poll would frame the question of reform: What will reform require? What would good or meaningful reform be? What changes to the Constitution, if any, are necessary to effect this reform?

The output of these deliberative polls would reflect the views of ordinary citizens about how or whether our Constitution should change. Because the participants are randomly selected, there's no chance of special-interest lobbying. Because they are representative, there's no chance of packing the process from one side or the other. First, region by region and then, if it takes off, state by state within regions, this experiment in a deliberative convention would give Americans a baseline to evaluate the capacity of American citizens to govern. And as these conventions succeed in demonstrating sanity and good sense (and I am certain they would), the support for a similar convention to propose amendments to the Constitution would grow.

For this is the core assumption I have about what this Article V convention should be: It should not be a convention of experts. Or politicians. Or activists. Or anyone else specific. It should be a convention of randomly selected voters called to a process of informed deliberation, who then concur on proposals that would be carried to the states. Delegates to this convention would have their salaries and expenses covered by the convention. Employers would be mandated to hold the jobs of the delegates. The convention would convene in a remote place, far from Washington, and maybe far from the Internet. And delegates would then be charged with the duty the law had placed upon them: to propose amendments to the Constitution.

I recognize that of all the insanity strewn throughout this book, this will strike readers as the most extreme. Ordinary citizens? *Are you crazy?* Proposing amendments to our Constitution? When two-thirds of Americans can't even identify what the Bill of Rights is?[28]

Whether you would agree with the final step in this plan or not isn't important just now. My purpose here is not to convince you of this ultimate step. I'm only trying to describe an interim step—that as the push for an Article V convention is made in each state, shadow conventions in each state should also be convened. If those shadows produce garbage, then my idea is garbage. But if those shadow conventions produce a series of sensible proposals, then, I suggest, we'll be in a position to ask whether we should make the experiment the model.

For, after all, the competition is not very great here. Given the insanely low quality of work coming from at least our federal legislature (states are actually more interesting and more encouraging), I'd be willing to make a very substantial bet that these amateur citizen conventions will impress America much more than the professional legislature does. Politics is that rare sport where the amateur contest is actually more interesting than the professional. We should at least give it a chance.

So, in a single line, this strategy goes like this: A platform for pushing states to call for a federal convention would begin by launching as many shadow conventions as is possible. In schools, in universities—wherever such deliberation among citizens could occur. The results of those shadow conventions would be collected, and posted, and made available for critique. And as they demonstrated their own sensibility, they would support the push for states to call upon Congress to remove the shadow from these conventions. Congress would then constitute a federal convention. That convention—if my bet proves correct—would be populated by a random selection of citizens drawn from the voter rolls. That convention would then meet, deliberate, and propose new amendments to the Constitution. Congress would refer those amendments out to the states for their ratification.

And so, again, what's the chance this might work? I think, comparatively, quite good: with enough entrepreneurial state representatives, let's say 10 percent at a minimum.

# CHAPTER 21

# *Choosing Strategies*

I've outlined four strategies for effecting the change we need. None are likely to succeed alone. But which makes the most sense? And why should we pursue any of them if none are likely to succeed?

To understand the challenge, we need to keep the enemy in focus and understand how it will react. As the movement to kill the system of dependence that is D.C. grows, the resistance will grow as well. There are too many people whose livelihoods depend upon the status quo. Some of them would be happy to see the system change. Most will fight like hell to protect it.

So, what does that fact say about the best strategy to defeat the status quo?

Insurgent movements have to fight the war on unconventional turf. If the issue gets decided finally within institutions that depend upon things staying the same, things will stay the same. But if we can move the battle outside the Beltway, to venues where the status quo has no natural advantage, then even small forces can effect big change.

That's the advantage to the three unconventional strategies. Each of them—running nonpolitician candidates, running reform presidential candidates, calling for an Article V convention—is something that hasn't happened before. The structures for controlling what happens in American politics haven't developed to control these contexts. Thus, the chance to evade the power of the status quo is greater with these three. And if I had the power to launch this war, I would launch it by launching all three at once.

Even then, however, the chances are still not great. We've had small examples of status quo defeats, but certainly nothing as big as dislodging the power of K Street. Any sane soul who looked at this cause would have to conclude that the odds are overwhelmingly against us. So, why do it? Why waste your time?

I was asked this question quite pointedly once, after a lecture at Dartmouth. "What's the point?" the sympathetic listener asked. "It all seems so hopeless."

And for the first time in my life, in the middle of a public lecture, I was so choked by emotion that I thought I had to stop. For the picture that came into my head as I struggled for a response to this fair yet devastating question was the image of my (then) six-year-old boy, and the thought, the horror, of a doctor's telling me that he had terminal cancer and that "there was nothing to be done." I painted that picture to that Dartmouth audience. And I then asked this: "Would you give up? Would you do nothing?"

Because of course I understand the futility in fighting. Of course I can read the odds—I typed them, by hand! I feel the dismissive impatience of those inside the system whenever I talk about changing the system. I can almost feel them roll their eyes as they hear about a fight to change the status quo.

But I also know love. And I know what love says to the rational. Love makes the odds irrelevant. It is a commitment to doing whatever can be done—sometimes destructively so—to beat the odds and save the soul who taught you that love.

We forgive this irrationality, especially when it comes to kids. Indeed, we celebrate it. Think of the story of John and Aileen Crowley (retold in the 2010 film *Extraordinary Measures*), who did everything humanly possible to drive research for a cure to the disease that doomed their kids. Or of Denzel Washington in *John Q* (2002) taking a hospital hostage to force them to transplant his heart to his son. Or of Harrison Ford in *Air Force One* (1997), playing a U.S. president who sells the interest of America to terrorists so as to save his twelve-year-old daughter. These are all heroes acting insanely, but for a reason we all understand well.

Why not the same for country?

I wouldn't compare my love for my family and my love for my

nation, except to say that the irrational parts in each feel very much the same. Or at least one irrational part that I would hope you saw as the same: we should be willing to do whatever we can, the odds be damned, to save both when we see, when we finally see, the threat that stands above both.

The poor do this all the time for us—not just the poor, but many, many who are poor. We call them soldiers. They volunteer to fight wars for democracy. They put their lives on the line, literally, for an argument that is, in my humble opinion, vastly more attenuated to the end of saving democracy than anything I've described here.

The war I've endorsed won't kill anyone. And it is a war we can't rely on poor people to fight alone.

So you pick your poison. You tell me which hopeless strategy is best. Or you come up with a better one. But don't tell me this is hopeless. Hopelessness is precisely the reason that citizens must fight.

# *Conclusion*

## Rich People

Arnold Hiatt was the chairman of Stride Rite Shoes, a company that has spread many beautiful designs, none as important as Keds. He is also one of the Democratic Party's largest contributors. In 1996 he was its second-largest contributor, maxing out to support close to forty congressional candidates who had each promised they would support campaign finance reform. Many of those candidates won. Their cause, however, has not been won. Yet.

In the spring of 1997, President Bill Clinton wanted to thank the largest contributors to the Democratic Party. He also wanted to hear their ideas for what he should do with the last four years of his presidency. Thirty of the top contributors were invited to the Mayflower Hotel. None of them knew of course that Clinton would be frittering away almost two-thirds of that four-year term because of a fling with an intern. That was all to come. Instead, he was then still riding high as the Comeback Kid who had beaten back the Republican Revolution to become the first Democratic president since Franklin Delano Roosevelt to be reelected after a full first term. *FDR, Clinton, Obama .. H. Clinton*

At the end of the dinner, Clinton gave some remarks. He then asked the guests to give him their remarks about what he should be doing, and how he should be governing. One by one, the guests stood and offered their ideas. The president listened and took notes. The evening appeared to be having its intended effect: the fat cats were being attended to; their purr was warming up nicely.

Hiatt was the last to speak. Sitting two seats from the president, he stood, looked the president straight in the eyes, and said (as it was told to me and as best as I can reconstruct, with just a little poetic license taken with the words that Hiatt has kept in the form of notes only):

> Mr. President, I know you're an admirer of Franklin Delano Roosevelt. So I want you to put yourself in FDR's shoes in 1940—the year when Roosevelt realized that he was going to have to convince a reluctant nation to wage a war to save democracy.
>
> Because that, Mr. President, is precisely what you need to do now—to convince a reluctant nation to wage a war to save democracy.

The war that Hiatt pushed, however, was not a war against Fascists. It was a war against fat cats, against people like the people in that room. People who believed that they were entitled to direct public policy merely because they were rich. People who had convinced the American people that democracy did not work, because the politicians listened to them, the fat cats, and not to the people. Hiatt challenged the president to recognize that "current campaign finance practices are threatening this nation in a different, but no less serious way." "Only your leadership," he said, "and your office can turn this around."

There was silence when Hiatt finished. No doubt, some were uncomfortable. Hiatt remembers the president being "gracious." The only published account reports him as being less than charitable: "Clinton's response effectively slashed Hiatt to pieces," according to Peter Buttenwieser, "humiliating him in front of the group."[1]

When I first heard this story, this simple act of courage moved me beyond words. I didn't know Hiatt. I hadn't heard of this effort to get Clinton to persuade a reluctant nation to wage a war to save democracy. But I could feel how impossibly difficult it must have been to utter those words, then and there. It was an act of courage, impossible for most of us if only because it was certain to alienate Hiatt from his friends.

For Hiatt's challenge effectively divided those Democrats into two very different camps: one supporting fundamental reform and the other preferring the status quo. Whether or not Hiatt was the only member of the reform camp, there was a certain majority that liked the status quo.

Over the past four years, as I've worked to recruit supporters to this campaign, I've come to recognize these two camps. What unites them is a basic commitment to liberal politics. Not radical, leftist policies, but Democratic policies far from the extremes of the GOP.

But what divides them, these fat cats of the Democratic Party, is the question of whether they should continue to have the power over the Democratic Party that they have, and hence, for those brief moments when the party controls our government, power over the government as well.

Some among these fat cats love the life they now have—a life in which they can get any senator on the phone, or even the president, in a pinch. They love the world in which the most powerful person in the world, the president, invites them to dinner.

I don't mean that they love this world of power merely because they like power. Maybe that's why they like it, but that's not how they understand it. Instead, these insanely rich people actually believe that their views about patent policy are better than those of people who have studied the question for thirty years. Or that their insights about health care are worth more than the views of doctors or nurses. They are convinced they are wise because the market made them rich. And they believe that a president should consider himself privileged to listen to their very comfortably funded wisdom.

As I've tried to convince these people to fight for a world where they don't have this power, I have grown accustomed to a certain deflated recognition. You can walk them through the thousand reasons why this system of government is corrupt; you can get them to acknowledge the million times when bad influences have produced insanely bad policies; you can bring them to acknowledge the poison that this economy of influence is for democracy, and the rule of law. Yet, in the end, they resist. They just can't imagine giving up their own power.

Sometimes they're quite honest about it. I remember one soul, the certain inheritor of billions, telling me flat out, "I like my influence. I like being able to get senators on the phone." (He has subsequently flipped, and is now a strong supporter of small-dollar-funded elections.)

But sometimes they're just oblivious, and their obliviousness brings out the worst in me. I remember once talking to one about the principle of "one person, one vote"—the Supreme Court's doctrine that forces states to ensure that the weight of one person's vote is equal to the weight of everyone else's. He had done work early in his career to push that principle along, and considered it, as he told me, "among the most important values now written into our Constitution." "Isn't it weird, then," I asked him, "that the law would obsess about making sure that on Election Day, my vote is just as powerful as yours, but stand blind to the fact that in the days before Election Day, because of your wealth, your ability to affect that election is a million times greater than mine?" My friend—or at least, friend until that moment—didn't say a word.

That's one side of this divide. On the other is a very different group: again, insanely rich, but souls who are keen to give up their power. Not because they hate the attention of the president of the United States (though, I imagine, depending upon the president, there are those sorts, too). And not because their own business wouldn't benefit from the sort of access and interest their position now gives them (for, of course, for many of these people, a good and effective relationship with the government is a key driver of their bottom line). But rather, because they recognize that in a democracy their power is wrong. Not their wealth. Their power. There's nothing wrong with getting rich. There's everything in the world to praise about being successful in business, or sports, or the arts. But the idea that in a democracy you should be able to trade your wealth into more influence over what the government does is just wrong. It denies the basic principle of "one person, one vote." It says some votes are more equal than others, and solely because of the money those voters have.

That's an important qualification. The egalitarianism that democracy demands is not that there be no influential people. It is that influence be tied to something relevant to the democracy. I was once told of the conversion story of one young, connected (as in to the most powerful people in our society) soul. She described a day on Capitol Hill when the group she led was trying to lobby to get a special provision added to the health care bill to benefit children. The idea was to get senators to talk to the nation's leading expert on children and health. Though the group had planned the day for weeks, they couldn't get any confirmed meeting with any representative or senator of any significance. Everyone promised they would meet if they could, but as the day of the meeting approached, the members were all too busy.

The morning of their seemingly doomed tour, this connected soul made a single telephone call to the chief fund-raiser for one of the senators. Within minutes, the calendar of that senator, and other members', had been cleared, and the group got their meetings. Of course, no promise had been made. It was a simple request for a favor. But because of who she was—a powerful, intelligent, connected soul—the favor was immediately granted.

As the group left the Capitol after the meeting—literally, as they were walking down the steps behind the building—the connected woman who had made the call got a telephone call herself. It was from the chief fund-raiser for one of the senators they had just met. "Do you think you might help the senator out by holding a small event in LA?" As she reflected to me later on, this is a system where "the most important person on the issue of children's health had practically no access at all, yet I, merely because of wealth and connections to wealth, have all the access I want. This," she said to me, "is wrong."

These rich people—people like this woman, or Arnold Hiatt

or Alan Hassenfeld (chairman of Hasbro) or Jerry Kohlberg (co-founder of Kohlberg & Company) or Edgar Bronfman, Jr. (CEO of Warner Music Group) or Vin Ryan (founder of Schooner Capital)—recognize that there's something wrong with their power. Each of them came to see this in different ways. But now they all see it. And some, such as Hiatt and Hassenfeld, have now made it their life's work to dismantle their own power, and the power of people like them, so as to restore this republic.

There's something astonishing and hopeful about these good rich souls. I'm never much moved by large charitable gifts from the very rich, for rarely do those gifts actually change the comfortable life that the giver leads. Much more impressive to me is the family of four, struggling to make ends meet, which manages nonetheless to commit to the United Way, or to put a significant amount in the church collection plate each week.

But the sacrifice of these good rich souls is a real sacrifice. If they succeed in changing the way political power in America is controlled, they will have a significantly different life. This isn't one less vacation house in the Bahamas. This would be a move from quintessential insider to just one of "the People."

Even more striking is that any number of them could, on their own, fund the reform that would save this republic. If this is a "war to save democracy," then the total cost of this war would be less than half as much as the Pentagon spends *every single day*. For $1 billion, a campaign to save this democracy could be waged and won. There are at least 371 billionaires in America, 157 of whom are worth more than $2 billion.[2] One of them could fund the campaign that would make this republic free again. Or ten of them. Or a hundred. Real change is within their grasp.

Because this isn't a problem like racism or sexism. It's simply a problem of incentives. It won't take generations of relearning, or the awakening of some kind of social awareness. It will simply require making it make sense for politicians to opt into a different system to fund their elections (as, for example, 80 percent of candidates in Maine now do, and more than that in Connecticut). Nor is this a problem like cancer or AIDS. We know precisely what would cure this problem, and we could produce that cure tomorrow. All it would take is resources, and the imagination to recognize just how far these resources could go to recovering this republic.

It wouldn't even have to be individuals. Think about the freedom now secured (mistakenly, in my view, but in war, you take what you can get) by *Citizens United*.

I recently had the chance to hear Google's Eric Schmidt speak. It was the first time I had seen him in a relatively intimate (and hence serious) context. Schmidt was describing all the incredible projects that Google was undertaking: world-changing technologies that anyone else would have thought impossible. There was a certain imagination that defined each of these projects. An imagination that said, "You say it's impossible. Watch."

So I asked Schmidt about the subject of this book. I pointed to the string of governmental policies that Google disagreed with, from copyright to network neutrality to antitrust to immigration. I suggested the obvious link to the corruption I have described here. And I asked him if he thought Google could just ignore these differences, treating them like flies buzzing around a picnic, or if Google would try to resolve the differences by pushing to get these policies changed.

For the first time that evening, a small idea was uttered by the representative of this extraordinary company. Schmidt spoke of invigorating the Google PAC, and pushing harder to get their side of the issue better heard.

And I thought, Wow. This is a Google solution to this, the most important problem facing this republic? This is the most they can imagine?

For *Citizens United* has handed a company like Google an enormous opportunity. We live in Google's infrastructure. *Citizens United* means that the company is free to deploy that infrastructure to political ends however it wishes. Indeed, given the failure of Congress to mandate disclosure of independent expenditures, Google could deploy its infrastructure to push particular political ends without even acknowledging it. A single decision by the powers that be could ramp up a campaign to radically strengthen and make more rational the way democracy functions. For almost nothing.

Tempting as these fantasies are, however, they are just fantasies. We can't wait for some deus ex machina to save our republic. Our republic is ours to save. Or better, it is only ours if we save it. It won't be billionaires. It won't be geniuses with brilliant code. And it certainly won't be politicians.

For our politicians are Yeltsin. Their problem is an <u>addiction</u>. This magnificent republic melts away, and they can't stop themselves long enough to save it. They can't stop themselves because they are being pulled in a way that they can't yet control. They are being pulled, and they don't resist.

We all understand this pull. We all know addiction. There isn't a person among us who hasn't suffered, or caused, Yeltsin's harm, if only at the level of a family or among friends.

So think about that harm. Recognize its nature. Think about the alcoholic and his plight. He might be losing his family, his job, and his liver. Each of these is a critically important problem, indeed, among the most important problems a person could face. But we all recognize that to solve any of these "most important" problems, he must solve his alcoholism first. It's not that alcoholism is the most important problem. It's not. <u>It is just the first problem</u>.

So, too, with us. There is no end to the list of problems we as a nation face. Whether big government or bad health care; complicated taxes or global warming; a ballooning deficit or decaying schools. But we won't solve these problems until we solve our first problem first: a dependency that has corrupted the core of our democracy. We can love the agents of that corruption. We can even reelect them. But we must get them to change.

The only souls that can do this <u>are citizens.</u> Not politicians. Not former politicians. Not wannabe politicians. But citizens. Indeed, <u>citizens who swear off elected</u> politics.

~~For we need~~ a politics that is not about politicians. We need a people who devote themselves to saving this republic without others wondering whether they are simply trying to secure a job for themselves. We need a way to engage that is not about just listening. We need to take responsibility for the government we ask the politicians to run. We need to fix it, and then give it back to them to run.

We citizens. You. Me. Us.

We need to launch a generation that stops simply hacking at the branches of evil, to steal from Thoreau one last time, and learns again to strike at the root. We need a generation of rootstrikers.

When Ben Franklin walked out of Independence Hall, the work of the Constitutional Convention completed, he was stopped by a woman and asked, "Mr. Franklin, what have you wrought?"

"A Republic, madam," Franklin replied, "*if you can keep it.*"

A republic.

*Meaning*: "A representative democracy."

*Meaning*: A government "dependent upon the People *alone*."

We have lost that republic.

We must act to get it back.

# Afterword to the Paperback Edition

This was a depressing book to write. The time since I completed it has been much more promising.

Less than two months after I sent the final draft to my publisher, Occupy Wall Street was born. And in the year since the book was first published, through the scores of talks that I have given about it and the problem it describes, I have been confirmed in my conviction, confirmed that the fight to restore this republic is something in which people want to engage. On both the Right and the Left, Americans understand that our government has been captured. On both the Right and the Left, they are looking for a way to release it. The only question is how: How do we move from the recognition this book evinces to the change most Americans want?

The remedies that I outline here haven't yet convinced most that change is possible. As I have read the reactions, both in formal reviews and throughout social media, most are eager to accept the conclusion that Congress won't change itself. But most are pessimistic about the other three options as well. There have been but a few protest congressional candidates. The only presidential candidate to focus his campaign on this issue was not invited to a single primary debate. And we've not yet seen a groundswell around the idea of calling a constitutional convention, though here too, there has been some progress.

Yet in the year since this book was published, we have seen the rise of the one force that could make a difference here, through the one tool that might indeed rebalance the power between status quo and change.

Over the course of the last year, repeatedly, the Internet has enabled effective political movements to arise and have consequence. In January, an extraordinary coalition of Internet-based companies, activists, and nonprofits, such as Wikipedia, produced enough Internet-based pressure to force Congress to back away from what seemed an almost certain legislative change reinforcing the war against Internet-based "piracy." The SOPA/PIPA success surprised everyone, including me, and has only encouraged more Internet-based activism for other less Internet-based causes. After Rush Limbaugh's inexcusably offensive verbal attack on a Georgetown student, activists rallied tens of thousands to call on advertisers to withdraw from Limbaugh's show. They did, and Limbaugh was forced to apologize. After a tragic shooting of a black youth by an apparent vigilante emboldened by Florida's "stand your ground" law, activists rallied tens of thousands more to get supporters of a key group pushing such legislation—the American Legislative Exchange Council (ALEC)—to pressure them to stop that work. They did, and ALEC formally ended its lobbying work in areas of social and civil rights legislation.

These campaigns have become so normal now that it is hard to see just how abnormal they were before. They have become terrifying to some, as these repeated instances of "cyberbullying" (as one tech company described it) threaten to change fundamentally the way policy making in Washington happens.

But this isn't thuggery. It is instead the slow awakening of Hobbes's sleeping giant—the sovereign. These growing movements of political action begin to teach the sovereign how to act. They teach coordination. And as the sovereign gets practiced in that coordination, the battles it can take on become more challenging. Bringing down Limbaugh is tiny as compared with the fight that would restore this republic. But the skills required for the latter begin with the practice necessary to the former.

This is the only source of hope. And as it relates to restoring this republic, I still believe it will be expressed through one of the three extraordinary means that I describe in this book. But though the most democratically authentic of the three—relative to the nature of this power—would be the movement to force an Article V convention, I now think the most likely is the idea I describe in Chapter 19: the regent presidency.

Much of this book is highly critical of President Obama. As I've reflected upon that criticism, I have come to see it as perhaps true but unfair. It is true that Obama failed to carry through with the reform that his campaign promised. But it is unfair if the office is structurally incapable of initiating the reform that Obama promised and that the republic desperately needs.

That impossibility was brought home to me in a story I heard shortly after I completed the final draft for this book. Someone close to the administration described a particularly poignant scene (from the perspective of this book): When Obama was presented with his first budget, he found a document littered with more than nine thousand earmarks. Obama threatened, I was told, to veto the bill, as a way to signal the reform that he wanted. But he was persuaded by his Capitol Hill lobbyists that he "couldn't do that." There was no way, Obama was told, that he could so directly alienate his own party.

When I first heard that story, I took it to be a measure of Obama's betrayal of the cause that he had fought for. But on reflection I recognized through it the real wisdom in Hillary Clinton's campaign. Clinton had famously rejected both Obama and John Edwards's challenge to "take up that fight," as Obama put it, to "change the way Washington works." At first I heard her rejection as cluelessness. I read it now as my own cluelessness. Clinton wasn't saying, "There's nothing wrong with lobbyists, or the way this system works." Clinton was saying, "Who could be so naive as to believe a president could change the way this system works?"

I was just so naive. That naiveté led me to Obama, who too may have been just so naive. And while my more stubborn half (of me, I'm not talking about my spouse) continues to believe that there was a strategy that perhaps only this president could have effected that would have brought about the change he described, a more realistic view might just conclude that Clinton was right. That it is pandering at best to imagine an ordinary president leading such a movement for reform—if, for no other reason, because it ignores the single most important yet unexpected feature of our constitutional design: political parties.

The framers of our constitution did not envision the government we have built. They worked incredibly hard to build a machine that would embed its own mechanisms of independence. Those mechanisms would assure legislative, executive, and judicial branches with the will and the means to remain independent of one another. A jealous self-interest within each branch would preserve that independence. Each would identify with its own. None would have any motive to bend or sell out to the other.

Over the past two and a quarter hundred years there has been much that has tested their theory. But nothing has disproven it more effectively than the emergence of the one thing they thought we would never have—political parties. Like molasses poured into the gearbox of a sports car, political parties have jammed the functioning of the machine our framers designed. There isn't a jealous interest that defends Congress's power from the executive branch, or the other way around. There is instead a necessary conspiracy of powers, as the party in power, bridging both branches, conspires to negotiate the relationship between the executive and the legislative branches so as to secure the continued victory of that party in the next presidential cycle.

It is a measure of our own cultural denial that we don't recognize the significance of the framers' mistake in failing to anticipate parties, and acknowledge how fundamentally it has changed, and weakened, their design. Congress is a failed institution, especially under the pressures I've described here, in part because there is no competing institution with the will to hold it to account. If the president's party controls Congress, criticism is an embarrassment (since it reflects on his party). If the president's party does not control Congress, criticism is embarrassing (since it reflects his own weakness). The framers imagined a power that could call other powers to account. The judicial branch has done that sporadically and sometimes effectively. But the congressional-presidential complex does that at most once a century—Watergate, Reconstruction—if we're lucky.

On this view, Obama couldn't "take up that fight" to "change the way Washington works," because there was no way to win that fight, nor any way to lose that fight and still win. A president is elected for many reasons. This fight would mean, in the short term at least, that none of his other objectives would be achieved. He might strive to explain that failure in terms of this more fundamental battle. But few would even recognize the link. Few would even remember the commitment to wage that battle. The bottom line would be the bottom line: What did you get done? The failure to get anything done would render his administration a failure, regardless of the merits of the fight. It could never pay, in other words, to make reform the issue—except, of course, as a strategy to get a candidate elected.

The conclusion from this might well be that change is impossible. Or at least, change through ordinary means is impossible. But I read it as another reason to consider the regent presidency.

It may well be that the only way to effect the change this republic needs is through a president who commits to that change, and makes that commitment real by committing to resigning once that change is effected—what I've called a "regent president." The reasons are even clearer in light of the failure of Obama to achieve the reform that he promised. An ordinary president is elected for many different reasons. A regent president is elected for one reason. For an ordinary president to take on the challenge of reform, he must sacrifice all the other reasons that he's been elected. For a regent president to take on the challenge of reform, he simply carries through with the commitment that his election represents. For an ordinary president to have the mandate to effect the reform this republic needs, his election must be clearly tied to issues of reform, more clearly than any other issue. For a regent president, that mandate is automatic: If indeed he was elected, he was elected to effect this change.

Similarly with interbranch relations: The fact of political parties means that there's no such thing as one branch against another. Each branch needs the other in the ongoing dance of policy making. Except in extraordinary moments, neither can afford all-out war on the other.

But the regent president needs no ongoing policy dance. He has but one demand. And if he comes to office with a sufficiently strong mandate, combined with the accumulated power of his office, the regent president might well have the ability to force onto Congress the kind of reform that would end its systematic corruption. Once that reform is completed, the regent resigns. And his resigning is essential, both to make credible that the only reason he was elected was to effect this change, and because the sort of soul capable of making this change is not the kind of president best able to facilitate the ongoing dance of executive-legislative policy making.

I wish it were not so. The populist in me would much rather see the energy the Internet has begun to channel mature into a cross-partisan (as in, one that cuts across partisan divisions) movement that forces a citizen-populated Article V convention onto the constitutional stage. But I fear we are still a people looking for a leader, not for leaders, even if that leader will depend fundamentally upon the support of the very many leaders that the Net now feeds.

The strength of the regent president has also been confirmed to me by the relative weakness of the one candidate in this election who made reform the central message—Buddy Roemer.

Roemer was easily the most qualified candidate in the 2012 republican primary. A four-term Congressman and former governor, he had more governmental experience than any other candidate. And as a businessman with twenty years in the private sector, he also had more private-sector experience than any except Herman Cain.

Yet Roemer was not invited to even a single presidential debate because he adopted a strategy that most believed would only ensure his defeat: a commitment to taking no more than $100 from anyone, and to abjuring any PAC or Super PAC support. Roemer took that commitment to make credible his claim that he would be "free to lead" as a president. How else could he distinguish himself, Roemer believed, from a field filled with special-interest money? But if most vote for the person they believe most likely to win, virtue here was poisonous. As one pundit put it to me, "[Roemer's election] would be amazing. And a cold day in hell."

Unlike Roemer, however, a candidate to become a regent president does not need unilateral disarmament to be credible. The device of a single-purpose mission makes the commitment clear. No one could doubt what the candidate's purpose would be, nor would there be any ambiguity about achieving it. The reform promised would be named. When that reform was enacted, the regent would resign. If he didn't, any credibility (and hence political power) would be lost.

This fact thus frees the regent to adopt a fully conventional style for campaigning. He can accept contributions from anyone. He need not object to any Super PAC support. And no doubt, while there is something sweetly ironic about accepting money from the very rich in order to end a corruption enabled by the very rich, it is a thin and forgivable irony, at least for souls like us. We wage war to secure peace, Quakers notwithstanding. A candidate for the regent presidency would likewise wage a war with financial influence to end the corrupting dependency upon money that so infects our political system today.

But how would a regent's campaign work? Why would anyone accept it?

My assumption is that they wouldn't—until they had to. No doubt the existing panoply of candidates for president would ignore any idea of the regent. But if the regent candidate(s) began to gain traction, the ordinary candidates would face a difficult choice: either fight the emerging reformer(s), or embrace the idea of the reformer, and fight to be (a short-term) vice president. For at some point, the ordinary candidates for president might recognize that the job could be much better once the corrupting influence of money had been removed.

The reason is crucial to understand, but on rereading, I don't think the book makes it clearly enough.

My focus throughout *Republic, Lost* was upon the dependency that has developed between Congress and the funders of Congress's campaigns. But I didn't do enough to understand the character of those funders. The striking and destabilizing fact about the funders that Congress depends upon is how few they are. This isn't the "one percent." It is a tiny slice of the 1 percent that funds the most significant portion of congressional campaigns. Only 0.26 percent of America gives more than $200 in a congressional campaign. Just 0.05 percent gives the maximum in any single election. The 1 percent of the 1 percent—0.01 percent—give more than $10,000 in an election cycle. And 196 Americans—the .0000063 percent of America—gave almost 80 percent of the money spent by Super PACs in the first quarter of 2012.

In a country of more than 300 million, these are small numbers. In their tininess, they reveal the great instability that is our current republic. They mean that for any issue of any significance to any interest with any access to significant resources, there is a tiny number of Americans who can effectively block legislation that would affect those interests. This is why we won't see any reform on a wide range of interests that are important to either the Left or the Right—because on those issues, there are ample resources that might be marshaled to block such reform.

The point is not about "the rich." The point is about any interest with access to resources threatened by reform. That may be "the rich"—think about the absurd fight about whether hedge-fund managers should pay more than 15 percent on their "carried earnings," roughly half the amount paid by the rest of wealthy America. Or it may simply be a large industry with a great deal at stake— think about the fight described in Chapter 10 between banks and retailers over the "bank swipe fee." No doubt banks and retailers

are not poor. But equally, no doubt, they are n
They are industries with a great deal to lose by a c
willing to invest a great deal to avoid that loss.

So long as we outsource the funding of elections 
we will be hostage to the preferences of that tiny p            .
Our current system—destined after this election to seem to most
as normal—thus assures that our republic will remain hostage to
their policies.

Such a government cannot long survive. The capacity for a small
minority to block any changes that might affect them means that
this government has been "debilitated." If the only changes that are
allowed are those that hurt the vast majority, without resources,
then the very idea of democratic government has been lost. The
tyranny of the majority has been displaced by a tyranny of the
minority—the tiny minority that funds the elections.

Wikipedia tells us that a regent is selected when the ruler "is a
minor, not present, or debilitated." Debilitated is precisely what our
government has become. We should follow this crowd-sourced wisdom and begin the process now of identifying a plausible regent
for 2016. But even that may be too late. Our problems certainly
seem more urgent. In the meantime, we should do everything else
that we can to push for reform, and to witness the swearing-in of a
regent in 2017 to accomplish it.

# Acknowledgments

I am grateful to many for their generous help.

I was aided in the research by an army of scholars and some soon-to-be lawyers, including Jennifer Campbell, Alissa Del Riego, Dominic DeNunzio, Ronak Desai, Ryan Doerfler, Ann Donaldson, Paul Dumaine, Jacob Eisler, Rachel Goldstein, Jeremy Haber, Lauren Henry, Jason Iuliano, Rohit Malik, Randy Maas, Bryson Morgan, Benjamin Sadun, Shaina Lee Trotta, and Chinh Vo. Matthew Wansley helped organize that army and did exceptional work on his own for an extended period.

My understanding of these issues was also affected substantially by students in four corruption seminars that I taught, two at Stanford, one at Harvard, and one at the University of Cincinnati. Paul Gowder helped me pull together the first of these seminars. Joel Hyatt co-taught the second at Stanford and has guided my thinking and work here substantially.

Michael Nelson, Michael Powell, Larry Pressler, and Ken Silverstein offered insights in a series of interviews. Mark McKinnon, Trevor Potter, and Nick Allard helped introduce the world of lobbying, as well as others less eager to be named. David Post showed me Jefferson on corruption. Zephyr Teachout's work about the Framers generally has been essential to my own. I am grateful to her, and eager to read her forthcoming book, *Benjamin Franklin's Snuff Box* (to be published in 2012).

Help with ideas and references was also provided by a wide range of Tweeps, including @JMHeggen, @EDUCAUSEeq, @gfish, @mrtnzlngr, @bobblakley, @bobblakley, @heydan, @dlnorman, @xt1, and @dclauzel.

Without the program Freedom (macfreedom.com), this book would not have been completed.

Early drafts of the manuscript were read by a wide range of colleagues and friends, including Eric Beerbohm, John Coates, Congressman Jim Cooper, Stephen Erickson, Chris Hayes, Judge Richard Posner, Susannah Rose, Alex Whiting, Tim Wu, and Jonathan Zittrain. Congressman Cooper's writing deserves special note. I have never received harsher comments on anything I have written. The criticism was valuable and correct, but I am especially grateful for the integrity it represents.

I presented a draft of part of this work at the Yale Legal Theory Workshop, and the Edmond J. Safra Center for Ethics Faculty Workshop.

Jef Pollock of Global Strategy Group provided survey research about attitudes toward Congress. MapLight helped frame a set of the influence data. Except where noted, Jin Suk designed the graphics that appear in the text.

None of this work would have been possible without the endless support of the Edmond J. Safra Center for Ethics, and Lily Safra especially. Nor without Szelena Gray, who has lent me her enormous talent. I am endlessly grateful to her, for her, and for her work.

This book is dedicated to "the million Arnold Hiatts this revolution will need." That includes, of course, Hiatt himself. It also includes an extraordinary collection of the believers in this cause who have taught me most everything I know about the issue and the challenge it presents: David Donnelly, Ellen Miller, Daniel Newman, Nick Nyhart, John Rauh, Micah Sifry, Josh Silver, and Daniel Weeks. I am also thankful to the amazing team that helped build Change Congress, Fix Congress First, and now Rootstrikers, including Monica Walsh, Japhet Els, Aaron Swartz, Adam Green, Stephanie Taylor, friends at Blue State Digital, and now Joey Mornin. I am especially grateful to the funders of those organizations, including especially Marc Andreessen, Matt and Cindy Cutts, Mike Klein, Kathleen McGrath and J. J. Abrams, David Mills, Dan Nova, Deborah Salkind, Richard Senn, Jonathan and Jennifer Soros, and the thousands of others who offered whatever they could to make change possible.

No dedication, however, could rightly acknowledge the sacrifice this work has forced on those I love most, Bettina and my three kids, Willem, Teo, and Tess. However important this issue is, it is as nothing compared to them.

# *Appendix*

## What You Can Do, Now

This is not a book about changing Congress written by a candidate for Congress. I promise (and indeed, have promised my first child if I break that promise). As I've described, this book is a call for a politics without politicians. That means we need a way to motivate citizens that doesn't in the end connect to some campaign for some important national office. It needs to be about ideals, or principles, not about a person and his or her inevitable flaws.

That campaign begins by spreading a certain kind of understanding, a recognition of how a wide range of issues get affected by one common influence: campaign cash. The group I helped start, Rootstrikers.org, works to spread that recognition by asking supporters to tag stories that evince this connection, and help spread those stories to as many souls as possible.

These stories sometimes simply present themselves: journalists, encouraged in part by fantastic resources provided by groups such as OpenSecrets.org, FollowTheMoney.org, OpenCongress.org, and MapLight, are increasingly including references to the obvious issue of campaign funding as they describe almost every issue of public policy.

But the stories sometimes require people to connect the dots. Rootstrikers.org asks citizens to help others see the connection, and spread this understanding. It also asks people from many different political perspectives to contribute to this common understanding. I recognize that the issues that upset friends on the Right will upset me less, and vice versa. But if we can begin to see that there is a common root, we might begin to address that common root.

So the first most important thing that you can do is to make it a practice to point: Whenever you see a money-in-politics story, tag it on Twitter with #rootstrikers. Or add it to Rootstrikers.org, and ask others to comment. Or put it on your Facebook wall or, ideally, your blog. Describe it in a way that helps others understand the issue. Help build a constant campaign driven by citizens to educate all of us about this issue.

The understanding that will grow from this grass-roots effort must then manifest itself in specific organizations driving for specific reforms. I've described my own preferred reform. But the most prominent recent example of reform like this was the effort to enact the Fair Elections Now Act. PublicCitizen.org, PublicCampaign.org, and CommonCause.org were the most engaged and effective organizations pushing to enact that act. They continue to push politicians to sign the Voters First Pledge at VotersFirstPledge.org.

These groups have inspired a new organization, which launched in the summer of 2011. The Fund for the Republic (Fundforthe Republic.org) promises to gather a politically diverse mix of rich people who commit to spending a great deal of their wealth to reform this system. Of all the organizational developments that have happened, this is among the most promising, as the Fund for the Republic is led by one of the very best organizers in this field, and has the potential to rally a great deal of support.

The second most important thing you can do is to demand that candidates for Congresss take a pledge to support small-dollar-funded campaigns. Whenever they speak publicly, get this question asked. Only by making this issue a constant focus of campaigns will we get enough representatives to commit to doing something about it. Let there never be another public meeting of a congressman or a candidate for Congress without this question asked, and asked again. And when it is asked, record it and post it on YouTube or blip.tv or Vimeo, and point us and others to the response.

For the Internet is the only tool we can rely upon just now. For at least the next five years, it will be the one tool that gives grass-roots movements an edge. You can be confident that this medium, too, will evolve. That soon it will feel as professional as magazine ads or television commercials. But for now there is enormous credibility that comes from authentic engagement. We can build that engagement, one click at a time.

There is also important work to do now to support the idea of a convention. Most important immediately is to push for mock conventions. You can find out how to support a mock convention at CallAConvention.org. These mock conventions, I believe, will begin to show Americans that we're not so dumb. That, in fact, the work we do as amateurs to reform this democracy is much better than the work the professionals do. If there were five hundred mock conventions in the next four years, there would be a strong national movement to support a constitutional convention. In the end, I confess, this may be the only real path to reform. We should educate the people to practice it well.

Finally, there is critical work to be done now to build understanding across the insane political divide that defines politics in America today. There are entities whose business model depends upon dividing us: Fox News, MSNBC, the Tea Party, BoldProgressives.org. But the souls who are fans of each of these extraordinary institutions must begin to see that we are more than these institutions allow us to be. However far from my views a member of the Tea Party is, we still agree about certain fundamentals: that it is a republic we have inherited; that it ought to be responsive to "the People alone"; that this one is not.

This isn't just a hypothesis for me. I've seen it firsthand. I stood in the middle of a national Tea Party convention. I recognized the people around me. They may not have agreed with me about gay rights. I don't know if they did, for their convention was not focused on that kind of issue. We certainly didn't agree about taxes or the need to "end government regulation." But we were united in the view that this republic can do better.

We need to remember how different our forebears were. Two hundred-plus years later, they all look the same to us. But they had very different values and radically different ideas about what their republic should be.

They put those differences aside, and saved their nation from ruin. We must do the same. Not after the next election. Now.

# *Notes*

Throughout these notes there are references to links (e.g., "link #23") on the Web. As anyone who has used the Web knows, these links can be highly unstable. I have tried to address this instability by redirecting readers to the original source through the website associated with this book. For each link below, you can go to Republic.Lessig.org and locate the original source. If the original link remains alive, you will be redirected to that link. If the original link has disappeared, you will be redirected to a cached copy of the original source. I have used the wonderful resource WebCitation .org to store the cached version.

## Introduction

1. "Congress Ranks Last in Confidence in Institutions," July 22, 2010, available at link #1.
2. Ronald J. Pestritto and William J. Atto, *American Progressivism: A Reader* (Lanham, Md.: Lexington Books, 2008), 40–41, quoting "Who Is a Progressive," April 1912 speech, reprinted in *Outlook* 100, April 1912.
3. Richard L. McCormick, "The Discovery That Business Corrupts Politics: A Reappraisal of the Origins of Progressivism," *American Historical Review* 86 (1981): 247, 270. There is some contest among historians about how new this awareness was. Richard Hofstadter, for example, argues "there was nothing new." But as McCormick powerfully describes, there was much about the mechanism to the emerging type of corruption that was not understood generally, or broadly. And when it was understood, it sparked a powerful political response. Ibid., 265. Beginning in 1906, "both major parties gushed in opposition to what the Republicans now called 'the domination of corporate influences in public affairs.' " Ibid., 263.
4. Jeffrey H. Birnbaum, *The Money Men: The Real Story of Fund-raising's Influence on Political Power in America* (New York: Crown Publishers, 2000), 29. See also the extremely compelling account by Jack Beatty in *Age of Betrayal* (New York: Vintage, 2007).
5. Pestritto and Atto, *American Progressivism*, 215, quoting Roosevelt's "The New Nationalism," Oct. 1910.
6. McCormick, "The Discovery that Business Corrupts Politics," 247, 265.
7. Speech of Theodore Roosevelt, April 14, 1906, available at link #2.

8. John Joseph Wallis, "The Concept of Systematic Corruption in American History," in Edward Glaeser and Claudia Goldin, eds., *Corruption and Reform* (Chicago: University of Chicago Press, 2006), 21 and 23, available at link #3.

Professor Michael Johnston is the dean of corruption studies. His *Syndromes of Corruption* (2005) captures better the dynamic of corruption that I am describing. While his work is comparative, and addresses the full range of corruption, including quid pro quo corruption, the mechanism he describes in a number of nations is close to the conception of "dependence corruption" described later.

## Chapter 1. Good Souls, Corrupted

1. The first prominent reports of Yeltsin's drunkenness came from a trip to the United States in 1989. Those reports were later discredited, including by the U.S. reporter who first reported them. Leon Aron, *Yeltsin: A Revolutionary Life* (New York: St. Martin's, 2000), 324, 344–48.
2. Taylor Branch, *The Clinton Tapes* (New York: Simon and Schuster, 2009), 56.
3. Ibid., 198.
4. See e.g., "The Scientific Basis of Influence and Reciprocity: A Symposium," June 12, 2007, Washington, D.C. (Association of America's Medical Colleges).
5. Dennis Thompson's work goes the furthest in distinguishing institutional from individual corruption. His conception of institutional corruption, however, is more strongly tied to private interest than my own. See "Two Concepts of Corruption," 12, n. 11 (Paper presented at an E. J. Safra Lab workshop, Nov. 2010). In my view, if an institution has an intended dependency, we should be able to call deviation from that dependency "corruption," regardless of whether or not it is motivated by private interest. Dependency corruption as I describe it later thus violates the independence of an institution. But not only because it "tend[s] to promote private interests." Ibid., 2.
6. As will become clear in the balance of this book, the term *dependence corruption* describes the process of governance. It doesn't point to a particular tainted result. It is thus distinct from the three end-state types of corruption described by Burke, quid pro quo, monetary influence, and distortion, in the sense that it could exist even if there were none of these three end-state corruptions present. See Thomas F. Burke, "The Concept of Corruption in Campaign Finance Law," *Constitutional Commentary* 14 (1997): 127, 131.
7. See Godfrey Davies, "Charles II in 1660," *Huntington Library Quarterly* 19 (1956): 245, 254–55. ("For about two years, 1654 to 1656, Charles lived at Cologne, in moderate comfort so long as the French paid him a pension.") See also Clyde L. Grose, "Louis XIV's Financial Relations with Charles II and the English Parliament," *Journal of Modern History* 1 (1929): 177, 204.
8. As Pierce Butler described at the convention, "A man takes a seat in parliament to get an office for himself or friends, or both; and this is the great source from which flows its great venality and corruption." Notes of Robert Yates (June 22, 1787), in *Records of the Federal Convention of 1787*, vol. 1, ed. Max Farrand, 1966, 379, quoting Butler.

## Chapter 2. Good Questions, Raised

1. Nena Baker, *The Body Toxic* (New York: North Point Press, 2008), 153.
2. Ibid., 142.

3. Ibid.
4. House of Representatives, Congress of the United States, Committee on Energy and Commerce (2009).
5. Denise Grady, "In Feast of Data on BPA Plastic, No Final Answer," *New York Times*, Sept. 6, 2010, D1, available at link #4.
6. Baker, *The Body Toxic*, 155, quoting Pete Mayers.
7. Grady, "In Feast of Data on BPA Plastic."
8. Baker, *The Body Toxic*, 142.
9. Trevor Butterworth, "Science Suppressed: How America Became Obsessed with BPA," Statistical Assessment Service, June 12, 2009, available at link #5. See also Gina Kolata, "Flaws in the Case Against BPA," *New York Times*, June 30, 2009, posted to *TierneyLab*, available at link #6.
10. "Spin the Bottle," *Harper's*, Dec. 2009, at link #7.
11. Baker, *The Body Toxic*, 144.
12. Ibid.
13. Ibid.
14. Kevin Stein et al., "Prevalence and Sociodemographic Correlates of Beliefs Regarding Cancer Risks," *Cancer* 110 (2007): 1141, available at link #8.
15. The most significant biologic effect here is damage to DNA. As Devra Davis writes, the "first time anyone had seen direct evidence that cell-phone-type radiation adversely affected DNA" was 1994. Devra Davis, *Disconnect: The Truth About Cell Phone Radiation, What the Industry Has Done to Hide It, and How to Protect Your Family* (New York: Dutton Adult, 2010), 229. Since then there have been many other studies, including an "extraordinary review" that concluded "cell phone radiation does damage DNA."
16. Frank Jordans, "Study on Cell Phone Link to Cancer Inconclusive," available at link #9. The World Health Organization's International Agency for Research on Cancer (IARC) recently concluded that the radio frequency used by cell phones is possibly carcinogenic. See Press Release No. 208, May 31, 2011, available at link #10.
17. Ibid.
18. Ibid.
19. Davis, *Disconnect*, 229.
20. Anke Huss, Matthias Egger, Kerstin Hug, Karin Huwiler-Müntener, and Martin Röösli, "Source of Funding and Results of Studies of Health Effects of Mobile Phone Use: Systematic Review of Experimental Studies," *Environmental Health Perspectives* 115 (2007): 1, 3.
21. Ibid.
22. See generally Dennis F. Thompson, "Understanding Financial Conflicts of Interest," *New England Journal of Medicine* 329 (1993): 573; "Conflicts of Interest," Responsible Conduct of Research, available at link #11 (last visited June 21, 2011); Michael McDonald, "Ethics and Conflict of Interest," The W. Maurice Young Center for Applied Ethics (Oct. 21, 2007), available at link #12.
23. For a related analysis in the context of public health research, see Katherine A. McComas, "The Role of Trust in Health Communication and the Effect of Conflicts of Interest Among Scientists," *Proceedings of the Nutrition Society* 67 (2008): 428n, available at link #13.

24. Robert C. Brooks, *Corruption in American Politics and Life* (New York: Dodd, Mead and Company, 1910), 93.

25. Dennis F. Thompson, *Ethics in Congress: From Individual to Institutional Corruption* (Washington, D.C.: The Brookings Institution, 1995), 124.

26. I don't mean to suggest that this is an easy question to answer. This is the lesson of Peter Morgan and Glenn Reynolds's powerful book, *The Appearance of Impropriety* (New York: Free Press, 1997). In example after example, Morgan and Reynolds demonstrate the political system's inability to distinguish real from fabricated political conflicts. This problem will only grow as the political environment becomes more poisonous. I don't pretend to offer any solution to bad faith, though as I emphasize in "Against Transparency" (*New Republic*, Oct. 9, 2009), the most obvious solution is to eliminate the suggestion that there may be a conflict.

27. Florence T. Bourgeois, Srinivas Murthy, and Kenneth D. Mandl, "Outcome Reporting Among Drug Trials Registered in ClinicalTrials.gov," *Annals of Internal Medicine* 153 no. 3 (Aug. 3, 2010): 158–66, 159, available at link #14.

28. Eli Pariser, *The Filter Bubble: What the Internet Is Hiding from You* (forthcoming, New York: Penguin Press, 2011), 28.

29. Top 1000 Sites—DoubleClick Ad Planner, available at link #15. The $150 million is calculated as follows: $1 per thousand page views, an estimated fourteen billion page views per month, times twelve months is at least $150 million.

30. Interview with author, May 4, 2007.

31. "Therefore I Travel, Company Profile of Lonely Planet," Tony Wheeler, Lonely Planet, available at link #16.

32. Adam Smith, *The Wealth of Nations*, vol. 1, ed. Edwin Cannan (Chicago: University of Chicago Press, 1976), 477 (book IV, chapter II: "Of Restraints upon the Importation from foreign Countries of such Goods as can be produced at Home").

## Chapter 3. 1 + 1 =

1. Paul Krugman, "Boiling the Frog," *New York Times*, July 13, 2009, at A19.

## Part II. Tells

1. Marc J. Hetherington, *Why Trust Matters: Declining Political Trust and the Demise of American Liberalism* (Princeton, N.J.: Princeton University Press, 2005), 9.

## Chapter 4. Why Don't We Have Free Markets?

1. Karl Weber, ed., *Food, Inc.: How Industrial Food Is Making Us Sicker, Fatter, and Poorer—and What You Can Do About It* (New York: Public Affairs Press, 2009), 228–29; Centers for Disease Control and Prevention, National Diabetes Fact Sheet (2007), 10–11, available at link #17.

2. Neil H. White, "Obesity, Type 2 Diabetes Rates Growing Rapidly Among Children," Washington University in St. Louis (website), Mar. 11, 2005, available at link #18 ("In 1985, experts estimated that about 1 to 2 percent of children with diabetes had Type 2").

3. Thomas Frieden, William Dietz, and Janet Collins, "Reducing Childhood Obesity Through Policy Changes: Acting Now to Prevent Obesity," *Health Affairs* 29, no. 3 (2010): 357–63, cited in Ellen-Marie Whelan, Lesley Russell, and Sonia Sekhar,

*Confronting America's Childhood Obesity Epidemic: How the Health Care Reform Law Will Help Prevent and Reduce Obesity*, Center for American Progress, 2010, 1.

4. See Centers for Disease Control and Prevention, National Diabetes Fact Sheet 8 (2007).

5. Whelan, Russell, and Sekhar, "Confronting America's Childhood Obesity Epidemic."

6. Heidi Adams, "Obesity in America: One Nation, Overweight," Oct. 31, 2008, available at link #19. See also "Reason for Increase in Number of Children with Type 2 Diabetes," MSN Health Network, July 28, 2008, available at link #20. See also "Type 2 Diabetes in Children and Adolescents," Consensus Statement, *Diabetes Care* 23, no. 3 (2000): 381–89.

7. National Center for Health Statistics, "Prevalence of Overweight, Obesity, and Extreme Obesity Among Adults: United States, Trends 1976–80 through 2005–2006" (2008), 3, available at link #21.

8. National Center for Health Statistics, "Health, United States, 2009: With Special Feature on Medical Technology" (2009), 303, available at link #22.

9. Eric A. Finkelstein et al., "Annual Medical Spending Attributable to Obesity: Payer- And Service-Specific Estimates," *Health Affairs* 28 (2009): 822.

10. Dana E. King et al., "Adherence to Healthy Lifestyle Habits in US Adults, 1988–2006," *American Journal of Medicine* 122 (2009): 528, 530.

11. James E. Tillotson, "Food Brands: Friend or Foe?" *Nutrition Today* (March–April 2002): 78, 79.

12. For this dynamic described, see David Kessler, *The End of Overeating* (New York: Rodale, 2009), 12.

13. Michael Pollan, *The Omnivore's Dilemma* (New York: Penguin Press, 2006), 104.

14. Ibid., 103–4.

15. Sarah Kate Coleman, "The Facts About High Fructose Corn Syrup," Jan. 13, 2010, available at link #23.

16. James Bovard, "Archer Daniels Midland: A Case Study in Corporate Welfare," Cato Policy Analysis, Cato Institute (1995), 1, available at link #24.

17. Ibid.

18. Kenneth Bailey, "Congress's Dairy Dilemma," *Regulation* (Winter 2001): 32. There were eleven. There now are ten. See U.S. Dep't of Agric., Econ. Res. Serv., Dairy: Policy (2009), available at link #25. See also Jasper Womach, "Agriculture: A Glossary of Terms, Programs, and Laws," Cong. Research Serv. Report for Congress, No. 97-905 (2005): 165, available at link #26.

19. Charles Lewis and the Center for Public Integrity, *The Buying of the Congress* (New York: Avon Books, 1998), 227.

20. Larry Rohter, "Brazil's Shrimp Caught Up in a Trade War," *New York Times*, March 10, 2004. The government had found "dumping." Mark Drajem, "U.S. Sets Shrimp Tariffs on Thailand, India, Ecuador, Brazil," Bloomberg (July 29, 2004), available at link #27.

21. Chana Joffe-Walt, "Why U.S. Taxpayers Are Paying Brazilian Cotton Growers," NPR, *All Things Considered*, Nov. 9, 2010, available at link #28.

22. David E. Sanger, "Dole at Forefront of Trade Battle to Aid Donor's Banana Empire," *New York Times*, Dec. 5, 1995, at A1, B9.

23. Brian M. Riedl, "Agriculture Lobby Wins Big in New Farm Bill," Backgrounder No. 1534, Heritage Foundation (April 9, 2002), available at link #29.

24. Press Release, White House, "President Announces Temporary Safeguards for Steel Industry" (Mar. 5, 2002), available at link #30. See also "Counting the Cost of Steel Production: Hearing Before the Subcomm. on Trade of the H. Comm. on Ways and Means, 106th Cong." (1999) (statement of Daniel Griswold, Cato Inst.), available at link #31.

25. Brink Lindsey, Mark Groombridge, and Prakash Loungani, "Nailing the Homeowner: The Economic Impact of Trade Protection of the Softwood Lumber Industry," Trade Pol'y Analysis no. 11, Cato Inst. (July 6, 2000), available at link #32.

26. Raghuram Rajan and Luigi Zingales, *Saving Capitalism from the Capitalists* (New York: Crown Business, 2003), 230.

27. Brian M. Riedl, "Seven Reasons to Veto the Farm Bill," Backgrounder No. 2134, Heritage Foundation (May 12, 2008), 1-2, available at link #33.

28. Brian M. Riedl, "How Farm Subsidies Harm Taxpayers, Consumers, and Farmers, Too," Backgrounder No. 2043, Heritage Foundation (June 20, 2007), 8.

29. Ibid., 8-9. The subsidies here are for the period 1995-2005.

30. Rajan and Zingales, *Saving Capitalism from the Capitalists*, 229-30.

31. Jason Lee Steorts, "The Sugar Industry and Corporate Welfare," *Review*, July 18, 2005, available at link #34. See also "Sugar Manufacturing Industry Profile," First Research (2011).

32. Bovard, "Archer Daniels Midland"; Chris Edwards, "Agricultural Regulations and Trade Barriers Downsizing the Federal Government," available at link #35.

33. See World Wildlife Foundation Global Freshwater Program, "Sugar and the Environment: Encouraging Better Management Practices in Sugar Production" (2005), 9, available at link #36.

34. James Bovard, "The Great Sugar Shaft," The Future of Freedom Foundation, Freedom Daily (April 1998), available at link #37.

35. Int'l Trade Admin., U.S. Dep't Com., Employment Changes in U.S. Food Manufacturing: The Impact of Sugar Prices (2006), 2.

36. Bovard, "The Great Sugar Shaft."

37. Daniel J. Ikenson, "America's Credibility Goes 'Timber!'" *Free Trade Bulletin* (2005), available at link #38.

38. Edwards, "Agricultural Regulations and Trade Barriers Downsizing the Federal Government," 8.

39. United States Corn Subsidies, EWG Farm Subsidy Database, available at link #39; Donald Carr, "Corn Subsidies Make Unhealthy Food Choices the Rational Ones," Grist, Sept. 21, 2010, available at link #40.

40. Pollan, *The Omnivore's Dilemma*, 48-53; Elanor Starmer and Timothy A. Wise, "Feeding at the Trough: Industrial Livestock Firms Saved $35 Billion from Low Feed Prices," 07-03 Global Development and Environment Institute Policy Brief 2 (2007), available at link #41. ("Factory hog operations saw the price of feed drop to 26% below production costs during the 1997-2005 period.")

41. Elanor Starmer and Timothy A. Wise, "Living High on the Hog: Factory Farms, Federal Policy, and the Structural Transformation of Swine Production," Global Development and Environment Institute Working Paper 07-04 (2007), 1, 3. A second factor they point to is lax enforcement of environmental rules.

42. Ibid.

43. "Food and Water Watch, Another Take: Food Safety Consequences of Factory Farms," in Weber, ed., *Food, Inc.* In May 2011, a coalition of environmental groups filed suit against the FDA to force it to enforce its own findings about the dangers from routine antibiotic use. Tom Laskawy, "Groups Sue FDA to Stop Big Ag Antibiotic Abuse—and It Just Might Work," Grist, May 26, 2011, available at link #42.

44. Pollan, *The Omnivore's Dilemma*, 74, 78-79; Weber, ed., *Food, Inc.* See also Donald Kennedy, "Cows on Drugs," *New York Times*, April 18, 2010, available at link #43.

45. Pew Commission on Industrial Farm Animal Production, "Putting Meat on the Table: Industrial Farm Animal Production in America" (2008), 13, available at link #44 ("Food-borne pathogens can have dire consequences when they do reach human hosts. A 1999 report estimated that E. Coli O157:H7 infections caused approximately 73,000 illnesses each year, leading to over 2,000 hospitalizations and 60 deaths each year in the United States....Costs associated with E. Coli O157:H7-related illnesses in the United States were estimated at $405 million annually: $370 million for deaths, $30 million for medical care, and $5 million for lost productivity....Animal manure, especially from cattle, is the primary source of these bacteria, and consumption of food and water contaminated with animal wastes is a major route of human infection. Because of the large numbers of animals in a typical IFAP [International Federation of Agricultural Producers] facility, pathogens can infect hundreds or thousands of animals even though the infection rate may be fairly low as a share of the total population. In some cases, it may be very difficult to detect the pathogen; Salmonella enterica [SE], for example, is known to colonize the intestinal tract of birds without causing obvious disease,...although the infected hen ovaries then transfer the organism to the egg contents. Although the frequency of SE contamination in eggs is low (fewer than 1 in 20,000 eggs), the large numbers of eggs—65 billion—produced in the United States each year means that contaminated eggs represent a significant source for human exposure." Citations omitted.)

46. The three-year-old's story is told in *Food, Inc.* The dance instructor's, in Michael Moss, "The Burger That Shattered Her Life," *New York Times*, Oct. 3, 2009, A1, available at link #45.

47. A Cato Institute study estimated that it took seven barrels of oil to produce eight barrels of corn-derived ethanol. The Monitor's View, "Corn Lobby's Tall Tale of a Gas Substitute," *Christian Science Monitor*, May 12, 2006, available at link #46.

48. Bovard, "Archer Daniels Midland."

49. Coalition for Balanced Food and Fuel, "Expert Economist Says National Ethanol Policy Continuing to Drive Meat and Poultry Prices Higher" (2008), available at link #47. See also Thomas E. Elam, "Biofuel Support Policy Costs to the U.S. Economy" (2008), 3, available at link #48.

50. Federal Priorities Project, Federal Priorities Database, available at link #49.

51. Center for Responsive Politics, OpenSecrets.org, "Sugar Cane and Sugar Beets: Long-Term Contribution Trends," available at link #50.

52. Center for Responsive Politics, OpenSecrets.org, "Crop Production & Basic Processing: Long-Term Contribution Trends," available at link #51.

## Chapter 5. Why Don't We Have Efficient Markets?

1. Copyright Office, Copyright Law of the United States and Related Laws Contained in Title 17 of the United States Code vi-x (2009), available at link #52.
2. U.S. Energy Information Administration, "Emissions of Greenhouse Gases Report 2008" (Dec. 2009), 24, available at link #53.
3. Robert N. Stavins and Kenneth Richards, "The Cost of U.S. Forest Based Carbon Sequestration," Pew Center on Global Climate Change (2005), ii, available at link #54; David Biello, "Future of 'Clean Coal' Power Tied to (Uncertain) Success of Carbon Capture and Storage," *Scientific American*, March 14, 2007, available at link #55; Center for American Progress, "ACCCE Company Profits," available at link #56. Profit of Coal and Petroleum industry as reported in U.S. Industry Quarterly Review: Energy 30 (Global Insight Inc., 2004).
4. Conrad Schneider and Jonathan Banks, "The Toll from Coal," Clean Air Task Force, Sept. 2010, 4, 10, available at link #57.
5. According to MapLight, coal-mining companies and employees contributed $2,344,731 to legislators from the top five coal-producing states (Wyoming, West Virginia, Kentucky, Pennsylvania, and Montana) between 2005 and 2010. One-third of that sum went to twenty-five Democrats.
6. Center for Responsive Politics, OpenSecrets.org, "Pro-Environment Groups Outmatched, Outspent in Battle over Climate Change Legislation," available at link #58.
7. See OpenSecrets.org. Data aggregates campaign and lobbying expenditures for "Print & Publishing" (see links #32 and #33) plus "TV/Movies/Music" (see links #34 and #35) versus campaign and lobbying expenditures for Public Knowledge, Open Internet Coalition, Digital Future Coalition, and the National Humanities Alliance (links #36 and #37) and (links #38 and $39).

## Chapter 6. Why Don't We Have Successful Schools?

1. Jessica Shepherd, "World Education Rankings: Which Country Does Best at Reading, Maths and Science?" *Guardian*, Dec. 7, 2010, available at link #59.
2. This claim is not uncontroversial. Vivek Wadhwa argues, for example, that the statistics fail to take into account critical thinking skills and innovation, see Vivek Wadhwa, "U.S. Schools Are Still Ahead—Way Ahead," *Businessweek*, Jan. 12, 2011, available at link #60; and Diane Ravitch points out that a 1991 report argued that the U.S. education system had been "stead[ily] improving." See Diane Ravitch, "Is U.S. Education Better Than Ever?" Huffington Post (Dec. 5, 2007), available at link #61, (referring to C. C. Carson, R. M. Huelskamp, and T. D. Woodall, "Perspectives on Education in America: An Annotated Briefing," *Journal of Education Research* 86 [May 1993]: 259). But the OECD's Programme for International Student Assessment (PISA), an international survey conducted in 2000, 2003, 2006, and 2009, reports that the United States is worse off than in 2000 as compared to other nations. And according to the National Assessment of Educational Progress (NAEP), the U.S. reading and math performance has remained largely flat since the early 1970s. See National Center for Education Statistics, "Trend in NAEP Reading Average Scores for 17-year-old Students" (2008), available at link #62 (documenting change in average scaled reading score of 285 in 1971 to 286 in 2008); National Center for Education Statistics, "Trend in Mathematics

Average Scores for 17-year-old Students" (2008), available at link #63 (documenting change in average scaled mathematics score of 304 in 1973 to 306 in 2008).

3. William Dobbie and Roland G. Fryer, Jr., "Are High-Quality Schools Enough to Close the Achievement Gap? Evidence from a Bold Social Experiment in Harlem," Harvard University (2009), available at link #64. See also David Brooks, "The Harlem Miracle," *New York Times*, May 7, 2009, at A31, available at link #65.

4. Eric A. Hanushek, "Teacher Deselection," in *Creating a New Teaching Profession*, Dan Goldhaber and Jane Hannaway, eds. (Washington, D.C.: Urban Institute Press, 2009), 168, 172, 173.

5. See Steven G. Rivkin, Eric A. Hanushek, and John F. Kain, "Teachers, Schools, and Academic Achievement," *Econometrica* 73 (Mar. 2005): 417, available at link #66 (measuring the importance of effective teachers), and Scholastic and Bill & Melinda Gates Foundation, "Primary Sources: America's Teachers on America's Schools" (2010), available at link #67 (same); William Dobbie and Roland G. Fryer, Jr., "Are High-Quality Schools Enough to Close the Achievement Gap? Evidence from a Bold Social Experiment in Harlem" (2009), available at link #64 (evaluating effectiveness of Harlem Children's Zone program); Joshua D. Angrist, Susan M. Dynarski, Thomas J. Kane, Parag A. Pathak, and Christopher R. Walters, "Who Benefits From KIPP?" NBER working paper (2010), available at link #68 (evaluating effectiveness of KIPP Academy); Martha Abele, Mac Iver, and Elizabeth Farley-Ripple, "The Baltimore KIPP Ujima Village Academy, 2002–2006: A Longitudinal Analysis of Student Outcomes," Center for Social Organization of Schools, Johns Hopkins University (2007), available at link #69 (same).

6. See the resources at Ounce of Prevention, Publications, available at link #70.

7. Center for Responsive Politics, OpenSecrets.org, Teachers' Unions: Long-Term Contribution Trends, available at link #71; Center for Responsive Politics, OpenSecrets.org, Democrats for Education Reform Expenditures, 2010 Cycle, available at link #72; Center for Responsive Politics, OpenSecrets.org, Democrats for Education Reform Expenditures, 2008 Cycle, available at link #73; Center for Responsive Politics, OpenSecrets.org, Democrats for Education Reform Expenditures, 2006 Cycle, available at link #74.

## Chapter 7. Why Isn't Our Financial System Safe?

1. My claim is not that the failures I describe in this chapter were the most important cause of the economic collapse, or even that properly handled, they would have avoided the economic collapse. Certainly the biggest drivers beyond the low interest rates were the trade imbalance and currency distortions with foreign trading partners. Jeffrey A. Frieden and Menzie D. Chinn, *Lost Decades: The Making of America's Debt Crisis and the Long Recovery* (forthcoming: Sept. 2011). But the argument here is about the rationality of this part of our financial policy, however significant this part is.

2. David Moss, "Reversing the Null: Regulation, Deregulation, and the Power of Ideas," Harvard Business School Working Paper, No. 10-080, Oct. 2010, 3, available at link #75. This graph was derived from Moss's more extensive original with permission from the author.

3. David Moss, "An Ounce of Prevention: Financial Regulation, Moral Hazard, and the End of 'Too Big to Fail,'" *Harvard Magazine* (Sept.–Oct. 2009): 25.

4. See Richard A. Posner, *The Crisis of Capitalist Democracy* (Cambridge, Mass.: Harvard University Press, 2010); and Richard A. Posner, *A Failure of Capitalism: The Crisis of '08 and the Descent into Depression* (Cambridge, Mass.: Harvard University Press, 2009).

5. Posner, *The Crisis of Capitalist Democracy*, 169.

6. These are described generally in David Moss, "An Ounce of Prevention," 25. See also Jacob S. Hacker and Paul Pierson, *Winner-Take-All Politics: How Washington Made the Rich Richer and Turned Its Back on the Middle Class* (New York: Simon and Schuster, 2010), 68.

7. Financial Crisis Inquiry Commission, Financial Crisis Inquiry Report (2011), 45, available at link #76.

8. Here, too, technology was critical. Technology not only enabled the crafting of complex mortgage-backed securities, but it also allowed mortgage lenders to lend on the basis of a portfolio of borrowers rather than the judgment about the creditworthiness of one borrower at a time. See, e.g., William R. Emmons and Stuart I. Greenbaum, "Twin Information Revolutions and the Future of Financial Intermediation," in Y. Amihud and G. Miller, eds., *Mergers and Acquisitions* (1998), 37–56; and Mitchell Petersen and Raghuram G. Rajan, "Does Distance Still Matter? The Information Revolution in Small Business Lending," *Journal of Finance* 57 (Dec. 2002): 2533–70.

9. Frank Partnoy, *Infectious Greed: How Deceit and Risk Corrupted the Financial Markets* (New York: Times Books, 2003), 110–13. The crisis was caused when the Fed surprised markets by raising interest rates.

10. Ibid., 145.

11. Gillian Tett, *Fool's Gold: How the Bold Dream of a Small Tribe at J. P. Morgan Was Corrupted by Wall Street Greed and Unleashed a Catastrophe* (New York: Free Press, 2009), 39.

12. Kevin P. Phillips, *Arrogant Capital: Washington, Wall Street, and the Frustration of American Politics* (New York: Little, Brown, and Co., 1995), 97.

13. Tett, *Fool's Gold*, 40.

14. Hacker and Pierson, *Winner-Take-All Politics*, 197.

15. Financial Services Modernization (Gramm-Leach-Bliley) Act of 1999, Pub. L. 106-102, 113 Stat. 1338 (codified in scattered sections of 12 and 15 U.S.C.).

16. Partnoy, *Infectious Greed*, 141.

17. Tett, *Fool's Gold*, 40.

18. See SEC Rule 3a-7 [17 CFR 270.3a-7], adopted in 57 Fed. Reg. 56,256 (Nov. 27, 1992). For discussion of the Dodd-Frank Reform Bill, see "Elizabeth Warren, TARP Watchdog and New Deal 2.0 Contributor," in Lynn Parramore, "Disappointing and Inspiring: Roosevelt Fellows and Colleagues React to FinReg," Huffington Post (June 25, 2010), available at link #77; Marshall Auerback, "A Proposal for Genuine Financial Reform," New Am. Found. (Feb. 2010), available at link #78.

19. Roger Lowenstein, *The End of Wall Street* (New York: Penguin Press, 2010), 58.

20. Ibid., 58–59.

21. Ibid., 59.

22. The President's Working Group on Financial Markets, Over-the-Counter Derivatives Markets and the Commodity Exchange Act (1999), 1, available at link #79.

23. Tett, *Fool's Gold*, 75.

24. Financial Crisis Inquiry Commission, Financial Crisis Inquiry Report (2011), xxiv, available at link #76.

25. And according to Louise Story of the *New York Times*, the secrecy serves an important (anti)competitive purpose as well. See Louise Story, "A Secretive Banking Elite Rules Trading in Derivatives," *New York Times,* Dec. 11, 2010, available at link #80.

26. Financial Crisis Inquiry Commission has likewise pointed to lack of "price transparency" as a factor that exacerbated the crisis. See Financial Crisis Inquiry Commission, Financial Crisis Inquiry Report (2011), 267.

27. Partnoy, *Infectious Greed*, 46.

28. Financial Crisis Inquiry Commission, Financial Crisis Inquiry Report (2011), 40.

29. Partnoy, *Infectious Greed*, 46.

30. Ibid., 402.

31. Financial Crisis Inquiry Commission, Financial Crisis Inquiry Report (2011), 53.

32. Posner, *The Crisis of Capitalist Democracy*, 192-93.

33. Ibid., 251 (emphasis added).

34. Ibid., 168.

35. Ibid., 264 (emphasis added).

36. Financial Crisis Inquiry Commission, Financial Crisis Inquiry Report (2011), 211 (quoting Moody's COO Andrew Kimball).

37. Ibid., xvii.

38. Raghuram G. Rajan, *Fault Lines: How Hidden Fractures Still Threaten the World Economy* (Princeton, N.J.: Princeton University Press, 2010), 152.

39. Marcus Miller, Paul Weller, and Lei Zhang, "Moral Hazard and the U.S. Stock Market: Analyzing the 'Greenspan Put,'" CSGR Working Paper no. 83/01 (2001), available at link #81. Financial Crisis Inquiry Commission reached a similar conclusion. See Financial Crisis Inquiry Commission, Financial Crisis Inquiry Report (2011), 60-61. See also Rajan, *Fault Lines*, 112-14.

40. Rajan, *Fault Lines*, 148.

41. Simon Johnson and James Kwak, *13 Bankers* (New York: Pantheon Books, 2010), 151-52. The change was in the Federal Deposit Insurance Corporation Improvement Act of 1991.

42. Ibid., 180. In a later analysis, Kwak writes "that the ['too big to fail'] subsidy exists, even after controlling for other factors that explain bank funding costs, and that it is in the range of 50 to 73 basis points." James Kwak, "Who Is Too Big to Fail?" Presented at "New Ideas for Limiting Bank Size," conference of the Fordham Corporate Law Center, Fordham Law School, New York, March 12, 2010, 26.

43. Financial Crisis Inquiry Commission, Financial Crisis Inquiry Report (2011), 58.

44. Rajan, *Fault Lines*, 122.

45. Ibid., 143, citing Michiyo Nakamoto and David Wighton, "Citigroup Chief Stays Bullish on Buyouts," *Financial Times,* July 9, 2007.

46. Ibid., 148.

47. Paul Krugman, "Zombie Financial Ideas," *New York Times*, Opinion Blogs: *The Conscience of a Liberal*, Mar. 3, 2009, available at link #82.

48. As my colleague Mark Roe has argued, another example of too much regulation may have been the decision by Congress of when to give derivatives high

priority in bankruptcy, which forced the government to intervene to avoid the catastrophic costs of derivatives being the primary debt paid by defaulting banks. See Mark J. Roe, "The Derivatives Market's Payment Priorities as Financial Crisis Accelerator," ECGI Law Working Paper No. 153/2010 (Jan. 2011); Harvard Public Law Working Paper No. 10-17, available at link #83.

49. Johnson and Kwak, *13 Bankers*, 58.
50. Hacker and Pierson, *Winner-Take-All Politics*, 185.
51. John Kenneth Galbraith, *The Economics of Innocent Fraud: Truth for Our Time* (New York: Houghton Mifflin Harcourt, 2004), x.
52. Johnson and Kwak, *13 Bankers*, 9–10.
53. Rajan, *Fault Lines*, 181.
54. Financial Crisis Inquiry Commission, Financial Crisis Inquiry Report (2011), xviii.
55. Hacker and Pierson, *Winner-Take-All Politics*, 226.
56. Ibid., 226–27.
57. Ibid., 227.
58. Partnoy, *Infectious Greed*, 146.
59. Ibid., 145–46.
60. Tett, *Fool's Gold*, 244.
61. Ibid., 213.
62. Sewell Chan, "Financial Crisis Was Avoidable, Inquiry Finds," *New York Times*, Jan. 25, 2011, 3.
63. Rajan, *Fault Lines*, 154.

## Chapter 8. What the "Tells" Tell Us

1. Survey, Global Strategy Group (Jan. 11, 2011), on file with author.

## Chapter 9. Why *So Damn Much Money*

1. Robert Kaiser, *So Damn Much Money* (New York: Knopf Books, 2009), 356.
2. Norman J. Ornstein, Thomas E. Mann, and Michael J. Malbin, *Vital Statistics on Congress 2008* (Washington, D.C.: Brookings Institution Press, 2008), 19.
3. Arianna Huffington, *Third World America* (New York: Crown Publishers, 2010), 130.
4. Kaiser, *So Damn Much Money*, 115.
5. R. Sam Garrett, "The State of Campaign Finance Policy: Recent Developments and Issues for Congress," Cong. Res. Serv. (April 29, 2011), available at link #84. ("House and Senate campaigns' fund-raising and spending have generally increased steadily since the early 1990s. Specifically, receipts more than doubled, from $654.1 million in 1992 to approximately $1.8 billion in 2010. Disbursements rose similarly, from $675.1 million to approximately $1.8 billion.") In my view, the relevant question is much more pragmatic: Does the demand force members to spend more time raising money than before? Whether spending is constant relative to income or not, its nominal amount has increased, forcing more time to be spent on fund-raising. See Stephen Ansolabehere, John M. de Figueiredo, and James M. Snyder, "Why Is There So Little Money in U.S. Politics?" *Journal of Economic Perspectives* 17 (2003): 105.
6. Randall Bennett Woods, *LBJ: Architect of American Ambition* (New York: Simon and Schuster, 2006), 434.

7. History buffs are always fascinated by the strange coincidences between Lincoln and Kennedy (described and dismantled at Barbara Mikkelson and David P. Mikkelson, "Linkin' Kennedy," Snopes.com (Sept. 28, 2007), available at link #85. The more interesting historical intertwining, in my view, is between the two presidents Johnson. Andrew Johnson, a southern Democrat, was the most important force blocking the Radical Republicans from achieving their objectives for Reconstruction. Lyndon Johnson, a southern Democrat, is, in my view, the most important political force correcting that deep injustice.

8. House: Federal Election Commission, Financial Activity of All U.S. House of Representatives Candidates: 1988–2000, available at link #86; Senate: Federal Election Commission, Financial Activity of All U.S. Senate Candidates: 1988–2000, available at link #87; Political Party Committees: Campaign Finance Institute, Hard and Soft Money Raised by National Party Committees: 1992–2010, available at link #88.

9. Kaiser, *So Damn Much Money*, 272.

10. Thomas Stratmann, "Some Talk: Money in Politics: A (Partial) Review of the Literature," *Public Choice* 124 (2005): 135, 148.

11. See John C. Coates, IV, " 'Fair Value' as an Avoidable Rule of Corporate Law: Minority Discounts in Conflict Transactions," *University of Pennsylvania Law Review* 147 (1999): 1251, 1273–77 (reviewing idea of a "control premium").

12. Kaiser, *So Damn Much Money*, 201.

13. See Gary C. Jacobson, "Modern Campaigns and Representation," in Paul J. Quirk and Sarah A. Binder, eds., *The Legislative Branch* (Oxford University Press, 2005), 118.

14. Federal Election Campaign Act of 1971, as amended in 1974, 2 U.S.C. § 431 (1974).

15. James J. Sample, "Democracy at the Corner of First and Fourteenth: Judicial Campaign Spending and Equality" (Aug. 20, 2010), 10 (forthcoming in *NYU Annual Survey of American Law*); Hofstra Univ. Legal Studies Research Paper No. 10-29, available at link #89.

16. Samuel Issacharoff, "On Political Corruption," *Harvard Law Review* 124 (2010): 119–20.

17. Sample, "Democracy at the Corner of First and Fourteenth," 10; Hofstra University Legal Studies Research Paper No. 10-29, available at link #89.

18. Huffington, *Third World America*, 127.

19. Dan Clawson, Alan Neustadtl, and Mark Weller, *Dollars and Votes: How Business Campaign Contributions Subvert Democracy* (Philadelphia, Pa.: Temple University Press, 1998), 91.

20. Hacker and Pierson, *Winner-Take-All Politics*, 224.

21. Ibid., 160.

22. Bertram Johnson, "Individual Contributions: A Fundraising Advantage for the Ideologically Extreme?" *American Politics Research* 38 (2010): 890, 906.

23. Shigeo Hirano, James M. Snyder, Jr., Stephen Ansolabehere, and John Mark Hansen, "Primary Competition and Partisan Polarization in the U.S. Senate," National Science Foundation 2008, 4, finds that primaries don't contribute to polarization in the Senate, but this is not inconsistent with the claim about gerrymandered safe seats in the House. Unlike the House, the boundaries of the Senate are set by state lines.

24. Morris P. Fiorina and Samuel J. Abrams, *Disconnect: The Breakdown of Representation in American Politics* (Norman, Okla.: University of Oklahoma Press, 2009), 47.
25. Hacker and Pierson, *Winner-Take-All Politics*, 159.
26. Ibid.
27. Fiorina and Abrams, *Disconnect*, 87.
28. Jeffrey H. Birnbaum, *The Money Men: The Real Story of Fund-raising's Influence on Political Power in America* (New York: Crown Publishers, 2000), 11.
29. Fiorina and Abrams, *Disconnect*, 168.
30. "Top Industries: Senator Max Baucus 2003–2008," Center for Responsive Politics, OpenSecrets.org, available at link #90.
31. Hacker and Pierson, *Winner-Take-All Politics*, 238.
32. Kaiser, *So Damn Much Money*, 151.
33. Martin Schram, "Speaking Freely," Center for Responsive Politics (1995), 151.
34. Kaiser, *So Damn Much Money*, 19.
35. Richard W. Painter, *Getting the Government America Deserves* (Oxford University Press, 2009), 181.
36. This theory has received new support from Google's Ngram Viewer. See link #91.
37. William N. Eskridge, Jr., "Federal Lobbying Regulation: History through 1954," in *The Lobbying Manual*, ed. William J. Luneburg et al., 4th ed. (2009), 7 n.7.
38. *Trist v. Child*, 88 U.S. 451 (1874).
39. Ken Silverstein, *Turkmeniscam: How Washington Lobbyists Fought to Flack for a Stalinist Dictatorship* (New York: Random House, 2008), 56.
40. Ibid., 57.
41. Ibid., 57–58.
42. Kenneth G. Crawford, *The Pressure Boys: The Inside Story of Lobbying in America* (Julian Messner, Inc., 1939), 3.
43. Thompson, *Ethics in Congress*, 2.
44. Crawford, *The Pressure Boys*, 25–26.
45. Thompson, *Ethics in Congress*, 2.
46. Painter, *Getting the Government America Deserves*, 27.
47. Crawford, *The Pressure Boys*, 27. Crawford states this letter is from "Edwards," but there was no "G. W. Edwards" who served in Congress. George Washington Edmonds served from 1913 to 1934. See Edmonds, George Washington, (1864–1939), in Biographical Directory of the United States Congress, available at link #92.
48. This idea is framed in Richard L. Hall and Alan V. Deardorff, "Lobbying as Legislative Subsidy," *American Political Science Review* 100, no. 1 (Feb. 2006): 69, and described later.
49. Kaiser, *So Damn Much Money*, 291.
50. Silverstein, *Turkmeniscam*, 55.
51. Kaiser, *So Damn Much Money*, 291.
52. Rob Porter and Sam Walsh, "Earmarks in the Federal Budget Process," Harvard Law Sch. Fed. Budget Policy Seminar, Briefing Paper No. 16 (May 1), 18, available at link #93.
53. Thompson, *Ethics in Congress*, 3. See also Fiorina and Abrams, *Disconnect*, 90 ("politics today is much 'cleaner' ").

54. Justin Fox and Lawrence Rothenberg, "Influence Without Bribes: A Non-Contracting Model of Campaign Giving and Policymaking," Working Paper 10/4/10.
   There are others who have developed models that might explain influence without assuming quid pro quo bribes. See, e.g., Brendan Daley and Erik Snowberg, "Even If It's Not Bribery: The Case for Campaign Finance Reform," unpublished working paper (Feb. 12, 2009), 1, available at link #94 ("We develop a dynamic multi-dimensional signaling model of campaign finance in which candidates can signal their ability by enacting policy and/or by raising and spending campaign funds, both of which are costly. Our model departs from the existing literature in that candidates do not exchange policy influence for campaign contributions, rather, they must decide how to allocate their efforts between policymaking and fund-raising. If high-ability candidates are better policymakers and better fund-raisers then they will raise and spend campaign funds even if voters care only about legislation. Voters' inability to reward or punish politicians based on past policy allows fund-raising to be used to signal ability at the expense of voter welfare. Campaign finance reform alleviates this phenomenon and improves voter welfare at the expense of politicians. Thus, we expect successful politicians to oppose true campaign finance reform. We also show our model is consistent with findings in the empirical and theoretical campaign finance literature"); Filipe R. Campante, "Redistribution in a Model of Voting and Campaign Contributions," unpublished working paper (Aug. 2010), available at link #95 ("even though each contribution has a negligible impact, the interaction between contributions and voting leads to an endogenous wealth bias in the political process, as the advantage of wealthier individuals in providing contributions encourages parties to move their platforms closer to those individuals' preferred positions").

55. I am not aware of any other work drawing upon Hyde, to model the lobbying behavior of Congress, but Phebe Lowell Bowditch does use it to understand the patronage system in Ancient Rome. See *Horace and the Gift Economy of Patronage* (Berkeley: University of California Press, 2001).

56. Lewis Hyde, *The Gift: Creativity and the Artist in the Modern World* (1979), 3.

57. Lawrence Lessig, *Remix: Making Art and Commerce Thrive in the Hybrid Economy* (New York: Penguin, 2008), 117–76.

58. Hyde, *The Gift*, 56.

59. Dan Clawson and his colleagues put the point similarly,

> Campaign contributions are best understood as gifts, not bribes. They are given to establish a personal connection, open an avenue for access, and create a generalized sense of obligation. Only rarely—when the normal system breaks down—does a contributor expect an immediate reciprocal action by a politician. Even then, the donor would normally use circuitous language to communicate this expectation.

Clawson, Neustadtl, and Weller, *Dollars and Votes*, 61–62.

The sociologist Clayton Peoples has picked up on their analysis:

> A true relationship can build between contributors and legislators, and this starts with the initial contribution. Clawson et al. (1998) note that PAC officers

tend to deliver contributions in person so that they can start building a relationship (p. 33). The relationships begun with initial contributing grow stronger with subsequent interactions. Part of this stems from the overlapping activities of PAC associates and legislators, or the "focused organization" of their ties to use Feld's (1981) terminology. PAC personnel "inhabit the same social world as [lawmakers] and their staffs..." and therefore contact occurs frequently since they "live in the same neighborhoods, belong to the same clubs, share friends and contacts, [etc.]" (Clawson et al. 1998: 85–86). This leads to genuine social relationships described by some as "friendship" and characterized by mutual trust. One PAC officer Clawson et al. (1998) interviewed said, "It's hard to quantify what is social and what is business.... Some of those [legislators] are my best friends on the Hill. I see them personally, socially...they always help me with issues" (pp. 86–87). Other PAC officers provide similar statements. For instance, one officer contends, "The [legislator] that is your friend, you are going to be his primary concern. The PAC certainly is an important part of that..." (p. 85). This leads Clawson et al. to conclude, "What matters is...a relationship of trust: a reputation for taking care of your friends, for being someone whom others can count on, and knowing that if you scratch my back, I'll scratch yours" (p. 88).

Clayton D. Peoples, "Contributor Influence in Congress: Social Ties and PAC Effects on U.S. House Policymaking," *Sociology Quarterly* 51 (2010): 649, 653–54.

Tolchin and Tolchin made a similar point in their powerful book *Pinstripe Patronage: Political Favoritism from the Clubhouse to the White House and Beyond*: "Lobbyists and members of Congress often become tied to each other through relationships based on mutual favors. These ties have become much stronger in recent years as election "reform" necessitates more and more fundraising interdependence." Martin Tolchin and Susan J. Tolchin, *Pinstripe Patronage: Political Favoritism from the Clubhouse to the White House and Beyond* (Boulder, Colo. Paradigm Publishers, 2010), 89.

60. Thomas M. Susman, "Private Ethics, Public Conduct: An Essay on Ethical Lobbying, Campaign Contributions, Reciprocity, and the Public Good," *Stanford Law and Policy Review* 19 (2008): 10, 15 (quoting Paul H. Douglas, *Ethics in Government* [1952], 44).

61. Tolchin and Tolchin, *Pinstripe Patronage*, 2.

62. Kaiser, *So Damn Much Money*, 297.

63. Ibid.

64. Susman, "Private Ethics, Public Conduct," 10, 15–17.

65. Michele Dell'Era, Lobbying and Reciprocity, working paper, Nov. 2009, 19.

66. Lawrence Lessig, "Democracy After *Citizens United*," *Boston Review* (Sept./Nov. 2010), 15.

67. Kaiser, *So Damn Much Money*, 72.

68. Painter, *Getting the Government America Deserves*, 155. ("Campaign contributions are involved in earmarks, sometimes from lobbyists and sometimes from other persons and entities that benefit from earmarks.")

69. Kaiser, *So Damn Much Money*, 124.

70. Silverstein, *Turkmeniscam*, 137.

71. Birnbaum, *The Money Men*, 169–70.

72. Ibid., 50.
73. Ibid., 169.
74. Kaiser, *So Damn Much Money*, 193-94.
75. Ibid., 172.
76. Ibid., 167.
77. Association of American Medical Colleges, "The Scientific Basis of Influence and Reciprocity: A Symposium" (2007), 10-12, available at link #96.
78. This idea is developed in Bruce Ackerman and Ian Ayres, *Voting with Dollars: A New Paradigm for Campaign Finance* (New Haven: Yale University Press, 2002), 25-44.
79. Martin Schram, "Speaking Freely," 94.
80. Kaiser, *So Damn Much Money*, 353.
81. See Bård Harstad and Jakob Svensson, "Bribes, Lobbying and Development," *American Political Science Review* 46 (2011): 105.
82. Raquel M. Alexander, Stephen W. Mazza, and Susan Scholz, "Measuring Rates of Return on Lobbying Expenditures: An Empirical Case Study of Tax Breaks for Multinational Corporations," *Journal of Law and Policy* 25 (2009): 401, 404.
83. Brian Kelleher Richter, Krislert Samphantharak, and Jeffrey F. Timmons, "Lobbying and Taxes," *American Journal of Political Science* 53 (2009): 893, 907.
84. John M. de Figueiredo and Brian S. Silverman, "Academic Earmarks and the Returns to Lobbying," *Journal of Law and Economics* 49 (2006): 597, 598.
85. Frank Yu and Xiaoyun Yu, "Corporate Lobbying and Fraud Detection," *Journal of Finance and Quantitative Analysis* 46 (forthcoming 2011), available at link #97.
86. Matthew D. Hill, G. W. Kelly, G. Brandon Lockhart, and Robert A. Van Ness, "Determinants and Effects of Corporate Lobbying," unpublished working paper (Sept. 3, 2010), 3-4, available at link #98.
87. Silverstein, *Turkmeniscam*, 74.
88. Hacker and Pierson, *Winner-Take-All Politics*, 118.
89. Huffington, *Third World America*, 129.
90. Radley Balko, "Washington's Wealth Boom," FOXNews.com (Jan. 12, 2009), available at link #99.
91. Robert Reich, "Everyday Corruption," lecture given at the Edmond J. Safra Center for Ethics, April 5, 2010 (on file with author).
92. Kaiser, *So Damn Much Money*, 20.
93. American Bar Association, "Lobbying Law in the Spotlight: Challenges and Proposed Improvements," Task Force on Federal Lobbying Laws Section of Administrative Law and Regulatory Practice (Jan. 3, 2011), vi, available at link #100.
94. Ibid., 20 (emphasis added). The ABA acknowledged that it drew on Susman, "Private Ethics, Public Conduct," 10.
95. Painter, *Getting the Government America Deserves*, 202.
96. Clawson, Neustadtl, and Weller, *Dollars and Votes*, 64.
97. Brooks, *Corruption in American Politics and Life*, 228.
98. Daniel Hays Lowenstein, "On Campaign Finance Reform: The Root of All Evil Is Deeply Rooted," *Hofstra Law Review* 18 (1989): 325.
99. Joseph Mornin, "Lobbyist Money: Analyzing Lobbyist Political Contributions and Disclosure Regimes" (June 25, 2011), available at link #101.

100. The FEC has likewise radically narrowed the range of contributions that must be reported, by requiring a specific record indicating a bundle was intended. See Kevin Bogardus, "Bundling Rule Doesn't Capture All the Fund-raising by Lobbyists," The Hill (2009), available at link #102.

101. Richard A. Posner, "Orwell Versus Huxley: Economics, Technology, Privacy, and Satire," in *Philosophy and Literature* 24 (2000): 1, 3.

102. Clawson, Neustadtl, and Weller, *Dollars and Votes*, 84.

103. List of Current Members of the United States House of Representatives by Seniority, available at link #103.

104. Jeffrey Birnbaum, "Hill a Stepping Stone to K Street for Some," *Washington Post*, July 27, 2005, available at link #104.

105. Justin Elliot and Zachary Roth, "Shadow Congress: More Than 170 Former Lawmakers Ply the Corridors of Power as Lobbyists," TPMMuckraker (June 1, 2010), available at link #105.

106. See Public Citizen, "Ca$hing In: More Than 900 Ex-Government Officials, Including 70 Former Members of Congress, Have Lobbied for the Financial Services Sector in 2009" (2009), available at link #106.

107. Birnbaum, *The Money Men*, 190–91.

108. Silverstein, *Turkmeniscam*, 68.

## Chapter 10. What *So Damn Much Money* Does

1. Tom Coburn, "Just Say No to Earmarks," *Wall Street Journal*, Feb. 10, 2006.

2. Brad Smith on *The Sound of Ideas*, WCPN (March 29, 2011), 8:20, available at link #107.

3. *The Federalist* No. 10 (James Madison), ed. Henry Cabot Lodge (New York: G. P. Putnam's Sons, 1888), 57 ("A republic, by which I mean a government in which the scheme of representation takes place"); *The Federalist* No. 14 (James Madison), 77 ("The true distinction between these forms was also adverted to on a former occasion. It is, that in a democracy, the people meet and exercise the government in person; in a republic, they assemble and administer it by their representatives and agents"); *The Federalist* No. 39 (James Madison), 233–34 ("[W]e may define a republic to be, or at least may bestow that name on, a government which derives all its powers directly or indirectly from the great body of the people, and is administered by persons holding their offices during pleasure, for a limited period, or during good behavior. It is *essential* to such a government that it be derived from the great body of the society, not from an inconsiderable proportion, or a favored class of it; otherwise a handful of tyrannical nobles, exercising their oppressions by a delegation of their powers, might aspire to the rank of republicans, and claim for their government the honorable title of republic. It is *sufficient* for such a government that the persons administering it be appointed, either directly or indirectly, by the people; and that they hold their appointments by either of the tenures just specified") (emphasis in the original).

4. Zephyr Teachout, "The Anti-Corruption Principle," *Cornell Law Review* (2008), 341, 377. Here and throughout I have drawn heavily upon Professor Teachout's original framing of this issue. Her work made clearer the sense in which the current Congress was a "corruption" of the framing design. Teachout has

extended her analysis in a forthcoming book, *Benjamin Franklin's Snuff Box* (forthcoming, 2012).

5. See, e.g., Gordon S. Wood, *Empire of Liberty: A History of the Early Republic, 1789-1815* (Oxford University Press, 2009), 429 ("For some American leaders, however, the ink on the Declaration of Independence was scarcely dry before they began expressing doubts about the possibility of realizing the high hopes and dreams of the Revolution); Kurt T. Lash, "Rejecting Conventional Wisdom: Federalist Ambivalence in the Framing and Implementation of Article V," *American Journal of Legal History* 38 (1994): 197, 225 ("In the decade following the Revolution, the track record of the state legislatures provided less reason to see society in terms of majorities acting for the common good and more reason to see competing factional interests that had to be controlled through institutional safeguards").

6. See Dennis Thompson, "Two Concepts of Corruption," *George Washington Law Review* 73 (2005): 1036, 1038. ("The democratic process is the modern surrogate for the consensus on the public good that traditional theorists hoped citizens could recognize.")

7. *The Federalist* No. 52 (James Madison), 328. See Glenn Fung, "The Disputed Federalist Papers: SVM Feature Selection via Concave Minimization," Proc. 2003 Conf. on Diversity in Computing, 42–46, available at link #108 (presenting the results of a quantitative word analysis suggesting that Madison wrote Federalist 52 and noting that "[t]his result coincides with previous work on this problem using other classification techniques").

8. That the very notion of corruption requires an appropriate baseline from which to measure is familiar. See, e.g., Thomas F. Burke, "The Concept of Corruption in Campaign Finance Law," *Constitutional Commentary* 14 (1997): 127, 128 ("Corruption is thus a loaded term: you cannot call something corrupt without an implicit reference to some ideal.... [O]ne must have some underlying notion of the pure, original or natural state of the body politic").

9. Teachout, "The Anti-Corruption Principle," 341, 359-60.

10. See New Jersey Constitution of 1776, article XX, cited in John Joseph Wallis, "The Concept of Systematic Corruption in American History," in Glaeser and Goldin, eds., *Corruption and Reform*, 34, available at link #109.

11. Adrian Vermeule, "The Constitutional Law of Official Compensation," *Columbia Law Review* 102 (2002): 501, 509-10.

12. Teachout, "The Anti-Corruption Principle," 341, 362-63.

13. Notes of James Madison (Aug. 13, 1787), in vol. 2 of *Records of the Federal Convention*, 267, 279.

14. By setting the baseline to "dependence upon the people alone," I don't mean to be fixing upon any particular theory of what that representation should be. In particular, my formulation is meant to be agnostic between a "sanction model" of representation and a "selection model." See Jane Mansbridge, "A 'Selection Model' of Political Representation," *Journal of Political Philosophy* 17 (2009): 369. With both models, there is at least a moment when a representative is accountable. That moment establishes the dependency, however that dependency is expressed.

15. See John Armor, "Congress for Life," Inner Self, available at link #110 (last visited June 21, 2011).

16. Robert L. Trivers, "The Evolution of Reciprocal Altruism," *Quarterly Review of Biology* 46 (1971): 35.

17. Brooks, *Corruption in American Politics and Life*, 274.

18. Melvin Urofsky, *Louis D. Brandeis: A Life* (New York: Pantheon, 2009), 159.

19. Survey, Global Strategy Group (Jan. 11, 2011), on file with author. See also Hart Research Associates, "Protecting Democracy from Unlimited Corporate Spending: Results from a National Survey among 1,000 Voters on the *Citizens United* Decision" (2010) (finding that 95 percent strongly agree or somewhat agree that "[c]orporations spend money on politics to buy influence/elect people favorable to their financial interests"), 7. See also Eric Zimmermann, "Poll: 70 Percent Believe Congress Is Corrupt," The Hill's blog *Briefing Room* (Aug. 10, 2010), available at link #111 (reporting the results of a Rasmussen poll that "[v]oters are more likely to trust the integrity of their own representative, but not by much. A majority, 56 percent, think their own lawmakers can be bought"). See also "Poll: Half of Americans Think Congress Is Corrupt," CNN (Oct. 19, 2006), available at link #112 (finding that, four years before the Rasmussen poll, 49 percent of Americans said "most members of Congress are corrupt" and 22 percent said their individual legislator was corrupt); "Distrust, Discontent, Anger and Partisan Rancor: The People and Their Government," Pew Research Center (2010), 51, available at link #113.

20. Schram, "Speaking Freely," 89.

21. Ibid., 31.

22. Ibid., 16.

23. Ibid., 23.

24. Larry Makinson, "Speaking Freely," Center for Responsive Politics (2003).

25. Bill Bradley, "Government and Public Behavior," *Public Talk*: Online Journal of Discourse Leadership, available at link #114.

26. Makinson, "Speaking Freely," 44.

27. Ibid.

28. For a review, see Frank R. Baumgartner and Beth L. Leech, *Basic Interests* (Princeton, N.J.: Princeton University Press, 1998). F. R. Baumgartner, Jeffrey M. Berry, Marie Hojnacki, David C. Kimball, and Beth L. Leech, *Lobbying and Policy Change: Who Wins, Who Loses, And Why* (Chicago: University of Chicago Press, 2009), 320. See also Lowenstein, "On Campaign Finance Reform," 307–8 (summarizing skeptics' view).

29. Baumgartner, Berry, Hojnacki, Kimball, and Leech, *Lobbying and Policy Change*, 194.

30. Stephen Ansolabehere, John M. de Figueiredo, and James M. Snyder, "Why Is There So Little Money in U.S. Politics?" 105.

31. Ibid., 114; Stephen Ansolabehere, John M. de Figueiredo, and James M. Snyder, "Why is There So Little Money in U.S. Politics?" (Center for Competitive Politics, June 2002), 114, available at link #115.

32. Ansolabehere, Figueiredo, and Snyder, "Why Is There So Little Money in U.S. Politics?" (2003), 105.

33. Ansolabehere, Figueiredo, and Snyder, "Why Is There So Little Money in U.S. Politics?" (2002), 20.

34. Ibid.

35. Ibid.

36. Center for Competitive Politics, "Fairly Flawed: Analysis of the 2009 Fair Elections Now Act (H.R. 1826 and S. 752)," *Policy Briefing* 2 (2009): 4.

37. As Richter and his colleagues write, "[T]he inordinate attention given to PAC contributions is essentially an exercise in 'looking under the lamppost' since PAC data have been readily available since the 1970s, whereas lobbying data have only become available recently...While focusing on contentious bills has its merits, crafty politicians have a variety of tools at their disposal to deliver favors, including attaching riders to mundane bills and exercising their power to steer bills in the congressional committee process. By not considering outcomes more broadly defined than roll-call votes on specific bills, existing research has arguably failed to detect some important benefits firms receive." Brian Kelleher Richter, Krislert Samphantharak, and Jeffrey F. Timmons, "Lobbying and Taxes," *American Journal of Political Science* 53 (2009): 894 (citations omitted).

38. Stratmann, "Some Talk: Money in Politics," 135, 146.

39. Sanford C. Gordon, Catherine Hafer, and Dimitri Landa, "Consumption or Investment? On Motivations for Political Giving," *Journal of Politics* 69 (2007): 1057.

40. Sanjay Gupta and Charles W. Swenson, "Rent Seeking by Agents of the Firm," *Journal of Law and Economics* 46 (2003): 253.

41. Atif Mian, Amir Sufi, and Francesco Trebbi, "The Political Economy of the U.S. Mortgage Default Crisis" (GSB Res. Pap 08-17 2009), 4, available at link #116.

42. As Lowenstein summarizes the skepticism, "When one takes into account all the defects and difficulties inherent in these studies, it becomes increasingly difficult to regard their mixed results as a clean bill of health for the campaign finance system." Lowenstein, "On Campaign Finance Reform," 322.

43. "As one Republican senator said: '[Fundraising] devours one's time—you spend two or three years before your re-election fund-raising. The other years, you're helping others.'" Peter Lindstrom, "Congressional Operations: Congress Speaks—A Survey of the 100th Congress," Center for Responsive Politics (1988), 80 (quoting unnamed Republican congressman).

"As I spoke to political consultants, they all said I should not even consider running for the Senate if I weren't prepared to spend 80 or 90 percent of my time raising money. It turned out that they were absolutely correct" (Rep. Mike Barnes [D-Md.; 1979–1987]). Philip M. Stern, *Still the Best Congress Money Can Buy* (Washington, D.C.: Regnery Publishing, updated and rev. ed., 1992), 130.

"The high costs of running for office at the congressional and statewide level has [*sic*] forced 55 percent of statewide and more than 43 percent of U.S. House candidates to devote at least one-quarter of their time to fund-raising." Paul S. Hernson and Ronald A. Faucheux, "Candidates Devote Substantial Time and Effort to Fundraising" (2000), available at link #117.

Senator Robert Byrd, former majority leader, similarly observed: "To raise the money, Senators start hosting fundraisers years before they next will be in an election. They all too often become fundraisers first, and legislators second." 133 Cong. Rec. 115 (daily ed. Jan. 6, 1987).

Former Senate majority leader George Mitchell explained that senators constantly wanted him to reschedule votes because "they [were] either holding or attending a fund-raising event that evening." Schram, "Speaking Freely," 37–38.

Representative Jim Bacchus explained that he chose not to run for reelection because he would have had to abandon the job he had "been elected to do in order to raise a million dollars and be a virtual full-time candidate." Schram, "Speaking Freely," 43.

44. Makinson, "Speaking Freely," 86.
45. Carrie Budoff Brown, "Senate Bill Weighs in at 2,074 Pages," *Politico* (Nov. 18, 2009), available at link #118.
46. Ernest Hollings, "Stop the Money Chase," *Washington Post*, Feb. 19, 2006, available at link #119.
47. Andy Plattner, "Nobody Likes the Way Campaigns Are Financed, but Nobody's Likely to Change It, Either," *U.S. News & World Report*, June 22, 1987, 30.
48. Anthony Corrado, "Running Backward: The Congressional Money Chase," in Norman J. Ornstein and Thomas E. Mann, eds., *The Permanent Campaign and Its Future* (Washington, D.C.: American Enterprise Institute; Brookings Institution, 2000), 75.
49. Norman J. Ornstein and Thomas E. Mann, "Conclusion," in Ornstein and Mann, eds., *The Permanent Campaign*, 221–22.
50. Norman J. Ornstein and Thomas E. Mann, "When Congress Checks Out," *Foreign Affairs* (Nov.–Dec. 2006), 67, 70; see also Paul J. Quirk, "Deliberation and Decision Making," in Paul J. Quirk and Sarah A. Binder, eds. *The Legislative Branch* (Oxford University Press, 2005), 314, 336 (effect on oversight panels).
51. Numbers drawn from Norman J. Ornstein, Thomas E. Mann, and Michael J. Malbin, *Vital Statistics on Congress 2008* (Washington, D.C.: Brookings Institution Press, 2008). See also Thomas E. Mann and Norman J. Ornstein, *The Broken Branch* (Oxford University Press, 2006), 18 ("In the 1960s and 1970s, the average Congress had an average of 5,372 House committee and subcommittee meetings; in the 1980s and 1990s the average was 4,793. In the … 108th, the number was 2,135").
52. Numbers drawn from Ornstein, Mann, and Malbin, *Vital Statistics on Congress 2008*. See also Mann and Ornstein, *The Broken Branch*, 18.
53. Gordon S. Wood, *Empire of Liberty: A History of the Early Republic, 1789–1815* (Oxford University Press, 2009), 1272–73.
54. Steven S. Smith, "Parties and Leadership in the Senate," in Quirk and Binder, eds., *The Legislative Branch* (Oxford University Press, 2005), 274–75.
55. Andrew Seidman, "Former Members of Congress Lament Current Partisanship," *McClatchy* (June 16, 2010), available at link #120.
56. Makinson, "Speaking Freely," 39–40.
57. Ibid., 6.
58. Lee Hamilton, "Will the House Come to Order?" *The American Interest Online* (Sept.–Oct. 2006), available at link #121.
59. To complain about distraction is not to betray doubt, as Daniel Ortiz puts it, about voters. A voter, like any employer, could well want his agent to stay focused on

the job, if only to avoid the necessity of extra monitoring. See Daniel R. Ortiz, "The Democratic Paradox of Campaign Finance Reform," *Stanford Law Review* 50 (1997) (arguing support for campaign finance reform is premised upon doubt about voters). The same applies to Issacharoff and Karlan's claim that a concern about "corruption" is really a concern about a "corruption of voters." For again, if the focus is on a distorted process, even if the voters could compensate for that distortion, they are rational to avoid the distraction that forces them to compensate. The fact that I double check the cash drawer does not mean I have no good reason to avoid hiring a kleptomaniac. See Samuel Issacharoff and Pamela S. Karlan, "The Hydraulics of Campaign Finance Reform," *Texas Law Review* 77 (1998): 1723–26.

Relatedly, Issacharoff and Karlan point to the "well-known feature of American political participation: there is a strong positive correlation between an individual's income and education level and the likelihood that she will go to the polls and cast a ballot." Ibid., 1725. In fact the connection to policy outcomes is more complicated. As I describe below, see text at n. 104: policy tracks income, but the richest are not the most highly educated.

60. Baumgartner, Berry, Hojnacki, Kimball, Leech, *Lobbying and Policy Change*, 257–58.
61. This table is based, with permission, on Figure 12.1 in ibid., 258. I have re-created it using a subset of the data drawn from Table 1.4 in ibid.
62. Ibid., 258.
63. Richard L. Hall and Alan V. Deardorff, "Lobbying as Legislative Subsidy," *American Political Science Review* 100 (Feb. 2006): 69.
64. Center for Responsive Politics, OpenSecrets.org, Lobbying Database, available at link #122.
65. Hall and Deardorff, "Lobbying as Legislative Subsidy," 81.
66. Or as Baumgartner et al. report, almost everyone. See Laura I. Langbein, "Money and Access: Some Empirical Evidence," *Journal of Politics* 48 (1986): 1052; Kevin M. Esterling, "Buying Expertise: Campaign Contributions and Attention to Policy Analysis in Congressional Committees," *American Political Science Review* 101 (2007): 93; Clawson, Neustadtl, and Weller, *Dollars and Votes*.
67. Makinson, "Speaking Freely," 59. See also Thompson, *Ethics in Congress*, 117.
68. Declaration of Paul Simon, *McConnell v. FEC*, No. 02-0582 (D.D.C. 2002).
69. Clawson, Neustadtl, and Weller, *Dollars and Votes*, 8.
70. Schram, "Speaking Freely," 62.
71. Hall and Deardorff, "Lobbying as Legislative Subsidy," 80.
72. Ibid., 81.
73. Ibid.
74. Johnson and Kwak, *13 Bankers*, 191–92.
75. Hall and Deardorff, "Lobbying as Legislative Subsidy," 69 (emphasis added).
76. U.S. Senate, Roll Call Vote on H.R. 6124, Food, Conservation, and Energy Act of 2008, available at link #123; U.S. House of Representatives, Office of the Clerk, Final Vote Result for Roll Call 417, available at link #124.
77. "The Cash Committee: How Wall Street Wins on the Hill," Huffington Post (Dec. 29, 2009), available at link #125.
78. Schram, "Speaking Freely," 12.

79. Ibid., 18.
80. Ibid., 48-49.
81. Ibid., 93.
82. Birnbaum, *The Money Men*, 171.
83. Clawson, Neustadtl, and Weller, *Dollars and Votes*, 67.
84. Hall and Deardorff, "Lobbying as Legislative Subsidy," 79.
85. Tolchin and Tolchin, *Pinstripe Patronage*, 78. This shape-shifting is also related to an argument by Harvard professor Jane Mansbridge about why contribution studies are not likely to measure influence. As she describes, interest groups funding campaigns will fund candidates who already believe in the policies the groups favor. This produces not "quid pro quo distortion," as Mansbridge describes it, but "selection distortion," eliminating even the need for shape-shifting as the change happens as the member is selected. Jane Mansbridge, "Clarifying the Concept of Representation," unpublished manuscript, May 2011.
86. General Interim Report of the House Select Committee on Lobbying Activities, H.R. Rep 3138, 81st Congress 2nd Session, 62.
87. Baumgartner, Berry, Hojnacki, Kimball, Leech, *Lobbying and Policy Change*, 2.
88. Interview with Larry Pressler, June 16, 2011 (on file with author).
89. The foundational work is George Stigler's, "The Theory of Economic Regulation," *Bell Journal of Economics and Management Science* 2 (1971): 3, and Richard Posner's, "Taxation by Regulation," *Bell Journal of Economics and Management Science* 2 (1971): 22. See also Richard A. Posner, "Theories of Economic Regulation," *Bell Journal of Economics and Management Science* 5 (1974): 335; Sam Peltzman, "Toward a More General Theory of Regulation," *Journal of Law and Economics* 19 (1976): 211; Burton Abrams and R. Settle, "The Economic Theory of Regulation and Public Financing of Presidential Elections," *Journal of Political Economy* 86 (1978): 245; James Q. Wilson, *The Politics of Regulation* (1980). Steven Croley's is perhaps the best recent effort to summarize and extend this analysis as it affects agency regulation in particular. See *Regulation and the Public Interests: The Possibility of Good Regulatory Government* (2008).
90. Luigi Zingales, *Preventing Economists' Capture* (2011), 2.
91. See generally Keith T. Poole and Howard Rosenthal, *Congress: A Political-Economic History of Roll Call Voting* (Oxford University Press, 1997).
92. Larry M. Bartels, "Economic Inequality and Political Representation," working paper (2005), available at link #126.
93. Martin Gilens, "Inequality and Democratic Responsiveness," *Public Opinion Quarterly* 69 (2005): 778, 781-82. Gilens's argument has been criticized by Stuart Soroka and Christopher Wlezien; see "On the Limits to Inequality in Representation," *PS: Political Science and Politics* 41 (2008): 319-27. But as Gilens writes in response to Soroka and Wlezien, his results and Bartels's are consistent with those of a wide range of scholars, who all find "that more privileged subgroups of Americans have greater—and sometimes dramatically greater—sway over government policy." Martin Gilens, "Preference Gaps and Inequality in Representation," *PS: Political Science and Politics* 42 (2009): 335-41, 335.
94. Gilens, "Inequality and Democratic Responsiveness," 778, 788.

95. Ibid.
96. Hacker and Pierson, *Winner-Take-All Politics*, 3.
97. Ibid.
98. Ibid., 16.
99. Ibid., 24.
100. Ibid., 194.
101. Ibid., 19.
102. Ibid., 21.
103. Rajan and Zingales, *Saving Capitalism from the Capitalists*, 92.
104. Ibid.
105. Gilens, "Inequality and Democratic Responsiveness," 778, 792.
106. Joseph E. Stiglitz, "Of the 1%, by the 1%, for the 1%," *Vanity Fair*, May 2011, 2, available at link #127.
107. Tyler Cowen, "The Inequality That Matters," *The American Interest* (Jan.-Feb. 2011), 4-5, available at link #128.
108. Huffington, *Third World America*, 17-18.
109. Sarah Anderson et al., "Executive Excess 2008: How Average Taxpayers Subsidize Runaway Pay," 15th Annual CEO Compensation Survey, Institute for Policy Studies and United for a Fair Economy (Aug. 25, 2008), 1, available at link #129.
110. Barry Lynn, *Cornered: The New Monopoly Capitalism and the Economics of Destruction* (Hoboken, N.J.: Wiley, 2010), 130.
111. Ibid., 130-31.
112. Hacker and Pierson, *Winner-Take-All Politics*, 151.
113. Gilens, "Inequality and Democratic Responsiveness," 778, 793-94.
114. Kaiser, *So Damn Much Money*, 355.
115. *Kirkpatrick v. Preisler*, 394 U.S. 526, 530 (1969).
116. Federal Election Commission: Contribution Limits 2009-10, available at link #130.
117. Birnbaum, *The Money Men*, 72.
118. This point is emphasized powerfully in Edward B. Foley, "Equal-Dollars-per-Voter: A Constitutional Principle of Campaign Finance," *Columbia Law Review* 94 (1994): 1204, 1226-27 ("Voting is only the final stage of the electoral process. It is preceded not only by the agenda-formation stage . . . but also by . . . the "argumentative stage." . . . [W]e must acknowledge that a citizen does not have equal input in the electoral process if she is denied an equal opportunity to participate in [these earlier stages]"). It is also the insight that animates David Strauss's. See David A. Strauss, "Corruption, Equality, and Campaign Finance Reform," *Columbia Law Review* 94 (1994): 1373 ("[E]ach dollar contribution . . . is a fraction of an expected vote"). Strauss pushes the analogy (with all of its strengths and weaknesses) directly to the Court's redistricting cases. In my view, what's missing from this analysis is the recognition of how equality (and not just corruption) is derivative from the idea of the proper dependency within a representative democracy—upon "the People alone."
119. Ansolabehere, de Figueiredo, and Snyder, "Why Is There So Little Money in U.S. Politics?" (2003), 125-26.
120. Gilens, "Inequality and Democratic Responsiveness," 778, 794.

121. Atif Mian, Amir Sufi, and Francesco Trebbi, "The Political Economy of the U.S. Mortgage Default Crisis," National Bureau of Economic Research (2010), 4–6.

122. Nancy L. Rosenblum, *On the Side of the Angels* (Princeton, N.J.: Princeton University Press, 2008), 251.

123. Ibid., 252.

124. Birnbaum, *The Money Men*, 70.

125. Hacker and Pierson, *Winner-Take-All Politics*, 252.

126. Ibid., 252, quoting Naftali Bendavid, *The Thumpin': How Rahm Emanuel and the Democrats Learned to Be Ruthless and Ended the Republican Revolution* (New York: Doubleday, 2007), 157.

127. Schram, "Speaking Freely," 19.

128. Birnbaum, *The Money Men*, 3–4.

129. Zach Carter and Ryan Grim, "Swiped: Banks, Merchants and Why Washington Doesn't Work for You," Huffington Post (April 28, 2011), available at link #131.

130. Ibid.

131. Baumgartner, Berry, Hojnacki, Kimball, Leech, *Lobbying and Policy Change*, 257, 214. Baumgartner and his colleagues craft an extensive empirical analysis of the relationship between lobbying and policy outcomes. The short form of the conclusion is that a "direct correlation between money and outcomes...is simply not there" (214). "While no one doubts that money matters, and while there is no question that the wealthy enjoy greater access," that doesn't mean, they argue, that the wealthy "can necessarily write their ticket." But this conclusion follows because of the relationship between short-term lobbying and long-term structures. While "the wealthy" "often do not" "win in Washington," that's "not because they lack power, but because the status quo already reflects that power" (194, 20). The status quo "reflects a rough equilibrium of power...and a quite unfair equilibrium...with much greater benefits going to the privileged and wealthy than to the needy and the poor" (23). "So to see that money cannot automatically purchase shifts in the status quo does not mean that the status quo might not already reflect important biases in politics" (214).

132. Lowenstein, "On Campaign Finance Reform," 323. (Addressing skepticism about the proven effects of money on results, Lowenstein writes: "The question of campaign finance is a question of conflict of interest...in the course of a relationship of trust.")

133. "The People and Their Government: Distrust, Discontent, Anger and Partisan Rancor," The Pew Research Center (April 18, 2010), 2, available at link #132.

134. Birnbaum, *The Money Men*, 10.

135. National Election Studies: The ANES Guide to Public Opinion and Electoral Behavior, University of Michigan Center for Political Studies, available at link #133.

136. New Judicial Watch/Zogby Poll: "81.7% of Americans Say Political Corruption Played a 'Major Role' in Financial Crisis," Judicial Watch (Oct. 21, 2008), available at link #134.

137. Jeanne Cummings, "SCOTUS Ruling Fuels Voters' Ire," *Politico* (Feb. 9, 2010), available at link #135. See also University of Texas, "Money and Politics Project U.S. National Survey" (2009), available at link #136 (finding that 79 percent of

respondents believe that the source of a candidate's campaign contributions has a high degree of influence on how a candidate votes on legislation).

138. Huffington, *Third World America*, 129.

139. As Mark Warren has written, "If low trust instead indicates disaffection from the institutions that manage distrust, then the kind of distrust necessary for a democracy to work—engaged monitoring of political officials—is replaced by disengagement, undermining the transformative capacities of democratic institutions." Mark E. Warren, "Democracy and Deceit: Regulating Appearances of Corruption," *American Journal of Political Science* 50 (2006): 160, 165.

140. Birnbaum, *The Money Men*, 10.

141. Steven J. Rosenstone and John Mark Hansen, *Mobilization, Participation, and Democracy in America* (1993). I am particularly grateful to Bryson Morgan for helping me frame this distinction.

142. See R. Michael Alvarez, Thad E. Hall, and Morgan Llewellyn, "On American Voter Confidence," *University of Arkansas-Little Rock Law Review* 29 (2007): 705; Robert F. Bauer, "Going Nowhere, Slowly: The Long Struggle Over Campaign Finance Reform and Some Attempts at Explanation and Alternatives," *Catholic University Law Review* 51 (2002): 741, 763 ("Studies conclusively show that nonvoting does not stem from a rejection of, or hypothesized alienation from, the political process, but from a lack of interest in it"); David M. Primo and Jeffrey Milyo, "Campaign Finance Laws and Political Efficacy: Evidence from the States," *Election Law Journal* 5 (2006): 1 (relationship between campaign finance laws and perception of democratic rule), available at link #137; John Samples, "Three Myths about Voter Turnout in the United States," Cato Institute (Sept. 14, 2004) ("The asserted line of causality from campaign finance to distrust of government does not exist. Given that, campaign finance cannot cause declines in voter turnout"), available at link #138.

143. Rosenstone and Hansen, *Mobilization, Participation, and Democracy in America*, 144. This conclusion is confirmed by Kevin Chen, *Political Alienation and Voting Turnout in the United States: 1960-1988* (Lewiston, N.Y.: Edwin Mellen Press, 1992), 214, 217.

144. Thomas E. Patterson, *The Vanishing Voter* (New York: Knopf, 2002), 183.

145. Rock the Vote, Wikipedia, available at link #139.

146. August 2010 Rock the Vote survey, question #15.

147. "What Do Elected Officials Think About the Role of Money in Politics?" Democracy Matters, available at link #140 (last visited June 21, 2011).

148. Hetherington, *Why Trust Matters*, 149.

149. Thompson, *Ethics in Congress*, 125-26.

## Chapter 11. How *So Damn Much Money* Defeats the Left

1. Speech of Barack Obama, Indianapolis, Ind., Oct. 8, 2008.

2. Obama: "'No Welfare for Wall Street': Nominee Is Inclined to Support Congress $700B Bailout Package If It Also Protects Main Street," CBS News *Face the Nation* (Sept. 28, 2008), available at link #141.

3. Speech of Barack Obama, San Diego, Calif., May 2, 2007.

4. Speech of Barack Obama, Washington, D.C., April 15, 2008.

5. Speech of Barack Obama, Columbia, S.C., Jan. 26, 2008.

6. Speech of Barack Obama, Indianapolis, Ind., April 25, 2008.

7. Ibid.

8. Speech of Barack Obama, Philadelphia, Pa., April 2, 2008.

9. Ben Smith, "Hillary Defends Lobbyists, Opens Doors for Rivals," *Politico* (Aug. 4, 2007), available at link #142.

10. Speech of Barack Obama, Indianapolis, Ind., April 25, 2008.

11. This point is related to Richard Posner's point about the willingness of monopolies to protect their monopoly. See Richard A. Posner, "The Social Costs of Monopoly and Regulation," *Journal of Politcal Economy* 83 (1975): 807.

12. Crawford, *The Pressure Boys*, 7.

13. Lynn, *Cornered*, 5-7, 258-59, n. 23.

14. The theory of regulatory capture raises questions about whether cartel-like industries will use their power to extract rents in the market or through government. And indeed, as Posner writes, the strongest examples of successful rent seeking come from relatively competitive industries. See Posner, "Theories of Economic Regulation," 335, 343-45. The success of the "deregulation" movement may have now shifted the rent-seeking game toward the focus that now concerns Rajan and Zingales.

15. Rajan and Zingales, *Saving Capitalism from the Capitalists*, 296.

16. *Eastern Railroad Presidents Conference v. Noerr Motor Freight, Inc.*, 365 U.S. 127 (1961); *United Mine Workers v. Pennington*, 381 U.S. 657 (1965).

17. Obama for America, "Barack Obama and Joe Biden's Plan to Lower Health Care Costs and Ensure Affordable, Accessible Health Coverage for All" (2008), 5-6, available at link #143.

18. Emphasis added.

19. "Top Industries: Most Profitable," CNN Money, available at link #144.

20. Pub. L. No. 108-173, 117 Stat. 2066 (2003) (codified as 42 U.S.C.A. § 1395w-101 et seq.).

21. 2009 Annual Report of the Boards of Trustees of the Federal Hospital Insurance and Federal Supplementary Medical Insurance Trust Funds, Centers for Medicare and Medicaid Services (2009), 120, available at link #145.

22. The Medicare Prescription Drug, Improvement, and Modernization Act of 2003 expressly prohibits the Centers for Medicare and Medicaid Services within the Department of Health and Human Services from (i) interfering with negotiations among drug manufacturers, prescription drug plans, and pharmacies, (ii) requiring prescription drug plans to use a particular formulary instituting a price structure for the reimbursement of drugs provided under Part D. Medicare Prescription Drug, Improvement, and Modernization Act of 2003, Pub. L. No. 108-173, sec. 101(a) (2), § 1395w-111, 117 Stat. 2066, 2092-99 (2003) (codified as 42 USC § 1395w-111[i] [2006]).

23. 153 Cong. Rec. S4634 (daily ed., April 18, 2007) (statement of Sen. Obama).

24. Obama for America, "Barack Obama and Joe Biden's Plan to Lower Health Care Costs."

25. Jonathan Cohn, "How They Did It," *New Republic*, June 10, 2010, 14, 15.

26. Ibid., 14, 18.

27. Speech of Barack Obama, Indianapolis, Ind., April 25, 2008.

28. Speech of Barack Obama, Columbia, S.C., Jan. 26, 2008.

29. Cohn, "How They Did It," 14, 21.

30. Ibid.

31. Ibid., 14, 25.

32. Speech of Barack Obama, Washington, D.C., April 15, 2008.

33. Ezra Klein, "Twilight of the Interest Groups," *Washington Post*, Mar. 19, 2010, available at link #146.

34. Speech of Barack Obama, San Diego, Calif., May 2, 2007.

35. Glenn Greenwald, "Industry Interests Are Not in Their Twilight," *Salon* (Mar. 20 2010), available at link #147.

36. Oliver Hart and Luigi Zingales, "Curbing Risk on Wall Street," *National Affairs* 3 (Spring 2010), 20–21, available at link #148.

37. Johnson and Kwak, *13 Bankers*, 180.

38. Hart and Zingales, "Curbing Risk on Wall Street," 20, 21.

39. "Trade Offs—National Priorities Project: Bringing the Federal Budget Home," available at link #149 (last visited June 21, 2011) (Select "State: United States"; "Program: proposed Unemployment Compensation in FY2012"; "Trade Off: All").

40. Hacker and Pierson, *Winner-Take-All Politics*, 1.

41. Krugman, "Zombie Financial Ideas"; Martin Wolf of the *Financial Times* has described it similarly. See Hacker and Pierson, *Winner-Take-All Politics*, 67.

42. Luigi Zingales, "A Market-Based Regulatory Policy to Avoid Financial Crisis," *Cato Journal* 30, no. 3 (Fall 2010): 535.

43. Luigi Zingales has another method not tied to controlling the size of banks. See ibid., 536.

44. Sebastian Mallaby has argued—powerfully, in my view—that these criticisms of Wall Street banks don't extend to hedge funds. That's not because hedge funds are populated with "saints," as Mallaby puts it, but because their "incentives and culture are ultimately less flawed than those of other financial companies." Sebastian Mallaby, *More Money Than God* (New York: Penguin Press, 2010), 375. I agree with this. The problem the past ten years has revealed is not innovation. It is innovation deployed in a context in which the risks are not borne by the gamblers. Hedge funds are not that.

45. Johnson and Kwak, *13 Bankers*, 214–15.

46. Roger Lowenstein, *The End of Wall Street* (New York: Penguin Press, 2010), 291.

47. Tyler Cowen, "The Inequality That Matters," *The American Interest* (Jan.-Feb. 2011), 6, available at link #150.

48. Hacker and Pierson, *Winner-Take-All Politics*, 282.

49. Mallaby, *More Money Than God*, 378.

50. MapLight, H.R. 4173: Dodd-Frank Wall Street Reform and Consumer Protection Act, available at link #151; MapLight, S. 3217: Restoring American Financial Stability Act of 2010, available at link #152; Center for Responsive Politics, OpenSecrets .org, Commercial Banks, available at link #153; Center for Responsive Politics, OpenSecrets.org, Finance/Credit Companies, available at link #154; Center for Responsive Politics, OpenSecrets.org, Securities and Investment Companies, available at link #155; Center for Responsive Politics, OpenSecrets.org, Savings and Loan Institutions, available at link #156; Center for Responsive Politics, OpenSecrets.org, Credit Unions, available at link #157.

51. Hacker and Pierson, *Winner-Take-All Politics*, 66.

52. Center for Responsive Politics, OpenSecrets.org, Pro-Environment Groups Outmatched, Outspent in Battle over Climate Change Legislation, available at link #58.

53. The heart of the bill was a mandate that major sources of carbon emissions obtain a pollution permit for each ton of carbon dioxide or its equivalent that they emit. Sponsors emphasize that it required "electric utilities to meet 20% of their electricity demand through renewable energy sources and energy efficiency by 2020." The bill included new spending on "clean energy technologies and energy efficiency, including energy efficiency and renewable energy ($90 billion in new investments by 2025), carbon capture and sequestration ($60 billion), electric and other advanced technology vehicles ($20 billion), and basic scientific research and development ($20 billion)." It also established new energy-saving standards for new buildings and appliances. "American Clean Energy and Security Act," Wikipedia, available at link #158.

54. Center for Responsive Politics, OpenSecrets.org, Lobbying Database, available at link #159.

55. Ryan Lizza, "As the World Burns: How the Senate and the White House Missed Their Best Chance to Deal with Climate Change," *The New Yorker*, Oct. 11, 2010, 12.

56. Robert Reich, "Everyday Corruption," *The American Prospect* (June 21, 2010), 8, available at link #160.

57. Speech of Barack Obama, Philadelphia, Pa., April 2, 2008.

## Chapter 12. How *So Damn Much Money* Defeats the Right

1. Loren Collins, "The Truth About Tytler," available at link #161. Something like this was certainly a concern among our Framers. John Adams, for example, feared that if democratic equality were taken too far, "debts would be abolished first; taxes laid heavy on the rich, and not at all on the others; and at last a downright equal division of everything be demanded, and voted." Hacker and Pierson, *Winner-Take-All Politics*, 77. Tocqueville, too: "The government of the democracy is the only one under which the power which votes the taxes escapes the payment of them." Alexis de Tocqueville, *Democracy in America*, ed. Francis Bowen, trans. Henry Reeve (Sever and Francis, 1863; 1835), 272.

2. See "How Dismal Is the Financial Future for America and Europe?" available at link #162.

3. U.S. Department of the Treasury, "The Debt to the Penny and Who Holds It," available at link #163 (figure obtained on Sept. 23, 2010). Brian Riedl, "New CBO Budget Baseline Shows that Soaring Spending—Not Falling Revenues—Risks Drowning America in Debt," The Heritage Foundation, Aug. 19, 2010, available at link #164 (calculations based on Congressional Budget Office baseline calculations).

4. Hacker and Pierson, *Winner-Take-All Politics*, 78.

5. Timothy F. Geithner et al., 2009 Annual Report of the Boards of Trustees of the Federal Hospital Insurance and Federal Supplementary Medical Insurance Trust Funds, 24, available at link #145.

6. Cohn, "How They Did It," 14.

7. Peter S. Goodman, "Treasury Weighs Fixes to Foreclosures Program," *New York Times*, Jan. 22, 2010, at B1. Treasury indicates it lowered the burden by $5.9 billion.

"Making Home Affordable," U.S. Dep't. of the Treasury, available at link #165 (last visited June 21, 2011).

8. American Bar Association, "Lobbying Law in the Spotlight: Challenges and Proposed Improvements," Task Force on Federal Lobbying Laws Section of Administrative Law and Regulatory Practice (Jan. 3, 2011), vi, available at link #100.

9. Carter and Grim, "Swiped."

10. Scott Rasmussen, "50% Say 'Rigged' Election Rules Explain High Reelection Rate for Congress," Rasmussen Reports 2009, available at link #166.

11. Ibid.

12. Schram, "Speaking Freely," 135–36.

13. Birnbaum, *The Money Men*, 66.

14. Clawson, Neustadtl, and Weller, *Dollars and Votes*, 37.

15. Ibid.

16. Birnbaum, *The Money Men*, 194.

17. Clawson, Neustadtl, and Weller, *Dollars and Votes*, 36.

18. Kaiser, *So Damn Much Money*, 315.

19. Schram, "Speaking Freely," 134.

20. Evan Halper, "Maker of Tax Software Opposes State Filing Help," *Los Angeles Times*, available at link #167.

21. Ibid.

22. Brian Kelleher Richter, Krislert Samphantharak, and Jeffrey F. Timmons, "Lobbying and Taxes," *American Journal of Political Science* 53 (2009): 893, 896.

23. Ibid.

24. Ibid., 893, 905.

25. Ibid., 893, 907. And not just taxes. As they also conclude, "firms that lobby are the primary tax beneficiaries of research and development activities." Ibid., 906.

26. Ibid.

27. Michael J. Graetz, "Paint-by-Numbers Tax Lawmaking," *Columbia Law Review* 95 (1995): 609, 672.

28. Rebecca Kysar, "The Sun Also Rises: The Political Economy of Sunset Provisions in the Tax Code," *Georgia Law Review* 40 (2006): 335, 340.

29. Ibid., 335, 341.

30. Ibid., 335, 358.

31. Ibid., 335, 358–59.

32. Ibid.

33. Ibid., 335, 363–64.

34. Mancur Olson was the father of modern public choice theory. His book *The Logic of Collective Action* (1965) explains most powerfully just why special interests are so powerful.

35. Kysar, "The Sun Also Rises," 335, 365.

36. John D. McKinnon, Gary Fields, and Laura Saunders, " 'Temporary' Tax Code Puts Nation in a Lasting Bind," *Wall Street Journal*, Dec. 14, 2010, available at link #168.

37. Clawson, Neustadtl, and Weller, *Dollars and Votes*, 76.

38. Hacker and Pierson, *Winner-Take-All Politics*, 107.

39. Rajan and Zingales, *Saving Capitalism from the Capitalists*, 293.

40. Ibid., 276.

41. Ibid., 294.

42. Ibid., 10.

43. Adam Smith, *Wealth of Nations*, ed. Edwin Cannan, vol. 1 (Chicago: University of Chicago Press, 1976), 144, chapter X ("Of Wages and Profit in the Different Employment of Labour and Stock"), part II ("Inequalities Occasioned by the Policy of Europe").

44. Rajan and Zingales, *Saving Capitalism from the Capitalists*, 9.

45. Ibid.

46. Ibid.,13.

47. Ibid., 18.

48. Ronald J. Pestritto and William J. Atto, *American Progressivism: A Reader* (Lanham, Md.: Lexington Books, 2008), 274.

49. Urofsky, *Louis D. Brandeis*, 326.

50. Johnson and Kwak, *13 Bankers*, 1.

51. Pestritto and Atto, *American Progressivism*, 216.

52. Committee for Economic Development, "Investing in the People's Business: A Business Proposal for Campaign Finance Reform" (1999), 1.

53. Ibid.

## Chapter 13. How *So Little Money* Makes Things Worse

1. Ilya Zemtsov, *The Encyclopedia of Soviet Life* (Transaction Publishers, 1991), 177; John Löwenhart, James R. Ozinga, and Erik van Ree, *The Rise and Fall of the Soviet Politburo* (London: UCL Press, 1992), 118.

2. Matthew Eric Glassman and Erin Hemlin, "Average Years of Service for Members of the Senate and House of Representatives, 1st-111th Congresses, Cong. Res. Service (Nov. 2, 2010), available at link #169.

3. James R. Ozinga, Thomas W. Casstevens, and Harold T. Casstevens II, "The Circulation of Elites: Soviet Politburo Members, 1919-1987," *Canadian Journal of Political Science* 22 (1989): 609, 614.

4. Norman Ornstein, "District of Corruption," *The New Republic*, available at link #170.

5. Lisa Rein, "Federal Officials Fight Back over Criticism About Salaries," *Washington Post*, Aug. 17, 2010, available at link #171 (describing debate about higher pay for federal officials).

6. Erika Lovley, "Report: 237 Millionaires in Congress," *Politico* (Nov. 6, 2009), available at link #172; Center for Responsive Politics, OpenSecrets.org, Personal Finance Disclosure, available at link #173.

7. Eric Jackson, "Evan Bayh: Hypocrisy on the Public Option," TheStreet (Oct. 29, 2009), available at link #174.

8. Editorial, "Wife's WellPoint Conflict Puts Bayh's Interests in Question," *Indianapolis Star*, May 25, 2009, A13.

9. Leadership PACS, Open Secrets.org, available at link #175.

10. Birnbaum, *The Money Men*, 233-34. This is still possible under the current ethics rules. H. Comm. on Standards of Official Conduct, 110th Cong., House Ethics Manual 47-48 (Comm. Print 2008), available at link #176.

11. "Leadership PACs: PAC Contributions to Federal Candidates," Center for Responsive Politics (April 25, 2011), available at link #177.

12. See R. Jeffrey Smith, "Money Intended to Help Candidates Often Ends Up Funding PACs Themselves," *Washington Post*, June 2, 2010, available at link #178.

13. Marcus Stern and Jennifer LaFleur, "Leadership PACs: Let the Good Times Roll," ProPublica (Sept. 26, 2009), available at link #179.

14. Prime Minister's Public Service Division, Press Release, "Modest Year-End Payments for Civil Servants" (Nov. 26, 2009), available at link #180.

15. Daniel Schuman, "What's the Average Salary of House Staff?" Open House Project (Dec. 2, 2009), available at link #181; Erika Lovley, "2,000 House Staffers Make Six Figures," *Politico* (Mar. 26, 2010), available at link #182.

16. William P. Barrett, "There's Something About Mary," *Forbes*, Mar. 11, 2009, available at link #183; "Securities and Exchange Commission Salaries," Simply Hired (accessed Sept. 16, 2010), available at link #184.

17. "Salaries in Investment Banking," available at link #185.

18. Though the issue is not uncontested. See Eugene Kiely, "Are Federal Workers Overpaid? Both Sides in Great Pay Debate Are Misleading the Public," FactCheck .org (Dec. 1, 2010), available at link #186.

19. See generally Keith A. Bender and John S. Heywood, "Out of Balance? Comparing Public and Private Sector Compensation over 20 Years" (2010), available at link #187.

20. Jeffrey H. Birnbaum, "The Road to Riches Is Called K Street," *Washington Post*, June 22, 2005, available at link #188; Jeanne Cummings, "The Gilded Capital: Lobbying to Riches," *Politico* (June 26, 2007), available at link #189; Arthur Delaney and Ryan Grim, "On K Street, an Ex-Senate Staffer Is Worth $740,000 a Year," Huffington Post (Sept. 24, 2010), available at link #190.

21. Ornstein, "District of Corruption," 1.

22. See a comparable case of Joel Oswald, who works for Williams and Jensen and has twenty financial services clients, available at link #191; Public Citizen and the Center for Responsive Politics, "Banking on Connections: Financial Services Sector Has Dispatched Nearly 1,500 'Revolving Door' Lobbyists Since 2009" (2010), available at link #192.

23. Birnbaum, *The Money Men*, 191.

24. Kaiser, *So Damn Much Money*, 343–44.

25. Eric Lichtblau, "Lobbyist Charged with Hiding Political Donations," *New York Times*, Aug. 5, 2010, A12, available at link #193; "104 Will Get You $300 Million," *New York Times*, Feb. 19, 2009, A30, available at link #194. Ryan J. Reilly and Alex Sciuto, "Despite Donations to Girl Scouts, PMA Lobbyist Gets 27 Months," TPM-Muckraker (Jan. 7, 2011), available at link #195.

26. Judy Sarasohn, "Special Interests; Of Revolving Doors and Turntables," *Washington Post*, Feb. 17, 2000, A29; Recording Industry Association of America, Wikipedia, available at link #196.

27. Lichtblau, "Lobbyist Charged with Hiding Political Donations"; "104 Will Get You $300 Million."

28. Jordi Blanes i Vidal, Mirko Draca, and Christian Fons-Rosen, "Revolving Door Lobbyists," Center for Economic Performance Working Paper No. 993 (Aug. 2010).

## Chapter 14. Two Conceptions of "Corruption"

1. Randal C. Archibold, "Ex-Congressman Gets 8-Year Term in Bribery Case," *New York Times*, Mar. 4, 2006, available at link #197.

2. David Stout, "Ex-Louisiana Congressman Sentenced to 13 Years," *New York Times*, Nov. 13, 2009, available at link #198.

3. *Buckley v. Valeo*, 424 U.S. 1, 27 (1976).

4. See J. Mark Ramseyer and Eric B. Rasmussen, "Skewed Incentives: Paying For Politics as a Japanese Judge," *Judicature* 83 (2000): 190.

5. James J. Sample, "Justice for Sale," *Wall Street Journal* online (Mar. 22, 2008), available at link #199.

6. Justice Sandra Day O'Connor, "How to Save Our Courts," *Parade*, Feb. 24, 2008, available at link #200.

7. Ibid. (emphasis added).

8. Sample, "Justice for Sale," A24.

9. James J. Sample, "Democracy at the Corner of First and Fourteenth: Judicial Campaign Spending and Equality" (Aug. 20, 2010), 23 (forthcoming in *NYU Annual Survey of American Law*); Hofstra Univ. Legal Studies Research Paper No. 10-29, available at link #89.

10. David Pozen, James Sample, and Michael Young, "Fair Courts: Setting Recusal Standards," 11, available at link #201.

11. Sample, "Democracy at the Corner," 20; Hofstra Univ. Legal Studies Research Paper No. 10-29, available at link #89.

12. Report of Stanford Law Student, Spring 2009, on file with author.

13. Stephen J. Ware, "Money, Politics and Judicial Decisions: A Case Study of Arbitration Law in Alabama," *Capital University Law Review* 30 (2002): 583, 584.

14. Adam Liptak and Janet Roberts, "Campaign Cash Mirrors a High Court's Rulings," *New York Times*, Oct. 1, 2006, A1.

15. Adam Liptak, "Looking Anew at Campaign Cash and Elected Judges," *New York Times*, Jan. 29, 2008, A14, available at link #202.

16. It isn't quite accurate historically to speak of both the House and Senate in this way, since the Senate was originally appointed by state legislatures. My analysis translates the view of the House to the norms for the now-elected Senate.

17. Sam Issacharoff advances a distinct conception of corruption that roughly parallels my sense of dependence corruption. He focuses upon the "clientelist" relation between "elected officials and those who seek to profit from relations to the state," Samuel Issacharoff, "On Political Corruption," *Harvard Law Review* 124 (2010): 121, the result of which is a "distortion of political outcomes as a result of the undue influence of wealth" (Ibid., 122).

18. *Buckley v. Valeo*, 424 U.S. 1, 47 (1976).

19. Clawson, Neustadtl, and Weller, *Dollars and Votes*, 4.

20. "Geography Data 2008 Race: Massachusetts Senate," Center for Responsive Politics (July 13, 2009), available at link #203.

21. Spencer Overton, "The Participation Interest," *Georgetown Law Journal* (Forthcoming, 2012): 6.

22. Ibid., 3–4.

23. John Joseph Wallis, "The Concept of Systematic Corruption in American History," University of Maryland and National Bureau of Economic Research (2005), 4.

24. Ibid., 23.

25. Ibid., 3–4.
26. Ibid.
27. Ibid., 52.
28. Ibid., 50, quoting Benjamin Parke DeWitt.
29. This recognition was born at the turn of the century, as "muckrakers" made the corporate control of politics tangible and widely known for the first time. As Richard McCormick describes, "[t]hat businessmen systematically corrupted politics was incendiary knowledge; given the circumstances of 1905, it could hardly have failed to set off an explosion." "The Discovery That Business Corrupts Politics: A Reappraisal of the Origins of Progressivism," 247, 270. Progressives split on what to do about this fundamental fact of American politics—with the followers of Roosevelt arguing for bigger government to match the influence of business, and followers of Wilson/Brandeis arguing for stronger laws to limit the size of business. Whether any solution was possible, TR's was particularly naive. But my point is not the wisdom in the remedies; it is the commonality of the motivation. See also Brooks, *Corruption in American Politics and Life* (1910) (pointing to campaign contributions as the source of corruption, and advancing a small-dollar alternative). For an outstanding early history of the influence of money in elections, see Anthony Corrado, *The New Campaign Finance Source Book* (2004), chap. 1, available at link #204.
30. Wallis, "The Concept of Systematic Corruption in American History," 48.
31. Ibid.
32. Huffington, *Third World America*, 58–59; Hacker and Pierson, *Winner-Take-All Politics*, 51.
33. See Barry Ritholtz, *Top 10 Hedge Fund Managers 2009 Salary*, The Big Picture (April 1, 2010), available at link #75; Hacker and Pierson, *Winner-Take-All Politics*, 228.
34. Kaiser, *So Damn Much Money*, 267. See also Hacker and Pierson, *Winner-Take-All Politics*, 207.
35. Ibid., 267.
36. Ibid., 272.
37. Ibid., 264.
38. "Tom DeLay Convicted of Money Laundering," FOXNews.com (Nov. 24, 2010), available at link #205.
39. Kaiser, *So Damn Much Money*, 270–71.
40. Ibid., 149.
41. Ibid., 346.
42. Center for Responsive Politics, available at link #206 (last visited June 21, 2011) (For the 2010 election cycle, independent expenditures totaled $210,912,167. Just four years prior, in 2006, independent expenditures totaled $37,394,589).
43. It is for this reason that I am skeptical of the utility of efforts to try to "reverse" *Citizens United* by denying corporate personhood. The root problem is an influence that drives representatives away from a focus on "the People alone." Even if a reform were to achieve the reversal of corporate personhood, that wouldn't by itself change the existing skew of influence.
44. Of course not all courts are this enlightened. In *Miles v. City of Augusta*, 710 F.2d 1542 (11th Cir. 1983), the Court refused "to hear a claim that" a talking cat's First

Amendment rights had been infringed, finding the cat not a "person" under the Fourteenth Amendment.

45. 494 US 652, 660 (1990).

46. Eric Uslaner has a compelling argument about how corruption relates to inequality. See Eric M. Uslaner, *Corruption, Inequality and Trust, Handbook on Social Capital*, Gert Tinggaard Svendsen and Gunnar Lind, eds. (2011). But the argument is causal. My point here is conceptual: the corruption of representative democracy is distinct from inequality in speech or resources within a representative democracy.

47. Birnbaum, *The Money Men*, 34.

48. Wallis, "The Concept of Systematic Corruption," 37.

49. John G. A. Pocock, *Virtue, Commerce, and History: Essays on Political Thought and History, Chiefly in the Eighteenth Century* (Cambridge University Press, 1985), 78.

50. Not every Framer was necessarily convinced of this need. Indeed, Alexander Hamilton, faced with the real task of inspiring a nation to pay its bills (both the government to pay its debtors, and the people to pay their taxes), thought the British form of "corruption" may actually be quite useful for a republic. According to a suggestion by Senator William Maclay (D-Pa.; 1789–1791), in order to secure the votes to get Congress to assume the Revolutionary War debts, Hamilton gave congressmen with inside knowledge the chance to send "stagecoaches all over the South and West buying up federal and state notes at fractions of their face value." Painter, *Getting the Government America Deserves*, 164. Jefferson complained to Washington directly about this. In his *Anas*, Jefferson reports telling Washington:

> That it was a fact, as certainly known as that he and I were then conversing, that particular members of the legislature, while those laws were on the carpet, had feathered their nests with paper, had then voted for the laws....
>
> [That this was a case of] a legislature legislating for their own interests, in opposition to those of the people....
>
> [T]hat these measures had established corruption in the legislature, where there was a squadron devoted to the nod of the Treasury, doing whatever he had directed, and ready to do what he should direct....
>
> [That] there was great difference between the little accidental scheme of self interest, which would take place in every body of men, and influence their votes, and a regular system for forming a corps of interested persons, who should be steadily at the orders of the Treasury....
>
> I confirmed [Washington] in the fact of the great discontents to the south; that they were grounded on seeing that their judgments and interests were sacrificed to those of the eastern States on every occasion, and their belief that it was the effect of a corrupt squadron of voters in Congress, at the command of the Treasury....

Thomas Jefferson, *The Complete Anas*, ed. Franklin B. Sawvel (Round Table Press, 1903; 1792), 54–55, 85, 91, 104–5.

51. *Citizens United v. Fed. Election Comm'n*, 130 S. Ct. 676, 910 (2010) (quoting *McConnell v. Fed. Election Comm'n*, 540 U.S. 93, 297 [2003] [opinion of Kennedy, J.]) (emphasis added).

52. Speech of Barack Obama, Feb. 10, 2007, available at link #207.

53. *Citizens United v. Fed. Election Comm'n*, 130 S. Ct. 676, 910 (2010).

54. "Congress Ranks Last in Confidence in Institutions," July 22, 2010, available at link #1.

## Part IV. Solutions

1. 145 Cong. Rec. 25517 (daily ed., Oct. 15, 1999) (statement of Sen. Tom Daschle citing Sen. Barry Goldwater).

2. Casey Bayer, "Jon Stewart and Bill O'Reilly Bond over Campaign Corruption," *Christian Science Monitor*, Sept. 28, 2010, available at link #208.

## Chapter 15. Reforms That Won't Reform

1. Clifford D. Tyree, "History and Description of the EPA Motor Vehicle Fuel Economy Program" (EPA Report No. EPA-AA-CPSB-82-02) (1982), 2–3. I was inspired to this powerful and subtle view of transparency by Archon Fung, Mary Graham, and David Weil, *Full Disclosure: The Perils and Promise of Transparency* (Cambridge University Press, 2007).

2. Center for Responsive Politics, Top 100 Contributors: Representative Michael E. Capuano 2009–2010, OpenSecrets.org, available at link #209.

3. Public Citizen, "Disclosure Eclipse: Nearly Half of Outside Groups Kept Donors Secret in 2010"; "Top 10 Groups Revealed Sources of Only One in Four Dollars Spent 3" (Nov. 18, 2010), available at link #210.

4. Marcos Chamon and Ethan Kaplan, "The Iceberg Theory of Campaign Contributions: Political Threats and Interest Group Behavior" (April 2007), 2–5, available at link #211.

5. Interview with Larry Pressler, June 16, 2011 (on file with author).

6. "Cause for Concern: More than 40% of Hill Staffers Responding to Public Citizen Survey Say Lobbyists Wield More Power Because of *Citizens United*," Public Citizen (May 2011), 6–9, available at link #212.

7. See Jack Beatty, *Age of Betrayal* (New York: Vintage, 2007), 216.

8. Bruce Ackerman and Ian Ayres, *Voting with Dollars: A New Paradigm for Campaign Finance* (New Haven: Yale University Press, 2004), 48–50, 102–4. Ian Ayres first introduced the idea of an anonymous donation booth with Jeremy Bulow in "The Donation Booth: Mandating Donor Anonymity to Disrupt the Market for Political Influence," *Stanford Law Review* 50 (1998): 837.

9. In 1972, Dade County established the "Dade Judicial Trust Fund" for all Dade County judicial elections. The trust was blind, the funds were solicited from all practicing members of the bar in Dade County, and the funds were distributed on a pro rata basis to each "qualified" judicial candidate in the county. The trust failed soon after it was adopted due to (i) a lack of attorney participation (donations), and (ii) criticism that the fund distributed funds to *all* qualified judicial candidates, thereby disallowing attorneys from directing contributions to particular candidates. In 1972 the fund received just over $30,000 from three hundred attorneys. In 1974 the fund received just over $61,000, and was disbanded shortly

thereafter. See Roy A. Schotland, "Elective Judges' Campaign Financing: Are State Judges' Robes the Emperor's Clothes of American Democracy?" *Journal of Law and Politics* 2 (1985): 57, 124, 100–104 (admitting that "[d]espite having begun this project enthusiastic about non-disclosure of lawyers' giving as a reform measure, after considering these factors, I find it neither worth doing nor doable"). See also Leona C. Smoler and Mary A. Stokinger, "Note: The Ethical Dilemma of Campaigning for Judicial Office: A Proposed Solution," *Fordham Urban Law Journal* 14 (1986): 353, 364.

## Chapter 16. Reforms That Would Reform

1. Brooks, *Corruption in American Politics and Life*, 228.
2. For a review of these different reforms, see U.S. Gov't Accountability Office, "GAO-10-390, Campaign Finance Reform: Experiences of Two States That Offered Full Public Funding for Political Candidates" (2010), available at link #213 (supplemental report available at link #214); Michael G. Miller, "After the GAO Report: What Do We Know About Public Election Funding?" working paper (2010), available at link #215; Stevin M. Levin, "Keeping it Clean: Public Financing in American Elections," Center for Governmental Studies (2006), available at link #216; Neil Malhorta, "The Impact of Public Financing on Electoral Competition: Evidence from Arizona and Maine," *State Politics and Policy Quarterly* 8 (2008): 263–81; Peter L. Francia and Paul S. Herrnson, "The Impact of Public Finance Laws on Fundraising in State Legislative Elections," *American Political Research* 31 (Sept. 2003): 5; Raymond La Raja, "Candidate Emergence in State Legislative Elections: Does Public Funding Make a Difference?" paper prepared for the Temple-IPA State Politics and Policy Conference (May 2008), available at link #217; Kenneth R. Mayer and Timothy Werner, "Public Election Funding, Competition, and Candidate Gender," *PS: Political Science and Politics* XL, no. 4 (Oct. 2007), available at link #218; Thomas Stratmann, "The Effect of Public Financing on the Competitiveness of Elections," George Mason University–Buchanan Center Political Economy, CESifo (Center for Economic Studies and Ifo Institute for Economic Research) working papers series, May 7, 2009, available at link #219; Maine Comm'n on Gov. Ethics and Election Practices, "Maine Clean Election Act: Overview of Participation Rates and Payments, 2000–2008" (2008), available at link #220; Conn. State Elections Enforcement Comm'n, "The Status of the Citizens' Election Fund as of December 31, 2009" (2009), available at link #221; Conn. State Elections Enforcement Comm'n, "Projected Levels of Candidate Participation and Public Grant Distribution for the 2010 Citizens' Election Program," available at link #222; and Kenneth R. Mayer and Timothy Werner, "Electoral Transitions in Connecticut: The Implementation of Clean Elections in 2008," paper presented at the Annual Meeting of the American Political Science Association, available at link #223.
3. The leading scholarship examining campaign finance reform is varied and deep. Among the leading articles are Samuel Issacharoff and Pamela S. Karlan, "The Hydraulics of Campaign Finance Reform," *Texas Law Review* 77 (1998): 1705; Lillian R. BeVier, "Money and Politics: A Perspective on the First Amendment and Campaign Finance Reform," *California Law Review* 73 (1985): 1045; Bradley A. Smith, "Faulty Assumptions and Undemocratic Consequences of Campaign

Finance Reform," *Yale Law Journal* 105 (1996): 1049; David A. Strauss, "Corruption, Equality, and Campaign Finance Reform," *Columbia Law Review* 94 (1994): 1369; Edward B. Foley, "Equal-Dollars-Per-Voter: A Constitutional Principle of Campaign Finance," *Columbia Law Review* 94 (1994): 1204; Richard L. Hasen, "Clipping Coupons for Democracy: An Egalitarian/Public Choice Defense of Campaign Finance Vouchers," *California. Law Review* 84 (1996): 1; Daniel Hays Lowenstein, "On Campaign Finance Reform: The Root of All Evil Is Deeply Rooted," *Hofstra Law Review* 18 (1989): 301; Fred Wertheimer and Susan Weiss Manes, "Campaign Finance Reform: A Key to Restoring the Health of Our Democracy," *Columbia Law Review* 94 (1994): 1126; Andrea Prat, "Campaign Spending with Office-Seeking Politicians, Rational Voters, and Multiple Lobbies," *Journal of Economic Theory* 103 (Mar. 2002): 162; Stephen Coate, "Pareto-Improving Campaign Finance Policy," *American Economic Review* 94 (June 2004): 628; Lillian R. BeVier, "Campaign Finance Reform: Specious Arguments, Intractable Dilemmas," *Columbia Law Review* 94 (1994): 1258; Bradley A. Smith, "Money Talks: Speech, Corruption, Equality, and Campaign Finance," *Georgetown Law Journal* 86 (1997): 45; Daniel R. Ortiz, "The Democratic Paradox of Campaign Finance Reform," *Stanford Law Review* 50 (1997): 893; Kathleen M. Sullivan, "Against Campaign Finance Reform," *Utah Law Review* (1998): 311; and Spencer Overton, "Donor Class: Campaign Finance, Democracy, and Participation," *University of Pennsylvania Law Review* 153 (2004): 73.

The proposal I advance here is focused less on restricting speech than the reforms criticized by Smith and BeVier. It shares the concern with corruption advanced by Lowenstein. Like Issacharoff and Karlan, I view the challenge as dynamic: What is the economy of influence reform will produce? Like Sullivan, I avoid reforms that would restrict important First Amendment values. And like Overton, I believe a key value must be the promotion of participation. Strauss brilliantly demonstrates how corruption, which is a derivative concept, derived from a concern about unequal power in the electoral speech market. As my analysis makes clear, however, while I agree with his diagnosis, I believe it is a mistake to frame the concern as one of equality alone. As I describe, equality, too, is a derivative concept, derived from the notion of a democracy "dependent upon the People alone."

4. As will be clear, the mode of reform that I am pushing does not "call for greater regulation" of speech. See Issacharoff and Karlan, "The Hydraulics of Campaign Finance Reform," 1711, as I share their concern that such reforms "exacerbate the already disturbing trend toward politics being divorced from the mediating influence of candidates and political parties." Ibid, 1714. The thrust of the reforms I advance here would increase the available speech resources within an election, and does not depend upon restricting the speech of anyone.

5. David Leonhardt, "Who Doesn't Pay Taxes?" *New York Times Economix Blog* (April 13, 2010), available at link #224; see also Congressional Budget Office, Historical Effective Federal Tax Rates: 1979–2006 (April 2009), available at link #225.

6. For readers of Bruce Ackerman and Ian Ayres, *Voting with Dollars*, this solution will seem familiar. I draw heavily upon their insights, though the contours to my framework are different. The idea of a voucher was also described extensively by Richard Hasen in "Clipping Coupons for Democracy." Hasen distinguishes between a "level[ing]-up" and a "level[ing]-down" approach. Ibid., 20. A voucher

system is the former; limits on expenditures or contributions are the latter. Hasen's own proposal mixes both. Ibid., 20-27, though he wrote this before the Court made it clear that Congress has no power to limit independent campaign expenditures in the name of "equality." Ibid., 39-44. See *Citizens United v. Fed. Election Comm'n*, 130 S. Ct. 676 (2010) (reversing *Austin v. Michigan Chamber of Commerce*, 494 U.S. 652 [1990]).

As Hasen notes, Senator Lee Metcalf proposed a voucher plan in 1967. Hasen, "Clipping Coupons for Democracy," 20.

7. Brooks, *Corruption in American Politics and Life*, 263.
8. See *Randall v. Sorrell*, 548 U.S. 230 (2006), which invalidated Vermont's limit of $400 to candidates.
9. Spencer Overton, "The Participation Interest," *Georgetown Law Journal* (Forthcoming: 2012): 3-4.
10. See *Cato Handbook for Policymakers*, chap. 26.
11. Nathaniel Persily and Kelli Lammie, "Perceptions of Corruption and Campaign Finance: When Public Opinion Determines Constitutional Law," *University of Pennsylvania Law Review* 153 (2004): 119, available at link #226.
12. This is strong insight in Issacharoff and Karlan, "The Hydraulics of Campaign Finance Reform," *Texas Law Review* 77 (1998): 1705. For the best mapping of the complexities, see the work of Anthony Corrado, especially *The New Campaign Finance Sourcebook* (Washington, D.C.: Brookings Institution Press, 2005) (with Thomas E. Mann, Daniel R. Ortiz, and Trevor Potter).
13. Brooks, *Corruption in American Politics and Life*, 99.

## Chapter 18. Strategy 2

1. This idea was suggested to me by Matt Gonzalez, Ralph Nader's vice-presidential candidate.

## Chapter 19. Strategy 3

1. Jake Tapper and Sunlen Miller, "President Obama's $8 Billion Earmark Rerun: Lesson Not Learned?" ABCNews, *Political Punch* (Dec. 15, 2010), available at link #227.
2. Speech of Governor Buddy Roemer, Harvard University, March 24, 2011.
3. See Paolo E. Coletta, *William Jennings Bryan: Political Evangelist, 1860-1908* (Lincoln: University of Nebraska Press, 1864), 272.

## Chapter 20. Strategy 4

1. Teachout, "The Anti-Corruption Principle," 341, 348 (citing Notes of James Madison [Aug. 14, 1787] *The Records of the Federal Convention of 1787*, vol. 2, pp. 282, 288).
2. Ibid., 349 (citing Patrick Henry, "Speech on the Expediency of Adopting the Federal Constitution" [June 7, 1788], in *Eloquence of the United States*, ed. E. B. Williston, vol. 1 [1827], 178, 223).
3. Ibid., 348 (citing Notes of Robert Yates [June 23, 1787], in *The Records of the Federal Convention of 1787*, vol. 1, pp. 391, 392).

4. *The Federalist* No. 40 (James Madison), 240–41 (quoting the Congress's charge to the Constitutional Convention).

5. Lash, "Rejecting Conventional Wisdom," 197, 221–22.

6. Ibid., 197, 212.

7. Paul J. Weber and Barbara A. Perry, *Unfounded Fears* (Santa Barbara, Calif.: Praeger, 1989), 56–60.

8. Congressional Research Service, CRS 95-589 A, "Amending the U.S. Constitution: By Congress or by Constitutional Convention" (May 10, 1995), 11, available at link #228; Cyril F. Brickfield, "Problems Relating to a Federal Constitutional Convention," Committee on the Judiciary, House of Representatives (July 1, 1957), 7.

There are some who question whether the threat of a convention really did cause the Senate to act. See James Kenneth Rogers, "The Other Way to Amend the Constitution," *Harvard Journal of Law and Public Policy* 30 (2007): 1005, 1008 (citing Russell L. Caplan, *Constitutional Brinksmanship: Amending the Constitution by National Convention* (1988), 65: [T]here remains no evidence that the convention threat by itself forced the Senate to approve the [Seventeenth A]mendment. At least as influential was the growing quota of senators chosen by popular vote"); Kris W. Kobach, "Rethinking Article V: Term Limits and the Seventeenth and Nineteenth Amendments," *Yale Law Journal* 103 (1994): 1971, 1976–80 (arguing that the growing proportion of senators elected by popular vote was the "most influential [factor] in finally winning a formal amendment to the U.S. Constitution").

This wasn't the only time a convention threat forced a constitutional amendment. Indeed, the threat of a second constitutional convention "was a key factor in Congress proposing the Bill of Rights." James Kenneth Rogers, "The Other Way to Amend the Constitution," *Harvard Journal of Law and Public Policy* 30 (2007): 1005, 1008. And beyond the Seventeenth Amendment, there are three other amendments in the twentieth century "that may be traced to convention call movements": the Twenty-first Amendment (repealing Prohibition), Twenty-second Amendment (setting limits on presidential terms), and the Twenty-fifth Amendment (clarifying presidential succession). Weber and Perry, *Unfounded Fears* (Santa Barbara, Calif.: Praeger, 1989), 75. Other issues inspiring a large convention movement have included petitions on the income tax (between 1939 and 1963), polygamy (1906–1916), and legislative reapportionment (1963–1969). Weber and Perry, *Unfounded Fears*, 61–67. Michael J. Molloy, "Confusion and a Constitutional Convention," *Western State University Law Review* 12 (1985): 793, 794.

9. The most ambitious recent discussion of a call for a constitutional convention is Larry Sabato's *A More Perfect Constitution* (2007), which describes twenty-three proposals for changes that he would have a convention consider. A call for partial public funding of elections is among Sabato's proposals.

10. See Sanford Levinson, *Our Undemocratic Constitution: Where the Constitution Goes Wrong (And How We the People Can Correct It)* ("Most liberals these days appear to be fully Madisonian in being close to terrified of the passions of their fellow citizens. They envision a runaway convention that would tear up the most admirable parts of the convention...") (Oxford University Press, 2008), 174–75;

Larry Greenley, "States Should Enforce, Not Revise, the Constitution!" *New American* (Nov. 29, 2010), available at link #229 (warning that a constitutional convention "may become a 'runaway convention' that drastically alters our form of government, or throws out the Constitution altogether and establishes an entirely new system of governance"); but see "Amending the Constitution by the Convention Method," Heritage Foundation (Mar. 8, 1988), 4–89, available at link #230 (debunking the "myth of the runaway convention").

11. Bruce Ackerman, "Unconstitutional Convention," *New Republic* (Mar. 3, 1979), 8; Russell L. Caplan, *Constitutional Brinksmanship: Amending the Constitution by National Convention* (Oxford University Press, 1988); David Castro, "A Constitutional Convention: Scouting Article Five's Undiscovered Country," *University of Pennsylvania Law Review* 134 (1986): 939; Walter E. Dellinger, "The Recurring Question of the 'Limited' Constitutional Convention," *Yale Law Journal* 88 (1979): 1623; Walter E. Dellinger, "Who Controls a Constitutional Convention? A Response," *Duke Law Journal* (1979): 999; Gerald Gunther, "The Convention Method of Amending the United States Constitution," *Georgia Law Review* 14 (1979): 1; Lash, "Rejecting Conventional Wisdom," 197; Michael J. Molloy, "Confusion and a Constitutional Convention," *Western State University Law Review* 12 (1985): 793; John T. Noonan, "The Convention Method of Constitutional Amendment: Its Meaning, Usefulness, and Wisdom, *Pacific Law Journal* 10 (1979): 641; Michael B. Rappaport, "Reforming Article V: The Problems Created by the National Convention Amendment Method and How to Fix Them," *Virginia Law Review* 96 (2010): 1509; James K. Rogers, "The Other Way to Amend the Constitution: The Article V Constitutional Convention Amendment Process," *Harvard Journal of Law and Public Policy* 30 (2007): 1005; Ronald D. Rotunda and Stephen J. Safranek, "An Essay on Term Limits and a Call for a Constitutional Convention," *Marquette Law Review* 80 (1996): 227; Laurence H. Tribe, "Issues Raised by Requesting Congress to Call a Constitutional Convention to Propose a Balanced Budget Amendment," *Pacific Law Journal* 10 (1979): 627; William W. Van Alstyne, "Does Article V Restrict the States to Calling Unlimited Conventions Only? A Letter to a Colleague," *Duke Law Journal* (1978): 1295; William W. Van Alstyne, "The Limited Constitutional Convention: The Recurring Answer," *Duke Law Journal* (1979): 985.

12. Weber and Perry, *Unfounded Fears*, 74–75.

13. William W. Van Alstyne, "The Limited Constitutional Convention: The Recurring Answer," *Duke Law Journal* 4 (1979): 985, 987. See also Lash, "Rejecting Conventional Wisdom," 197, 202 (describing Randolph plan).

14. Weber and Perry, *Unfounded Fears*, 59–60.

15. The argument for the power of Congress to control a convention was laid out fully more than fifty years ago by Cyril Brickfield, an attorney working for the House Committee on the Judiciary. After an exhaustive analysis of the history of constitutional conventions, Brickfield concludes that a convention exercises its will "within the framework set by the congressional act calling it into being." Cyril F. Brickfield, "Problems Relating to a Federal Constitutional Convention," Committee on the Judiciary, House of Representatives (July 1, 1957), 18. "A convention," Brickfield writes, "is an instrument of government and acts properly only when it stays within the orbit of its powers." "[T]o act validly," it would "have to stay

within the designated limits of the congressional act which called it into being" (Ibid., 18). That conclusion is only buttressed by the express statement of the Necessary and Proper Clause (Ibid., 19).

16. Constitutional Convention Implementation Act of 1985, Senate Bill 40, 99th Cong. 1st Sess. (1985).

17. Senate Bill 40, §7(a).

18. Walter E. Dellinger, "The Recurring Question of the 'Limited' Constitutional Convention," *Yale Law Journal* 88 (1979): 1623, 1633.

19. This was the basis for Judge John A. Jameson's conclusion in 1867 that conventions could be limited. See Weber and Perry, *Unfounded Fears*, 60.

20. Lash, "Rejecting Conventional Wisdom," 197, 213.

21. Indeed, some members thought even talking about proposals beyond amending the articles of convention "must end in the dissolution of the powers" of the convention. Weber and Perry, *Unfounded Fears*, 23-24.

22. Ibid., 26.

23. Ibid., 107-8.

24. Hacker and Pierson, *Winner-Take-All Politics*, 109.

25. Ibid.

26. Ibid.

27. See, for example, James S. Fishkin, *The Voice of the People* (New Haven, Conn.: Yale University Press, 1995). For a related device, see Mark E. Warren, "Two Trust-Based Uses of Minipublics in Democracy," American Political Science Association meeting (Sept. 2009).

28. "Poll Finds Only 33% Can Identify Bill of Rights," *New York Times*, Dec. 15, 1991, A33. See also Pew Research Center for the People and the Press, "Well Known: Twitter; Little Known: John Roberts" (2010), available at link #231.

## Conclusion

1. Makinson, "Speaking Freely," 153.

2. "The 400 Richest Americans 2009," available at link #232.

# Index

# About the Author

Lawrence Lessig is the Roy L. Furman Professor of Law and Leadership at Harvard Law School, and director of the Edmond J. Safra Center for Ethics at Harvard University. Prior to rejoining the Harvard faculty, Lessig was a professor at Stanford Law School, where he founded the school's Center for Internet and Society, and at the University of Chicago. He clerked for Judge Richard Posner on the Seventh Circuit Court of Appeals and for Justice Antonin Scalia on the U.S. Supreme Court.

Lessig serves on the boards of Creative Commons; MapLight; Brave New Film Foundation; the American Academy, Berlin; AXA Research Fund; and iCommons.org; and on the advisory board of the Sunlight Foundation. He is a member of the American Academy of Arts and Sciences, and the American Philosophical Association, and has received numerous awards, including the Free Software Foundation's Freedom Award and Fastcase 50 Award. He has also been named one of *Scientific American*'s Top 50 Visionaries.

Lessig holds a BA in economics and a BS in management from the University of Pennsylvania, an MA in philosophy from Cambridge, and a JD from Yale.

# ABOUT TWELVE

TWELVE

TWELVE was established in August 2005 with the objective of publishing no more than twelve books each year. We strive to publish the singular book, by authors who have a unique perspective and compelling authority. Works that explain our culture; that illuminate, inspire, provoke, and entertain. We seek to establish communities of conversation surrounding our books. Talented authors deserve attention not only from publishers, but from readers as well. To sell the book is only the beginning of our mission. To build avid audiences of readers who are enriched by these works—that is our ultimate purpose.

For more information about forthcoming TWELVE books, please go to www.twelvebooks.com.